INFORMATION INDIA : 1994-95 & 1995-96

CONCEPTS IN COMMUNICATION INFORMATICS & LIBRARIANSHIP (CICIL)

For a list of titles in this series, *see* pp. 320-323 at the end of this Book.

About the Authors

S.P. Agrawal (*b.* 1929) was Director, National Social Science Documentation Centre, ICSSR, Government of India and Member Secretary, Indian Association of Social Science Institutions. He was also the Vice-Chairman of the Asia and Pacific Information Network in Social Sciences (APINESS). In 1988 he was awarded the degree of Doctor of Philosophy in Education (*Honoris Causa*) by International University Foundation. Presently, he is Member, IFLA Round Table on Research in Reading, International Committee for Social Science Information and Documentation, Board of Studies of National Archives of India and Hindi Advisory Committee, Ministry of Coal, Government of India. He is also Fellow of the Society of Ethnobotanists. Born and brought up in the cradle of freedom movement, which he joined at the tender age of twelve, he gained an insight into political problems and developed a sense of responsibility which bore fruit as an information scientist. He has written extensively on various aspects of Education, Indian Polity and Library and Information Science.

J.C. Aggarwal (*b.* 1928), former Deputy Director of Education/Executive Director of Delhi Bureau of Textbooks, Delhi Administration has a varied experience in the field of education. He has singly/jointly authored about 130 books on Education, Social Sciences and current problems. In collaboration with S.P. Agrawal, he has written *Documentation Encyclopaedia of UNESCO and Education* (in two parts); *Women's Education in India; National Policy on Education, Agenda for India 2001;* and *Vocational of Education in India; Uttar Pradesh : Past, Present and Future; Modern History of Punjab; Modern History of Jammu & Kashmir*, etc.

His other recent publications include : *Year-book of Indian Education, 1991: World Overview; Ramamurti Report 1990 on National Policy on Education in India;* and *Survey of Educational Documents in the World since 1983*, etc.

CONCEPTS IN COMMUNICATION
INFORMATICS & LIBRARIANSHIP-76

GENERAL EDITOR: **S. P. AGRAWAL**

INFORMATION INDIA : 1994-95 & 1995-96 Global View

S.P. AGRAWAL
former Member Secretary
Indian Association of Social Science Institutions, and Director, National Social Science Documentation Centre, ICSSR, Government of India

J.C. AGGARWAL
former Executive Director
Delhi Bureau of Textbooks, Delhi Administration
NEW DELHI

CONCEPT PUBLISHING COMPANY, NEW DELHI -110059

ISBN 81-7022-656-2

First Published 1997

Published and Printed by
Ashok Kumar Mittal
Concept Publishing Company
A/15-16, Commercial Block, Mohan Garden
New Delhi-110059 (India)
Phones: 5554042, 5504042
Fax: 091-(11)-5598898

GENERAL EDITOR'S INTRODUCTION

Information India was first brought out in 1989 under CICIL series which covers a wide range of disciplines—interrelated but at the same time including a very wide stretch of topics for investigation, research and study. It is of great consolation that previous editions of Information India placed in the hands of the discerning readers as also reviewers have been received well. In all humility, we assume that these annuals have fulfilled a long felt need.

The focus of the present volume is on India as it was in 1994-95 & 1995-96. As many as 18 out of the total of 27 chapters, under suitable divisions, are devoted to various aspects of the country. The chapters are, by and large, a combination of descriptive accounts and vital statistics. *Information India* is now accompanied by 3D companiom volume — *Development/Digression Diary of India.*

S.P. Agrawal

PREFACE

In this compilation it has been endeavoured to give all important facets of not only India but also the world as a whole.

Challenges facing the world, comparative country profile relating to Economic and Social Development and Significant International Reports have been included.

Relating to India, it has been attempted to provide almost all embracing facts and figures with regard to various sectors of development since 1947. Detailed account has been given about important aspects, as well as other topical areas which are of significant in any discussion on India.

It is observed that data collected by various national and international organisations from different sources and also used here, do not necessarily relate to the same year in a few cases.

S.P.Agrawal
J.C.Aggarwal

CONTENTS

General Editor's Introduction v

Preface vii

PART I : WORLD OVER VIEW

1. The Progress of Nations : A Fact Sheet 3
   - 1.1 Human World of Differences and Contrast : Challenges Facing the World *3*
   - 1.2 Meeting the Challenges : Tasks Ahead *14*
2. World Summit for Social Development : Copenhagen Declaration and Programme of Action (1995) 32
3. Advancement of Women : Fourth World Conference on Women (FWCW, 1995) 42
4. Human Development 51
5. Economic and Social Development : Comparative Country Profile 58
6. Select International Reports (1994-95 and 1995-96) 69

   A. 1994-95

   - 6.1 AIDS : International Conference (1994) *69*
   - 6.2 Drug Control : International Narcotics Control Board INCB Report (1994) *71*
   - 6.3 Economic and Social Survey : UN Report (1994) *73*
   - 6.4 Population : UNFPA Report (1994) *75*
   - 6.5 Population : Population Conference (1994) *77*
   - 6.6 Children : The State of The World's Children Report (1996) *78*
   - 6.7 Development : UNCTAD's Least Developed Countries Report (1995) *81*
   - 6.8 Development : World Development Report (1995) *83*
   - 6.9 Disasters : World Disasters Report (1995) *84*
   - 6.10 Employment : ILO Report on World Employment (1995) *86*
   - 6.11 Health : WHO Report (1995) *87*
   - 6.12 Investment : UNCTAD World Investment Report (1995) *89*
   - 6.13 Population : State of World Population Report (1995) *92*
   - 6.14 Poverty : Oxfarm Poverty Report (1995) *93*
   - 6.15 Refugees : UN High Commissioner for Refugees UNHCR Report (1995) *95*
   - 6.16 Trade and Development : UNCTAD's Report (1995) *97*
   - 6.17 World Bank : Annual Report (1995) *100*
7. Nations of the world 104

PART II : INDIA 1994-95 AND 1995-96

8. Land and Its People 117
9. India Since Independence (From 1993-94 Information India) 124

9.1 Achievements *124*
9.2 Progress made and Tasks Ahead *127*
9.3 Concluding observations *132*

10. Eighth Five Year Plan 133
11. State of Indian Economy 141
12. Balance of Payment, External Debt and Foreign Trade 153
13. Fiscal and Budgetary Developments 164
14. Inflation, Prices and Public Distribution System 178
15. Monetary Policy 184
16. Poverty Alleviation and Employment 189
17. Agriculture including Rural Development 199
18. Defence 214

18.1 National Security Environment *214*
18.2 Army *219*
18.3 Navy *220*
18.4 Air Force *221*
18.5 Defence Public Sector Undertakings *223*
18.6 Recruitment and Training *224*

19. Education and Culture 226
20. Energy (Coal, Electricity and Petroleum Policy) 237
21. Industry 247
22. Polity 260
23. Radio, Doordarshan and Media Policy 265
24. Science and Technology 273

24.1 Research and Development (R & D) *273*
24.2 Atomic Energy *274*
24.3 Technology *275*

25. Social Welfare (Including, Child and Women Development) 280

25.1 Welfare of Scheduled Castes, Scheduled Tribes, Minorities and the Disabled *280*
25.2 Child Development *284*
25.3 Women *288*

26. Transport and Communications 300
27. Diverse Issues 310

27.1 Environmental Conservation and Protection *310*
27.2 Housing *313*
27.3 Labour *314*
27.4 Medical and Health Care *315*
27.5 Population and Family Welfare *316*
27.6 Sports and Physical Education *318*
27.7 Youth Programmes *319*

CICIL List 320

PART ONE

WORLD OVER VIEW

1

THE PROGRESS OF NATIONS
A Fact Sheet

1.1 HUMAN WORLD OF DIFFERENCES AND CONTRASTS : CHALLENGES FACING THE WORLD

Widespread Poverty

Worldwise, one out of every five people—more than one billion in all—lives below the poverty line, and an estimated 13 million to 18 million die annually of poverty-related causes;

The ranks of those suffering extreme poverty will quadruple within one life time if current economic and demographic trends continue;

Entire nations are afflicted : developing country debt is offering. At $ 1.4 million, it is nearly double that of a decade ago. Servicing this debt means a net cash outflow from South to North and slashed social budgets which mean that the poorest in society bear the brunt of the burden.[1]

The Widening Income Gap

The annual per capita income in industrialized countries stands at $ 20,000 as compared to only $ 50 in the least developed countries of the world.[2]

The top 20 per cent of income earners receive 83 per cent of world income, while the bottom 20 per cent receive only 1.5 per cent.[3]

Internationally, the poorest 40 or 50 countries have seen their share of world income decline to the point where a fifth of the world's people now share less than 1.5 per cent of world income.[4]

Within individual nations, developing or industrialised, the poorest sections of the community are being increasingly marginalised; in the 44 developing nations and 20 industrialized countries for which figures are available, the poorest fifth non-share, on average little more than 5 per cent of national income, whilst the richest fifth claim between 40 per cent and 60 per cent.[5]

This tendency is not confined to the developing world ; in many industrialised nations a significant fraction of the population is also being excluded from social and economic progress. During the decade of the 1980s, for example, 4 million more American children fell below the official poverty line even as average incomes rose and the economy as a whole grew by 25 per cent.[6]

Similarly, in the United Kingdom, the proportion of the employed who earn less than half the average national income has doubled in the last three decades.[7]

An underclass is therefore, being created, undereducated and unskilled, standing beneath the broken bottom ranges of social and economic progress, victims of past poverty, of falling real wages, and of the fraying of social safety nets in 1980s.[8]

Unemployment and Decreasing Productive Employment

Out of a 1994 global population totaling some 5.3 billion people, 2.8 billion constitute the global workforce. Of these more than 120 million are estimated to be unemployed.[9]

One out of every 10 people of working age cannot find work paying a decent living.[10]

An estimated 30 per cent of the labour force—over 800 million people are not productively employed, that is, they are either hunting vainly for jobs or are underemployed, working at tasks that do not allow them to make ends meet. There are 700 million people in the underemployed category; these people constitute the majority of the 1.1 billion "absolutely poor" in the world.[11]

Twenty per cent of the world's total wage earners receive only 2 per cent of the world's income.[12]

World-wide, almost 40 per cent of rural women work without wages on their families' farms. Even when paid, rural women earn far less than men for the same work.[13] One out of 10 persons in the 24 major industrialized countries is unemployed.[14]

Sixty per cent of the overall population in developing countries live in rural areas, depending primarily on agriculture for their livelihood.[15]

Even though export crop prices have declined substantially in recent years, as the dominant sector of the economy, agriculture accounts for the bulk of the labour force and contributes an average 40 per cent of Gross Domestic Product.[16]

Some thirty million people, most of the women in developing countries, live hand to mouth lives in the so-called informal employment sector, without any sort of social security, insurance, disability or retirement benefits.[17]

In most regions of the world, unemployment and underemployment are rising rapidly.[18]

The average unemployment in industiralized countries is predicted to reach 8.6 per cent in 1994; Western Europe is expected to reach 12 per cent, while Eastern Europe may reach 15 per cent.[19]

Exacerbated by two decades of economic crises, the urban unemployment rate in Sub-Saharan Africa stands at almost 20 per cent with the vulnerable in formal sector comprising over 60 per cent of the urban labour force; in rural areas, underemployment affects well over half the labour force.[20]

In North Africa and the Middle East, unemployment ranges between 10 to 20 per cent, with youth being hardest hit.[21]

In Latin America, despite stringent structural adjustment policies, urban unemployment has once again climbed to 7 per cent, the level as in 1980.[22]

In South and East Asia, 50 per cent of the world's 1.1 billion poor live in South Asia, while another 15 per cent live in East Asia.[23]

Crime

Reported crime has grown at a world-wide average of 5 per cent each year since the 1980s; in the USA alone, there are 35 million crimes committed annually.[24]

Escalation of crime has been particularly swift in developing countries and countries in transition; for example the Russian Interior Ministry reported in 1994 that the country was beset by more than 5,600 gangs, almost 10 times more than in 1990.[25]

Illegal drug trafficking rakes in profit of some $ 500 billion a year—a sum equal to thc combined gross national products of two-thirds of the UN Member States put together.[26]

Criminal justice systems struggle to cope with increasingly complex and sophisticated types of crime, such as stock price manipulation, insider trading and credit card frauds.[27]

Domestic Violence

Violence in the home is both a symptom and a result of the breakdown of family values. Children are tragic victims. So a women, who are at more risk of being killed by their male partners than by any other kind of assault.[28]

Conflict

Conflict a symptom of disintegration, has claimed more than 20 million lives since 1945. Over the last decade, conflicts within countries have increased; of the 82 armed conflicts between 1989 and 1992, 79 were domestic, many along ethnic lines; 90 per cent of casualties were civilian.[30]

Migration

Conflict also produces refugees and forced migration. Migration itself has become a business. The International Organization for Migration reports that smuggling of migrants in after as lucrative as trafficking in drugs.[31]

Mounting fear of unemployment has led a number of major immigration countries to further restrict the flow of an estimated 30-35 million economically active migrants, 1.3 per cent of the global work force.[32]

Debt Crisis

External debt in developing countries nearly doubled over the past decade, reaching $ 1.4 trillion in 1992, resulting in a development standstill and increasing unemployment.[33]

Increasing Tension and Increasing Exclusion

These two different kinds of threat-increasing tension and increasing exclusion—are not separate issues.[34] It may be that, as one historian has written, "In all epoches men of one creed, class, race or state have tended to despise, hate and fear even of alien identities,"[35] but it is also the case that such tendencies are more likely to be kept within bounds by social and economic progress, by a reasonably equitable distribution of its benefits, and by the evolution of stable democracies, laws and institutions. No circumstances can wash the blood from the individual hands that have committed this year's crimes in Bosnia or Rwanda, but it would be a mistake to conclude that the root of such atrocities in ethnic and tribal hatred alone.[36]

New Crisis in Human Security

The Secretary-General of the United Nations, Boutros Boutros-Ghali, has argued that direct aggression by one country against another has now become rare, and that the traditional concept of security—the territorial security of states that was the original purpose of the United Nations has been largely achieved.[37] But within these states, there is to-day a "new cirsis in human security."[38] As Boutros Boutros-Ghali has said, "A shared commitment to social progress in the answer to shared threats of poverty, unemployment and social disintegration. It is time to shift from providing security through arms, to ensuring security through development.[39]

Suffering of Children

At one time, wars were fought between armies; but in the wars of last decade far more children than soldiers have been killed and disabled. Over that period, approximately 2 million children have died in wars, between 4 and 5 million have been physically disabled, more than 5 million have been forced into refugee camps and more than 12 million have been left homeless.

These are statistics of shame. And they cast a long shadow over future generation and their struggle for stability and social cohesion.

But the broader view must also recognise that armed conflict is not the only force which is affecting the normal development of million of children in the 1990s. More quietly, the continued economic and social marginalization of the poorest nations, and of the poorest communities within nations, is depriving far larger members of children of the kind of childhood which would enable them to become past of tomorrow's solutions rather than tomorrow's problems.[40]

One-third of the developing world's children suffer from protein-energy malnutrition.[41]

An estimated 250,000 children a year lose their eyesight because they lack vitamin A.[42]

At least 50 million children have impaired development because they lack iodine. Lack of iodine causes an estimated 100,000 infants a year to be born as cretins. In total, 1.6 billion people are at risk with consequences ranging from goitre to reduced mental and physical performance.[43]

Millions of infants are exposed to illness, poor growth, and early death by the decline in breast feeding.[44]

The three greatest threats to the health of children in the developing world are measles, diarrhoea, and pneumonia. Helped by poor nutrition, these three diseases kill approximately 7 million children a year and leave millions more malnourished.[45]

Every year 1 million children are killed by measles.

Diarrhoea disease still kills almost 3 million children every year despite the availability of the low-cost remedy known as oral rehydration therapy (ORT).[46]

Over 3 million children die from pneumonia.[47] Six lakhs new born die of tetanus.[48]

The annual tragedy of half a million children losing their sight was only the tip of a very much larger problem.[49]

In some areas of Africa, 25 to 35 per cent of pregnant women attending antenatal clinics are HIV-positive. One in three of their babies will be born with the virus. All well develop AIDS and most will die before the age of five. So far, approximately 1 million children have been infected and half a million have already died—almost all of them in Africa. Two-thirds of all new cases of HIV are now occurring in Africa where 9 million children will be orphaned in the 1990s and where recent gains in child survival are being reversed. AIDS has already become the biggest single killer of the nation's under-fires. But the situation in some countries in Asia is giving almost as much cause for concern.[50]

Abuse Against Women and Their Inequality

The death of half a million women a year in pregnancy and childbirth is described in this report as one of the least-protested scandals of the late 20th century. But it is rivaled by another of the great hidden issues—the violence inflicted on women by their male partners.[51]

Surveys in recent years indicate that almost a quarter of the world's women are violently abused in their own homes, Community-based surveys have yielded higher figures — up to 50 per cent in Thailand, 60 per cent in Papua New Guinea and The Republic of Korea, and 80 per cent in Pakistan and China. In the United States, domestic violence is the biggest single cause of injury to women accounting for more hospital admissions than rapes, muggings and road accidents combined.[52]

Many of the victims come to accept beatings as an inevitable accompaniment of a woman's inferior status in home and society.[53]

In the established industrial societies, the progress of recent years has still left most women a long way short of equality. Compared with men, they are underrepresented in the professions and in politics, underpaid in the workforce, and overworked by the multiple responsibilities of their domestic, child caring, and income-earning roles.[54]

In the developing world, discrimination can take harsher forms, ranging from female genital mutilation to the lifelong discrimination in nutrition and health and health care that is eventually revealed by the statistics on low-birth-weight.[55]

Women's share of seats in the world's parliaments has fallen from 13 to 10 per cent since the worldwide situation was last assessed in 1991, according to the Inter-Parliamentary Union.[56]

Educational Gap

Pupil Teacher Ratio Gap : The number of pupils per teacher in the world's primary schools varies from almost a dozen in Norway or Sweden to over 90 in the Central African Republic. Generally class sizes in the developing world are at least two to three times larger than classes in industrialised countries.[57]

Spending Gap : There are enormous differences between the amounts that different nations spend per pupil at all levels of education, ranging from over $ 2400 per head in the industrialized nations to less than $ 60 in sub-Saharan Africa.[58]

Adult Literacy Differences : Adult literacy rate varies from 99 per cent (almost 30) countries to less than 50 per cent (almost 30 countries); the lowest being 19per cent in Dfibouti.[59]

Discrepancies between Boys and Girls in Primary Schooling : The discrepancies between boys and girls in primary schooling mean that 14 million more girls than boys are out of school.[60]

For most of the developing world, where average literacy rates stand at 75 per cent for men, 55 per cent for women, the literacy gap in a reasonable overall guide to the degree of inequality between the sexes.[61]

Family Planning Gap

There are to-day an estimated 120 million women in the developing world who do not want to become pregnant but who are not using family planning. As a result, one pregnancy in every five is unwanted.[62] Only 40 out of 129 countries have family planning statistics dating from the 1990s—and about one third have no data at all for the last ten years.[63]

The education of girls has been shown to be one of the most powerful determinants of falling family size. Educated women usually have more opportunities, more awareness of family planning, and more decision-making power. They are also more likely to marry late to postpone the first pregnancy to leave more time between births and to have fewer children in total.[64]

Fertility rates have been falling for many years in every region of the world except Africa—where the first signs of decline are now becoming visible in countries such as Botswana, Kenya and Zimbabwe.[65]

Teenage pregnancy threatens the health and educational opportunities of girls, and child death rates in the developing world are approximately 50 per cent higher for babies born to girls under the age of 18.[66]

Population Disparities

When world population eventually stabilises, there will be more than double today's number of people on the planet, according to World Bank Projections. Although most industrialized countries are already close to zero population growth, many developing countries are expected to keep on growing well into the 21st century.[67]

China and India will vie for the title of most populous nation. [68]

More than half of the nations of sub-Saharan Africa will see their present populations increase five-fold before stabilizing.[69]

Unequal People's Participation

Only ten per cent of the world's people participate fully in the events and processes that shape their lives.[70]

Economies

Economies are growing but leaving people behind, which will result in a deficit of a billion jobs by the year 2000.[71]

Minorities

Minorities get a small piece of the pie, even in the world's richest country. Whites in the USA rank first in human development, while African, American and Hispanics rank belong some developing countries.[72]

Political Power

Political power stays in national capitals, particularly in the developing world. On average, less than ten per cent of total national spending in developing countries in delegated to local government, versus 40 per cent in industrial countries.[73]

Rural Poverty

The prevailing approach to development and poverty alleviation in the developing world is not working—or at least is not working well enough. Of the approximately 4 billion people living these, some 2.6 billion are in rural areas, and of these, close to one billion—almost a fifth of the global's total population live below the poverty line, 40 per cent more than just two decades ago. This is in spite of very substantial flows of assistance to poor countries.[74]

Rural poverty has many faces and can be measured in many ways. At the national level, four indices are used to indicate the overall rural poverty status:

- — Food Security Index (FSI) that attempts to portray the composite food security situation of a country by relating food production and consumption variables;
- — Integrated Poverty Index (IPI) that combines the head-count measure of poverty with the income-gap ratio, income distribution below the poverty line and the annual per capita GNP growth;
- — Basic Needs Index (BNI) that calculates such factors as adult literacy, primary school enrolment, population per physician, infant mortality rate and access to such services as health care, potable water and sanitation;
- — Relative Welfare Index (RWI), which is the arithmetic average of the other three indices.

On the basis of the above indices for 1988, countries can be classified and ranked.

- — *Food security* : Only 15 to 114 developing countries had a high food security status; 44 had a medium status and 55 and a low status. In Latin

America and the Caribbean, 17 of 32 countries are ranked low, in sub-Saharan Africa 19 of 45, in Asia 12 of 24 and in the Near East and North Africa 7 of 13.

—*Integrated Poverty* : Out of 114 developing countries, 22 have a low poverty status, 26 a medium status and 66 a high poverty status. Of the latter, 36 are in sub-Saharan Africa, 14 each in Asia and Latin America and the Caribbean, and 2 in the Near East and North Africa.

—*Basic Needs* : 40 countries fall in the low category, 50 in the medium and 24 in the high. In 1985-87, less than half of the rural population in 114 developing countries had access to safe water and sanitation, while only 60 per cent had access to health services.[75]

The rate of increase of rural poverty at present exceeds demographic growth and is expected to continue to accelerate well into the 21st century unless drastic measures are taken.[76]

Nearly 60 per cent of the rural poor in the developing world are women, over 550 million in all. In Asia alone, the number of poor rural women has reached 374 million, more than the entire population of Western Europe.[77]

The population process is a major factor in rural poverty in many countries, especially in the 37 countries where the annual population growth is over 3 per cent.[78]

Between 1965 and 1988, the availability of arable land per head agricultural population has been on the decline in every region of the developing world except Latin America and the Caribbean.[79]

The percentage of the agricultural work force that is engaged in wage labour varies from about 5 per cent in sub-Saharan Africa to 50 per cent in some Latin American countries and from 65 to 70 per cent in a number of Asian countries.[80]

Every year an estimated 6-7 million ha of agricultural land become unproductive through erosion; another 1.5 million ha are lost through waterlogging, salinization and alkalization; deforestation of tropical forests and woodland occurs at a rate of 11 million ha; over 70 per cent of all range lands and drylands are severely to moderately desertified.[81]

The landless and near landless, who number some 324 million, are both the largest and poorest group among the rural population in the developing world.[82]

In Latin America to-day, fewer than 10 per cent of landowners own almost 90 per cent of the land.[83]

In the Philippines, the proportion of rural workers who are landless has risen from 10 per cent in the 1950s to 50 per cent in the 1990s.[84]

In Bangladesh, the poorest 60 per cent of landowners have seen their share of the nation's farm land fall from 25 per cent in 1960 to 10 per cent in 1980. In Tanzania, the poorest 20 per cent of the population share only 2.44 per cent of national income, 2.7 per cent in Kenya and 3.98 per cent in Zimbabwe; in all three of those countries over 60 per cent of national income accrues to the richest 20 per cent of the people.[85]

Internationally, inequality has now reached monstrous proportions. Overall the richest fifth of the world now has almost 85 per cent of the world's GNP while the poorest fifth has just 1.5 per cent.[86]

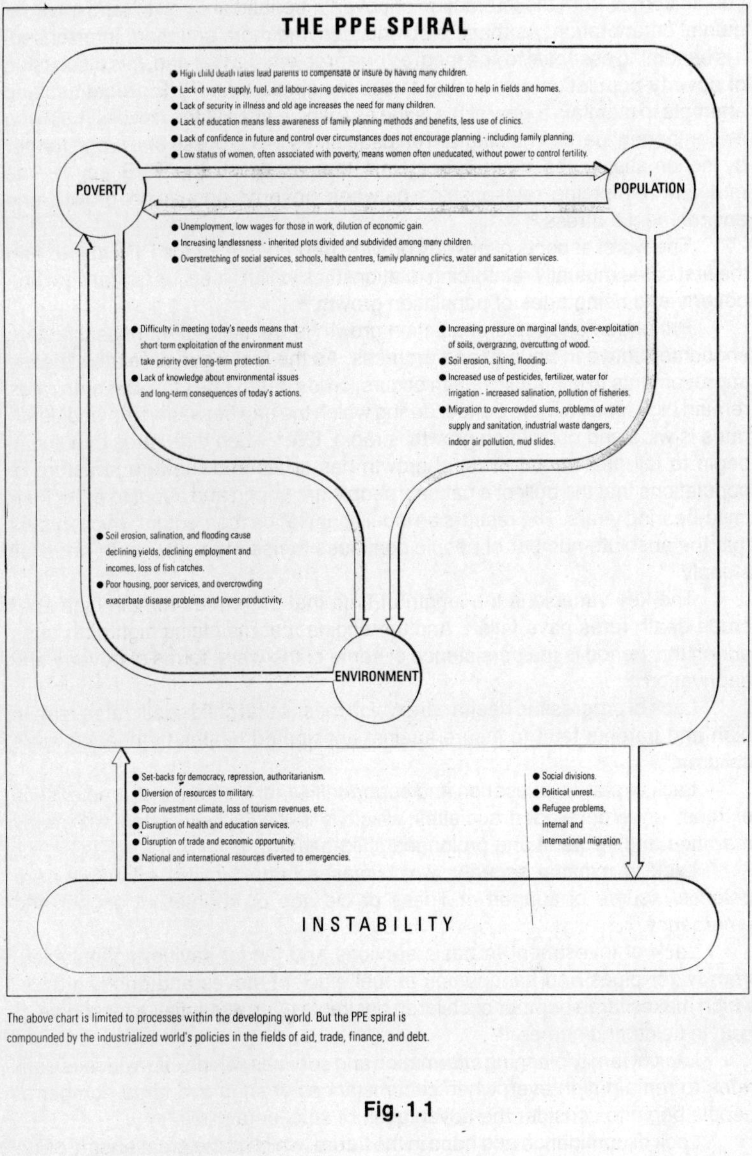

The above chart is limited to processes within the developing world. But the PPE spiral is compounded by the industrialized world's policies in the fields of aid, trade, finance, and debt.

Fig. 1.1

PPE Spiral (Poverty-Population-Environment Spiral)

Within an international economic framework that disables rather than enables the poorer countries and peoples, the principal threat to world's poorest billion people comes from the interaction of poverty, population growth, and environmental deterioration. As these problems become more and more interrelated, it is becoming essential to see them as one problem. To that end, this discussion of poverty-population-environment uses the single term 'PPE problems', and attempts to maintain a view of the issue as a whole even at the risk of simplifying its component parts. The diagram on page takes this process one stage further by schematising the main synergisms that made up the PPE spiral—the mutually reinforcing relationships between poverty, population growth and environmental stress.[87]

The worst aspects of poverty provide the impetus for the PPE spiral. And the first of the mutually reinforcing relationships which it sets up is that between poverty and rising rates of population growth.[88]

Prolonged and rapid population growth is the child of an unsatisfactory encounter between poverty and progress. As the first wave of relatively easy improvements in the public health occurs, crude death rates fall. But birth rates remain high for a variable period, during which the gap between birth and death rates is wide and population growth is rapid. Even when birth rates eventually begin to fall, the period of rapid growth has so altered the age structure of populations that the bulk of a nation's people are young and about to enter their child-bearing years. The result is an inbuilt population momentum which means that the absolute number of people continues to rise even after birth rates fall steaply.[89]

The key variable is the length of time that birth rates remain high after crude death rates have fallen. And the engine that maintains high birth rates during this period is the persistence of some of the worst forms of poverty and deprivation.[90]

Lack of progress in health care which means that child death rates remain high and parents tend to insure against anticipated deaths by hearing more children.[91]

Lack of status, education and opportunities for women, a characteristics of most underdeveloped societies which is strongly associated with early marriage and frequent and prolonged child-bearing.[92]

Lack of minimal security, which makes large families attractive as a potential source of support in illness or old age or in times of danger and emergency.[93]

Lack of investment in basic services and labour-saving technologies, from water-pipes and handpumps to fuel efficient stoves and grinding mills, which makes large number of children desirable even essential, as a source of help in fields and homes.[94]

Lack of family planning information and services, which often causes birth rates to remain high even when circumstances change and large number of people begin to consider the advantages of smaller families.[95]

Lack of confidence and hope in the future, which is the great enemy of life planning in general and family planning in particular.[96]

In sum, poverty is the coiled spring that powers population growth.[97]

Several recent studies have explored the relationship between poverty and environmental pressure.[98]

A Silent Crisis : A World of Contrasts

Behind the blaring headlines of the world's many conflicts and emergencies, there lies a silent crisis—a crisis of underdevelopment, of global poverty, of ever-mounting population pressures, of thoughtless degradation of environment.[99]

Despite all our technological break through, we still live in a world where a fifth of the developing world's population goes hungry every night, a quarter lacks access to even a basic necessity like safe drinking water, and a third lives in a state of object poverty—at such a margin of human existence that words simply fail to describe it.[100]

We also live in a world of disturbing contrasts—where so many go hungry, there is so much food to waste; where so many children do not live to enjoy their childhood, there are so many inessential weapons. Global military spending despite a welcome decline, still equals the combined income of one-half of humanity each year. And the richest billion people command 60 times the income of the poorest billion.[101]

Poor nations and rich are afflicted by growing human distress—weakening social fabrics, rising crime rates, increasing threats to personal security, spreading narcotic drugs and a growing sense of individual isolation.[102]

The threats to human society are no longer just personal or local or national. They are becoming global : with drugs, AIDS, terrorism, pollution, nuclear proliferation. Global poverty and environmental problems respect no national border. Their grim consequences travel the world.[103]

The same speed that has helped unify the world has also brought many problems to our doorsteps with devastating suddenness. Drug dealers can launder money rapidly through many countries—in a fraction of the time it takes their victims to detoxify. And terrorists operating from a remote safe haven can destroy life on a distant continent.[104]

The basic question of human survival on an environmentally fragile planet has gained in urgency as well. By the middle of the next century—still in the lifetimes of to-day's children—the world population may double and the world economy may quadruple. Food production must triple if people are to be adequately fed, but the resource base for sustainable agriculture is eroding. Energy must be provided too, but even at today's level of use, fossil fuels threaten climatic stability. The destruction of the world's forests and the loss of biological wealth and diversity continue relentlessly.[105]

Several nation-states are beginning to disintegrate. While the threats to national survival may emerge from several sources—ethnic, religious, political—the underlying causes are often the lack of socio-economic progress and the limited participation of people in such progress.[106]

People go hungry not because food is unavailable—but because they cannot afford it.[107]

1.2 MEETING THE CHALLENGES : TASKS AHEAD

New Role of UN: Against this background of human achievement and distress we must seek a new concept of human security in the decades ahead. We must seek a new paradigm of sustainable human development that can satisfy the expanding frontiers of this human security. We must seek a new framework of development cooperation that brings humanity together through a more equitable sharing of global economic opportunities and responsibilities. And we must seek a new role for the United Nations so that it can begin to meet humanity's agenda not only for peace but also for development.[108]

Shared Commitment: A shared commitment to social progress is the answer to shared threats of poverty, unemployment, and social disintegration ... It is time to shift from providing security through arms, to ensuring security through development.[109]

Sustainable Development: There is to-day a considerable agreement that the way forward lies along the path of democratic politics and marked-friendly economics; of government action to ensure that growth benefits the many and not just the few; of meeting human needs and investing in human capacities through better health, nutrition, and education; of the restructuring of government expenditures and aid programmes in favour of basic social services and employment opportunities for the poor; of ending the discrimination against women and girls that is so unacceptable in principle and so ruinous of development efforts in practice; of reducing fertility through a comprehensive approach combining family planning information and services, lowered child death rates, improved levels of education, and the empowerment of women to decide how many children to have and when; of rethinking unjust and unsustainable patterns of consumption and pollution in industrialized nations; of significant cuts in arms expenditures and an increase in the resources available for environmentally sustainable development, of a reorientation of economic assistance towards countries that spend less on military capacity and more on meeting the basic needs of the poorest; of debt cancellation and reduction for the least developed nations; of a new level of international effort to assist sub-Saharan Africa to resume its progress; and of a significant increase in the level and efficiency of investment in the developing world.[110]

The search for human security lies in development, not in arms.[111]

Sustainable human development is development that not only generates economic growth but distributes its benefits equitably; that regenerates the environment rather than destroying it, that empowers people rather than marginalizing them. It gives priority to the poor, enlarging their choices and opportunities, and provides for their participation in decisions affecting them. It is development that is pro-poor, pro-nature, pro-jobs, pro-democracy, pro-women and pro-children.[112]

Children at the Centre

The 1990 World Summit for Children, bringing to-gether representatives of over 150 governments including 71 heads of state, had formally adopted a series of goals for the year 2000, including a one-third reduction in child deaths, a halving of child malnutrition, immunization levels of 90per cent, control of the major childhood diseases, the eradication of polio, the elimination of micronutrient deficiencies, a halving of maternal mortality rates, primary school education for at least 80per cent of children, the provision of clear water and safe sanitation to all communities, and the universal ratification of the new convertion on the Rights of the Child.[113]

Unless the investment in children is made all of humanity's most fundamental long-term problems will remain fundamental long-term problems.[114]

Improvments in child survival, which increase the predictability of the family building process, trigger the transition from natural to controlled fertility behaviour.[115]

The effort to reduce child illness and malnutrition and to reach the goals of the World Summit for Children is crucial not only for its own sake but also as a means of helping to slow population growth and make possible environmentally sustainable development in the 21st century and beyond.[116]

World Summit for Children on the Development of Children

The following is the full list of year 2000 goals which the world's political leaders agreed upon—as being technically and financially feasible—at the World Summit for Children on 30 September, 1990.

Overall goals 1990-2000

- A one-third reduction in under-five death rates (or a reduction to 70 per 1,000 live births—whichever is lower).
- A halving of maternal mortality rates.
- A halving of severe and moderate malnutrition among the world's under-fives.
- Safe water and sanitation for all families.
- Basic education for all children and completion of primary education by at least 80 per cent.
- A halving of the adult illiteracy rate and the achievement of equal educational opportunity for males and females.
- Protection for the many millions of children in especially difficult circumstances and the acceptance and observance, in all countries, of the recently adopted Convention on the Rights of the Child. In particular, the 1990s should see rapidly growing acceptance of the idea of special protection for children in time of war.

Protection for Girls and Women

- Family planning education and services to be made available to all couples to empower them to prevent unwanted pregnancies and births which are 'too many and too close' and to women who are 'too young or too old'. Such services should be adapted to each country's cultural, religious, and social traditions.
- All women to have access to prenatal care, a trained attendant during childbirth and referral facilities for high-risk pregnancies and obstetric emergencies.

- Universal recognition of the special health and nutritional needs of females during early childhood, adolescence, pregnancy, and lactation.

Nutrition

- A reduction in the incidence of low birth weight (under 2.5 kg) to less than 10 per cent.
- A one-third reduction in iron deficiency anaemia among women.
- Virtual elimination of vitamin A deficiency and iodine deficiency disorders.
- All families to know the importance of supporting women in the task of exclusive breastfeeding for the first four to six months of a child's life.
- Growth monitoring and promotion to be institutionalized in all countries.
- Dissemination of knowledge to enable all families to ensure house-hold food security.

Child Health

- The eradication of polio.
- The elimination of neonatal tetanus (by 1995).
- A 90 per cent reduction in measles cases and a 95 per cent reduction in measles deaths, compared to pre-immunization levels.
- Achievement and maintenance of at least 90 per cent immunization coverage of one-year-old children and universal tetanus immunization for women in the child-bearing years.
- A halving of child deaths caused by diarrhoea and a 25 per cent reduction in the incidence of diarrhoeal diseases.
- A one-third reduction in child deaths caused by acute respiratory infections.
- The elimination of guinea worm disease.

Education

- In addition to the expansion of primary school education and its equivalents, today's essential knowledge and life skills could be put at the disposal of all families by mobilizing today's vastly increased communications capacity.[117]

Rights of the Child

The Convention on the Rights of the Child (1989) says that all children have a right to survival, health care and education. Convention also demands protection against exploitation and abuse—in the home, at work, and in wars.

There are many who say that the international Convention on the Rights of the Child is just another piece of paper, another list of pious intentions, another example of the international community sinking its gums into the great issues of the day. But if people and their organizations in all countries continue to mobilize behind the Convention, campaigning to hold 150 governments to their promise, then it will eventually become a standard below which any civilized nation—rich or poor—will be ashamed to fall.[118]

By incorporating the right of every child to survive and to develop normally, and to receive at least basic health care and a primary education, the Convention on the Rights of the Child bridges, for the first time, the ideological gap which has always separated economic and social rights from civil and political rights. And it stands as an internationally agreed minimum standard for the treatment of children everywhere.[119]

In less than 5 years, the vast majority of the World's Nations—167 altogether have ratified the convention on the Rights of the Child. Nine more have signed the document—indicating an intention to ratify in the near future. Only 14 nations (including Saudi Arabia and the United States) have neither signed nor ratified as of fall 1994.[120]

A universally accepted code for the treatment of children is a major step forward. It provides an unchallangeable platform for advocacy and action on behalf of children in all countries and in all circumstances, and it prepares the way for the next and obviously more difficult stage—the stage of moving from universal acceptance to universal observance.[121]

Education

Measuring quality in education is even more difficult than measuring quantity.[122]

Advancing literacy is one indicator. But literacy can be difficult to define, and mainly reflects educational achievement in the past.[123]

Starting school at the right stage is also important—as children learn best when lessons are geared to the right age and stage of development.[124]

Finally, the ratio of teachers to school-age children, and the average amount spent per pupil are also indicators of the efforts being made.[125]

In many countries, the poor quality of the education on offer, combined with limited job opportunities and the need for children to help their families in fields and homes, means that large numbers drop out of school before completing even one or two years. In South Asia and South America, for example, more than 95 per cent of children enrol in grade I of primary school but only about 50 per cent reach grade 5.[126]

The experience of several countries over recent years has shown the great gains that can be made and sustained at an affordable cost.[127]

The principal elements of these successful strategies appear to be : The use of parateachers in preschools and primary schools, short teacher training periods, regular support and supervision of teacher performance, small school units close to the communities served; low capital costs of school buildings; active involvement of communities and parents; relevant basic curricula presented in an interesting way; school calendars and time tables that take into account the seasonal demands for children to help in agriculture; and the support of local non-governmental organizations.[128]

The links between educational advance and resolving PPE problems are many. To begin with, education, like health, helps people to loosen the hold of poverty. Many studies, particularly those initiated by the World Bank in recent years have demonstrated this effect. In agriculture, for example, studies in Malaysia, the Republic of Korea and Thailand, and more recently in Bangladesh, India, Nepal, Pakistan, and several Latin American countries, have shown that farmers with schooling are more productive than similarly situated farmers without education.[129]

Overall increases in literacy levels and in primary school enrolment have been found to be strongly associated with more rapid increases in per capita incomes and with greater economic equality.[130]

Women's Education and Power

Education can give a woman more awareness, more choice and more confidence. It raises her value and status in the eyes of her husband, her family and her community.[131]

It is this powerful set of practical, affordable, and mutually reinforcing changes—in education, family planning, health, and women's technologies—that could do most to bring about the beginnings of a transformation for many millions of women in the developing world.[132]

The right of women to hold title to land and to inherit must be ensured and protected.[133]

The biggest answer is known to us already. Of all the social and economic forms of investment which affect fertility behaviour, the level of education of women stands out as the most consistent... In several high-fertility traditional societies, women who have completed primary school and above have about three children less than their unschooled or moderately schooled (1 to 3 years) counterparts. The observed reduction in marital fertility is linked to delayed marriage, effective contraceptive use and plausibly, the higher expectations held by educated mothers for their children... A girl with secondary education typically marries at 21. A girl with none marries at 17. If the higher age were global, there would be close to 1 billion fewer of us before our planet reached population stability.[134]

There is widespread agreement that the education of girls is one of the most important investments that any developing country can make in its own future.[135]

In the long term, almost every other aspect of progress, from nutrition to family planning, from child health to women's rights, is profoundly affected by whether or not a nation educates its girls.[136]

The educational progress of nations is judged by the percentage of girl children who reach at least grade 5 of primary school. [137]

More Schooling, Fewer Births

The education of girls has been shown to be one of the most powerful determinants of falling family size. Educated women naturally have more opportunities, more awareness of family planning, and more decision-making power. They are also more likely to marry late to postpone the first pregnancy, to leave more time between births, and to have fewer children in total.[138]

Family Planning

Almost all the world's political leaders have agreed that family planning should be made available to all couples by the end of the century reaching that goal would bring immeasurable benefits to the lives of millions of women and children.[139]

The world now has enough knowledge and experience to be able to meet the existing demand for family planning, and to increase that demand, in ways that are totally human and totally respectful of human rights. We must now use that knowledge and experience as the basis for a major renewal of the family planning effort. And we must do this for the sake of the women and children of to-day—and for the world of tomorrow.[140]

Population Control and Human Development

The population issue is one of today's major planetary problems towards the solution of which education must contribute... An education concerning population issues should be provided to both sexes and all age groups, at all levels and in both formal and non-formal education...[141]

Every birth in the developed countries puts as much pressure on resources as tens of births in the developing countries.[142]

Whereas a few centuries ago the population doubled in 300 years, it will now double within a few decades. At the same time, environmental, social and cultural deterioration is accelerating. The world's population increases by more than 90 million people every year. As population growth increases in turn the demand for goods and services, environmental degradation may well grow dramatically.[143]

Those regions of the world with the highest population growth rates are experiencing rapid transformations, especially of their agricultural land, thus destroying natural habitats. In other areas, where population is not increasing, consumption is increasing instead. Over-consumption puts pressure on the global resources and generates pollution and waste.[144]

On the other hand, the rapid industrialization of some areas stimulates migration to these areas which can further accentuate environment and social problems. Population increases combined with consumption increases may lead to human, economic and environmental disaster. The increasing consumption of an increasing number of persons, mainly in the developed countries, is damaging the shared resources that support humanity. Rapid population growth, especially in developing countries, undermines the efforts made by these countries to attain acceptable living standards. The problems of over-consumption and overcrowding cross all borders and are linked to all the problems facing the inhabitants of the planet Earth.[145]

Reduction of world population growth and gradual stabilization of the number of people living in our world are today indisputable objectives of the international community.[146]

UNESCO and the UN population Fund (UNFPA) organized the First International Congress on Population Education and Development (Istanbul, April 1993). The Congress reviewed trends in population education over the past two decades, and adopted a Declaration on the role of population education in human development and an action framewrokd for strengthening and institutionalizing population education during the 1990s and beyond.[147]

Because tomorrow's parents have already been born and the impacts of fertililty decline won't be felt fore several decades, the world has to prepare itself to cope with a global population of 8 to 9 billion people in 2025. Therefore, the measures to be taken must not be confined to the sole objective of reducing fertility.[148]

On the one hand, we must personally and in daily life help modify prevailing sexual and gender roles and stereotypes and replace them with new roles based on partnership. On the other hand we must demand that policy-makers take measures to reduce and eliminate inequalities in all aspects of life (economic, sexual, social, etc). This requires active collaboration with those organizations whose objectives are to :

— work for environmentally, socially and culturally sustainable societies, at both the local and global scales;
— defend universal access to information, education and debate about gender, the roles of men and women, reproduction and family planning;
— formulate strategies for maintaining and improving living standards and satisfying people and communities needs;
— foster decision-making, at all levels, that takes into account men and women equitably;
— ensure that women have access to locally and individually adapted, high-quality comprehensive reproductive health services, and that these services are provided free of incentives and obstacles;
— support policies encouraging responsible parenting and gender equality in family responsibilities; and
— favour suitable legislation in favour of women's education, professional training, paid employment, access to loans, and the right to own land and other goods.

Furthermore, Each of Us Can

— support and work with organizations committed to the task of promoting women's health and reproductive rights, and organizations linked to the communities they serve;
— exercise the right to take part in the design, implementation and control of policies and programmes related to the local community; and
— put pressure on the media to avoid the use of sexist stereotypes and messages encouraging over-consumption.[149]

Social Expenditure

Most countries could in fact go a long way towards the meeting of basic needs by a fairer allocation of existing social expenditure. In Indonesia, for example, government spending on the health of the richest 10 per cent amounts to three times more than on the poorest 10 per cent.[150]

Similarly in India, 75 per cent of government health spending is allocated to curative services in urban areas where 25 per cent of the population lives, and 12,000 medical doctors a year are being trained at the cost of a public whom they do not serve 80 per cent of graduates go straight into private practice in urban areas.[151]

The same case can be made in education.[152]

Such distortions are common across the spectrum of basic social services of the $ 10 billion to $ 12 billion a year that is currently spent on water supply and sanitation, for example, 80 per cent is allocated to relatively high cost systems-water treatment plants, pumping stations, individual household water supplies, and highly mechanized sewage system—serving mostly the better off communities.[153]

Proposals that these expenditure patterns should be shaken up and redirected in favour of the poor are not the product of some radical imagination. The World Bank, for example, has made a significant contribution to this aspect of the current consensus. In its *World Development Report* 1993, the Bank concluded, governments in developing countries should spend far less—on average, about 50 per cent less—than they now do on less cost—effective interventions and instead double or triple spending on basic public health programmes.[154]

Similarly, on water supply, the Bank argues that government can also improve the use of public resources by eliminating widespread subsidies for water and sanitation that benefit the middle class.[155]

The principal technologies for meeting children's needs at relatively low cost are already available. The social capacity is largely in place. And the financial cost is frankly negligible in relation to what humanity has at stake in this race. It has been estimated by UNDP, UNEPA, and UNICEF, for example, that the total cost of providing basic social services in the developing countries, including health, education, family planning, clean water, and all of the other basic social goals agreed on at the World Summit for Children, would be in the region of an additional $ 30 billion to $ 40 billion-a year, two thirds of which could come from the developing countries themselves. The world spends more than this on playing golf.[156] The United States share of this bill S. N. 80 P. 62, 1995 would be less than is spent, nationally on advertising tobacco. The United States spends $ 25 billion a year on its prison services alone.[157] Germany finds more than $ 30 billion each year to meet the social costs of reunification. Japan is about to invest approximately ten times as much in an optical fibre network for the next century.[158]

Expanding Water and Sanitation Facilities

Reports from 93 nations suggest that progress commensurate with reaching the goal of clean water for all is being made in approximately 40 countries. For safe sanitation, perhaps only a third of the developing countries are likely to reach the goal on present trends.[159] This effort is a continuation of the International Drinking Water Supply and Sanitation Decade (1981-1990), which saw the proportion of families with access to safe drinking water rise from

38 to 66 per cent in South-East Asia, from 66 to 80 Latin America and from 32 to 42 per cent in Africa.[160]

In India, the percentage of rural people with access to safe water has risen from just over 30 per cent in 1980 to about 80 per cent in 1992, and on present trends will reach almost 100 per cent by 1997 or 1998.[161]

Fundamental Changes in Development Consensus : Agricuiturai and Land Reforms

Poor-oriented and labour intensive patterns of growth, most families could be enabled to meet their own needs.[162]

One of the gravest of past errors has been in associating development with industry, notably primary industry. And farm prices, in frequent cases, have been deliberately kept low as a favour to the urban population. This has been a disastrous error, redeemed too often only in later hunger. It is noteworthy that the developed states, all of them in the past, strongly favoured their farmers and still do...[163]

Closely associated with agricultural development is land reform. No century in recent times has flourished under an economic and political system of great landlords or even of small ones. Both economic progress and political democracy require that economic independence be accorded to the men and women who till the land.[164]

Governments must improve the conditions of the landless poor through land distribution and land texure reform, and accompany these with improved access to credit, supplies and equipment, irrigation and water systems, markets and extension services. International financial agencies can assist in the process by providing the financial resources needed for land surveys, settlement of conflicting claims and land improvement. The rights of women to hold title to land and to inherit must be ensured and protected.[165]

Hopeful Signs

The necessary task of drawing attention to human needs has unfortunately given rise to the popular impression that the developing world is a stage upon which no light falls and only tragedy is enacted. But the fact is that, for all the setbacks, more progress has been made in the last 50 years than in the previous 2,000. Since the end of the Second World War, average real incomes in the developing world has more than doubled; infant and child death rates have been more than halved, average like expectancy has increased by about a third; the proportion of the developing world's children starting school has risen to more than three quarters; and the percentage of rural families with access to safe water has increased from less than 10 per cent to almost 60 per cent.[166]

Over that same time, much of the world has also freed itself from colonialism, brought apartheid in all its forms to the edge of extinction, and largely freed itself from the iron grip of fascist and totalitarion regimes.[167]

In the decades ahead, a clear opportunity exists to make the breaks through against what might be called the last great obscenity—the needless malnutrition, disease and illiteracy that still cast a shadow over the lives, and the futures of the poorest quarter of the world's children.[168]

Progress in Child Welfare

Four years after the 1990 World Summit for Children, practical progress is made in a large measure. More than 100 of the developing nations, with over 90per cent of the developing world's children, are making significant progress towards the goals. Malnutrition has been reduced; immunization levels are generally being maintained or increased; measles death are down by 80 per cent compared to pre-immunization levels; large areas of the developing world have become free of polio; iodine deficiency are being overcome; the use of oral rehydration therapy (ORT) is rising (preventing more than a million child deaths a year); guinea worm disease has been reduced by some 90 per cent and complete eradication is insight; thousands of hospitals are actively supporting breast feeding; progress in primary education is being resumed; and the Convention on the Rights of the Child has become the most widely and rapidly ratified convention in history. Such progress means that approximately 2.5 million few children will die in 1996 than in 1990. It also means that tens of millions will be spared the insidious sabotage wronght on their development by malnutrition. And it means that at least three quarters of a million few children each year will be disabled, blinded, crippled, or mentally retarded.[169]

Expansion of Primary Education

According to a mid-1994 review by UNICEF, 42 of 95 countries have achieved or are on target to achieve the 1995 goal of a one-third reduction in the gap between 1990 primary school completion rates and the 80per cent target set for the year 2000. New commitments to the 80per cent goal have been made in 1993 and 1994 by the Presidents or Prime Ministers of nine of the most populous nations of the developing world. China, Indonesia and Mexico have already achieved a minimum of four years of schooling for at least 80per cent of their children. Brazil, Egypt and India could reach the goal if the accelerated efforts now being in all three countries are continued. Bangladesh, Nigeria and particularly Pakistan face a massive—but not impossible-task; all three have renewed their efforts to expand primary education in the 1990s.[170] Meanwhile, the World Bank has honoured the promise of gometin by tripling lending for primary education to nearly $ 1 billion a year in 1993.[171]

Progress in Family Planning

In the early 1990s fewer than 15 million couples in the developing world outside China were using contraception. To-day, some 380 million couples in the developing world are talking charge of their fertility—over half of all couples in the child-bearing years. There is no doubt that the world is in transition, social and demographic. We are on the way to creating a world in which mankind's success in reducing death rates is matched by a move towards fewer, healthier and planned births. Such a world will be one in which women everywhere have a right to control their own fertility. It will be one in which reproductive health is a matter of universal care and concern. It will be a world where population growth rates no longer fuel urban and environmental pressures which help perpetuate gross disparities of wealth and poverty and which lead to continuing destruction of the spaceship in which we travel.[172]

Reconsideration of Priorities : Cut in Military Spending

The governments of developing countries should allocate at least 20 per cent of their expenditures to meeting priority human needs for adequate nutrition, clean water, safe sanitation, basic health care, primary education, and family planning information and services, and that the industrialized nations should restructure existing aid programmes in order to also allocate a minimum of 20per cent to these same basic priorities (this is now an agreed position of UNDP, UNICEF, and UNFPA).[173]

Both developing and industrialized nations should agree to a targeted annual reduction rate for military spending (UNDP) suggests a 3 per cent per year reduction, which would yield approximately $ 460 billion in the second half of this decade.[174]

The case for such restructuring has become a major part of to-day's consensus on social development.[175]

New Concept of Security

Governments and peoples need to reconsider their older definitions of what constitutes a threat to national and international security. Regardless of whether the cold war is over or whether an end can be brought to Middle East rivalries, these now exist vast non-military threats to the safety and well-being of the peoples of this planet which deserve attention...just as nation-state rivalries are being overtaken by bigger issues, we may have to think about the future on a far broader scale than has characterized thinking about international politics in the past.[176]

International Aid

To ease the financial famine and to support the developing world in reaching the basic human goals that have been agreed, will demand considerable vision on the part of leaders in industrialized nations. But it will also require the courage and tenacity to hold fast to that vision in the face of all the immediate problems and pressures crowding the agendas of political leader in the 1990s. At least 20 per cent international aid should be allocated to meeting the minimum human needs of the poorest people.[177]

Improbable or not, something like the Marshall Plan—a Global Marshall Plan, if you will—is now urgently needed. The scope and complexity of this plan will far exceed those of the original; what is required now is a plan that combines large-scale, long-term, carefully targeted financial aid to developing nations, massive efforts to design and then transfer to poor nations the new technologies needed for sustainable economic progress, a world-wide programme to stabilize world population, and binding commitments by the industiral nations to accelerate their own transition to an environmentally responsible pattern of life.[178]

The Marshall Plan took the broadest possible view of Europe's problems and developed strategies to serve human needs and promote sustained economic progress; must now do the same on a global scale.[179]

Almost every commission report, and conference of the last 20 years has repeated. The industiralized nations should fulfil their pledge to give at least 0.7per cent of GNP in official development assistance. Currently, only Norway, Sweden, Denmark and the Netherlands are doing so.[180]

New Design for Development Cooperation

The 1994 Human Development Report's new design for development cooperation in the coming decades envisions a scenario where

— aid is regarded as an essential investment by the rich nations in their own human security.
— developing countries are compensated for trade and immigration barriers imposed by the rich nations.
— polluting nations are made to pay for over-use of the global commons.
— the potential peace divided of nearly $ 500 billion between 1995 and 2000 in earmarked primarily for the human development agenda.
— and global compacts are negotiated in specific areas between rich and poor nations—population, environment, drug control—based on two-way cooperation, not on one-way conditionality coercision.

It is in these above contexts that the 1994 Human Development Report suggests a six-point agenda.

1. A World Social Order, to arrive at a new social contract among all nations and all people.
2. A reduction of 3per cent a year in future global military spending, with 20 per cent of the savings by rich nations and 10 per cent by poor nations earmarked for global human security.
3. A 20 : 20 compact for human development—to provide basic education, primary health care, safe drinking water and essential family planning services to all people over the next decade—by earmarking 20 per cent of the existing developing country budgets and 20 per cent of the existing aid allocation to these basic human priority concerns (this is easily the most important and most feasible policy recommendations of the Human Development Reports).
4. A global security fund—financed from global taxes such as the 'Tobin Tax' on speculative movements of international funds an international tax on the consumption of non-renewable energy, global environmental permits and a tax on arms trade.
5. A new framework of development cooperation, to graduate from the present aid relationship to a more mature developing partnership—by

including trade, technology, investment and labour flows in a broader design to be negotiated among nations, and

6. An Economic Security Council in the United Nations, as the highest decision-making forum to consider basic issues of human security such as global poverty, unemployment, food security, drug trafficking, global pollution, international migration and a new framework of sustainable human development.[181]

The Role of the United Nations

In 50 years of working for development and collaborating with governments and aid agencies in over 150 developing countries, the United Nations family of organization has built up an enormous fund of experience and expertise in almost area of social development. This capacity too, must now be more fully exploited for the implementation of to-day's development consensus. The United Nations can play a key role in responding to new threats to human security in the 21st century—just as it has played a key role in helping to achieve the territorial security of states in the 20th century.[182]

This mixture—which I term a new paradigm for development action is—I believe of widespread applicability, just as the success of immunization over the 1980s has led on to a broader agenda of goals for improving the health and welfare of children, so this model could also be applied to other areas of international action; to new approaches to peacemaking and conflict prevention; to human development focused on the eradication of poverty; to strengthening of human rights and democratic processes; to environmental protection and sustainable development; to management of global economic and financial relationships. It will require stronger leadership from the international agencies. It will certainly require support from the governments concerned. It will require new means by the United Nations agencies for reaching out to win understanding and support from the publics in individual countries, using the media to explain their mission and to mobililze a greater sense of effectiveness. But above all it will require an abandonment of the cynism towards international action and some resurgence of hope and belief in the humanitarian mission of the United Nations and of international action move generally. Such vision is not beyond us, and such vision has...always been present at the most creative periods of the international agencies.[183]

Becoming Involved

Being involved in a cause larger than oneself is a deep human need from which we have been diverted by the particular direction that progress has taken in recent times. If so, it is a need of which George Bernard Shaw has left us a powerful reminder.[184] This is the true joy in life, the being used for a purpose recognised by yourself as a mighty one. I am of the opinion that my life belongs to the whole community and as long as I live it is my privilege to do for it whatever I can. Life is no brief candle to me. It is a sort of splendid torch which I have got hold of for the moment, and I want to make it burn as brightly as possible before handing it on to future generations.[185]

Words and Actions

In the past, the international development effort has lacked any real urgency; there have been no deadlines attached, no imperative other than the humanitarian, no spur other than the nag of conscience, no consequences of failure other than for the poor themselves. All this is now changing. Development now has a deadline. And failure to meet it will bring consequences not just for the poor but for all. Implementing to-day's development consensus is, therefore, becoming not only a moral minimum for our civilization but a practical minimum for ensuring its survival.[186]

Taken together, all of these factors may mean that the world is about to fulfil the promise held out by the historian Arnold Toynbee who wrote, in the years before the cold war descended upon the world that "our age is the first generation since the down of history in which mankind dared to believe it practical to make the benefits of civilization available to the whole human race."[187]

NOTES AND REFERENCES

1. *UN Newsletter*, August 1994, New Delhi.

2., 3. *UN Newsletter*, November 1994, New Delhi.

4. United Nations Development Programme, *Human Development Re port 1994*, UNDP, New York, 1994.

5. World Bank, *World Development Report 1994 : Infrastructure for Development*, World Bank, Washington, D.C., 1994.

6. Johnson, Clifford M., and others, *Child Poverty in America*, Children's Defense Fund, Washington, D.C., 1991.

7. United Nations Department of Public Information, 'The Job Crisis', DPI/1485-94, backgrounder 1, press kit for World Summit for Social Development, United Nations, New York, July 1994.

8. *The State of the World's Children 1995*, UNICEF New York, 1995.

9. to 11. *UN Newsletter*, August 1994, New Delhi.

12 , 13. *UN Newsletter*, November 1994, New Delhi.

14 to 23. *UN Newsletter*, August 1994, New Delhi.

24 to 29. *UN Newsletter*, November 1994, New Delhi.

30 to 32. *UN Newsletter*, August 1994, New Delhi.

33. *UN Newsletter*, November 1994, New Delhi.

34. *The State of the World's Children 1995.*

35. Brogan, Hugh, *The Pelican History of the United States*, Penguin Book/ Viking, 1987, p. 107.

36. *The State of the World's Children 1995.*

37. Boutros-Ghali, Boutros, address to second session of the Preparatory Committee for the World Summit for Social Development, New York, 22 August 1994.

38. *The State of the World's Children 1995.*

39. Boutros-Ghali, Boutros, *op. cit.*

40. *The State of the World's Children 1995.*

41 to 48. *The Progress of Nations*, UNICEF, 1994.

49 to 53. *The State of the World's Children 1995.*

54 to 69. *The Progress of Nations*, UNICEF, 1994.

70 to 73. *Human Development Report 1993*, UNDP, 1994.

74. *Press Release*, November 23, 1992. International Fund for Agricultural Development (IFAD), Italy.

75 to 82. *The State of World Rural Poverty*, synopses 1 to 8. IFAD, 1992.

83. Harison, Paul, *The Third Revolution*, Penguin Books London, 1992.

84. 'Philippines : The Answer's a Tomato', *The Economist*, 21 May 1994, p. 86.

85. World Bank, *World Development Report 1994*, *op. cit.*, table 30, p. 220.

86. United Nations Development Programme *Human Development Report*, 1994.

87 to 90. *The State of the World's Children 1994*, UNICEF.

91. Ross, John A., and others. *Family Planning and Child Survival Programmes as Assessed in 1991.* Population Council, New York, 1992.

92. Le Vine, Robert A., and others. 'Women's Schooling and Child care in the Demographic Transition : A Mexico Case Study', *Population and Development Review*, Vol. 17, No. 3. September 1991.

93. Clay, Daniel C., and Vander Haar, Jane E., 'Patterns of Intergenerational Support and Child bearing in The Third World', *Population Studies*, Vol. 47, 1993.

94. *Ibid.*

95 to 96. United Nations, Department of International Economic and Social Affairs, "Family Building by Fate or Design : A Study of Relationships between Child Survival and Fertility". ST/ESA/SER.R/74, United Nations, New York, 1987.

97. *The State of The World's Children 1994.* UNICEF.

98. Leonard, Jeffrey, ed., *Environment and the Power* : Development Strategies for *a Common Agenda.* Overseas Development Council, Washington, D.C., 1989 World Commission on Environment and Development (Brundt land Commission, *Our Common Future*, Oxford University Press, 1987.

99 to 108. *Human Development Report* 1994. UNDP.

109. Boutros-Ghali, Boutros, *op. cit.*

110. *The Need to Increase The Efficiency of Investment* is a principal theme of the World Bank's *World Development Report 1994.*

111. *Human Development Report 1994.*

112. Administrator of the United Nations Development Programme (UNDP), quoted in *The State of the World's Children 1995.*

113. United Nations Children's Fund, *First Call for Children : World Declaration and Plan of Action from the World Summit for Children, and Convention on the Rights of the Child,* UNICEF, New York, December 1990.

114. *The State of the World's Children* 1995.

115. United Nations, Department of International Economic and Social Affairs, 'Family Building by Fate or Design : A Study of Relationships between Child Survival and Fertility'. United Nations, New York, 1987.

116. *Earth Summit,* Rio de Janeiro, 1992.

117. United Nations Children's Fund. 'World Declaration on the Survival, Protection and Development of Children' and Plan of Action for Implementing The World Declaration on the Survival, Protection and Development of Children in the 1990's, UNICEF, New York, 1991.

118. *The Progress of Nations.* UNICEF, 1994.

119. United Nations Children's Fund, *First Call for Children : World Declaration and Plan of Action from The World Summit for Children, and Convention on The Rights of The Child.* UNICEF, New York, December 1990.

120 &121. *The State of the World's Children 1995.* UNICEF, 1995.

122 to125. *The Progress of Nations.* UNICEF, 1994.

126. *The Progress of Nations 1993,* UNICEF, 1993.

127. Anderson, Mary B., *Education for All : What Are We Waiting For?* UNICEF, New York, 1992.

128. *The State of the World's Children,* 1994.

129. Carnoy, Martin, *The Case for Investing in Basic Education.* UNICEF, New York, 1992.

130. United Nations Development Programme. *Human Development Report 1992.* UNICEF, 1992.

131. *The Progress of Nations 1994.*

132. Gertrude Mongella, (Secretary General of the Fourth World Conference on Women 1995).

133. United Nations, 'Outcome of The World Summit for Social Development : Draft Declaration and Draft Programme of Action'. Note by The Secretary General to the Preparatory Committee for The World Summit for Social Development, New York, June 3, 1994.

134. Catley—Carlson, Margaret, Present Population Council Explosions, Eclipses and Escapes : Charting a Course on Global Population Issues : 1993 Paul Hoffman Lecture for United Nations Development Programme, New York, June 7, 1993.

135 to 139. *The Progress of Nations 1994.*

140. Catley—Carlson, Margaret, *op. cit.*

141. *Istanbul Declaration,* First International Congress on Population Education and Development, 14-17 April 1993.

142 to 149. *All of Us,* No. 3, November 1993. Centre UNESCO de Catalunya, Barcelona (Spain), 1993.

150. World Bank, *World Development Report 1993 : Investing in Health.* World Bank, Washington, 1993.

151. Rohde, Jon., Chatterjee, Meera and Morley, David, eds. *Reaching Health for All.* Oxford University Press, 1993.

152. World Bank, *World Development Report 1991.* World Bank, Washington, D.C., 1991.

153. United Nations Children's Fund and World Health Organization, 'Achieving of Mid-decade Goals for Water Supply and Sanitation'. JC H PSS/94/2.11, UNICEF-WHO Joint Committee on Health Policy, Speical Session, Geneva, 27-28 January 1994.

154 &155. World Bank, *World Development Report 1993.*

156. 'In The Bunker'. *The Economist*, January 8, 1994.

157. Rothman, David J., 'The Crime of Punishment', *New York Review of Books*, February 17, 1994.

158. 'The Future of Entertainment Networks', *PC* Magazine (U.K. Edition), Vol. 3, No. 10, October 1994.

159. *The State of the World's Children 1995*, UNICEF.

160. World Health Organization, *The International Drinking Water Supply and Sanitation Decade : End of Decade Review.* WHO/CWS/92. 12. WHO, Geneva, 1992.

161. *The State of the World's Children 1995*, UNICEF.

162. Overseas Development Council, 'Growth from Below : A People-Oriented Development Strategy'. Development Paper No. 16, ODC., Washington, D.C., December 1973.

163 and 164. Galbraith, John Kenneth, 'The Challenge to The South : Seven Basic Principles', in *Facing the Challenge : Responses to the Report of The South Commission.* South Centre/Zed Books, London, 1993.

165. United Nations, 'Outcome of The World Summit for Social Development : Draft Declaration and Draft Programme of Action', A/CONF, 166/PC/9. 13. Note by the Secretary-General to the Preparatory Committee for The World Summit for Social Development United Nations, New York, June 3, 1994.

166 to 168. *The State of the World's Children 1993*, UNICEF.

169. *The Progress of Nations.* UNICEF, 1994.

170. *The State of the World's Children 1995*, UNICEF, 1995.

171. Pasker, Davia and Jespersen, Eva, 20/20 : *Mobilising Resrouces for Children in the 1990's*, UNICEF Staff Working Papers, No. 12, UNICEF, New York, 1994.

172. Rowley, John and Mahler, Halfdan, 'Family Planning Can Contribute to Health For All', in Rohde, Jon, Chatterjee, Meera and Morley, David, eds, *Reaching Health For All.* Oxford University Press, 1993.

173 &174. *The State of the World's Children 1995.*

175. United Nations Development Programme, United Nations Po-pulation Fund and United Nations Children's Fund, *The 20/20 Initiative : Achieving,*

Universal Access to Basic Social Services, for Sustainable Human Development. UNDP, New York, 1994.

176. Kennedy Paul, *Preparing for The Twenty-first Century.* Random House, New York, 1993.
177. *The State of the World's Children 1994.*
178. Gore, Al., *Earth in The Balance* Plume Books, New York, 1993.
179. *Ibid.*
180. Organisation for Economic Cooperation and Development, Press Release, cited in James Gustave Speth, UNDP Administrator, memorandum to UNICEF Executive Director, June 29, 1994.
181. *UNDP India News*, Vol. 3, No. 1, August 10, 1994, New Delhi.
182. *The State of the World's Children 1995.*
183. Jolly, Richard 'The United Nations : A Development Agenda for The 21st Century', 1994 Ashley Lecture, Clare Hall, Cambridge, England, March 10, 1994.
184. *The State of the World's Children 1995.*
185. Shaw, George Bernard, *Man and Superman*, Penguin Books/Viking, 1950.
186. *The State of the World's Children 1995.*
187. Arnold Toynbee quoted in *The State of the World's Children 1994.*

2

WORLD SUMMIT FOR SOCIAL DEVELOPMENT, COPENHAGEN DECLARATION AND PROGRAMME OF ACTION (1995)

Introduction

As a part of the collective thinking, the international community under the leadership of the United Nations, has given a good deal of thought to the position of the individual human being and his development.

The 1990 World Summit for Children held at New York, the first of the major summits on development issues agreed on a series of measurable goals to be achieved by the close of the 20th Century. These goals included major progress against malnutrition, preventable disease and illiteracy among the children of the developing world. In all, 20 specific goals were agreed upon and eventually endorsed by over 150 Presidents and Prime Ministers of nations.

At the United Nations Conference on Envrionment and Development (Earth Summit) in Rio de Junerio, in 1992, the relationship between the human being and the environment was debated upon.

In 1993, at the World Conference on Human Rights in Vienna, the human being was looked upon as the bearer of rights.

In 1994, the human being as a collective being was the theme of the International Conference on Population and Development held at Cairo.

The World Summit for Social Development (WSSD) in 1995 at Copenhagen aimed at making social development a major priority for the international community. The focus of the 50-year organization i.e. the United Nations, shifted towards human development and human security.

The WSSD was attended by over 180 Heads of States or their senior representatives.

Copenhagen Declaration on Social Development

1. For the first time in history, at the invitation of the United Nations, we gather as Heads of State and Government to recognize the significance of social development and human well-being for all and to give to these goals the highest priority both now and into the 21st century.

2. We acknowledge that the people of the world have shown in different ways an urgent need to address profound social problems, especially poverty, unemployment and social exclusion, that affect every country. It is our task to address both their underlying and structural causes and their distressing consequences in order to reduce uncertainty and insecurity in the life of people.

3. We acknowledge that our societies must respond more effectively to the material and spiritual needs of individuals, their families and the communities in which they live throughout our diverse countries and regions. We must do so as a matter of urgency, but also as a matter of sustained and unshakeable commitment through the years ahead.

4. We are convinced that democracy and transparent and accountable governance and administration in all sectors of society are indispensable foundations for the realization of social and people-centred sustainable development.

5. We share the conviction that social development and social justice are indispensable for the achievement and maintenance of peace and security within and among our nations. In turn, social development and social justice cannot be attained in the absence of peace and security or in the absence of respect for all human rights and fundamental freedoms. This essential interdependence was recognized 50 years ago in the Charter of the United Nations and has grown ever stronger.

6. We are deeply convinced that economic development, social development and environmental protection are interdependent and mutually reinforcing components of sustainable development, which is the framework for our efforts to achieve a higher quality of life for all people. Equitable social development that recognizes empowering of the poor to utilize environmental resources sustainably is a necessary foundation for sustainable development. We also recognize that broad-based and sustained economic growth in the context of sustainable development is necessary to sustain social development and social justice.

7. We recognize, therefore, that social development is central to the needs and aspirations of people throughout the world and to the responsibilities of Governments and all sectors of civil society. We affirm that, in both economic and social terms, the most productive policies and investments are those that empower people to maximize their capacities, resources and opportunities. We acknowledge that social and economic development cannot be secured in a sustainable way without the full participation of women and that equality and euity between women and men is a priority for the international community and as such must be at the centre of economic and social development.

8. We acknowledge that people are at the centre of our concerns for sustainable development and that they are entitled to a healthy and productive life in harmony with the environment.

9. We gather here to commit ourselves, our Governments and our nations to enhancing social development throughout the world so that all men and women, especially those living in poverty, may exercise the rights, utilize the resources and share the responsibilities that enable them to lead satisfying lives and to contribute to the well-being of their families, their communities and humankind. To support and promote these efforts must be the overriding goals of the international community, especially with respect to those suffering from poverty, unemployment and social exclusion.

10. We make this solemn commitment on the eve of the fiftieth anniversary of the United Nations and with a determination to capture the unique possibilities

offered by the end of the cold war to promote social development and social justice. We reaffirm and are guided by the principles of the Charter of the United Nations and by agreements reached at relevant international conferences, including the World Summit for Children, held at New York in 1990, the United Nations Conference on Environment and Development, held at Rio de Janeiro in 1992, the World Conference on Human Rights, held at Vienna in 1993, the Global Conference on the Sustainable Development of Small Island Developing States, held at Bridgetown, Barbados, in 1994, and the International Conference on Population and Development, held at Cairo in 1994. By this Summit we launch a new commitment to social development in each of our countries and a new era of international cooperation between Governments and peoples based on a spirit of partnership that puts the needs, rights and aspirations of people at the centre of our decisions and joint actions.

11. We gather here in Copenhagen in a Summit of hope, commitment and action. We gather with full awareness of the difficulty of the tasks that lie ahead but with a conviction that major progress can be achieved, must be achieved and will be achieved.

12. We commit ourselves to this Declaration and Programme of Action for enhancing social development and ensuring human well-being for all throughout the world now and into the twnety-first century. We invite all people, in all countries and in all walks of life, as well as the international community, to join us in our common cause.

A. Current Social Situation and Reasons for Convening the Summit

13. We are witnessing in countries throughout the world the expansion of prosperity for some, unfortunately accompanied by an expansion of unspeakable poverty for others. This glaring contradiction is unacceptable and needs to be corrected through urgent actions.

14. Globalization, which is a consequence of increased human mobility, enhanced communications, greatly increased trade and capital flows and technological developments, opens new opportunities for sustained economic growth and development of the world economy, particularly in developing countries. Globalization also permits countries to share experiences and to learn from one another's achievements and difficulties, and promotes a cross-fertilization of ideals, cultural values and aspirations. At the same time, the rapid processes of change and adjustment have been accompanied by intensified poverty, unemployment and social disintegration. Threats to human well-being, such as environmental risks, have also been globalized. Furthermore, the global transformations of the world economy are profoundly changing the parameters of social development in all countries. The challenge is how to manage these processes and threats so as to enhance their benefits and mitigate their negative effects upon people.

15. There has been progress in some areas of social and economic development, *inter alia* :

(a) The global wealth of nations has multiplied sevenfold in the past 50 years and international trade has grown even more dramatically;

(b) Life expectancy, literacy and primary education, and access to basic health care, including family planning, have increased in the majority of countries and average infant mortality has been reduced, including in developing countries; and

(c) Democratic pluralism, democratic institutions and fundamental civil liberties have expanded. Decolonization efforts have achieved much progress, while the elimination of apartheid is a historic achievement.

16. Yet we recognize that far too many people, and particularly women and children, are vulnerable to stress and deprivation. Poverty, unemployment and social disintegration too often result in isolation, marginalization and violence. The insecurity many people, in particular vulnerable people, face about the future—their own and their children's—is intensifying:

(a) Within many societies, both in developed and developing countries, the gap between rich and poor has increased. Further, and despite the fact that some developing countries are growing rapidly, the gap between developed and many developing countries, particularly the least developed countries, has widened;

(b) More than one billion people in the world live in abject poverty, most of whom go hungry every day. A large proportion, the majority of whom are women, have very limited access to income, resources, education, health care or nutrition, particularly in Africa and the least developed countries;

(c) There are also serious social problems of a different nature and magnitude in countries with economies in transition and those experiencing fundamental political, economic and social transformations;

(d) The major cause of the continued deterioration of the global environment is the unsustainable pattern of consumption and production, particularly in industrialized countries, which is a matter of grave concern, aggravating poverty and imbalances;

(e) Continued growth in the world's population, its structure and distribution, and its relationship with poverty and social and gender inequality, challenge the adaptive capacities of Governments, individuals, social institutions and the natural environment;

(f) Over 120 million people worldwide are officially unemployed and many more are underemployed. Too many young people, including those with formal education, have little hope of finding productive work;

(g) More women than men live in absolute poverty, and the imbalance continues to grow, with serious consequences for women and their children. Women carry a disproportionate share of the problems of coping with poverty, social disintegration, unemployment, environmental degradation and the effects of war;

(h) One of the world's largest minorities, more than 1 in 10, are people with disabilities, who are too often forced into poverty, unemployment and social isolation. In addition, in all countries, older persons may be particularly vulnerable to social exclusion, poverty and marginalization;

(i) Millions of people worldwide are refugees or internally displaced persons. The tragic social consequences have a critical effect on the social stability and development of their home country, their host country and the respective regions.

17. While these problems are global in character and affect all countries, we clearly acknowledge that the situation of most developing countries, and particularly of Africa and the least developed countries, is critical and requires special attention and action. We also acknowledge that these countries, undergoing fundamental political, economic and social transformation, including those in the process of consolidating peace and democracy, require the support of the international community.

18. Countries with economies in transition, which are also undergoing fundamental political, economic and social transformation, require the support of the international community as well.

19. Other countries undergoing fundamental political, economic and social transformation require the support of the international community as well.

20. The goals and objectives of social development require continuous efforts to reduce and eliminate major sources of social distress and instability for the family and for society. We pledge our particular focus on and priority attention to the fight against worldwide conditions that pose severe threats to the health, safety, peace, security and well-being of our people. Among these conditions are chronic hunger, malnutrition, illicit drug problems, organized crime, corruption, foreign occupation, armed conflicts, illicit arms trafficking, terrorism, intolerance and incitement to racial, ethnic, religious and other hatreds, xenophobia, and endemic, communicable and chronic diseases. To this end, coordination at the national level and in particular at the regional and international levels should be further strengthened.

21. In this context, the negative impact on development of excessive expenditures, arms trade and investment for arms production and acquisition must be addressed.

22. Communicable diseases constitute a serious health problem in all countries and are a major cause of death globally; in many cases, their incidence is increasing. These diseases are a hindrance to social development and often the cause of poverty and social exclusion. The prevention, treatment and control of these diseases, covering a spectrum from tuberculosis and malaria to HIV/AIDS, must be given highest priority.

23. We can continue to hold the trust of the people of the world only if we make their needs our priority. We know that poverty, lack of productive employment and social disintegration are an offence to human dignity. We also know that they are negatively reinforcing and represent a waste of human resources and a manifestation of ineffectiveness in the functioning of markets and economic and social institutions and processes.

24. Our challenge is to establish a people-centred framework for social development to guide us now and in the future, to build a culture of cooperation and partnership and to respond to the immediate needs of those who are most affected by human distress. We are determined to meet this challenge and promote social development throughout the world.

B. Principles and Goals

25. We Heads of State and Government are committed to a political, economic, ethical and spiritual vision for social development based on human dignity, human rights, equality, respect, peace, democracy, mutual responsibility and cooperation, and full respect for the various religious and ethical values and cultural backgrounds of people. Accordingly, we will give the highest priority in national, regional and international policies and actions to the promotion of social progress, justice and the betterment of the human condition, based on full participation by all.

26. To this end we will create a framework for action to :

(a) Place people at the centre of development and direct our economies to meet human needs more effectively;

(b) Fulfil our responsibility for present and future generations by ensuring equity among generations and protecting the integrity and sustainable use of our environment;

(c) Recognize that, while social development is a national responsibility, it cannot be successfully achieved without the collective commitment and efforts of the international community;

(d) Integrate economic, cultural and social policies so that they become mutually supportive, and acknowledge the interdependence of public and private spheres of activity;

(e) Recognize that the achievement of sustained social development requires sound, broadly based economic policies;

(f) Promote democracy, human dignity, social justice and solidarity at the national, regional and international levels; ensure tolerance, non-violence, pluralism and non-discrimination in full respect of diversity within and among societies;

(g) Promote the equitable distribution of income and greater access to resources through equity and equality of opportunity for all;

(h) Recognize the family as the basic unit of society and acknowledge that it plays a key role in social development and as such should be strengthened, with attention to the rights, capabilities and responsibilities of its members. In different cultural, political and social systems various forms of family exist. It is entitled to receive comprehensive protection and support;

(i) Ensure that disadvantaged and vulnerable persons and groups are included in social development, and that society acknowledges and responds to the consequences of disability by securing the legal rights of the individual and by making the physical and social environment accessible;

(j) Promote universal respect for, and observance and protection of, all human rights and fundamental freedoms for all, including the right to development; promote the effective exercise of rights and the discharge of responsibilities at all levels of society; promote equality and equity between women and men; protect the rights of children and youth; and promote the strengthening of social integration and civil society;

(k) Reaffirm the right of self-determination of all peoples, in particular of peoples under colonial or other forms of alien domination or foreign occupation, and the importance of the effective realization of this right, as enunciated, *inter alia,* in the Vienna Declaration and Programme of Action adopted at the World Conference on Human Rights;

(l) Support progress and security for people and communities whereby every member of society is enabled to satisfy basic human needs and to realize his or her personal dignity, safety and creativity;

(m) Recognize and support indigenous people in their pursuit of economic and social development with full respect for their identity, traditions, forms of social organization and cultural values;

(n) Underline the importance of transparent and accountable governance and administration in all public and private national and international institutions;

(o) Recognize that empowering people, particularly women, to strengthen their own capacities is a main objective of development and its principal resource. Empowerment requires the full participation of people in the formulation, implementation and evaluation of decisions determining the functioning and well-being of our societies;

(p) Assert the universality of social development, and outline a new and strengthened approach to social development, with a renewed impetus for international cooperation and partnership;

(q) Improve the possibility of older persons achieving a better life;

(r) Recognize that the new infromation technologies and new approaches to access to and use of technologies by people living in poverty can help in fulfilling social development goals; and therefore, recognize the need to facilitate access to such technologies;

(s) Strengthen policies and programmes that improve, ensure and broaden the participation of women in all spheres of political, economic, social and cultural life, as equal partners, and improve their access to all resources needed for the full exercise of their fundamental rights;

(t) Create the political, legal, material and social conditions that allow for the voluntary repatriation of refugees in safety and dignity to their countries of origin, and the voluntary and safe return of internally displaced persons to their places of origin and their smooth reintegration into their societies; and

(u) Emphasize the importance of the return of all prisoners of war, persons missing in action and hostages to their families, in accordance with international conventions, in order to reach full social development.

27. We acknowledge that it is the primary responsibility of States to attain these goals. We also acknowledge that these goals cannot be achieved by States alone. The international community, the United Nations, the multilateral financial institutions, all regional organizations and local authorities, and all actors of civil society need to positively contribute their own share of efforts and resources in order to reduce inequalities among people and narrow the gap

between developed and developing countries in a global effort to reduce social tensions, and to create greater social and economic stability and security. Radical political, social and economic changes in the countries with economies in transition have been accompanied by a deterioration in their economic and social situation. We invite all people to express their personal commitment to enhancing the human condition through concrete actions in their own fields of activities and through assuming specific civic responsibilities.

C. Commitments

28. Our global drive for social development and the recommendations for action contained in the Programme of Action are made in a spirit of consensus and international cooperation, in full conformity with the purposes and principles of the Charter of the United Nations, recognizing that the formulation and implementation of strategies, policies, programmes and actions for social development are the responsibility of each country and should take into account the economic, social and environmental diversity of conditions in each country, with full respect for the various religious and ethical values, cultural backgrounds and philosophical convictions of its people, and in conformity with all human rights and fundamental freedoms. In this context, international cooperation is essential for the full implementation of the social development programmes and actions.

29. On the basis of our common pursuit of social development, which aims at social justice, solidarity, harmony and equality within and among countries, in full respect for national sovereignty and territorial integrity, as well as policy objectives, development priorities and religious and cultural diversity, and full respect for all human rights and fundamental freedoms, we launch a global drive for social progress and development embodied in the following commitments.

The WSSD included the following ten Commitments:

1. Commitment to create an economic, political, social, cultural and legal environment that will enable people to achieve social development.
2. Commitment to the goal of eradicating poverty in the world, through decisive national actions and international cooperation, as an ethical, social, political and economic imperative of mankind.
3. Commitment to promoting the goal of full employment as a basic priority of our economic and social justice, and to enabling all men and women to attain secure and sustainable livelihoods through freely chosen productive employment and work.
4. Commitment to promoting social integration by fostering societies that are stable, safe and just and based on the promotion and protection of all human rights, and on non-discrimination, tolerance, respect for diversity, equality of opportunity, solidarity, security and participation of all people, including disadvantaged and vulnerable groups and persons.
5. Commitment to promoting full respect for human dignity and to achieving equality and equity between men and women, and to

recognizing and enhancing the participation and leadership roles of women in political, civil, economic, social and cultural life and in development.

6. Commitment to promoting and attaining the goals of universal and equitable access to quality education, the highest attainable standard of physical and mental health and access of all to primary health care, making particular efforts to rectify inequalities relating to social conditions and without distinction as to race, national origin, gender, age or disability, respecting and promoting common and particular cultures, striving to strengthen the role of culture in development; preserving the essential bases of people centred sustainable development and contributing to the full development of human resources and to social development. The purpose of these activities is to eradicating poverty and, promoting full and positive employment and faster social integration.
7. Commitment to acclerating the economic, social and human resource development of Africa and the least developed countries.
8. Commitment to ensuring that when structural adjustment programmes are agreed to include social development goals in particular eradicating poverty, promoting full and productive employment and enhancing social integration.
9. Commitment to increase significantly and/or utilize more efficiently the resources allocated to social development in order to achieve the goals of the Summit through national action and regional and international cooperation.
10. Commitment to an improved and strengthened framework for international, regional and sub-regional cooperation for social development, in a spirit of partnership, through the United Nations and other multinational institutions.

Programme of Action

The Programme of Action outlines policies, actions and measures to implement the principles and fulfil the commitments enunciated in the Declaration adopted by the World Summit for Social Development. Important observations and recommendations for the mobilization of financial resources as given in the Programme of Action are given below :

1. The implementation of the Declaration and the Programme of Action of the Summit at the national level may require substantial new and additional resources, both in the public and the private sectors. Augmenting the availability of public resources for social development requires at the national level.

(a) Implementing macro-economic and micro-economic policies in accordance with national priorities and policies aimed at encouraging, greater domestic savings and investment required for public spending, through progressive, fair and economically efficient taxes that are cognizant of substainable development concerns, and through cutting back on subsidies that do not benefit the poor.

2. Reducing, an appropriate, excessive military expenditure and investment for arms production and acquisition, consistent with national security requirements in order to increase resources for social and economic developopment.

3. Giving high priority to social development in the allocation of public spending and ensuring predictable funding for the relevant programmes.

4. Striving for the fulfilment of the agreed target of 0.7 per cent of gross national product (GNP) for overall official assistance as soon as possible, and increasing the share of funding for social development programmes, commensurate with the scope and scale of activities required to achieve the goals of the Declaration and Programme of Action.

5. Agreeing on a mutual commitment between interested development and developing country partners to allocate, on average, 20 per cent of ODA and 20 per cent of the national budget, respectively, to basic social programmes.

6. The World Bank, the International Monetary Fund (IMF), the regional and sub-regional banks and funds, and all other international finance organizations should further integrate social development goals in their policies, programmes and operations, including by giving high priority to social-sector lending, where applicable, in their lending programmes.

Source : Department of Public Information of the United Nations, New York.

3

ADVANCEMENT OF WOMEN
Fourth World Conference on Women (FWCW, 1995)

Introduction

The Fourth World Conference on Women (FWCW) which took place at Beijing in China from 4-15 September 1995 was truly a UN world event.

It was attanded by 16,904 participants, which included representatives of 189 member states, 4035 NGO representatives, and 3245 professionals from the media. With the parallel NGO Forum, some 50,000 people took part in the events, making this the largest UN gathering in history.

The Beijing meeting was the sixth in a series of recent major UN conferences addressing the world's most pressing economic and social issues. The run of conferences began in 1990 with the World Summit for Children, and was followed in June 1992 by the UN Conference on Environment and Development (UNCED), the World Conference on Human Rights in June 1993, the Global Conference on the Sustainable Development of Small Island Developing States in April-May 1994, the International Conference on Population and Development (ICPD) in September 1994, and the World Summit for Social Development (WSSD) in March 1995.

The FWCW was also the fourth in a series of women's conferences, the first having been held in 1975 in Mexico City, the second in 1980 in Copenhagen, and the third in 1985 in Nairobi. These conferences put women's issues firmly and irrevocably on the public international agenda.

The Fourth World Conference on Women built upon the outcomes of both of these series of conferences.

The Declaration and Platform for Action

After two weeks of negotiating in working groups and contact groups, issues still outstanding included sexual orientation, religious and ethical values, criminalization of illegal abortions, inadequate references to development, and the Declaration. While not all the issues were included in the final text, they were eventually resolved in informal and high-level sessions, and the main committee finalized the text in the pre-dawn hours of 15 September. The Declaration contains 38 paragraphs outlining the principles which underlie the commitments of member states.

The Platform for Action is a long and detailed document made up of a mission statement, the global framework on the current situation facing women around the world, the 12 critical areas of concern mentioned earlier, and the strategic objectives and actions. It also contains a chapter on institutional arrangements, outlining measures governments can take at the national level, regional and subregional arrangements to be put in place in support of women, and national, regional and international measures to generate the resources required for the platform's implementation.

The adoption of the Platform for Action is considered a major step towards the achievement of gender equality, and the most comprehensive consensus statement on women ever made by the world's governments.

Many participants, particularly representatives of women's organizations, were pleased with the references to mainstreaming women's issues, reproductive health, sexual rights, education of girls, violence against women, women's rights, equal inheritance rights for girls and women and recognition of the need to measure unremunerated work. But they were less so with the outcomes on resources, the environment, the global economic system and the—albeit largely successful—efforts expended to retain agreements reached during previous conferences.

Source : *NGLS Round up*, Nov. 1995.

Beijing Declaration

1. We, the Government participating in the Fourth World Conference on Women.

2. Gathered here in Beijing in September 1995, the year of the fiftieth anniversary of the founding of the United Nations.

3. Determined to advance the goals of equality, development and peace for all women everywhere in the interest of all humanity.

4. Acknowledging the voices of all women everywhere and taking note of the diversity of women and their roles and circumstances, honouring the women who paved the way and inspired by the hope present in the world's youth.

5. Recognize the status of women has advanced in some important respects in the past decade but that progress has been uneven, inequalities between women and men have persisted and major obstacles remain, with serious consequences for the well-being of all people.

6. Also recognize that this situation is exacerbated by the increasing poverty that is affecting the lives of the majority of the world's people in particular women and children, with origins in both the national and international domains.

7. Dedicate ourselves unreservedly to addressing these constraints and obstacles and thus enhancing further the advancement and empowerment of women all over the world, and agree that this requires urgent action in the spirit of determination, hope, cooperation and solidarity now and to carry us forward into the next century.

We reaffirm our commitment to

8. The equal rights and inherent human dignity of women and men and other purposes and principles enshrined in the Charter of the United Nations, to the Universal Declaration of Human Rights and other international human

rights instruments, in particular the Convention on the Elimination of All Forms of Discrimination against Women and the Convention on the Rights of the Child, as well as the Declaration on the Elimination of violence against Women and the Declaration on the Right to Development.

9. Ensure the full implementation of the human rights of women and of the girl child as an inalienable, integral and indivisible part of all human rights and fundamental freedoms.

10. Build on consensus and progress made at previous United Nations Conferences and summits—on women in Nairobi in 1985, on children in New York in 1990, on environment and development in Rio de Janeiro in 1992, on human rights in Vienna in 1993, on population and development in Cairo in 1994 and on social development in Copenhagen in 1995 with the objective of achieving equality, development and peace.

11. Achieve the full and effective implementation of the Nairobi Foward-looking Strategies for the Advancement of Women.

12. The empowerment and advancement of women, including the right to freedom of thought, conscience, religion and belief, thus contributing men, individually or in community with others and thereby guaranteeing them the possibility of realizing their full potential in society and shaping their lives in accordance with their own aspirations.

We are convinced that

13. Women's empowerment and their full participation on the basis of equality in all spheres of society, including participation in the decision-making process and to power, are fundamental for the achievement of equality, development and peace.

14. Women's rights are human rights.

15. Equal rights, opportunities and access to resources, equal sharing of responsibilities for the family by men and women, and a harmonious partnership between them are critical to their well-being and that of their families as well as the consolidation of democracy.

16. Eradication of poverty based on sustained economic growth, social development, environmental protection and social justice requires the involvement of women in economic and social development, equal opportunities and the full and equal participation of women and men as agents and beneficiaries of people-centred sustainable development.

17. The explicit recognition and reaffirmation of the right of all women to control all aspects of their health, in particular their own fertility, is basic to their empowerment.

18. Local, national, regional and global peace is attainable and is inextricably linked with the advancement of women, who are a fundamental force for leadership, conflict resolution and the promotion of lasting peace at all levels.

19. It is essential to design, implement and monitor, with the full participation of women, effective, efficient and mutually reinforcing gender-sensitive policies and programmes including development policies and programmes, at all levels that will foster the empowerment and advancement of women.

20. The participation and contribution of all actors of civil society, particularly women's groups and networks and other non-governmental organisations and community-based organisations, with full respect for their autonomy, in cooperation with Governments, are important to the effective implementation and follow-up of the Platform for Action.

21. The implementation of the Platform for Action requires commitment from Governments and the international community. By making national and international commitments for action, including those made at the Conference, Governments and the international community recognize the need to take priority action for the empowerment and advancement of women.

We are determined to

22. Intensify efforts and actions to achieve the goals of the Nairobi Forward-looking Strategies for the Advancement of Women by the end of this century.

23. Ensure the full enjoyment by women and the girl child of all human rights and fundamental freedoms and take effective action against violations of these rights and freedoms.

24. Take all necessary measures to eliminate all forms of discrimination against women and the girl child and remove all obstacles to gender equality and the advancement and empowerment of women.

25. Encourage men to participate fully in all actions towards equality.

26. Promote women's economic independence, including employment and eradicate the persistent and increasing burden of poverty on women by addressing the structural causes of poverty through changes in economic structures, ensuring equal access for all women, including those in rural areas, as vital development agents, to productive resources, opportunities and public services.

27. Promote people-centred sustainable development, including sustained economic growth, through the provision of basic education, life long education, literacy and training, and primary health care for girls and women.

28. Take positive steps to ensure peace for the advancement of women and, recognizing the leading role that women have played in the peace movement, work actively towards general and complete disarmament under strict and effective international control, and support negotiations on the conclusion, without delay of a universal and multilaterally and effectively verifiable comprehensive nuclear-test ban treaty which contributes to nuclear disarmament and the prevention of the proliferation of nuclear weapons in all its aspects.

29. Prevent and eliminate all forms of violence against women and girls.

30. Ensure equal access to and equal treatment of women and men in education and health care and enhance women's sexual reproductive health as well as education.

31. Promote and protect all human rights of women and girls.

32. Intensify efforts to ensure equal enjoyment of all human rights and fundamental freedoms for all women and girls who face multiple barriers to their empowerment and advancement because of such factors as their race, age,

language, ethnicity, culture, religion or disability or because they are indigenous people.

33. Ensure respect for international law, including humanitarian law, in order to protect women and girls in particular.

34. Develop the fullest potential of girls and women of all ages, ensure their full and equal participation in building a better world for all and enhance their role in the development process.

We are determined to

35. Ensure women's equal access to economic resources, including land, credit, science and technology, vocational training, information, communication and markets, as a means to further the advancement and empowerment of women and girls, including through the enhancement of their capacities to enjoy the benefits of equal access to these resources, *inter alia* by means of international cooperation.

36. Ensure the success of the Platform for Action, which will require a strong commitment on the part of Governments, international organisations and institutions at all levels. We are deeply convinced that economic development, social development and environmental protection are interdependent and mutually reinforcing components of sustainable development, which is the framework for our efforts to achieve a higher quality of life for all people. Equitable social development that recognizes empowering the poor, particularly women living in poverty, to utilise environmental resources for sustainable development. We also recognize that broad-based and sustained economic growth in the context of sustainable development is necessary to sustain social development and social justice. The success of the Platform for Action will also require adequate mobilization of resources at the national and international levels as well as new and additional resources to the developing countries from all available funding mechanisms, including multilateral, bilateral and private sources for the advancement of women; financial resources to strengthen the capacity of national, subregional, regional and international institutions, a commitment to equal rights, equal responsibilities and equal opportunities and to the equal participation of women and men in all national, regional and international bodies and policy-making processes; and the establishment or strengthening of mechanisms at all levels for accountablity to the world's women.

37. Ensure also the success of the Platform for Action in countries with economies in transition, which all require continued international cooperation and assistance;

38. We hereby adopt and commit ourselves as Governments to implement the following Platform for Action, ensuring that a gender perspective is reflected in all our policies and programmes. We urge the United Nations system, regional and international financial institutions other relevant regional and international institutions and all women and men, as well as non-governmental organisation, with full respect for their autonomy, and all sectors of civil society,

in cooperation with Governments, to fully commit themselves and contribute to the implementation of this Platform for Action.
Source : UN Department of Public Information.

Strategic Objectives from the Platform of Action

Women and Poverty

- Review, adopt and maintain macroeconomic policies and development strategies that address the needs and efforts of women in poverty;
- Revise laws and administrative practices to ensure women's equal rights and access to economic resources;
- Provide women with access to savings and credit mechanisms and institutions;
- Develop gender-based methodologies and conduct research to address the feminization of poverty.

Education and Training of Women

- Ensure equal access to education;
- Eradicate illiteracy among women;
- Improve women's access to vocational training, science and technology, and continuing education;
- Develop non-discriminatory education and training;
- Allocate sufficient resources for and monitor the implementation of educational reforms;
- Promote lifelong education and training for girls and women.

Women and Health

- Increase women's access throughout the life cycle to appropriate affordable and quality health care, information and related services;
- Strengthen preventive programmes that promote women's health;
- Undertake gender-sensitive initiatives that address sexually transmitted diseases, HIV/AIDS, and sexual and reproductive health issues;
- Promote research and disseminate information on women's health;
- Increase resources and monitor follow-up for women's health.

Violence Against Women

- Take integrated measures to prevent and eliminate violence against women;
- Study the causes and consequences of violence against women and the effectiveness of preventive measures;
- Eliminate trafficking in women and assist victims of violence due to prostitution and trafficking;

Women and Armed Conflict

- Increase the participation of women in conflict resolution at decision making levels and protect women living in situations of armed conflicts or under foreign occupation;

- Reduce excessive military expenditures and control the availability of armaments;
- Promote non-violent forms of conflict resolution and reduce the incidence of human rights abuse in conflict situations;
- Promote women's contribution to forstering a culture of peace;
- Provide protection, assistance and training to refugee women in need of international protection and internally displaced women;
- Provide assistance to the women of the colonies and non-self-governing territories;

Women and the Economy

- Promote women's economic rights and independence, including access to employment and appropriate working conditions and control over economic resources;
- Facilitate women's equal access to resources, employment, markets and trade;
- Provide business services, training and access to markets, information and technology, particularly to low-income women;
- Strengthen women's economic capacity and commercial networks;
- Eliminate occupational and all forms of employment discrimination;
- Promote harmonization of work and family responsibilities for women and men;

Women in Power and Decision-Making

- Take measures to ensure women's equal access to and full participation in power structures and decision making;
- Increase women's capacity to participate in decision making and leadership;

Institutional Mechanisms for the Advancement of Women

- Create or strengthen national machineries and other governmental bodies;
- Integrate gender perspective in legislation, public policies, programmes and projects;
- Generate and disseminate gender-disaggregated data and information for planning and evaluation;

Human Rights of Women

- Promote and protect the human rights of women, through the full implementation of all human rights instruments, especially the Convention on the Elimination of All Forms of Discrimination against Women;
- Ensure equality and non-discrimination under the law and in practice;
- Achieve legal literacy;

Women and the Media

- Increase the participation and access of women to expression and decision-making in and through the media and new technologies of communication;
- Promote a balanced and non-stereotypes portrayal of women in the media;

Women and the Environment

- Involve women actively in environmental decision-making at all levels;
- Integrate gender concerns and perspectives in policies and programmes for sustainable development;
- Strengthen or establish mechanisms at the national, regional and international levels to assess the impact of development and environmental policies on women.

The Girl Child

- Eliminate all forms of discrimination against the girl child;
- Eliminate negative cultural attitudes and practices against girls;
- Promote and protect the rights of the girl child and increase awareness of her needs and potential;
- Eliminate discrimination against girls in education, skills development and training;
- Eliminate discrimination against girls in health and nutrition;
- Eliminate the economic exploitation of child labour and protect young girls at work;
- Eradicate violence against the girl child;
- Promote the girl child's awareness of and participation in social, economic and political life;
- Strengthen the role the family in improving status of the girl child.

Source : *NGLS*, November, 1995.

1945-95 : Fifty Years of UN Work for Women

1945 : The UN Charter declares the principle of equal rights for all "without distinction as to race, sex, language or religion."

1946 : The Commission on the Status of Women (CSW) is established by the UN Economic and Social Council.

1952 : The Convention on the Political Rights of Women.

1957 : The Convention on the Nationality of Married Women.

1962 : The Convention on the Consent to Marriage.

1967 : The General Assembly adopts the Declaration on the Elimination of All Forms of Discrimination Against Women.

1975 : The UN observes International Women's Year. First World Conference on Women is held in Mexico City.
The UN General Assembly declares 1976-85 United Nations Decade for Women.

1979 : The General Assembly adopts the Convention on the Elimination of All Forms of Discrimination Against Women.

1980 : Second World Conference on. Women (Copenhagen, Denmark); adopts a Programme of Action for the second half of the UN Decade for Women.

1981 : The Convention on the Elimination of All Forms of Discrimination Against Women comes into force.

1982 : The Committee on the Elimination of Discrimination Against Women (CEDAW) begins its work.

1985 : The Thrid World Conference on Women (Nairobi, Kenya); adopts the Forward looking Strategies for the Advancement of Women to the Year 2000.

1990 : CSW begins work on reviewing progress towards implementation of Nairobi Forward-looking Strategies.

1993 : World Conference on Human Rights (Vienna, Austria); recognizes women's rights as human rights and recommends appointment of a special Rapporteur on Violence Against Women.
Declaration on the Elimination of Violence against Women is adopted by the General Assembly.

1994 : Regional preparatory process for the Fourth World Conference on Women; regional meetings are held in Indonesia, Argentina, Austria, Jordan and Senegal.
International Conference on Population and Development (Cairo, Egypt) underscores the empowerment and autonomy of women as the basis for development.

1995 : World Summit for Social Development (Copenhagen, Denmark) calls attention to the pivotal role of women in addressing the problems of poverty, unemployment and social integration.
Fourth World Conference on Women (Beijing, China)

Source : *UN Newsletter,* May 27, 1995.

4

HUMAN DEVELOPMENT

Introduction

The UNDP's Human Development Reports since 1990 have stimulated international dialogue on models of development. The first Report introduced a new way of measuring human development—by combining indicators of life expectancy, educational attainment and income into a composite human development index, the HDI. Building upon this exercise, successive Human Development Reports emphasised the need to treat GNP growth as a means, not an end; to concentrate not on economic growth per se but its character and distribution; to accept the fact that high levels of economic growth need not automatically translate into high levels of human development.

HUMAN DEVELOPMENT REPORT 1994

The 1994 Report continued tradition and took it a step further. It explored the new frontiers of human security in the daily lives of the people—in their homes, in their jobs, in their streets, in their communities and in their environment.

Such a concept of security binds together all people and all nations, and it can be addressed only through sustainable human development strategies, not through the acquisition of ever-more-powerful weapons. It recognised that it is easier, more humane and less costly to deal with the new issues of human security upstream rather than down-stream. The Report identified some new indicators of human insecurity—food, job and income insecurity, human rights violations, ethnic or religious conflicts, inequity and military spending—that can help give an early warning on countries heading for trouble and alert the international community about the need for preventive diplomacy and development, in order to save a society from reaching a crisis point.

The Report identified many developing countries which are already heading towards social disintegration in the same way as Somalia and Nicaragua did in the 1990s. The Report also identified other countries which could follow the same path. Behind every failed state, there lies a long trail of failed development or unacceptably high socio-economic disparities. According to the Report, the new imperatives of global human security demand an entirely new system of global governance—particularly, a greatly strengthened role of the United Nations in the development field.

The 1994 Human Development Report also outlined a new design for development cooperation in the post-cold war era. It points out that even today, foreign aid is often linked to strategic allies from the past than to such specific global objectives of the future as poverty reduction, human development, slowing down population growth rate and improving the physical environment.

Only one-third of Official Development Assistance (ODA) is earmarked for 10 countries containing two-thirds of the world's absolute poor. Twice as much ODA per capita is given to the top 40 per cent income group in the world as to the bottom 40 per cent. The richer development countries of the Middle East get $ 21 per capita, compared with $ 6 per capita for the poorer countries of South Asia.

Egypt receives $ 280 in aid per poor person, while Bangladesh gets $ 19 and India only $ 7. India has 27 per cent of the world's absolute poor, but receives only 5 per cent of ODA. Less than 7 per cent of bilateral ODA is directed towards human priority concerns of primary health care, basic education, safe drinking water, nutrition programmes and family planning services. This shows the enormous scope that still exists to get more policy mileage and much better allocations out of existing aid funds.

At the same time the Report argued that the concept of development cooperation must be broadened to include all development flows, including trade, investment, technology and labour flows. It is simply unacceptable that while aid transfers so few resources to the developing world, much more is taken away through trade protection, immigration barriers and an increasing debt burden. In such a situation, it is critical for poor nations to bargain for a more equitable access to global market opportunities.

The Report's new design for development cooperation in the coming decades envisions a scenario where :

- aid is regarded as an essential investment by the rich nations in their own human security.
- developing countries are compensated for trade and immigration barriers imposed by the rich nations,
- polluting nations are made to pay for over-use of the global commons,
- the potential peace dividend of nearly $ 500 billion between 1995 and 2000 is earmarked primarily for the human development agenda,
- and global compacts are negotiated in specific areas between rich and poor nations—population, environment, drug control—based on two-way cooperation, not on one-way conditionality or coercion.

It is in these above contexts that the 1994 Human Development Report suggests a concrete six-point agenda for the consideration of the World Summit for Social Development that is to meet in Copenhagen in March next year :

- a World Social Charter, to arrive at a new social contract among all nations and all people,
- a reduction of 3 per cent a year in future global military spending, with 20 per cent of the savings by rich nations and 10 per cent by poor nations earmarked for global human security,
- a 20:20 compact for human development—to provide basic education, primary health care, safe drinking water and essential family planning services to all people over the next decade—by earmarking 20 per cent of the existing developing country budgets and 20 per cent of the

existing aid allocations to these basic human priority concerns (this is easily the most important and most feasible policy recommendation of the Human Development Reports),

- a global human security fund—financed from global taxes such as the 'Tobin tax' on speculative movements of international funds, an international tax on the consumption on non-renewable energy, global environmental permits and a tax on arms trade,
- a new framework of development cooperation, to graduate from the present aid relationship to a more mature development partnership—by including trade, technology, investment and labour flows in a broader design to be negotiated among nations, and
- an Economic Security Council in the United Nations, as the highest decision-making forum to consider basic issues of human security such as global poverty, unemployment, food security, drug trafficking, global pollution, international migration and a new framework of sustainable human development.

Canada ranked first in human development overall, while Barbados ranked first among developing countries. The other countries making up the 'top 10' on the HDI were, in descending order, Switzerland, Japan, Sweden, Norway, France, Australia, the United States of America, Netherlands, the United Kingdom and Germany.

India ranked 135 among 173 countries, with the corresponding ranks for its South Asian neighbours being 90 for Sri Lanka, 130 for Myanmar, 132 for Pakistan, 146 for Bangladesh, 149 for Nepal and 162 for Bhutan.

Source : *UNDP India News*, Vol. 3, No. 1, August 1994. New Delhi.

HUMAN DEVELOPMENT REPORT (1995)

The Human Development Report is best known for its HDI, or Human Development Index, which each year ranks countries according to life expectancy, educational attainment and adjusted real income. This year's innovations, however, show some countries fall dramatically in rank when disparities between the sexes are taken into account.

Four Nordic countries—Sweden, Finland, Norway and Denmark—score highest in terms of gender equality. More surprisingly, the human development rankings of Canada, the Netherlands and Spain fall significantly when gender is included. The highest ranking developing countries are the Caribbean nations of Barbados, the Bahamas and Trinidad and Tobago.

Gender-Related Development Index (GDI)

Using the new measure, the report concludes that :

- in no society do women fare as well as men; as many as 45 countries fall below a value of 0.5 on the index, out of a maximum possible value of 1.00;

- gender equality does not necessarily depend on income, and political commitment is more important; and
- there has been significant but uneven progress over the past two decades.

Gender Empowerment Measure (GEM)

By analyzing this measure, the report reveals that :

- in sharing political and economic opportunities, there is still a long way for women to go, in rich countries as well as in poor;
- some developing countries outperform much richer countries in the opportunities they afford women;
- the best record of women using their skills and education is in the Nordic countries, followed by Botswana, the Philipines and Uruguay;
- women have obtained the highest representation in parliament in Norway and Finland, with four-fifths of the seats held by men, worldwide, the average share of seats held by men in around 90%.

Strategy for Action

The report identifies a five-point strategy to accelerate progress in the field of gender equality.

Established Timeframe : National and international efforts must be mobilized to win legal equality within a defined period—say, the next ten years. To do this, a campaign should be launched for unconditional ratification of CEDAW, the Convention on the Elimination of All forms of Discrimination Against Women; CEDAW's implementation should be strengthened within the UN system; and an international NGO, World Women's Watch, should be set up to prepare country-by-country reports on discrimination and progress towards gender-related targets.

Economic and Institutional Changes : These could include encouraging men to participate in family care; flexible work schedules; expanding the concept of public services beyond education and health to child care; chaning tax and social security incentives; and changing laws on property, inheritance and divorce.

Women's Share in Decision-Making : The report says a critical 30% threshold should be regarded as a minimum share of decision making positions held by women at the national level. It recommends each nation identify a firm timetable for crossing this threshold.

Advancement of Women : Key programmes should embrace universal female education, improved reproductive health and more credit for women.

Access to Opportunities : National and international efforts should target programmes that enable people, particularly women, to gain greater access to economic and political opportunities. Some elements in this package could include basic social services for all; reproductive health care; credit for poor people; sustainable livelihoods for all; targeted programmes for poverty reduction; and capacity building and empowerment.

The report was commissioned by UNDP and written by an independent team of experts led by Mahbub ul Haq, former Finance and Planning Minister of Pakistan and now special advisor to the UNDP Administrator.

Source : *Go Between 53,* Aug./Sept. 95.

TABLE 4.1. Ranking of Countries on Human Development Index (HDI)

Rank 1991	*Rank 1992*	*Country*	*Rank 1991*	*Rank 1992*	*Country*
1	1	Canada	2	13	Switzerland
3	3	Japan	4	10	Sweden
5	7	Norway	6	8	France
7	11	Australia	8	2	USA
9	4	Netherlands	10	18	United Kingdom
11	15	Germany	12	14	Austria
13	12	Belgium	14	6	Iceland
15	16	Denmark	16	5	Finland
17	27	Luxumberg	18	17	Newzealand
19		Isreal	20	25	Barbados
21	19	Ireland	22	20	Italy
23	9	Spain	24	24	Hongkong
25	22	Greece	26	23	Cyprus
27	38	Czechoslovakia	28	71	Lithuania
29	43	Estonia	30	48	Lativa
31	50	Hungary	32	31	Korea, Rep. of
33	32	Uruguary	34	52	Russian Federation
35	39	Trinidad and Tobago	36	26	Bahamas
37	30	Argentina	38	33	Chile
39	28	Costa Rica	40	42	Belarus
41	34	Malta	42	36	Portugal
43	35	Singapore	44	41	Brunei Darussalam
45	54	Ukraine	46	47	Venezuela
47	49	Panama	48	65	Bulgaria
49	51	Poland	50	57	Colombia
51	61	Kuwait	52	53	Mexico
53	40	Armenia	54	58	Thailand
55	55	Antigua and Barbuda	56	56	Qatar
57	59	Malaysia	58	44	Bahrain
59	46	Fiji	60	60	Mauritius

(*Contd.*)

TABLE 4.1 (*Contd.*)

Rank 1991	*Rank 1992*	*Country*	*Rank 1991*	*Rank 1992*	*Country*
61	64	Kazakhistan	62	45	United Arab Emirates
63	63	Brazil	64	69	Dominica
65	88	Jamaica	66	92	Georgia
67	76	Saudi Arabia	68	66	Turkey
69	79	Saint Vinacent	70	37	Saint Kitts and Nevis
71	99	Azerbaijan	72	98	Romania
73	78	Syrian Arab Rep.	74	68	Ecuador
75	81	Moldova, Rep. of	76	82	Albania
77	84	Saint Luccia	78	67	Grenda
79	73	Libyan Arab Jamabiriya	80	86	Turkmenistan
81	75	Tunisia	82	64	Kyragzstan
83	62	Seychclles	84	87	Paraguay
85	77	Susinane	86	70	Iran, Islamic Rep. of
87	74	Botswana	88	29	Belize
89	72	Cuba	90	97	Sri Lanka
91	94	Uzbekistan	92	91	Oman
93	95	South Africa	94	111	China
95	93	Peru	96	96	Dominican Rep.
97	103	Tajikstan	98	80	Jordan
99	100	Philippines	100	106	Iraq
101	83	Korea, Dem. Rep. of	102	110	Mongolia
103	101	Lebanon	104	102	Samoa
105	104	Indonesia	106	109	Nicaragua
107	105	Guyana	108	112	Guatemala
109	85	Algeria	110	107	Egypt
111	117	Morocco	112	115	El Salvador
113	113	Bolivia	114	114	Gabon
115	116	Honduras	116	120	Viet Nam
117	124	Swiziland	118	118	Maldives
119	119	Vanuatu	120	131	Lestho
121	121	Zimbabwe	122	123	Cape Verde
123	122	Congo	124	127	Cameroon
125	130	Kenya	126	125	Solomon Islands
127	108	Nambia	128	133	Sao Tome and Principe
129	126	Papua New Guinea	130	132	Myanmar
131	135	Madagascar	132	128	Pakistan
133	138	Lao people's Den. Rep.	134	129	Ghana
135	134	India	136	145	Cote d Lvoire
137	148	Haiti	138	136	Zambia
139	141	Nigeria	140	143	Zaire
141	139	Comoros	142	137	Yemen

(*Contd.*)

TABLE 4.1 (*Contd.*)

Rank 1991	*Rank 1992*	*Country*	*Rank 1991*	*Rank 1992*	*Country*
143	152	Senegal	144	159	Liberia
145	140	Togo	146	146	Bangladesh
147	153	Combodia	148	147	Tanzania, U. Rep. of
149	151	Nepal	150	142	Equatroial Guinea
151	144	Sudan	152	165	Burundi
153	156	Rwanda	154	158	Uganda
155	164	Angola	156	155	Benin
157	157	Malawi	158	150	Mauritania
159	167	Mozambique	160	149	Central Africa Rep.
161	171	Ethopia	162	160	Bhutan
163	154	Djibonta	164	163	Guinea-Bissan
165	166	Somalia	166	161	Gambia
167	172	Mali	168	162	Chad
169	174	Niger	170	173	Sierra Leone
171	170	Afghanistan	172	169	Burkina Faso
173	168	Guinea	174	40	Slovakia

Sources :

1. Human Development Report 1994 (For 1991).
2. Human Development Report 1995 (For 1992).

5

ECONOMIC AND SOCIAL DEVELOPMENT
Comparative Country Profile

Introduction

The tables given in this chapter cover a wide range of economic and social statistics on the development of the nations of the world and provide a comparative study of the various facets of life. The United Nations Children Fund (UNICEF) has derived the data from several international agencies like the United Nations Population Fund, United Nations Statistical Office, World Bank, United Nations Educational Scientific and Cultural Organization, World Health Organisation, Food and Agricultural Organisation, International Monetary Fund, Organisation of Economic Cooperation and Developments, besides its own divisions and offices.

Following two symbols have been used :

. . Data not available.

x Indicates data that refer to years or periods other than those specified in the column heading, differ from the standard definition, or refer to only part of a country.

TABLE 5.1 : Basic Data

		Under-5 mortality rate		Infant mortality rate (under 1)		Total population (millions)	Annual no. of births (thousands)	Annual no. of under-5 deaths (thousands)	GNP per capita (US$)	Life expectancy at birth (years)	Total adult literacy rate	Primary school enrolment ratio (gross)	% share of household income 1980-93	
		1960	1994	1960	1994	1994	1994	1994	1993	1994	1990	1986-93	lowest 40%	highest 20%
1	Niger	320	320	191	191	8.9	459	147	270	46	12	29	..	
2	Angola	345	292	208	170	10.7	542	158	700	46	42	91	..	
3	Sierra Leone	385	284	219	164	4.4	214	61	150	39	27	48	..	
4	Mozambique	331	277	190	161	15.5	699	194	90	46	35	60	..	
5	Afghanistan	360	257	215	165	18.9	970	249	280x	43	27	24	..	
6	Guinea-Bissau	336	231	200	137	1.1	44	10	240	43	50	60	9	59
7	Guinea	337	223	203	131	6.5	326	73	500	44	31	42	..	
8	Malawi	365	221	206	140	10.8	535	118	200	46	52x	66	..	..
9	Liberia	288	217	192	144	2.9	138	30	450x	55	34	35	..	..
10	Mali	400	214	233	119	10.5	525	112	270	46	25	25	..	..
11	Gambia	375	213	213	129	1.1	46	10	350	45	34	69	..	..
12	Somalia	294	211	175	125	9.1	458	97	120x	47	24	11x	..	..
13	Zambia	220	203	135	114	9.2	402	82	380	49	73	95	15	50
14	Chad	325	202	195	119	6.2	269	54	210	47	43	65	..	..
15	Eritrea	294	200	175	117	3.4	146	29	100	50	..	..	..	..
16	Ethiopia	294	200	175	117	53.4	2562	511	100	47	31x	22	21	41

(Contd.)

TABLE 5.1: (Contd.)

		Under-5 mortality rate		Infant mortality rate (under 1)		Total population (millions)	Annual no. of births (thousands)	Annual no. of under-5 deaths (thousands)	GNP per capita (US$)	Life expectancy at birth (years)	Total adult literacy rate	Primary school enrolment ratio (gross)	% share of household income 1980-93	
		1960	1994	1960	1994	1994	1994	1994	1993	1994	1990	1986-93	lowest 40%	highest 20%
17	Mauritania	321	199	191	114	2.2	87	17	500	51	35	62	14	46
18	Bhutan	324	193	203	125	1.6	64	12	170	50	37	25	..	..
19	Nigeria	204	191	122	114	108.5	4855	927	300	50	49	76	15	49
20	Zaire	286	186	167	120	42.6	2002	372	220x	52	72	70	..	..
21	Uganda	218	185	129	111	20.6	1055	195	180	45	57	80	21	42
22	Cambodia	217	177	146	113	10.0	417	74	200x	51	35	..	..	..
23	Burundi	255	176	151	106	6.2	281	50	180	50	31	69	..	..
24	Central African Rep.	294	175	174	103	3.2	133	23	400	49	50	68	..	..
25	Burkina Faso	318	169	183	89	10.1	465	79	300	47	16	37	..	..
26	Madagascar	364	164	219	100	14.3	616	101	220	56	80	79	..	..
27	Tanzania, U. Rep. of	249	159	147	105	28.9	1228	195	90	52	62x	68	8	63
28	Lesotho	204	156	138	106	2.0	73	11	650	60	67	106	9	60

(Contd.)

TABLE 5.1: *Contd.*

		Under-5 mortality rate		Infant mortality rate (under 1)		Total population (millions)	Annual no. of under-5 births (thousands)	Annual no. of deaths (thousands)	GNP per capita (US$)	Life expectancy at birth (years)	Total adult literacy rate	Primary school enrolment ratio (gross)	% share of household income 1980-93	
		1960	1994	1960	1994	1994	1994	1994	1993	1994	1990	1986-93	lowest 40%	highest 20%
29	Gabon	287	**151**	171	91	1.3	49	7	4960	53	56	..	..	..
30	Côte d'Ivoire	300	**150**	195	90	13.8	682	102	630	51	34	69	18	44
31	Benin	310	**142**	184	85	5.3	253	36	430	47	30	66	..	..
32	Rwanda	191	**139**	115	80	7.8	340	47	210	47	54	77	23	39
33	Lao Peo. Dem. Rep.	233	**138**	155	94	4.7	211	29	280	51	52x	98	..	..
34	Pakistan	221	**137**	137	95	136.7	5461	748	430	61	34	46	21	40
35	Togo	264	**132**	155	83	4.0	177	23	340	55	45	111	..	..
36	Ghana	213	**131**	126	76	16.9	695	91	430	56	58	74	18	44
37	Haiti	260	**127**	170	74	7.0	246	31	370x	56	41	56	..	..
38	Sudan	292	**122**	170	74	27.4	1078	131	480x	53	40	51	..	..
39	India	236	**119**	144	79	918.6	26095	3103	300	60	48	102	21	41
40	Nepal	290	**118**	190	84	21.4	827	98	190	53	24	102	22	40
41	Bangladesh	247	**117**	151	91	117.8	4127	483	220	55	35	77	23	39
42	Senegal	303	**115**	174	60	8.1	344	40	750	49	29	59	11	59
43	Yemen	340	**112**	230	78	13.9	670	75	520x	50	39	78	..	..

(Contd.)

TABLE 5.1: (Contd.)

		Under-5 mortality rate 1960	Under-5 mortality rate 1994	Infant mortality rate (under 1) 1960	Infant mortality rate (under 1) 1994	Total population (millions) 1994	Annual no. of births (thousands) 1994	Annual no. of under-5 deaths (thousands) 1994	GNP per capita (US$) 1993	Life expectancy at birth (years) 1994	Total adult literacy rate 1990	Primary school enrolment ratio (gross) 1986-93	% share of household income 1980-93 lowest 40%	% share of household income 1980-93 highest 20%
44	Indonesia	216	111	127	71	194.6	4684	520	740	62	82	115	21	42
45	Bolivia	252	110	152	73	7.2	255	28	760	59	79	85	15	48
46	Cameroon	264	109	156	69	12.9	520	57	820	56	57	101	..	..
47	Congo	220	109	143	82	2.5	112	12	950	51	68	..	..	..
48	Myanmar	237	109	158	79	45.6	1457	159	220x	57	81	105	..	..
49	Libyan Arab Jamahiriya	269	95	160	64	5.2	216	21	5310x	63	70	..	..	..
50	Papua New Guinea	248	95	165	67	4.2	139	13	1130	56	68	73	..	..
51	Keyna	202	90	120	61	27.3	1201	108	270	56	72	95	10	62
52	Turkmenistan	..	87	..	70	4.0	124	11	1230x	65	98x	..	..	..
53	Tajikistan	..	81	..	63	5.9	212	17	470	70	98x	..	..	..
54	Zimbabwe	181	81	109	57	11.0	421	34	520	54	82	119	10	62
55	Namibia	206	78	129	62	1.5	55	4	1820	59	..	124	..	..
56	Mongolia	185	76	128	58	2.4	63	5	390	63	80	89	..	..
57	Iraq	171	71	117	57	19.9	751	54	1036x	66	52	89	..	..

(Contd.)

TABLE 5.1:(Contd.)

		Under-5 mortality rate		Infant mortality rate (under1)		Tolal population (millions)	Annual no. of births (thousands)	Annual no. of under-5 deaths (thousands)	GNP percapita (US$)	Life expec-tancy at birth (years)	Total adult literacy rate	Primary school enrolment ratio (gross)	% share of household income 1980-93	
		1960	1994	1960	1994	1994	1994	1994	1993	1994	1990	1986-93	lowest 40%	highest 20%
58	Guatemala	205	**70**	137	51	10.3	393	28	1100	65	53	79	8	63
59	South Africa	126	**68**	89	52	40.6	1247	85	2980	63	80x	109	9	63
60	Nicaragua	209	**68**	140	49	4.3	168	11	340	66	64x	102	12	55
61	Algeria	243	**65**	148	54	27.3	775	50	1780	67	55	99	18	47
62	Uzbekistan	..	**64**	..	52	22.4	678	43	970	69	97x	..	..	..
63	Brazil	181	**61**	118	51	159.1	3824	233	2930	66	81	106	7	68
64	Peru	236	**58**	143	41	23.3	627	36	1490	66	86	119	14	51
65	Philippines	102	**57**	73	44	66.2	1968	112	850	66	94	109	17	48
66	Ecuador	180	**57**	115	45	11.2	308	17	1200	69	87	116	..	..
67	El Salvador	210	**56**	130	42	5.6	187	11	1320	66	69	78	..	..
68	Morocco	215	**56**	133	46	26.5	746	42	1040	63	39	69	17	46
69	Kyrgyzstan	..	**56**	..	47	4.7	130	7	850	69	96x	..	10	57
70	Turkey	217	**55**	161	47	60.8	1608	88	2970	66	79	113	..	..
71	Botswana	170	**54**	117	42	1.4	53	3	2790	65	66	116	11	59
72	Honduras	203	**54**	137	41	5.5	199	11	600	67	69	105	9	64
73	Egypt	258	**52**	169	41	61.6	1733	90	660	63	48	101	..	..

(Contd.)

TABLE 5.1: (Contd.)

		Under-5 mortality rate		Infant mortality rate (under 1)		Total population (millions)	Annual no. of births (thousands)	Annual no. of under-5 deaths (thousands)	GNP per capita (US$)	Life expectancy at birth (years)	Total adult literacy rate	Primary school enrolment ratio (gross)	% share of household income 1980-93	
		1960	1994	1960	1994	1994	1994	1994	1993	1994	1990	1986-93	lowest 40%	highest 20%
74	Azerbaijan	..	**51**	..	35	7.5	159	8	730	70	97x	..	..	..
75	Iran, Islamic Rep. of	233	**51**	145	40	65.8	2244	114	2200x	67	62	109	..	..
76	Kazakhstan	..	**48**	..	41	17.0	323	16	1560	70	97x	..	..	..
77	Viet Nam	219	**46**	147	35	72.9	2194	101	170	65	91	108	19	44
78	Dominican Rep.	152	**45**	104	38	7.7	200	9	1230	69	80	95	12	56
79	China	209	**43**	140	35	1208.8	21513	925	490	68	78	121	17	42
80	Albania	151	**41**	112	34	3.4	79	3	340	72	..	101	..	..
81	Lebanon	85	**40**	65	33	2.9	76	3	2150x	68	91	111	..	..
82	Syrian Arab Rep.	201	**38**	136	32	14.2	574	22	1160x	67	66	107	..	..
83	Moldova	..	**36**	..	31	4.4	67	2	1060	68	96x	..	..	..
84	Saudi Arabia	292	**36**	170	31	17.5	618	22	7510x	69	59	78	..	..
85	Paraguay	90	**34**	66	28	4.8	155	5	1510	70	91	110	..	..
86	Tunisia	244	**34**	163	28	8.7	215	7	1720	68	60	120	16	46
87	Thailand	146	**32**	101	27	58.2	1102	36	2110	69	93	97	15	51
88	Armenia	..	**32**	..	27	3.6	70	2	660	72	99x	..	..	..

TABLE 5.1: (Contd.)

		Under-5 mortality rate 1960	Under-5 mortality rate 1994	Infant mortality rate (under 1) 1960	Infant mortality rate (under 1) 1994	Total population (millions) 1994	Annual no. of births (thousands) 1994	Annual no. of under-5 deaths (thousands) 1994	GNP per capita (US$) 1993	Life expectancy at birth (years) 1994	Total adult literacy rate 1990	Primary school enrolment ratio (gross) 1986-93	% share of household income 1980-93 lowest 40%	% share of household income 1980-93 highest 20%
89	TFYR Macedonia	177	**32**	120	27	2.1	32	1	820	72	..	..	..	..
90	Mexico	148	**32**	103	27	91.9	2473	79	3610	71	88	113	12	56
91	Russian Federation	..	**31**	..	28	147.4	1487	46	2340	68	99x	..	14	48
92	Korea, Dem. Peo. Rep.	120	**31**	85	23	23.5	559	17	970x	71	..	104	..	..
93	Romania	82	**29**	69	23	22.9	245	7	1140	70	97x	88	..	..
94	Georgia	..	**27**	..	23	5.5	84	2	580	73	99x	..	..	..
95	Argentina	68	**27**	57	24	34.2	685	18	7220	72	96	107	..	..
96	Oman	300	**27**	180	22	2.1	90	2	4850	69	..	100	..	..
97	Latvia	..	**26**	..	22	2.6	28	1	2010	69	99x	86	..	..
98	Ukraine	..	**25**	..	21	51.5	568	14	2210	70	98x	..	..	..
99	Jordan	149	**25**	103	21	5.2	199	5	1190	68	82	105	17	48
100	Venezuela	70	**24**	53	20	21.4	568	13	2840	72	90	99	14	50
101	Estonia	..	**23**	..	20	1.5	16	0	3080	69	100x	85	..	..
102	Yugoslavia	120	**23**	87	20	10.8	149	3	a	72	..	..	..	..

(Contd.)

TABLE 5.1: (Contd.)

		Under-5 mortality rate		Infant mortality rate (under1)		Tolal population (millions)	Annual no. of births (thousands)	Annual no. of under-5 deaths (thousands)	GNP percapita (US$)	Life expec-tancy at birth (years)	Total adult literacy rate	Primary school enrolment ratio (gross)	% share ofhousehold income 1980-93	
		1960	1994	1960	1994	1994	1994	1994	1993	1994	1990	1986-93	lowest 40%	highest 20%
103	Mauritius	84	**23**	62	19	1.1	23	1	3030	70	80	106	..	..
104	Belarus	..	**21**	..	18	10.2	116	2	2870	70	98x	..	..	..
105	Uruguay	47	**21**	41	19	3.2	54	1	3830	72	97	108	..	..
106	United Arab Emirates	240	**20**	160	17	1.9	41	1	21430	74	77x	118	..	..
107	Lithuania	..	**20**	..	17	3.7	48	1	1320	71	98x	92	..	..
108	Panama	104	**20**	67	18	2.6	63	1	2600	73	89	105	8	60
109	Trinidad and Tobago	73	**20**	61	17	1.3	26	1	3830	71	97x	95	..	..
110	Bulgaria	70	**19**	49	16	8.8	89	2	1140	71	..	90	21	39
111	Sri Lanka	130	**19**	90	15	18.1	367	7	600	72	89	107	22	39
112	Colombia	132	**19**	82	16	34.6	808	15	1400	69	90	117	11	56
113	Bosnia and Herzegovina	155	**17**	105	15	3.5	48	1	b	72	..	..	..	..
114	Poland	70	**16**	62	14	38.3	494	8	2260	71	99x	98	23	36
115	Costa Rica	112	**16**	80	14	3.4	86	1	2150	76	94	105	13	51

(Contd.)

TABLE 5.1: (Contd.)

		Under-5 mortality rate		Infant mortality rate (under 1)		Total population (millions)	Annual no. of births (thousands)	Annual no. of under-5 deaths (thousands)	GNP per capita (US$)	Life expectancy at birth (years)	Total adult literacy rate	Primary school enrolment ratio (gross)	% share of household income 1980-93	
		1960	1994	1960	1994	1994	1994	1994	1993	1994	1990	1986-93	lowest 40%	highest 20%
116	Chile	138	15	107	13	14.0	300	5	3170	74	94	96	10	60
117	Slovakia	..	15	..	13	5.3	75	1	1950	71	..	..	..	..
118	Malaysia	105	15	73	12	19.7	545	8	3140	71	80	93	13	54
119	Croatia	98	14	70	12	4.5	50	1	a	71	..	..	..	..
120	Hungary	57	14	51	13	10.2	120	2	3350	69	99x	89	26	34
121	Kuwait	128	14	89	12	1.6	42	1	19360	75	76	60	..	..
122	Jamaica	76	13	58	10	2.4	51	1	1440	73	83	106	16	48
123	Portugal	112	11	81	9	9.8	118	1	9130	75	85	120	..	..
124	Cuba	50	10	39	9	11.0	180	2	1170x	75	94	102	..	..
125	United States	30	10	26	8	260.6	4080	41	24740	76	..	104	16	42
126	Czech Rep.	..	10	..	9	10.3	136	1	2710	71	..	..	..	..
127	Belgium	35	10	31	8	10.1	121	1	21650	76	..	99	22x	36x
128	Greece	64	10	53	8	10.4	102	1	7390	78	93	97	..	..
129	Spain	57	9	46	8	39.6	378	4	13590	78	95	107	22	37
130	France	34	9	29	7	57.8	736	7	22490	77	..	106	17	42
131	Israel	39	9	32	7	5.5	111	1	13920	76	92x	94	18x	40x
132	New Zealand	26	9	22	7	3.5	60	1	12600	75	..	104	16	45
133	Korea, Rep. of	124	9	88	8	44.6	732	6	7660	71	97	102	20	42

(Contd.)

TABLE 5.1:(*Contd.*)

		Under-5 mortality rate		Infant mortality rate (under1)		Tolal population (millions)	Annual no. of births (thousands)	Annual no. of under-5 deaths (thousands)	GNP percapita (US$)	Life expectancy at birth (years)	Total adult literacy rate	Primary school enrolment ratio (gross)	% share of household income 1980-93	
		1960	1994	1960	1994	1994	1994	1994	1993	1994	1990	1986-93	lowest 40%	highest 20%
134	Slovenia	45	**8**	37	7	1.9	20	0	6490	73	..	..	..	..
135	Australia	24	**8**	20	7	17.9	262	2	17500	77	..	107	16	42
136	Italy	50	**8**	44	7	57.2	557	4	19840	77	97	95	19	41
137	Netherlands	22	**8**	18	6	15.4	199	2	20950	77	..	98	21	37
138	Norway	23	**8**	19	6	4.3	62	0	25970	77	..	99	19x	37x
139	Canada	33	**8**	28	6	29.1	435	3	19970	77	97x	107	18	40
140	Austria	43	**7**	37	6	7.9	94	1	23510	76	..	104	..	..
141	United Kingdom	27	**7**	23	6	58.1	777	6	18060	76	..	104	15	44
142	Switzerland	27	**7**	22	6	7.1	90	1	35760	78	..	105	17	45
143	Ireland	36	**7**	31	6	3.5	52	0	13000	75	..	103	..	..
144	Germany	40	**7**	34	6	81.3	778	5	23560	76	..	94	19	40
145	Denmark	25	**7**	22	6	5.2	65	0	26730	75	..	95	17	39
146	Japan	40	**6**	31	4	124.8	1259	8	31490	79	..	102	22x	38x
147	Hong Kong	52	**6**	38	5	5.8	63	0	18060	79	91x	104x	16	47
148	Singapore	40	**6**	31	5	2.8	43	0	19850	75	89x	107	15	49
149	Finland	28	**5**	22	4	5.1	66	0	19300	76	..	100	18	38
150	Sweden	20	**5**	16	4	8.7	124	1	24740	78	..	101	21	37

Countries listed in descending order of their under-five mortality rates (shown in bold type).
a : Range US$696 to US$2785.b : Range US$695 or less.
Source : *The State of World's Children 1996*, UNICEF (1996).

6

SELECT INTERNATIONAL REPORTS (1994-95 AND 1995-96)

A. 1994-95

6.1 AIDS : INTERNATIONAL CONFERENCE (1994)

More than 11,000 people from 128 countries gathered in the Japanese city of Yokohama for the conference, held from 7 to 11 August, 1944 to focus the world's attention on the rapidly increasing AIDS epidemic affecting Asia and women.

Addressing the opening meeting, Dr. Nakajima said : "the world has sufficient knowledge about HIV/AIDS to contain the spread of the pandemic through effective prevention. Fear, indifference and denial, along with poverty, have been our main enemy. Another major challenge must be to provide the necessary care and support to all people affected with HIV/AIDS."

According to the WHO, the cumulative number of HIV infections to date exceeds 17 million worldwide. If present trends continue, the figure will more than double to reach 30 to 40 million by the year 2000. The spread of the pandemic may be fastest in South and South-East Asia but even in East Asia and the Pacific, where total numbers remain low, estimated HIV infections are on the increase. These are alarming signals because today there is no effective cure for HIV/AIDS.

The Yokohama International Conference on AIDS can play a crucial role in mobilizing the political, financial and social support urgently needed worldwide to ensure full implementation of our global AIDS strategy, Dr. Nakajima said.

The WHO remains committed to strengthening its partnership with countries, communities and people living with HIV/AIDS. The WHO will also continue to promote research and accessibility of drugs and care for all, in particular for the poorest, he said.

Dr. Nakajima paid tribute to Japan for setting an example to the rest of the world in the fight against AIDS.

Also addressing the gathering, Dr. Michael Merson, Executive Director of the WHO Global Programme on AIDS, appealed to Asian leaders to face reality and make AIDS a national priority. The WHO predicts that if current trends continue, by the year 2000, more than 10 million Asians will have been infected with HIV.

> "In places where the epidemic is just moving into the early explosive phase—like much of Asia"—he said, "overriding need is to act now, without delay, to prevent or blunt the rise in infections. I appeal to all Asian leaders to face reality and make AIDS prevention a national priority. Do

whatever you need to do to overcome denial, and fight discrimination. Provide your most vulnerable citizens the information and means—condoms—to protect themselves. And do not believe as many others have believed—that it won't happen to you."

In the past 12 months, according to the WHO estimates, anonter 3 million men, women and children have been infected with HIV. The cumulative total stood at around 14 million a year ago. It now exceeds 17 million. In South and South-East Asia, HIV infections are now estimated at over 2.5 million—a million more than just a year ago. The HIV epidemic here is growing at an alarming rate. For example, estimated infections in Thailand have risen tenfold since early 1990. In India, they have tripled since 1992.

This is the first time that researchers, public health officials, service providers and activists have gathered in an Asian nation for the International AIDS Conference.

Holding the international AIDS Conference here in Yokohama could not be more timely, said Dr. Merson. HIV and AIDS are challenging this continent as never before. Enormous population movements, the inferior status of women and a reluctance to acknowledge the huge threat posed by AIDS make many Asian countries every vulnerable. But for all its vulnerability, Asia, is in a position of unique strength to curb the epidemic, given clear vision and strong political will.

Dr. Merson said that three social forces were driving the spread of HIV and blocking effective prevention and care—denial, discrimination and dismemberment. It is clear that until we overcome these societal factors...we will never bring the epidemic under full control, he said. Political leaders must find the courage to provide leadership despite the sensitivities and taboos around AIDS, discriminatory laws and practices must be abolished and those who are prowerless must be given the means to protect themselves.

With sufficient resources and political will, the WHO believed that millions of new infections can be avoided. There were signs in sub-saharan Africa that it was possible to encourage people to change their behaviour to avoid infection, Dr. Merson said. More and more condoms were being sold and distributed, and there was increasing anecdotal evidence that bars and discos that served as sex trade centres were losing clientele. Rates of sexually transmitted diseases reported from primary health clinics in Harare, Zimbabwe, showed a substantial downturn—63 per cent between 1990 and 1993. All of that pointed to encouraging changes in sexual behaviour.

And there were other examples of successful prevention efforts in many Asian countries. In India, for example, in Sonagachi, Calcutta, a project which worked with 6,000 sex workers had resulted in a marked increase in condom use. In Thailand, projects aimed at promoting 100 per cent condom use in the sex entertainment industry had been successful, particularly in Samut Sakhon.

In Manipur, India, Kuala Lumpur, and in Ho Chi Minh City in Viet Nam, there were examples of innovative projects which promoted harm-reduction strategies among intravenous drug users, including education and rehabilitation programmes. And in Asia, as elsewhere, programmes for effective prevention and care of sexually transmitted disease were being promoted and supported by international agencies, including the WHO.

There was also evidence of a growing realization of the potential benefits of HIV/AIDS education in schools, even in countries where it was difficult to talk about sex, HIV and AIDS and other sexually transmitted diseases, according to the WHO. School education projects had begun in Viet Nam, Malaysia, Philippines, India and Thailand, as had numerous projects targeting youth in Bangladesh, Mongolia, Nepal and Indonesia.

But in order to have a significant impact on the spread of HIV, such effective prevention measures must be scaled up dramatically, said Dr. Merson. To do that would require a financial as well as political commitment. The WHO calculated that implementing basic prevention programmes in Asia would cost between three-quarters to one-and-a-half billion dollars a year.

Let us not use cost as an excuse, said Dr. Merson. This represents less than 0.03 per cent of Asia's economic output. Or to put it another way, it is the equivalent of what Japan's workers produce in less than one hour. An investment of this kind would avoid an estimated 5 million infections by the year 2000 alone. And the preventive effect would be even stronger as Asia moves into the twenty-first century.

The economic benefit that could result from prevention on such a scale was difficult to estimate, he said, but it was clearly massive in comparison with the investment needed. Consider that by the year 2000, a Thai estimate put the loss to Thailand's economy alone at nearly $ 11 billion, and that it was estimated that AIDS would cost Asian economies between $ 38 and $ 52 billion.

Worldwide, over 6,000 people were becoming infected with HIV every day, more and more of them in Asia. Faced with such a rapid spread of the disease, Dr. Merson said the answers to the questions posed by HIV/AIDS lay in teamwork. "The answers—the global response—are up to us—researchers, government officials, clinicians, journalists, citizens of all nations, men and women living with and without AIDS. As we move forward, let us seek out and link up with all possible allies—people fighting for development, for equality, for human rights, for fairness, in whatever sphere of life. If we act together, we can persuade the powers that be that action cannot wait in Africa, in the Americas, in Europe, not the least in Asia, where time is fast running out", he concluded.

Source : *UN Newsletter*, August 20, 1994.

6.2 DRUG CONTROL : INTERNATIONAL NARCOTICS CONTROL BOARD INCB REPORT (1994)

Background on INCB

The INCB was established in 1968 as an independent and quasi-judicial control organ for the implementation of the United Nations drug control treaties, replacing predecessor bodies which had monitored earlier conventions since the time of the League of Nations. Although the Board's work is financed by the United Nations, it functions independently of Governments and of that

Organization on substantive issues. It endeavours to ensure that adequate supplies of drugs are available for medical and scientific uses and that leakages from licit sources to illicit traffic do not occur. At the same time it seeks to identify weaknesses in national and international control of drugs.

The Board's tasks, among which is the preparation of an annual report, are mandated by the international drug control Conventions. Its 13 members serve in their individual capacities. They are elected by the Economic and Social Council, with three chosen from a list of candidates nominated by the World Health Organization (WHO) and 10 from a list nominated by Governments.

Recommendations for increasing the effectiveness of the International Drug Control Conventions, based on an evaluation on the strengths and weaknesses of those treaties, are a key component of the 1994 Report of the International Narcotics Control Board (INCB), which was released on 17 February.

The Board which regularly reviews the world drug scene and international compliance with three international drug control conventions in its current report focuses on how effective those treaties have been in preventing drug abuse and illicit trafficking in narcotic drugs. The analysis was conducted in response to a request by the General Assembly that the Board cooperate with the Commission on Narcotic Drugs to examine the status of global drug control efforts, with a view to identifying areas of satisfactory progress and weakness.

The Board concludes that the treaties—the 1961 Single Convention on Narcotic Drugs and as amended by the 1972 Protocol, the 1971 Convention on Psychotropic Substances; and the 1988 Convention Against Illicit Traffic in Narcotic Drugs and Psychotropic Substances—are of crucial importance for effective international action, but points out a number of areas where their provisions are not effective enough or not wholly adequate to the present international drug situation, or are misunderstood.

The key to more effective international drug control, the Board argues, is not in amending those treaties or in drawing up new instruments, but by universal adherence to those treaties, proper and thorough implementation of their provisions on both the national and international levels and making sure that the international drug control system is dynamic enough to be capable of reacting rapidly to adapt to the fast-changing drug scene around the world.

Among the issues identified for further consideration by Governments are the strengthening of measures to control poppy straw, classifying of cannabis products according to their potency and solving the long-standing contradiction between the conventions and traditional forms of coca leaf use. The Board expresses doubt on the usefulness or feasibility of additional new treaty provisions on demand reduction.

The one main goal and one philosophy of the three treaties, the Report stresses, is to prevent the use of drugs for non-medical purposes. Thus the INCB continues "its stance, asserted in 1993, that there is no viable alternative" to policies based on the drug control treaties and that calls for "legalization" should be rejected.

In a section on adherence to the conventions, the Board draws attention to the fact that Austria, Belgium and Switzerland have not yet made good on their longstanding promise to accede to the 1971 Convention, stating that "the failure of those major manufacturing and exporting countries to control international trade in many psychotropic substances has had a negative impact on the effectiveness of the international drug control system."

Of particular concern to the Board in 1994 was an upsurge in the diversion of benzodiazepines—commonly prescribed tranquilizers—from licit sources to illicit markets. This pattern is partly to blame according to the Report, on the low priority accorded by some Governments to the control of those substances.

A further focus of attention was increased diversion and smuggling of precursors—raw materials and chemicals used in the illicit production of substances of abuse. The failure of a number of countries to monitor and report on trade in such substances was again cited as a major loophole being exploited by drug criminals.

Source : *UN Newsletter*, March 4, 1995.

6.3 ECONOMIC AND SOCIAL SURVEY : UN REPORT (1994)

"Policy-makers in the world's major economies should remain focused on the economic fundamentals and not be pressured into precipitate aotion to stabilize markets when they meet in Naples at the Group of Seven summit", said Jean-Claude Milleron, Under-Secretary-General of the United Nations and head of the UN Department of Economic and Social Information and Policy Analysis (DESIPA). "The fundamentals are encouraging", according to Mr. Milleron, "and the most effective way to reach calm waters is to stay the course."

Introducing the UN's World Economic and Social Survey 1994, released 5 July, Mr. Milleron backed its projection that world output will rise in 1994 and 1995 by the fastest rates since 1989, as long as the macroeconomic policy stances of the second quarter are maintained.

Growth is returning to the developed market economies, albeit on a modest scale, according to the Survey, and economic expansion in developing countries overall will continue at the rapid rate of the past two years. "Incomes of a large proportion of the population of the developing countries, still very low, are growing faster in recent years than considered likely even a decade ago", the UN report observes.

But it also finds sharp variations between countries and regions. Population growth in Africa will again outstrip the projected rise in output. In the economies in transition in eastern Europe, growth will be just over 2 per cent in 1994 and 3 per cent in 1995, while the outlook for most of the countries of the former Soviet Union is of falling output again in 1994 and 1995. Among the developed countries, the United States economy remains the greatest source of optimism, while Japan and western Europe are expected to emerge slowly from recession, with 1994 growth in the range of 1 to 2 per cent.

Prospects for the world economy clearly improved in early 1994, but a number of acute problems remain. The Survey points to the alarming levels of unemployment in Europe and the economies in transition, as well as most developing countries; the political and ethnic unrest and military conflicts which are inflicting misery and wreaking havoc with economic and social development; and the one-fifth of the world's population that lives in poverty.

The two final chapters of the Survey were prepared to assist in global preparations for two important United Nations meetings : the International Conference on Population and Development, to be held in September 1994 in Cairo, and the World Summit for Social Development, taking place in Copenhagen in 1995. Following are summaries of these chapters.

Global Unemployment

The high level of unemployment in most developed economies is mainly due to increased labour supply stemming largely from the greater participation of women in the work force : the growth of employment has been as high in recent decades—despite lower economic growth rates—as in the early post-war period.

Labour shortages have occurred in a few rapidly growing, newly industrializing economies, but in most developing countries high levels of structural unemployment persist. The economies in transition also are experiencing high levels of unemployment, with less skilled and younger workers particularly vulnerable. Many older workers are situated in enterprises in which the state is effectively acting as empolyer of last resort. A further complicating factor is the weakening of the substantial social safety net previously provided by state agencies or through regular employment.

Policies that stimulate investment, with its ability to add both to demand and employment-generating productive capacity, are needed to reduce unemployment in all three groups of countries. However, constraints on expansionary policies and the persistence of structural unemployment militate in favour of policies oriented towards specific labour-market barriers and rigidities. In addition, rapid technological change, while beneficial in the long run and stimulative of trade and investment, can disrupt employment patterns. Policies need to take into account such trade-offs while imparting greater flexibility and transparency to labour-market institutions, especially in those economies where such institutions are underdeveloped, the Survey recommends.

Population and Sustainable Development

In the 35-year period 1990 to 2025, in all regions of the world, the population is expected to grow more slowly than in the 35-year period 1955 to 1990. In the developed countries and in some developing countries, the slow-down in population growth will lead to major increase in the proportion of those over 65 in the population. This will have implications for the type of investments to be made, and also for government finances, as provisions will have to be made for the needs of the elderly. In the end, however, it is healthy economic growth that can assure adequate retirement incomes.

Technology and productivity increases have led to lower food and raw material prices in real terms—a far cry from the earlier specter of shortages. These trends are likely to continue. However, it is important that prices reflect the true scarcity of limited resources, such as fish or water, and also the costs of repairing environmental damage incurred by production.

Over the next 35 years, it is not the total number of people in the world, but rather their production and consumption patterns, that will determine the level of environmental degradation. This is especially the case as most of the world's present environmental degradation is caused by the developed countries, where population growth is stagnant. Only over a period of 100 year or more is growth in the size of developing country population expected to become a significant factor in determining levels of global pollution, and even then technological factors will have greater impact.

There is little reason to believe in a Malthusian-type trap, in which population growth consistently runs ahead of people's ability to sustain themselves. The crossover from wasteful and polluting patterns to those fostering sustainable development will be a key factor in the transition to the next century.

Source : *UN Newsletter*, August 13, 1994, New Delhi.

6.4 POPULATION : UNFPA REPORT (1994)

Empowerment is about choice. Choices about if and when to get married, choices about education and employment, choices about if and when to get pregnant, and ultimately about family size. According to the report, empowerment of individual women may be the key to social development.

Empowerment requires that husbands, partners, family members and communities help promote a healthy environment free from coercion, violence or abuse, in which women are free to use community services on a basis of equality. The report stresses the importance of equal access for girls to formal education, but says women also need speical training outside school; education for older women is important too because they play an influential role in the family and community.

The report says there is increasing evidence that free and equal access to health care, family planning and education is not only desirable in itself but a practical contribution to broader objectives such as environmental protection and economic development. In addition to broadening their options and improving their health, women's growing control over their fertility will also help achieve balanced population growth.

A slowdown in population growth, says the report, will relieve pressure on the environment and on other problem areas, and provide time for finding solutions. "For the countries concerned, even the difference of a decade in the transition to lower fertility can have a considerable impact on the quality of life, for example in providing education, quality health care and employment opportunities."

Highest Population Growth Ever

The report says world population will be six billion by 1998, up from 5.66 billion in mind-1994; latest United Nations projects place world population in the year 2025 at 8.5 billion and 10 billion by 2050. These projections assume a continued decline in fertility, however. Without it, population growth could surge in the first half of the next century to 12.5 billion by 2050.

The report says many of the actions needed to alleviate poverty, improve food supply, end malnutrition and provide adequate housing are the same as those needed achieve balanced population growth, for example, extending the range of choice available to individuals, especially women, and equalizing opportunities between the sexes from birth onwards. According to the report, individual needs and public policy are converging. "The priority for the remaining years of this century must be to ensure that they remain in harmony and that individual needs form the basis of public policy."

An Individual Pursuit

While governments are investing considerable resources to curb population growth, ultimate success or failure depends on the decisions of individual women and men in pursuit of their own personal interests, says the report.

The report cites Zimbabwe, Thailand and Colombia as examples of successful integrated policies. While conditions vary widely, the approaches are similar: providing freedom of choice leads to increased responsibility on the part of individuals.

In Zimbabwe, the average number of children per woman—close to eight in the late 1960s—has fallen to 5.4. This remarkable success is due in large part to community involvement, especially in guaranteeing women's participation in decision making at all levels. Since the country's independence, the government has made the advancement of women a cornerstone of its policy.

Thailand has given priority to population as an integral part of development, with growth rates declining from 3.5 per cent a year in 1960 to 1.4 per cent in 1991. Thailand, one of the world's fastest growing economies, has focused on social development and the empowerment of women, with Thai women among the most economically active in Asia.

Colombia, too, has faced a remarkable decline in population growth, with no formal policy to reduce fertility. In 1960, the average number of children per woman was about 7; that figure is now 2.9, one of the lowest levels in Latin America. Colombia places strong emphasis on cooperation with NGOs to implement its social policies, with one major NGO, PROFAMILIA, operating 48 clinics and providing 32 per cent of all modern methods used.

Future Needs

The report says the means to allow most of the world's women to plan their number of children already exist. The problem is that access to health care, particularly reproductive health care, is still inadequate. About 120 million women worldwide would like to plan their families, but have no access to modern contraceptives.

The report says it is possible to design successful strategies that meet individual needs—especially those of women—which also contribute to national development priorities. For countries, this entails increasing national investment in the areas of human development, especially in education, health and improving the status of women. The report calls these the "building blocks of sustainable economic development."

Extended globally, these national programmes "will contribute to slower overall population growth, and thus to a solution of the central issue for the 21st century: how to balance human needs and human numbers."

A Few Facts

Only a generation ago, fewer than one woman in five worldwide could plan her family. Today, three-quarters of all couples in industrialized countries and well over half those in the developing world use family planning. The 'reproductive revolution' has firmly established itself as the major force in population trends around the world.

Progress in providing modern health care has tended to obscure one tragic face: despite renewed attention to maternal health, pregnancy and its consequences claim the lives of 500,000 women a year.

Source : *Go Between 48, Oct/Nov 94*, NGLS, Geneva.

6.5 POPULATION : POPULATION CONFERENCE (1994)

On 13 September 1994, after 10 days of intense negotiations, delegates from 180 nations adopted the Porgramme of Action of the United Nations International Conference on Population and Development (ICPD), in Cairo, Egypt.

The 16-chapter Programme outlines a comprehensive strategy for stabilising world population growth and achieving sustainable development. It focuses on reproductive health needs; improving immigration and urbanisation policies; and empowering women.

According to the Programme, reproductive health strategies (including family planning, maternal health, the prevention of sexually transmitted diseases, and collecting and analysing population data), will cost US$ 17 billion in the year 2000. A loophole is left in the final text to the extent that "these are indicative cost estimates [which] should be reviewed and updated." Several African countries propor ed an amendment where governments would devote at least 20% of public sector expenditures to the social sectors, as well as 20% of official development aid. Known as the "20/20 initiative", this proposal was deflected by the European Union, Japan and others, to be revisited following the outcome of the World Summit for Social Development.

The Programme of Action marks a watershed in taking population programmes beyond family planning. Its approach is to link population with women's empowerment and economic development. It recognises the rights of couples and individuals to choose the number, spacing and timing of their children, and to have the information and means to do so. The fact that countries with very different cultural and religious attitudes to family planning have produced a consensus document is in itself laudable, and implies that the Programme can be implemented in all of the countries which support it.

Countries

There are 228 countries in the world. Three quarters of the world population live in the 23 largest. China (1.2 billion) and India (919 million) account for 38 per cent of the world population (see Table 6.1).

In 1994, 10 countries had a population of more than 100 million. These 10 countries encompass 60 per cent of the world population. Following China and India in population size are the United States of America (261 million), Indonesia (195 million), Brazil (159 million), the Russian Federation (147 million), Pakistan (137 million), Japan (125 million), Bangladesh (118 million) and Nigeria (108 million).

Thirteen countries have a population size between 50 million and 100 million persons. Those 13 countries combined have a population of 837 million and constitute 15 per cent of the world population. In this group, frive countries are in Asia (Viet Nam, the Philippines, the Islamic Republic of Iran, Turkey and Thailand), five in Europe (Germany, the United Kingdom, France, Italy and Ukraine), two in Africa (Egypt and Ethiopia) and one in Latin America and the Caribbean (Mexico).

Hence, just 23 of the 228 countries of the world hold 75 per cent of the world population. On the other hand, there are 77 countries with a population of fewer than 1 million in 1994.

Source : The Netwook, September, 1994.

6.6 CHILDREN : THE STATE OF THE WORLD'S CHILDREN REPORT (1996)

The *State of the World's Children* argues that respect for children and commitment to their welfare are key to humanitarian and political progress. It then sets out an Anti-War Agenda for action. Measures include :

— *Prevention :* a much more deliberate effort should be made to address the underlying causes of violence, including poverty, and to invest resources in mediation and conflict resolution.

— *Girls and women :* specific measures are needed to ensure their security because of the terrible threat of sexual violence and rape.

— *Child soldiers :* the minimum age for military recruitment specified in the Convention on the Rights of the Child is 15. UNICEF supports the adoption of an optional protocol to raise this age to 18.

— *Landmines :* their production, use, stockpiling, sale and export should be prohibited by international law.

— *War crimes :* recent years have seen the most barbaric acts of violence against children and other civilians. These must be denounced as they are revealed. International war crimes tribunals must have both the support and the resources to bring perpetrators to justice.

— *Children as 'zones of peace' :* the idea of negotiating temporary cease-fires to allow children in war zones to be vaccinated, or to allow food supplies to pass through enemy lines, has already proved its worth. It should be enshrined in international humanitarian law.

— *Sanctions :* these are used increasingly in international diplomacy to exert pressure on regimes. However, a 'child impact assessment' is needed whenever any set of sanctions is applied, and constant monitoring must then take place to gauge the impact of sanctions on children.

TABLE 6.1 : The 31 Largest Countries Ranked According to Population Size, 1950, 1994 and 2050

1950			1994			2050		
Rank	*Country*	*Population*	*Rank*	*Country*	*Population*	*Rank*	*Country*	*Population*
1.	China	555	1.	China	1 209	1.	India	1 640
2.	India	358	2.	India	919	2.	China	1 606
3.	United States of America	152	3.	United States of America	261	3.	Pakistan	381
4.	Russian Federation	103	4.	Indonesia	195	4.	United Staes of America	349
5.	Japan	84	5.	Brazil	159	5.	Nigeria	339
6.	Indonesia	80	6.	Russian Federation	147	6.	Indonesia	319
7.	Germany	68	7.	Pakistan	137	7.	Brazil	264
8.	Brazil	53	8.	Japan	125	8.	Bangladesh	239
9.	United Kingdom	51	9.	Bangladesh	118	9.	Ethiopia	194
10.	Italy	47	10.	Nigeria	108	10.	Zaire	164
11.	France	42	11.	Mexico	92	11.	Iran (Islamic Rep. of)	163
12.	Bangladesh	42	12.	Germany	81	12.	Mexico	161
13.	Pakistan	40	13.	Viet Nam	73	13.	Viet Nam	144
14.	Ukraine	37	14.	Philippines	66	14.	Philippines	130
15.	Nigeria	33	15.	Iran (Islamic Rep. of)	66	15.	Russian Federation	130
16.	Viet Nam	30	16.	Egypt	62	16.	Egypt	117

(Contd.)

TABLE 6.1 : (Contd.)

1950			1994			2050		
Rank	Country	Population	Rank	Country	Population	Rank	Country	Population
17.	Mexico	28	17.	Turkey	61	17.	Japan	110
18.	Spain	28	18.	United Kingdom	58	18.	Turkey	106
19.	Poland	25	19.	Thailand	58	19.	Myanmar	95
20.	Egypt	22	20.	France	58	20.	United Rep. of Tanzania	91
21.	Philippines	21	21.	Italy	57	21.	Kenya	90
22.	Turkey	21	22.	Ethiopia	53	22.	South Africa	90
23.	Republic of Korea	20	23.	Ukraine	51	23.	Sudan	85
24.	Thailand	20	24.	Myanmar	46	24.	Thailand	82
25.	Ethiopia	18	25.	Republic of Korea	45	25.	Uganda	70
26.	Myanmar	18	26.	Zaire	43	26.	Germany	65
27.	Argentina	17	27.	South Africa	41	27.	United Kingdom	62
28.	Iran (Islamic Rep. of)	17	28.	Spain	40	28.	Côte d'Ivoire	61
29.	Romania	16	29.	Poland	38	29.	Saudi Arabia	61
30.	Canada	14	30.	Colombia	35	30.	France	60
31.	South Africa	14	31.	Argentina	34	31.	Afghanistan	60

- *Emergency relief :* where there is long-term conflict, aid should be seen as part of a process to help rebuild a society's capacity and promote development.
- *Rehabilitation :* a much more deliberate effort needs to be made to demobilize both adult and child soldiers and rebuild communities to foster not just respite but reconciliation. An important part of this rehabilitation must be to address psychosocial damage to children.
- *Education for peace :* all countries should include methods of conflict resolution in their school curricula that develop mutual understanding and show how differences can be resolved without violence.

But while children continue to be affected by war, many of the promises set by the 1990 World Summit for Children are becoming reality. In the field of health, child mortality is down, immunization rates are up, polio is nearing eradication and oral rehydration therapy (ORT) is saving lives. In nutrition, there is progress against iodine deficiency disorders, Vitamin A needs are being met, and breastfeeding has been made friendlier. Primary school enrollment is up, more people have access to safe drinking water, and the elimination of guinea worm disease is in sight. Finally, 179 nations have ratified the Convention on the Rights of the Child.

Source : *Go Between 55,* Dec 95/Jan 1996.

6.7 DEVELOPMENT : UNCTAD'S LEAST DEVELOPED COUNTRIES REPORT (1995)

According to the report, the forecast of GDP growth is based on recent improvements in world commodity prices, the return of peace and stability in some LDCs affected by political difficulties, and the improved performance of certain LDCs which have been faring well in the last few years. These prospects are dampened by high population figures, with a combined population in the 48 LDCs estimated at 580 million for 1994.

Growth performances vary considerably, however. Twelve LDCs registered significant increases in per capita output in the first half of the 1990s, mostly because of expansion in agricultural production, a strong government commitment to development, and the support of the international community.

On the other hand, armed conflict, large-scale migration and breakdowns in governance in several LDCs have prompted economic and social upheaval and a fall in output. The report says LDCs should place greater emphasis on rebuilding and strengthening the state's capacity to perform essential functions, with an early and peaceful end to conflict the key condition to reactivating the development process in these countries.

Despite advances, performance in the productive sectors remains weak. For most LDCs, performance in agriculture, industry and infrastructure has not been encouraging. Agriculture continues to be characterized by slow production growth in relation to the growth of population, declines in terms of trade, and loss of market shares for traditional agricultural commodities. According to the report, achieving food security, which should remain a priority for LDCs, will require more arable land and improved production.

While manufacturing value added grew in about one-third of LDCs until the early 1990s, growth rate turned negative in the 1990s. Setbacks to manufacturing include low investment, import compression and the policy environment, including the impacts of adjustment and reform. Selective interventions are needed to remove constraints caused by structural deficiencies, market limitations, insufficient endowments and inadequate policies. On the infrastructure front, the report says more progress is needed. It sets out priorities for improving transport and communications infrastructure and services in LDCs, with the international community's financial and technical support.

Furthermore, development in most LDCs has been stymied by a persistent decline in human welfare and inadequate progress in mobilizing and developing their human capacities. In 1994, UNDP classified as many as 42 LDCs in the lower category of human development.

In 1990, the Second UN Conference on LDCs in Paris adopted the programme of action for the LDCs. But so far, donor countries have shown little progress in implementing the ODA targets adopted in the programme. According to preliminary estimates, ODA flows to LDCs from member countries of the OECD Development Assistance Committee (DAC) and from multilateral agencies declined in absolute terms by almost US$ 1.3 billion in 1993. The ODA/GNP ratio for DAC donors—the amount of ODA in relation to a country's GNP—as a whole declined to 0.07% the same year. Two DAC countries (France and Portugal) met the 0.15% ODA target in 1993, while four countries (Denmark, the Netherlands, Norway and Sweden) surpassed it, reaching 0.2%.

Budgetary belt-tightening in donor countries makes ODA prospects uncertain. The report insists LDCs be given priority in aid allocation and makes three broad recommendations :

- generous replenishment of the soft-term windows of the international financial institutions, as well as of grant-based multilateral programmes;
- tapping new sources of finance, such as special drawing rights allocations and IMF gold sales; and
- linking ODA more closely to LDCs' long-term socioeconomic objectives.

At end 1993, LDC debt stock stood at US$ 127 billion, an estimated 76% of their combined GDP. For almost half the LDCs, the size of the debt stock equalled or exceeded GDP.

According to the report, LDCs' national policies should focus on economic policy reforms and on mobilizing domestic resources. This implies developing human resources through education, training, health, nutrition, family planning and improving the status of women. Greater emphasis on the productive sectors would improve and diversify supply capacity. Governance-related priorities include popular participation; increased participation of the private sector and NGOs; civil service reform to strengthen national administrative and management capacity; and greater emphasis on the rule of low to resolve and avoid political and social conflicts.

Finally, the international community should support the efforts of LDCs by substantially improving volume and quality of ODA. New international debt strategies should be launched to cancel the LDCs' debt and allow them a clean start with regard to their external obligations. Priority should also be given to putting into action the decisions taken at the Marrakesh ministerial meeting of the Uruguay Round in favour of LDCs and the net food-importing countries and to setting up 'safety net' measures to enable LDCs to tide over possible unfavourable consequences of the Final Act of the Uruguay Round.

Source : *Go Between 51*, April/May 1995.

6.8 DEVELOPMENT : WORLD DEVELOPMENT REPORT (1995)

South Asia's economic reforms and market liberalization policies should enable the region's economies to grow at rates rivaling the East Asian tigers. The reforms are designed to raise private investment, reduce reliance on the public sector, promote exports, open markets, and attract foreign capital. This change in economic strategy toward market based development, which encourages firms and workers to invest in physical capital and new technologies and skills, will improve the quantity and quality of jobs for South Asia's 430 million workers, the World Bank says in a **World Development Report 1995** *Regional Perspective, Jobs, Poverty and Working Conditions in South Asia.*

South Asia is home to nearly one-fifth of the world's labour force. It is also the poorest region in the world. Today, close to 59 per cent of the population spends less than $ 30 per month (measured in terms of purchasing power parity). The key to alleviating these problems is more productive jobs. Low employment and low labour productivity are the major market problems facing the region, and the main cause of poverty. Low employment can take the form of high chronic unemployment, as in Sri Lanka where nearly 14 per cent of the labour force is unemployed, or it can be reflected in high rates of under-employment, as in Pakistan (15 %), Bangladesh (43 %), and Nepal (45 %).

The report draws four major conclusions :

A market-friendly development strategy that encourages investment, human development, and growth is essential to improving labour market outcomes, creating more jobs, and enhancing working conditions.

Integration with the global economy through a reduction in trade barriers and greater capital mobility will provide a multitude of new opportunities for South Asian workers.

Labour policies should complement, rather than supplant, market mechanisms. These policies should be based on labour's right to collective bargaining in a competitive environment and avoid privileges to small groups of workers at the expense of the majority, most of whom are in rural and informal sectors.

This is evident from the success of a means-tested pension program for agricultural workers in the Indian state of Kerala. The pension level and income ceiling for eligibility are set low enough to ensure that recipients will continue to require support from relatives. This system, which effectively subsidizes the cost of home care for the elderly has been credited with encouraging traditional informal support.

The relative stability and large agrarian sectors of South Asian economies provide flexibility in choosing the pace of implementing structural reforms, but governments' reform agendas need to be credible and deal with the legitimate concerns of workers who may lose in the short run.

Governments can play an important role in softening the short-run impact of economic reforms. For example, the Government of Sri Lanka has avoided forcibly retrenching public sector workers and instead has opted for voluntary departure. Prior to its privatization, the "Leather Corporation" shed workers by offering an attractive compensation package that ranged from 10 to 50 months of salary, depending on the years of service. This package was very popular and helped privatization of the enterprise succeed.

On the critical issue of child labour, the report states that while all countries in the region have laws against child labour, it is believed that there are millions of working children under fifteen in South Asia today. Some types of child labour are more harmful than others, and the vast majority of working children in South Asia are unpaid helpers on the family farm.

Child labour must be understood before policies can be designed to eliminate it. High rates of child labour labour are linked to poverty and underdevelopment and poor or unavailable education. Children in poor families work because the family needs the extra income, especially if the parents' major source of revenue is uncertain. The report points out that education is one of the key components in reducing the problem of child labour. While national and international conventions banning child labour have a symbolic value as an expression of society's desire to eradicate this practice, they cannot deliver results unless accompanied by measures to shift the balance of incentives away from child labour and toward education.

The report concludes that the right government policies can help workers seize opportunities the global economy provides and can minimize risks in stalled economic transitions. In South Asia, policies should encourage private savings and investment and promote exports. Governments should also ensure that labor market interventions, such as establishing a minimum wage, benefit all workers and not just the lucky few who have modern sector jobs. Microeconomic projections under assumptions of high investment and export growth show real wages increasing at more than 5 per cent a year. This projection and related analyses indicate that good choices by governments in domestic and international realms can advance the incomes of all workers, address both their rights and concerns, and help bring back into the fold those who are now unable to keep up or adjust on their own.

Source : *UN Newsletter*, July 8, 1995.

6.9 DISASTERS : WORLD DISASTERS REPORT (1995)

The International Federation of Red Cross and Red Crescent Societies is the world's largest and oldest humanitarian network, with national societies in 163 countries working through 128 million members.

It puts ethics at the center of the humanitarian debate. With the rapid increase in conflicts and consequently in the number of organizations offering assistance, it says the international aid business is one of the most unregulated markets in the world.

"This unregulated free-for-all cannot continue. If humanitarian assistance is to retain anything of its roots in caring and compassion for mankind, then it has to reassert and abide by its value set." And that value set is neutrality, impartiality and independence.

The report portrays disaster response as a growth industry, with more internal wars and more victims worldwide, 95% of them civilians. There are more people on the move—at least 17 million refugees, 26 million internally displaced persons, and 100 million economic migrants. Some 250-300 million people a year are affected by disasters—and that doesn't even include war victims.

According to OECD figures, says the report, "Ten years ago, humanitarian assistance accounted for just over one percent of total overseas development assistance, now it is up to six per cent."

The federation says that along with the NGO community and the UN system, it is being expected to deal with the fallout from rapid social and economic change around the world. "Organizations which traditionally saw their role as filling in gaps, providing innovative examples and easing the suffering of individuals now find their resources committed to long-term assistance programmes, sometimes for millions of people."

So while more conflicts mean more agencies in the field, there are few internationally agreed standards to regulate them, and as a result, they must aim for increasingly high standards in behaviour, professional practice and technology.

"This is a market which literally deals in life and death issues for millions of people, and spends thousands of millions of dollars of other people's money." The report says the issue here is not the actual number of agencies, but their quality and willingness to cooperate with one another.

The federation believes that to provide effective assistance, a three-point agenda is needed :

— values and operational principles must be clearly and unambiguously stated and put into practice;
— professional and technical standards must also be stated and put into practice; and
— governments must be strenuously lobbied to respect humanitarian norms and rules, without which there can be no assistance and protection.

It says that in situations of violence, humanitarian agencies have a duty to ensure that their practice allows them to deliver assistance to those who need it most, where they need it most and when they need it most. It says the practice of professionalism is essential, and backs the statement with its newly established Code of Conduct for relief workers, as well as with research, training and evaluation for better response.

Governments, too, have responsibilities, says the report. They must accept that humanitarian action is no substitute for diplomatic and political action to address the underlying causes of today's humanitarian crises.

The federation argues against an integrated approach to assistance. This is the approach which links humanitarian assistance to political and military intervention. "While it may make theoretical sense in the safety of an agency's headquarters, by linking humanitarian assistance with military force, albeit in the form of peacekeeping operations...humanitarian assistance is being drawn into the conflict. Agencies, rightly or wrongly, are perceived as taking sides and their ability to alleviate suffering is severely hampered."

It says humanitarian assistance is no longer a side issue in today's crises. It is a central issue, hotly fought over, heavily funded and often under attack. The only solution, it says, is for humanitarian assistance to be delivered by a neutral agency.

Code of Conduct

1. The humanitarian imperative comes first;
2. Aid is given regardless of the race, creed or nationality of the recipients and without adverse distinction of any kind. Aid priorities are calculated on the basis of need alone;
3. Aid will not be used to further a particular political or religious standpoint;
4. We shall endeavour not to act as instruments of government foreign policy;
5. We shall respect culture and custom;
6. We shall attempt to build disaster response on local capacities;
7. Ways will be found to involve programme beneficiaries in the management of relief aid;
8. Relief aid must strive to reduce future vulnerabilities to disaster as well as meeting basic needs;
9. We hold ourselves accountable to both those we seek to assist and those from whom we accept resources; and
10. In our information, publicity and advertising activities, we shall recognize disaster victims as dignified human beings, not hopeless objects.

Source : *Go Between 53,* Aug/Sept 1995.

6.10 EMPLOYMENT : ILO REPORT ON WORLD EMPLOYMENT (1995)

According to ILO, the world is facing its worst employment crisis since the Great Depression of the 1930s. In 1994, some 820 million people—30% of the global labour force—were unemployed or underemployed.

In industrialized countries, about 35 million workers are jobless and unemployment rates are in the two digits. Projections for 1995 unemployment rates stand at 24.4 per cent for Spain, 17.7 per cent for Finland, 15.4 per cent for Ireland, 12.2 per cent for France and 10 per cent for Germany and Russia. In Poland, unemployment is 16.9 per cent and in Hungary 11 per cent. Latin America reports high underemployment, making it a more severe problem than unemployment. As for sub-Saharan Africa, more than 60 per cent of its urban labour force works in unorganized activities in the 'informal' sector.

Barring a change in present policies, the report warns that prospects for job growth remain gloomy worldwide, with growth insufficient to cure Europe's endemic employment ills, reverse the decline in real US incomes, halt the spread of poverty and underemployment in developing countries or prevent the marginalization of an entire continent, Africa.

But ILO says unemployment in industrial countries can be cut by half in the next decade if the proper combination of macro and microeconomic policies are adopted nationally and internationally and lead to higher economic growth rates, with benefits eventually spreading to developing countries.

The report identifies four requirements for job growth: trade liberalization, increased international cooperation, export-led industrial development, and positive adjustment measures. It says the key to increasing jobs is the ability of markets to manufacture and export goods and services globally, and that the best way of liberalizing trade is to fully implement the GATT agreement. As for international cooperation, the report says financial inability and volatile currencies inhibit the investment needed to create jobs; these need to be dealt with at the international level because no single country can deal with these problems alone.

East and Southeast Asia—where 78% of exports are manufactured goods—are models for export-led industrial growth with employment growth rates up 2.3% in Hong Kong and 5.9% in Singapore over the last decade. ILO calls for positive measures to speed globalization, in contrast with protectionist defensive policies. The report argues for :

- liberalization of product markets and financial markets to eliminate distortions, in order to increase competitiveness and improve productivity and output;
- scaling down non-wage labour costs-like payroll taxes and social security-especially for low-wage workers;
- reforming unemployment systems in order to reduce long-term unemployment and generate incentives to the unemployed;
- constant retraining in order to improve worker productivity and employability; and
- aid and assistance to the most disadvantaged workers.

Source : *Go Between* 53, Aug/Sep. 1995.

6.11 HEALTH : WHO REPORT (1995)

According to the *World Health Report 1995*, "Poverty is the main reason why babies are not vaccinated, why clean water and sanitation are not provided, why curative drugs and other treatments are unavailable and why mothers die in childbirth. It is the underlying cause of reduced life expectancy, handicap, disability and starvation... Every year in the developing world 12.2 million children under five years die, most of them from causes which could be prevented for just a few US cents per child. They die largely because of world indifference, but most of all they die because they are poor."

At any one time around the world, two billion people are sick, and many of them will die needlessly from preventable illnesses. For example, the 12.2 million death toll for children under five could be cut to some 350,000 deaths if those children had access to the same health care facilities as exist in industrialized nations.

The challenge facing the report is to highlight some of these inequities and to tackle the wider questions of global health priorities. What exactly are they? Which are the major diseases? Which conditions cause most misery, although they may not be fatal? Who has the greatest health needs? Where should health resources be targeted?

The report focuses on the widening gap between rich and poor and their health. In the world's most developed countries, deaths among children under five are as low as six per 1000 live births. At the other extreme, in the poorest nations, the rate is 320 deaths. Rapid urbanization has made the urban poor more marginalized, and the number of international refugees and internally displaced persons increased by 40% between 1990 and 1993 from 30 million to 43 million.

The poorest of the poor are getting sicker or living in poorer health, even if people overall are living longer. A person in one of the least developed countries has a life expectancy of 43 years, compared with 78 in one of the most developed countries.

The Good News

The report says all isn't bad news on the health front, however. Globally, there have been significant gains in health in the past 25 years :

- 80% of children have been vaccinated against the five major childhood killer diseases;
- infant mortality fell 25% globally between 1980 and 1993;
- life expectancy at birth increased by more than four years to about 65 during 1980-1993; and
- population growth is expected to slow from 1.7% in 1990-95 to 1% in 2020-25.

Priorities for Action

Despite these encouraging trends, the gap between rich and poor widens, and solutions become ever more pressing. The *World Health Report 1995* highlights four priorities for international action in an effort to bridge that gap.

Value for Money

The first priority is to ensure 'value for money' by using available resources as effectively as possible and redirecting them to those who need them the most. The aim is to create self-help environments in which men and women can slove their own problems, establishing and sustaining a development process that will ensure a brighter future for their children.

Poverty Reduction

The second priority is poverty reduction through better health. Investing in health saves money as well as lives. Poverty should be tackled on two fronts; one to meet people's basic minimum needs, the other to provide opportunities for people to earn their way out of their difficulties through better health and increased productivity.

Public Health Policy

The thrid priority calls for integrated, intersectoral action in addressing all the determinants—individual behaviour, along with the working and living environment—or ill-health.

Capacity Building

The fourth priority is to strengthen national capabilities for emergency relief and humanitarian assistance in the health sector. The new policy of 'emergency management for sustainable development' will provide a bridge between relief work and development proper.

According to WHO, poverty should be tackled on two fronts. On the one hand by ensuring the poor—especially families with young children, and vulnerable groups such as the elderly—have access to primary health care; on the other, by enhancing the health potential of the current workforce and of school children, on whom future social and economic development will eventually depend.

This first annual report has three sections. The first, 'Status of World Health', assesses global health at different phases of the life cycle—children, adolescents, adults and the elderly—and reports on general health issues. The second, 'Contribution of WHO of World Health', analyzes WHO activities aimed at improving human health. The third, 'Charting the Future', indicates possible areas for priority action in international health during the remainder of this decade. In addition, a special section on 'The Evolution of WHO' reviews historical developments in international health and the ways in which WHO has moved to meet the challenges.

Source : *Go Between 52,* June/July 1995.

6.12 INVESTMENT : UNCTAD WORLD INVESTMENT REPORT (1995)

The *World Investment Report* is the annual review of issues related to foreign direct investment prepared by UNCTAD's Division on Transnational Corporations and Investment. It has become established, and highly regarded, as a store of key data on the latest developments in the rapidly growing arena of foreign direct investment. It also contains an in-depth analysis of leading policy questions related to the complex universe of transnational corporations. This year, the special topic of policy analysis is competitiveness.

The research in this Report shows that international investment by transnational corporations supersedes trade as the most important mechanism for international economic integration. International business investment has become a major engine of global growth. It is an important source of the competitiveness of corporations.

It appears highly likely that the levels of foreign direct investment will continue to rise in coming years, that the business globalization process will accelerate and that, consequently, foreign direct investment will be increasingly prominent on the agendas of international policy-makers. These trends will, in turn, result in ever closer linkages between national economies.

The most recent foreign direct investment trends, which are detailed in *WIR 95*, provide ample support for these conclusions. We are talking now about 40,000 transnational coporations, whose approximately 250,000 foreign affiliates have sales in excess of $ 5.2 trillion—a greater volume than all of world trade.

The largest transnational corporations have their headquarters in the developed countries; yet, as *WIR 95* shows, an increasing number of transnational corporations can be found in developing countries. Their importance in global foreign direct investment is growing, and we expect this trend to continue at a significant pace. Transnational corporations made direct investments in foreign countries amounting to $ 226 billion in 1994. The 1995 total is likely to amount to $ 235 billion. A record 37 per cent of the 1994 volume went into developing countries.

Today's *WIR* provides you with UNCTAD's ranking of the world's 100 largest transnational corporations, as well as, for the first time, UNCTAD's ranking of the 50 leading transnational corporations in developing countries. *WIR 95* also highlights the competitiveness of small - and medium-sized transnational enterprises, and it provides you with a sample of 50 of these corporations. Moreover, to deepen understanding of the full nature of corporate globalization we have, for the first time, created an UNCTAD composite index of transnationality. This takes into account the respective shares of foreign assets, foreign sales and foreign employment of transnational corporations. According to this index, incidentally, many small - and medium-sized enterprises are more transnationalized than a number of large transnational corporations.

The picture in foreign direct investment and globalization is changing rapidly: the stock of global foreign direct investment from 1991 to 1993 grew about twice as fast as world-wide exports of goods and services. The world stock of foreign direct investment is estimated to reach $ 2.5 trillion this year. One of the causes of this dynamism is the increasing effort on the part of governments to adopt policies to liberalize and facilitate inward foreign direct investment. The benefits that this investment can yield for an economy are increasingly being recognized throughout the world. Transnational corporations are bringing with them a package of tangible and intangible assets, including, capital, management, know-how, skills and access to international markets.

The liberalization process is progressing at a rapid speed. Between 1991 and 1994, a total of at least 373 changes took place in national foreign direct investment laws and regulations—368 of them in the direction of liberalization. These unilateral measures were complemented by over 900 bilateral investment protection treaties, of which 60 per cent have been concluded since 1990. A new trend tracked by UNCTAD in this context is the growing number of bilateral foreign direct investment treaties between developing countries. A more recent trend has been characterized by discussions and negotiations in multilateral fora with eventually aim at the establishment of a multilateral framework on foreign direct investment. In that context, discussions are exploring what could be the possible content of such a framework, its implications from the development perspective and the best multilateral approach to the issue. If such a framework were, indeed, to be established, it could well rival the importance of past trade agreements in terms of creating new parameters for international business transactions.

WIR 95 contains two chapters that focus on policy issues relating to inward and outward foreign direct investment, and there are many boxes and sections in the *Report* that highlight aspects of these issues. The *Report* notes that many governments are offering incentives to attract foreign direct investment, many of which are wasteful or distortive. This is an area in which international action is needed, and the *World Investment Report* outlines some options in this respect. *WIR 95* also shows that corporations become more efficient, thus more competitive, as they build transnational production systems. The process of liberalization by governments has made it extremely difficult for firms to withdraw into the safe havens of sheltered national markets. Markets are increasingly being contested by foreign direct investment, non-equity forms of international business and trade. Competition is the central characteristic of the nature of the globalizing and liberalizing world economy.

And this fact, in turn, is a stimulus for corporations to become still more transnational, to secure not only direct access to new markets, but also to obtain access to a broad array of factors of production which they utilize to convert global inputs into outputs for global markets. The result is the establishment of an international production system—the productive core of the globalizing world economy.

An important aspect of this international production system is that a good part of international economic exchanges are internalized, that is, takes place within the corporate systems of individual transnational corporations. This might sound like an obscure concept, but it is important. For example, the international production systems of transnational corporations constitute an internal market for the flow of goods and services, which now has a volume in global trade terms of approximately $ 1.6 billion. In other words, one-third of world trade today is accounted for by shipments of goods and services within transnational corporations systems themselves—and the percentage is rising.

The constant pressure for efficiency at the global level can have negative effects as well. There are hardships in particular locations when production is moved to more efficient locations. Also, if governments do not ensure that markets function properly—because of, for example, lack of competition or restrictive business practices—countries do not benefit to the extent they could from the increased competitiveness of transnational corporations. Looking at the global economy as a whole, however, the *World Investment Report 1995* sees greater positives than negatives from the current trends in foreign direct investment and transnational corporations.

These trends show, however, marked regional differences. There are also key differences within regions themselves. For example, we find the bulk of foreign direct investment in Central and Eastern Europe concentrated in just three countries : Hungary, Poland and the Czech Republic. We find that foreign direct investment in Africa remains low and seems to be passing by this region, although Africa has considerable potential; *WIR 95* shows, for example, that returns on investments in Africa by United States firms have been more constant and higher than returns on foreign direct investment in other regions. Asia, on the other hand, led by China, has had a stellar performance in terms of attracting foreign direct investment in 1994. Latin America has a foreign direct investment stock that awaits to be dynamized and integrated in regional and international transnational corporations production systems. The United States is the single largest home and host country for transnational corporations. We encourage you to look at the regional discussion in *WIR 95.*

In conclusion, the Report is a rich mine of detailed information on how transnational corporations are operating, the impact foreign direct investment has on the competitiveness of firms, and the implication this has for the economic performance of countries. In other words, it addresses a key issue of today's national and international policy discussions.

Source : *UNCTAD Bulletin,* Nov./Dec. 1995.

6.13 POPULATION : STATE OF WORLD POPULATION REPORT (1995)

The 20-year goals of the Programme of Action of last year's International Conference on Population and Development in Cairo for expanded access to education, particularly for girls; reduced infant, child and maternal mortality rates and the gender disparity in these rates; and increased access to quality reproductive health services, are the key to social and economic development.

World population is currently 5.7 billion. According to United Nations projections, annual population increments are likely to remain above 86 million until the year 2015. Projections for 2015 range from 7.1 billion to 7.83 billion, and for 2050 from 7.9 billion to 11.9 billion, the actual totals reached will largely be determined by success during the rest of this decade in promoting the goals of Cairo. The low level can be reached and world population can be stabilized at 7.9 billion by 2050 if the ICPD Programme of Action is fully implemented.

Where there has been great progress over the past 30 years—lowered birth and death rates as well as reductions in infant mortality and increases in life expectancy—the progress has also always been linked to higher levels of education and income, political support for population policies, and changes in attitudes towards family planning. Contraceptive use has increased five-fold since 1965-70.

However, there continues to be great diversity among countries and regions. Maternal death rates are 15 to 50 times greater in the developing world than in most developed countries. Half a million women die each year as a consequence of pregnancy and childbirth; most of these deaths could have been prevented. Many more women—a much large number than was previously thought—suffer from illness or impairment related to pregnancy and childbirth.

Unsafe abortion is a major threat to the health of women. World-wide, it is estimated that women have more than 40 million abortions each year. Between 26 and 31 million are performed legally, and some 20 million are performed under unsafe conditions, accounting for an estimated 67,000 deaths. An even larger number of women suffer long-term complications such as infection, pain and infertility.

In addition, female genital mutilation damages the health and lives of an estimated 85 to 114 million girls and women. This and other unsafe practices must be stopped.

In some countries, adolescents account for as much as 60 per cent of those hospitalized with abortion complications. Expanded and improved family planning services is the best way to deal with unsafe abortion.

Married or not, very young women face higher risks in pregnancy and childbirth than those who delay childbearing until after the age of 20. They are less likely to continue their education, and are more likely to have lower-paying jobs or to be jobless. They have a higher rate of separation and divorce.

Today, women in most societies cannot participate fully in economic and public life, have limited access to positions of influence and power, have narrower occupational choices and lower earnings than men, and must struggle to reconcile activities outside the home with their traditional roles. These inequities must be redressed to fulfill women's human rights and enable countries to progress towards sustainable development.

Men must be educated and encouraged to take responsibility for their sexual and reproductive behaviour and for family and household obligations.

"The best way to address global problems such as poverty and high population growth rates and to achieve sustainable development is for governments to invest in people.

Investing in people, in broadening their opportunities and enabling them to realize their potential as human beings, is the key to economic growth and sustainable development, as well as to population growth that the world can support.

Enabling people, through access to family planning, to choose when to have children, and freeing women from the danger and illness associated with reproduction and sexuality through the promotion of safe motherhood initiatives, the prevention of sexually transmitted diseases, including HIV/AIDS, are all part of reproductive health care which is essential to achieving these aims.

Source : *UN Newsletter*, July 15, 1995.

6.14 POVERTY : OXFAM POVERTY REPORT (1995)

The situation is far from encouraging. While one in four people is dirt poor, millions more live very close to the line. Thirty years ago the richest fifth of the world's population had incomes 30 times greater than the poorest fifth. Today, those incomes are 60 times greater.

The report also says Africa, with 10 per cent of the world's population, has less than 1 per cent of world trade. And, more than half the United Nations' budget goes to emergency relief, diverting money from development: in 1989, the figure for emergency relief was 25 per cent.

The good news is that life expectancy is increasing, infant mortality is falling, nutrition levels have improved, and more people are receiving more education. Most important, marginalized people are reclaiming their resources and decision making power, working with NGOs and other to move out of poverty. Many initiatives exist, ranging from influencing agreements signed by heads of state at UN conferences, to a campaign in Brazil bringing together churches, trade unions, NGOS, the private sector and local government against hunger, to community organizations in Zimbabwe working to conserve scarce water resources.

The report concludes that the best hope for ending poverty is for citizens and social movements in both South and North to exert pressure on governments. But the report does not say all action must be local; on the contrary, it recommends changes in inter-governmental institutions as well as in national policy. The report clearly says that many of the most significant causes of poverty lie in decisions and actions for removed from the poor's sphere of influence.

The report sees the UN as a key institution in the fight against world poverty. "Charged with finding solutions to international social and economic problems, and promoting and protecting human rights and fundamental freedoms, the UN will be able to carry out its role only if the steady erosion of its power and authority is reversed... This implies both political support and financial backing."

Institutional Reforms

The report recommends that ECOSOC play a stronger role in monitoring the impact of global economic policies on social development and basic rights. It also suggests a complaints mechanism, open to individuals and groups, to allow investigation of alleged denials of basic rights under the International Covenant on Economic, Social and Cultural Rights.

The report echoes many NGOs in recommending that social impact assessments of World Bank and IMF policies go beyond internal review mechanisms. Such a process would involve the wider UN system as well as outside experts. The report calls for greater transparency in information policy and institutional reform to allow developing countries, accountable for implementing structural adjustment programmes, to have a bigger say in shaping them.

Northern and international NGOs should strengthen the advocacy capacity of community based organizations and southern NGOs, and all NGOs should develop advocacy, research, networking, and policy dialogue with governments, multilateral agencies, and the corporate sector as an integral part of their work.

Conflict Resolution

The report says there is a need for lasting resolution to conflicts. While pointing out the many (essential) peace and reconstruction initiatives taking place at the local level, it also highlights the importance of international efforts. "Currently, the international community is foundering in attempts to find an appropriate response to conflict, having gone from counterproductive intervention in Somalia to inaction in the face of genocide in Rwanda", says the report. It warns that NGOs are in danger of "becoming a humanitarian cover for failure to address the more fundamental causes of conflicts."

The recommendations underline the importance of local and regional conflict mediation and conflict prevention initiatives. A UN Office for Preventive Diplomacy is one suggestion. It would ensure an early warning mechanism for coordinated UN responses. An enforceable code of conduct on international arms transfers is also recommended, as is a stronger mandate for the existing UN Register of Conventional Arms and a 1% tax on arms exports to fund UN conflict prevention initiatives.

Other Recommendations

The report contains many other recommendations. On trade, the report calls for stabilizing commodity markets at remunerative levels and organizing international negotiations, under UN auspices, to replace the existing GATT agreement on foreign investment and intellectual property rights with a more equitable arrangement. On gender equity, it calls for an end to all forms of discrimination, particularly in relation to land, credit, and control over productive resources. Northern countries are encouraged to follow the Dutch example by carrying out an assessment of their impact on the world environment and setting up time-bound commitments to reduce negative impacts. Reducing CO_2 emissions by 30% from 1990 levels by 2005 and much more stringent targets for energy use are also recommended. The report quotes a World Bank study which says energy-saving improvements that cut developing country energy use by even 20% would save about US$ 30 billion a year, or about 60% of the net flow of resources from developing countries for debt service in 1988.

The report was produced by Oxfam UK and Ireland (UKI), in collaboration with sister Oxfam organizations in Canada, New Zealand and the USA.

Source : *Go Between 53,* Aug/Sept 1995.

6.15 REFUGEES : UN HIGH COMMISSIONER FOR REFUGEES UNHCR REPORT (1995)

The report points to the changing nature and scale of modern conflict. Before the end of the Cold War, most conflicts were cross-border: now, they are internal. And five years ago, most civilian casualties were refugees who crossed international borders. Today, the number of internally displaced people—people who have fled their homes but not their country—has rocketed.

The report is clear about what is needed : "Lasting solutions to the problem of human displacement will only be found if a concerted effort is made to protect human rights, to keep the peace within and between states, to promote sustainable development, and to manage international migration."

Traditional approaches simply aren't enough anymore. Rather than waiting for civilians to cross borders to help them, UNHCR's new strategy is to tackle the problem early on. In other words, a focus on the country of origin has been added to that on country of asylum. Not only does this save and improve lives, it also makes economic sense.

This approach is already showing success. In Tajikistan, more than 600,000 people were displaced in a brutal but little-noticed civil war in 1992. UNHCR's work inside the country—a mixture of hands-on human rights monitoring and major assistance for reconstruction—has helped stabilize the situation rapidly and rehabilitate the most war-ravaged areas. By the summer of 1995, 96% of Tajik refugees and displaced people in Afghanistan and Tajikistan had returned home.

The report shows dealing with potential refugee problems earlier in the game also pays dividends. "What might have happened in Rwanda if the estimated US$ 2 billion spent on refugee relief in the first two weeks of the emergency had been devoted to keeping the peace, protecting human rights and promoting development in the period which preceded the exodus?"

"Does it really make sense for the industrialized states to spend up to US$ 10 billion a year on their asylum systems, while freezing development assistance allocations and pursuing economic policies which have the effect of obliging people in the less prosperous states to migrate in search of work?"

"If the international community is serious in its desire to resolve the refugee problem, why have the UN's human rights institutions remained the world body's poor relation, with a budget and operational capacity that is minuscule in relation to its relief and peacekeeping activities?"

The report says the day of the quick fix is over, as is that of short-sightedness. It suggests a number of sensible initiatives to move the issue of human displacement forward, including :

— the establishment of war crimes tribunals,
— deployment of human rights monitors,
— more effort by the international community to prevent conflict,
— commitments by governments to reduce arms expenditures,
— a greater role for financial institutions,
— rewards to states which observe democratic principles and human rights standards,
— more institution building, needed for conflict prevention, resolution, and the promotion of democracy,
— promotion of conventional development, since peace and economic growth go hand in hand,
— urgent tackling of related problems of land distribution, environmental degradation, population growth and food security, and
— more private investment and trade.

The report urges greater respect for human rights, both to prevent new refugee crises and to consolidate solutions to existing ones.

UNHCR recognizes it cannot resolve these broad problems alone, so it works closely with a wide range of non-traditional partners such as peacekeepers, human rights organizations and military airlift coordinators.

Still, the report says these new approaches must not undermine the institution of asylum, often the only solution for people fleeing danger. Instead, it says, efforts must be made to address the most pressing issues facing the world today, which are linked to the refugee problem—the protection of human rights, the resolution of conflicts, the promotion of economic and institutional development, thc conservation of the natural environment, and the management of international migration.

A Few Figures

— 28 countries host more than 100,000 refugees (the four with the most are Iran, Zaire, Pakistan and Germany)
— 23 countries have produced more than 100,000 refugees (led by Afghanistan, Rwanda and Liberia)
— there are up to 30 million displaced people worldwide
— Africa has the largest number of refugees (6.75 million)
— Africa also has the largest number of returnees (3.08 million)
— the top five donors worldwide are USA, EU, Japan, Sweden, UK
— the top five donors per capita are Norway, Sweden, Denmark, Netherlands, Switzerland

Source : *Go Between 55,* Dec 95/Jan 1996.

6.16 TRADE AND DEVELOPMENT : UNCTAD REPORT (1995)

The world economy will sustain most of its current momentum and grow by 2.9 per cent in 1995 (compared with 3.1 per cent in 1994), and the developing countries' growth will continue to outstrip that of industrialized economies, the UNCTAD Trade and Development Report 1995' forecasts.

However, UNCTAD points out that the growth in the United States and Latin America is slowing down. Moreover, the lingering effects of Mexico's currency crisis in late 1994 and the decline in the U.S. dollar have added uncertainty to the short-term economic outlook. UNCTAD's forecasts for 1995, which cover all the major economies and regions of the world, tend to be more conservative than the general consensus.

In the industrialized countries, economic growth will slow to 2.5 per cent this year from 3.1 per cent in 1994, because of a deceleration in the United States fo 2.7 per cent from 4.1 per cent, the report says.

Western European growth will hold steady at 2.8 per cent, but the high level of unemployment will continue to be a preoccupation. In Japan, recession will continue with minuscule growth contracting to 0.5 per cent from 0.6 per cent.

The developing countries' higher growth rate will be sustained, at 4.5 per cent (4.4 per cent in 1994) thanks to the bright outlook for developing countries in Asia. Growth in those countries is expected to accelerate to 6.0 per cent in 1995 from 5.3 per cent in 1994, boosted by intra-regional trade and investment. China's economy will slow slightly to 9.6 per cent after three years of roughly 12 per cent growth.

However, short-term prospects for Latin America have been seriously impaired by the impact of the Mexican financial crisis, and the region's economic growth will slow to 2.0 per cent from 3.7 per cent.

Prospects for the African countries, meanwhile, are mixed and uncertain. Much will depend on the evolution of commodity prices and world demand, on the one hand, and on the weather and political conflicts and civil wars on the other. Prices for commodities—including foods, tropical woods and a number of metals—are expected to be weak this year because of the slowdown of industrial expansion in many major markets, sluggish recovery in Western Europe, and increases in commodity supplies.

Growth should improve in Central and Eastern Europe, although the gap between the former USSR and other countries in the region will widen further. Outside the former USSR, expansion should occur at a rate of 4.5 per cent in 1995. Inside, a further output decline of 7-8 per cent is possible.

Growth in 1994 varied considerably among and within regions.

In its review of 1994, the report says the 3.1 per cent growth of the world economy stemmed from recovery in industrialized countries and strong expansion in developing countries and China. The overall 1994 economic recovery, which compared with growth of 1.7 per cent in 1993, was broadly based but growth varied considerably both among and within regions.

World trade ballooned nearly 9 per cent last year, the biggest increase in two decades, and trade within regions also rose markedly, particularly in Asia. When measured in U.S. dollars, trade grew even more rapidly because of the fall in the value of the dollar against other currencies. Imbalances in the trade of industrialized countries worsened, with the deficit in the United States growing due to economic recovery. The large surpluses of Germany and Japan also grew further.

Price increases for commodities such as coffee, cotton and aluminium stemmed largely from strong demand, disruptions in supply, and speculative trading, as well as the weak U.S. dollar. The big exception was oil, whose prices continued to decline. Tea, beef, bananas and other commodities also fared badly.

The 3.1 per cent growth rate of the economies of the industrialized world was more than double the 1.4 per cent rate of growth in the previous year and was due largely to a widening and deepening of the cyclical recovery in Western Europe. Inflation was kept in check, but worry about high Western European unemployment continued. For developing countries as a whole, the 4.4 per cent expansion was faster than the preceding year's 3.8 per cent.

Industrialized Countries

The **United States** economy's growth of 4.1 per cent in 1994 continued an upswing that began in 1991. The latest growth rate was the biggest increase in a decade, and compared with 3.0 per cent growth in 1993. It was virtually the first investment-led recovery since the 1970's. Unemployment fell, dropping to 6.1 per cent from 6.8 per cent in the previous year, and consumer price increases slowed down.

Exports rose a sharp 9.0 per cent, double the previous year's growth, because of the drop in the U.S. dollar, the rise in the Japanese yen, increased U.S. productivity, strong demand from developing countries, as well as Western

Europe's recovery. However, the 13.2 per cent increase in imports, which was fueled by consumer demand, was greater than the rise in exports.

Western Europe's strong turnaround to growth of 2.8 per cent in 1994 from a contraction of 0.5 per cent in 1993 exceeded expectations and more than compensated for two years of declines. Germany enjoyed 2.9 per cent economic growth compared with a drop of 1.3 per cent in 1993.

The main factor behind the economic recovery was strong export demand, especially from developing countries in Asia, as well as North America and Central and Eastern Europe. Machinery and capital equipment did particularly well.

Inflation, meanwhile, slowed down in Western Europe, and unemployment seemed to have stopped rising in some countries.

Japanese economic growth was weak and erratic. That country managed an increase of less than 1 per cent in 1994 for the second year in a row. The rapid rise in the yen and continued political uncertainty cancelled out the benefits of public spending and low interest rates.

The strong yen helped sustain the dollar value of Japanese exports, but their volume growth was small at 1.7 per cent. The yen's rise also encouraged imports, which grew a sharper 12.2 per cent.

Developing Countries

Growth of 5.3 per cent in 1994 compared with 4.8 per cent 1993 made the developing countries of **Asia** the most dynamic group in the world economy. On the whole, Asian countries benefited from the further rise of the yen which prompted Japanese industries to move labour-intensive manufacturing to other Asian countries. This has strengthened the already strong trade and investment links within the region. Trade continued to be buoyant, with a few countries recording volume increases of more than 30 per cent in imports and more than 20 per cent in exports.

China, which has become an important locomotive for growth in the region, maintained a growth rate of roughly 12 per cent—much the same as in the previous two years. The country suffered from severe drought in the North and heavy floods in the South. Despite an austerity programme, inflation surged, with retail prices rising to 21.7 per cent in 1993.

Latin America's three-year expansion continued for a fourth year, with 1994's growth of 3.7 per cent representing an acceleration over the previous year's 3.1 per cent. The region's modest annual growth rate of about 3 per cent up to 1994 was accompanied by increasing success in contolling inflation. However, massive inflows of foreign capital worsened the region's current account deficit—that is merchandise trade plus so-called invisible trade such as financial services. The region's retail price inflation, excluding Brazil, fell to 16 per cent in 1994, compared with 40 per cent in 1991. Brazil reduced its inflation to between 2 per cent and 3 per cent a month in the latter half of 1994 from monthly inflation of 50 per cent before.

The economic performances of **African** countries varied widely but taken together they grew at about 2.0 per cent in 1994 vs. 1.4 per cent in 1993. They were helped by price increases for a wide variety of non-oil commodities and good weather, but economic growth was slower than population growth, resulting in a further decline in per capita GDP. The continent has yet to how tangible signs of strong recovery and sustained growth. The situation remains precarious and contrasts sharply with trends in Asia and Latin America. Africa's share of world output and trade continued to shrink while its share of world population continued to rise. The continent not only suffers from the vagaries of weather, armed conflicts and political instability, its productivity also is low and its management inefficient. African countries have failed to diversify their economies, reduce their dependence on commodities exports, and mitigate their vulnerability to external economic factors.

Continuing a decline that began in 1990, economic output shrank 10.1 per cent in **Central** and **Eastern Europe** in 1994, compared with a drop of 9.4 per cent in 1993. Although its statistics might be exaggerated, the fall in output in the former USSR still exceeded expectations, with its gross domestic products (GDP) falling as much as 16 per cent against a drop of 11.5 per cent a year earlier. The poor performance was accompanied by a sharp acceleration of inflation caused by incoherent monetary and fiscal policies. However, Central and Eastern European exports rose sharply, with the Russian Federations' trade surplus hitting a record $ 20 billion. Russia's main exports are raw material and energy products. Progress also was achieved in curbing inflation elsewhere in this region.

Source : *UN Newsletter*, September, 16, 1995.

6.17 WORLD BANK : ANNUAL REPORT (1995)

Lending for basic social sector needs during fiscal year 1995 amounted to $ 3.9 billion, or 17.3 per cent of overall commitments of $ 22.5 billion, according to the World Bank's Annual Report 1995, published on 24 September. Social sector commitments include $ 2.1 billioin for education-sector projects; $ 1.2 billion for projects and components in the population, health, and nutrition sector, and $ 648 million for projects in the social sector. Energy (12.6 %), agriculture (11.8 %), financial sector (11.4 %), and transportation (9.5 %) also accounted for a substantial portion of total new commitments.

Adjustment lending amounted to 24 per cent of Bank commitments, up from the previous year's 12 per cent. The fiscal 1955 adjustment totals included $ 1.4 billion in rehabilitation-import loans and $ 375 million in debt-reduction loans. If these amounts had been excluded, adjustment lending would have been 16 per cent of the total. Adjustment lending was particularly low in fiscal 1994, because country conditions caused delays in adjustment operations in the Europe and Central Asia region.

The report notes that the Bank demonstrated its flexibility and responsiveness to diverse client needs in a number of dramatic ways during the year, through :

— approval of $ 1 billion in lending for financial reform in Mexico to assist the restructuring of the banking sector in the wake of the December 1994 peso crisis. This was coupled with a $ 500 million loan to support essential social programs to cushion the poor from the effects of the crisis;

— emergency assistance to Russia to contain and clean up a massive oil spill 1,000 miles northeast of Moscow near the Arctic Circle;
— financing the emergency recovery programs in Burundi and Rwanda; and
— provision of emergency assistance to Haiti to help that country's economic and social development.

The new lending commitments of $ 22.5 billion include both the market-rate loans made by the International Bank for Reconstruction and Development (IBRD) and the concessionary loans made through the International Development Association (IDA). Assistance to the poorest countries—those with a per capita gross national product of $ 695 or less (in 1993 U.S. dollars)—totaled $ 8.5 billion, $ 3.8 billion from IBRD and $ 4.7 billion from IDA. The largest borrowers of IDA credits were India, China, and Viet Nam. China was the largest overall borrower of IBRD/IDA funds, with close to $ 3 billion committed in the year.

IBRD loan commitments in FY 95 amounted to $ 16.9 billion—about three-quarters of the total—for 134 projects; $ 5.7 billion in IDA credits supported 108 projects. The respective totals for FY 94 were $ 14.2 billion for 124 IBRD projects and $ 6.6 billion for 104 IDA projects.

IBRD/IDA combined gross disbursements at the end of FY 95 were $ 18.5 billion, up from $ 15.9 billion in FY 94. IBRD gross disbursements totaled $ 12.8 billion, compared with $ 10.4 billion in FY 94; IDA gross disbursements were $ 5.7 billion, compared with $ 5.5 billion in the previous fiscal year.

Financial Results

IBRD achieved solid financial results and strengthened its balance sheet in fiscal 1995, posting $ 1.35 billion in net income for the year. Borrowings in the world's capital markets totaled $ 9.03 billion at an average cost swaps of 6.32 per cent. Reserves were strengthened and stood at 14.3 per cent of loans outstanding by year end. In addition, late in the fiscal year, the Executive Directors of the Bank, moving to respond to the expressed needs of the Bank's clients, agreed to expand the single currency loan program beyond its two-year pilot phase. The addition of the single currency loan option allows borrowers to select any currency or composite currency for which there is sufficient borrower demand and in which the IBRD can efficiently borrow from the market.

Environmentally Sustainable Development

The World Bank's vice presidency for environmentally sustainable development (ESD) has continued to recognize that development can be achieved and sustained only through the integration of economic, social, technical, and ecological dimensions. During the past year ESD played an active role in the appraisal of the recently approved Liepaja Environment Project in Lativa ($ 4 million) and the Klaipeda Environment Project in Lithuania ($ 7 million) and provided similar support to the Haapsalu and Matsalu Bays Environment Project in Estonia ($ 2 million). These three projects, all of which involve pollution control and environment management, constitute the Bank's first investments in support of the Baltic Sea Environment Program. Other projects have included lending $ 110 million to help develop an early warning flood protection component in the Yangtze Water Basin Project in China, and, through an IBRD/IDA "blend" loan providing $ 168 million to India to strengthen four state pollution-control boards and support the efforts of individual firms to abate pollution.

Private Sector Development

To meet the continued demands for support of private sector investment, the Bank continued in fiscal 1995 to deliver innovative operations support to local financial institutions and markets. The World Bank Group supports about $ 25 billion of private sector finance a year, or 10 per cent of all investment by private enterprise in developing countries. Financial sector adjustment loans in fiscal 1995 totaled $ 1.2 billion, and financial intermediation loans amounted to $ 1.8 billion. The Bank's financial intermediation loans of close to $ 2 billion support $ 4 billion in private investment. The adjustment loans helped create a competitive financial sector, which the intermediation loans helped feed. The Bank's private sector affiliate, the International Finance Corporation (IFC), through its loans, equity investments, and credit lines, provides $ 2.9 billion a year. And with a much bigger multiplier of about 6 to 1, the IFC supports roughly $ 18 billion worth of investment. Such operations provide support to a wide range of financial intermediaries strong enough to access growing private capital.

The World Bank's loan guarantee instruments were revitalized and amended during the year to catalyze the flow of private capital to infrastructure projects, when the Bank's Executive Directors approved the proposal "Mainstreaming of Guarantees as an Operational Tool of the World Bank". The new guarantee initiative broadens country eligibility to any Bank borrower, modifies fees, and simplifies procedures. Though large pools of equity capital are potentially available for investment in private sector infrastructure projects, debt financing has been constrained because private lenders are unwilling to assume certain sovereign risks. A World Bank partial risk guarantee helps address this constraint by protecting lenders from these risks.

Improving Results on the Ground

According to the report, the Bank further intensified its efforts to promote a strong implementation culture during the year under review. Supervision intensity per project increased by 8 per cent, and all six operational regions are now assigning high priority to implementation and obtaining results on the ground.

The region also continued to strengthen portfolio-management practices through various measures, including involving borrowers more closely in every aspect of portfolio management and using mid-term review and supervision mission findings to pursue mid-course corrections (project restructurings, for example) to increase the likelihood that projects will achieve their development objectives.

Implementation of the Bank's Disclosure Policy and Independent Inspection Panel

During calendar 1994, a total of 1,928 Bank documents were made available to the public. The number included 674 Project Information Documents, which provide details on every project in the Bank pipeline, and 601 Environmental Data Sheets, which are prepared and updated quarterly or all projects in the lending program. The Bank is currently intensifying its disclosure efforts by preparing a formal training module for new Bank staff that explains the rationale for the disclosure policy, its implications for operational work, and the procedures involved in carrying out the policy. The World Bank's independent Inspection Panel, established to receive and investigate complaints that the Bank had not followed its own policies it supports, became operational in September 1994. The panel complements the Bank's existing systems for quality control in project preparation and implementation. As such, it helps the Bank's Executive Board in its governance of the Bank and does not affect the President's accountability to the Executive Directors for the management of Bank operations. The panel reports directly to the Bank's Board.

Korea Graduates

While 25 countries have "graduated", or phased out their reliance on World Bank lending, the Republic of Korea became the first country ever to progress from being a purely concessional borrower from IDA to being on IDA donor and IBRD graduate. Korea reached the milestone with the signing on March 3, 1995 of its two final loan agreements with the IBRD.

At year end, the total number of IBRD members stood at 178; and IDA had 158 members.

Source : *UN Newsletter*, September 3, 1995.

7

NATIONS OF THE WORLD

S. No.	Country	Capital	Area (Sq. Km)	Population (thousands)
1	Afghanistan (As)	Kabul	647,497	20,100
2	Albania (Eu)	Tirana	28,748	3,400
3	Algeria (Af)	Algiers	2,381,741	27,900
4	Andorra (Eu)	Andorre laVielle	464	59
5	Angola (Af)	Luanda	1,246,699	11,100
6	Antigua & Barbuda (WI)	St. John's	442	80
7	Argentina (SA)	Buenos Aires	2,766,654	34,600
8	Armenia (EU)	Yerevan	29,800	3,600
9	Australia (Au)	Canberra	7,682,300	18,100
10	Austria (Eu)	Viena	93,853	8,000
11	Azerbaijan (Eu)	Baku	86,600	7,600
12	Bahamas (NA)	Nassau	13,939	300
13	Bahrain (As)	Manama	669	600
14	Bangladesh (As)	Dhaka	148,393	120,400
15	Barbados (WI)	Bridgetown	430	300
16	Belarus (Eu)	Minsk	207,600	10,200
17	Belgium (Eu)	Brussels	30,521	10,100
18	Belize (NA)	Belmopan	22,965	230
19	Benin (Af)	Porto Novo	112,622	5,400
20	Bermuda (NA)	Hamilton	53.3	61
21	Bhutan (AS)	Thimphu	46,500	1,665
22	Bolivia (SA)	La Paz	1,098,581	7,700
23	Bosinia-Herzegovina(Eu)	Sarajevo	51,129	3,500
24	Botswana (Af)	Gaborone	581,730	1,500
25	Brazil (SA)	Brasilia	8,511,965	161,800
26	Brunei (As)	Bander Seri Begawan	5,765	369
27	Bufgaria (Eu)	Sofia	110,912	8,900
28	Burkina Faso (Af)	Ouagadougou	274,200	10,300
29	Burundi (Af)	Bujumbura	27,834	6,400
30	Cambodia (AS)	Phnom Penh	181,035	10,300
31	Cameroon (Af)	Yaounde	475,442	13,200
32	Canada (NA)	Ottawa	9,976,139	29,500
33	Cape Verde (Af)	Praia	4,033	400
34	Cent. Af. Rep. (Af)	Bangui	622,984	3,300
35	Chad (Af)	N'Djamena	1,284,000	6,400

S. No.	Country	Capital	Area (Sq. Km)	Population (thousands)
36	Chile (SA)	Santiago	756,626	14,300
37	China (AS)	Beijing	9,561,000	1,221,500
38	Colombia (SA)	Bogota	1,138,400	35,100
39	Comoros (Af)	Moroni	1862	700
40	Congo (Af)	Brazzaville	342,000	2,600
41	Costa Rica (CA)	San Jose	51,100	3,300
42	Cote D'Ivoire (Af)	Abidjan	322,462	14,300
43	Croatia (Eu)	Zagreb	56,538	4,500
44	Cuba (WI)	Havana	114,524	11,000
45	Cyprus (As)	Nicosia	9,251	716
46	Czech Rep. (Eu)	Prague	78,864	10,400
47	Denmark (Eu)	Copenhagen	43,074	5,200
48	Djibouti (Af)	Djibouti	21,783	695
49	Dominica (WI)	Roseau	750	88
50	Dominican Rep (WI)	Santo Domingo	48,442	7,800
51	Ecuador (SA)	Quito	283,561	11,500
52	Egypt (Af)	Cairo	997,677	62,900
53	El Salvador (NA)	San Salvador	21,393	5,800
54	Eq. Guinea (Af)	Malabo	28,051	389
55	Eritrea (Af)	Asmara	117,600	3,500
56	Estonia (Eu)	Tallinn	45,100	1,607
57	Ethiopia (Af)	Addis Ababa	1,221,900	51,300
58	Figi (OC)	Suva	18,376	800
59	Finland (Eu)	Helsinki	337,032	5,100
60	France (Eu)	Paris	543,965	58,000
61	Gabon (Af)	Libreville	267,667	1,210
62	Gambia (Af)	Banjul	11,295	1100
63	Georgia (Eu)	Tbilisi	69,700	5,500
64	Germany (Eu)	Berlin	357,020	81,600
65	Ghana (Af)	Accra	238,537	17,500
66	Greece (Eu)	Athens	131,990	10,500
67	Grenada (WI)	St. George's	344	98
68	Guatemala (NA)	Guatemala City	108,889	10,600
69	Guinea (Af)	Conakry	245,857	6,700
70	Guinea-Bissau (Af)	Bissau	36,125	1,074
71	Guyana (SA)	Georgetown	214,969	800
72	Haiti (WI)	Port-au-Prince	27,750	7,200
73	Honduras (NA)	Tegucigalpa	112,088	5,600
74	Hong Kong (As)	Victoria	1,071	5,800
75	Hungary (Eu)	Budapest	93,033	10,500
76	Iceland (Eu)	Reykjavik	102,846	300
77	India (As)	New Delhi	3,287,263	935,700
78	Indonesia (As)	Jakarta	1,904,569	197,600
79	Iran (As)	Teheran	1,648,000	67,300

S. No.	Country	Capital	Area (Sq. Km)	Population (thousands)
80	Iraq (As)	Baghdad	438,446	20,400
81	Ireland (Eu)	Dublin	70,282	3,526
82	Israel (As)	Jerusalem	20,772	5,600
83	Italy (Eu)	Rome	301,253	57,200
84	Jamaica (WI)	Kingston	11,425	2,513
85	Japan (As)	Tokyo	377,765	125,200
86	Jordan (As)	Amman	97,740	5,400
87	Kazakhistan (As)	Almaty	2,717,300	17,200
88	Kenya (Af)	Nairobi	582,646	28,300
89	Kiribati (OC)	Bairiki	861	78
90	Korea, North (As)	Pyongyang	120,538	23,900
91	Korea, South (As)	Seoul	98,859	45,000
92	Kuwait (As)	Kuwait City	17,656	1,500
93	Kyrgyzstan (As)	Bishkek	198,500	4,700
94	Laos (As)	Vientiane	236,800	4,900
95	Latvia (Eu)	Riga	63,700	2,681
96	Lebanon (As)	Beirut	10,400	3,900
97	Lesotho (Af)	Maseru	30,355	2,100
98	Liberia (Af)	Monrovia	111,369	3,000
99	Libya (Af)	Tripoli	1,759,540	5,500
100	Liechtenstein (Eu)	Vaduz	160	30
101	Lithuania (Eu)	Vilnius (Vilna)	65,200	3,700
102	Luxembourg (Eu)	Luxembourg	2,586	400
103	Macao (as)	Macao	16	484
104	Macedonia (Eu)	Skopje	25,713	2,300
105	Madagascar (Af)	Antananarivo	587,341	14,800
106	Malawi (Af)	Lilongwe	118,784	11,100
107	Malaysia (As)	Kuala Lumpur	330,434	20,100
108	Maldives (As)	Male	298	252
109	Mali (Af)	Bamako	1,240,192	10,800
110	Malta (Eu)	Valletta	316	400
111	Marshall Is. (Oc)	Dalap-Uliga, Darrit	181	50
112	Mauritania (Af)	Nouakchott	1,030,700	2,300
113	Mauritius (IO)	Port Louis	2,040	1,141
114	Mexico (NA)	Mexico City	1,972,547	93,700
115	Micronesia (OC)	Palikir	702	111
116	Moldova (Eu)	Chisinau	33,700	4,458
117	Monaco (Eu)	Monaco	1.95	3
118	Mongolia (As)	Ulanbator	1,565,000	2,305
119	Montserrat (WI)	Plymouth	102	12
120	Morocco (Af)	Rabat	458,730	27,000
121	Mozambique (Af)	Maputo	783,030	15,900
122	Myanmar (As)	Yangon	676,533	46,500
123	Namibia (Af)	Windhoek	824,292	1,574

S. No.	Country	Capital	Area (Sq. Km)	Population (thousands)
124	Nauru (OC)	Yaren Nauru	22	10
125	Nepal (As)	Kathmandu	147,181	21,900
126	Netherlands (Eu)	Amsterdam	41,160	15,500
127	New Zealand (Au)	Wellington	269,057	3,600
128	Nicaragua (NA)	Managua	130,000	4,400
129	Niger (Af)	Niamey	1,267,000	9,200
130	Nigeria (Af)	Abuja	923,768	111,700
131	Norway (Eu)	Oslo	323,895	4,300
132	Oman (As)	Muscat	300,000	2,200
133	Pakistan (As)	Islamabad	796.095	140,500
134	Palau (As)	Karor	1632	18
135	Palestine (As)	Jericho	- NA	-NA
136	Panama (NA)	Panama City	77,082	2,600
137	Papua New Guinea (Au)	Port Moresby	462,840	4,300
138	Paraguay (SA)	Asuncion	406,752	5,000
139	Peru (SA)	Lima	1,281,215	23,800
140	Philippines (AS)	Manila	299,404	67,600
141	Poland (Eu)	Warsaw	312,677	38,500
142	Portugal (Eu)	Lisbon	92,072	9,900
143	Puerto Rico (WI)	San Juan	8,891	3,600
144	Qatar (As)	Doha	11,437	513
145	Romania (Eu)	Bucharest	237,500	22,800
146	Russia (Eu & As)	Moscow	17,075,000	147,000
147	Rwanda (Af)	Kigali	26,038	8,000
148	San Marino (Eu)	San Marino	61	24
149	Sahrawi Arab Rep (Af)	El & Alaiun	266,769	180
150	Sao Tome & Principe (Af)	Sao Tome	964	132
151	Saudi Arabia (As)	Riyadh	2,250,070	17,900
152	Senegal (Af)	Dakar	196,162	8,300
153	Seychelles (IO)	Victoria	308	73
154	Sierra Leone (Af)	Freetown	71,740	4,456
155	Singapore (As)	Singapore City	615	2,800
156	Slovakia (Eu)	Bratislava	49,039	5,400
157	Slovenia (Eu)	Ljubljana	20,251	1,980
158	Solomon Is. (OC)	Honiara	29,758	360
159	Somalia (Af)	Mogadishu	637,657	9,300
160	South Africa (Af)	Pretoria	1,221,027	41,500
161	Spain (Eu)	Madrid	504,750	39,600
162	Sri Lanka (As)	Colombo	65,610	18,400
163	St. Kitts—Nevis (WI)	Basseterre	269	42
164	St. Lucia (WI)	Castries	616	145
165	St. Vincent &The Grenadines(WI)	Kingstown	388	112
166	Sudan (Af)	Khartoum	2,505,813	28,100
167	Suriname (SA)	Paramaribo	163,820	410

S. No.	Country	Capital	Area (Sq. Km)	Population (thousands)
168	Swaziland (Af)	Mbabane	17,363	913
169	Sweden (Eu)	Stockholm	449,793	8,700
170	Switzerland (Eu)	Berne	41,293	7,200
171	Syria (As)	Damascus	185,180	14,700
172	Taiwan (As)	Taipei	35,981	21,300
173	Tajikistan (As)	Dushanbe	143,100	6,100
174	Tanzania (Af)	Dodoma	945,087	29,700
175	Thailand (As)	Bangkok	542,373	58,800
176	Togo (Af)	Lome	56,785	4,100
177	Tonga (OC)	Nukualofa	748	108
178	Trinidad & Tobago (WI)	Port-of-Spain	5,128	1,300
179	Tunisia (Af)	Tunis	164,150	8,900
180	Turkey (As)	Ankara	779,452	61,900
181	Turkmenistan (As)	Ashkhabad	488,100	4,100
182	Tuvalu (OC)	Funafuti	26	10
183	Uganda (Af)	Kampala	241,139	21,300
184	Ukraine (Eu)	Kiev	603,700	51,400
185	U.A.E. (As)	Abu-Dhabi	82,880	1,900
186	United Kingdom (Eu)	London	244,108	58,300
187	U.S.A. (NA)	Washington D.C.	9,372,614	263,300
188	Uruguay (SA)	Montevideo	176,215	3,200
189	Uzbekistan (As)	Tashkent	447,400	22,900
190	Vanuatu (OC)	Vila	14,760	174
191	Vatican City (Eu)	Vatican City	0.4	1
192	Venezuela (SA)	Caracas	912,050	21,800
193	Vietnam (As)	Hanoi	329,566	74,500
194	W. Samoa (OC)	Apia	2,835	204,000
195	Yemen (As)	Sana'a	531,000	14,500
196	Yugoslavia (Eu)	Belgrade	102,173	10,800
197	Zaire (Af)	Kinshasa	2,344,885	43,900
198	Zambia (Af)	Lusaka	752,620	9,500
199	Zimbabwe (Af)	Harare	390,272	11,300

Abbreviations used : Af—Africa, As—Asia, Au—Australia, Eu—Europe, NA—North America, SA—South America, WI—West Indies, OC—Oceania, IO—Indian Ocean.

The Hottest

Continents	*Max°F*	*Place*
Africa	136	Al'Aziziyah (Libya)
N. America	134	Death Valley (California)
Asia	129	Tirat Tsvi (Israel)
Australia	128	Cloncury (Queensland)
Europe	122	Seville (Spain)
S. America	120	Rivadavia (Argentina)
Antarctica	58	Esperanza (Palmer Peninsula)

The Coldest

Continents	*Min°F*	*Place*
Antarctica	- 127	Vostok Station
Asia	- 90	Oymyakon (Russia)
N. America	- 87	Northice Station (Greenland)
Europe	- 67	Ust'-Schugor (Russia)
S. America	- 27	Sarmeinto (Argentina)
Africa	- 11	Ifrane (Morocco)
Australia	- 8	Charlotte Pass (New South Wales)

The Wettest

Continents	*Average Annual Rainfall (Cm)*	*Place*
Asia	1143	Cherrapunji (India)
Africa	1028	Debundscha (Cameroon)
South America	899	Quibdo (Colombia)
North America	666	Henderson Lake (Br. Colombia)
Europe	464	Crkvice (Yugoslavia)
Australia	455	Tully (Queensland)

The Driest

Continents	*Av. Annual Rainfall (Cm)*	*Place*
South America	0.8	Arica (Chile)
Africa	0.3	Wadi Haffa (Sudan)
Antarctica	2.0	South Pole Station
North America	3.0	Bataques (Mexico)
Asia	4.6	Aden (P.D.R. Yemen)
Australia	10.3	Mulka (South Australia)
Europe	16.3	Astrakhan (Russia)

Basic Facts About The Earth

1.	Estimated Age of the Earth	4500 million years
2.	Estimated Surface Area of the Earth	510,100,500 sq km
3.	Estimated Land Surface (29.08%)	148,950,800 sq km
4.	Estimated Water Surface (70.92%)	361,149,700 sq km
5.	Estimated Mass of the Earth	5.888×10^{21} tons
6.	Density	5.515 Times that of water
7.	Volume of the Earth	1,083,208,840,000 cubic km
8.	Equatorial Circumference of the Earth	40067 km
9.	Polar (Meridianial) Circumference of the Earth	40000 kms
10.	Estimated Population (1995)	5.75 billion

11. Highest Point on Earth — Mt. Everest (Nepal)(8848 mt. above sea level)
12. Lowest Point on Earth — Dead Sea (Palestine) (397 mt. below sea level)
13. Greatest Ocean Depth — Mariana Trench (Pacific) (11776 mt)
14. Hottest Place on Earth — Al' Aziziyah (Libya)
15. Coldst place on Earth — Vostok Station (Antarctica)
16. Wettest place on Earth — Cherrapunji (India)
17. Driest place on Earth — Arica (Chile)
18. Earth revolves round the sun once in every 365 days, 5 hours, 48 minutes & 45.51 seconds.
19. Earth rotates round its axis once in 23 hours, 56 minutes & 4.091 seconds.
20. Distance of Earth from Sun — 148,800,000 km
21. Speed of Earth around the Sun — 107,220 km per hour
22. Speed of Earth in rotation around its axis — 1670 km per hour
23. Equatorial Diameter — 12754 km
24. Polar diameter — 12714 km

Continents

Continents	*Area Sq. Km (app)*	*Population est 1995*	*Highest Elevation (meters)*	*Lowest Elevation (meters below sea level)*
Africa	29,800,540	401,000,000	Killimanjaro (Tanzania) 5895	Lake Assai 156.1
Antarctica	14,245,000	–	Vinson Massif 5138.9	Sea level
Asia	41,667,920	2,316,312,000	Mt. Everest (Nepal) 8848	Dead Sea 397
Australia	7,687,120	13,800,000	Mt. Kosciusko (New South Wales) 2228.1	Lake Eyre (South Australia) 15.8
Europe	9,699,550	660,313,000	Ellbrus 5641.8	Caspian Sea 28
North America	24,320,000	342,700,000	Mt. McKinley (Alaska) 6194	Death Valley (California) 85.9
South America	17,599,050	219,000,000	Mt. Aconcagua (Argentina) 6958.8	Voudes Penin. 39.9

Volcanoes

	Name	*Hieght Mt.*	*Range or Location*	*Country*
1.	Ojos del Salado	6885	Andes	Argentina-Chile
2.	Guallatin	6065	Andes	Chile
3.	Cotopaxi	5897	Andes	Ecuador
4.	Lascar	5641	Andes	Chile
5.	Popocatepcti	5451	Altiplano de Mexico	Mexico
6.	Mauna Loa	4170	Hawaii	USA
7.	Rindjani	3726	Lombok	Indonesia
8.	Mt. Etna	330-8	Sicily	Italy

Peninsulas

	Name	*Areas in Sq. Km.*
1.	Arabia	3,250,000
2.	Southern India	2,072,000
3.	Alaska	1,500,000
4.	Labrador	1,300,000
5.	Scandinavia	800,300
6.	Liberian	584,000

Principal Rivers

	Name	*Length—Km.*
1.	Nlle	6690
2.	Amazon	6296
3.	Yangtze Chiang	5797
4.	Ob	5567
5.	Huang He	4667
6.	Yenisei	4506
7.	Parana	4498
8.	Irtish	4438
9.	Congo	4371
10.	Amur	4352
11.	Lena	4268
12.	Mackenzie	4241
13.	Niger	4184
14.	Mekong	4023
15.	Mississippi	3779
16.	Missouri	3726
17.	Volga	3687
18.	Purus	3207
19.	St. Lawrence	3058
20.	Brahmaputra	2897
21.	Indus	2897
22.	Danube	2842
23.	Ganga	2506

Chief Languages of The People

	Name		*Est. Total speaking people in million*
1.	Mandarin (China)	—	844
2.	English	—	437
3.	Hindi	—	338
4.	Spanish	—	331
5.	Russian	—	291
6.	Arabic	—	192
7.	Bengali	—	181
8.	Portuguese	—	171
9.	Malay-Indonesian	—	138
10.	Japanese	—	124
11.	French	—	119
12.	German	—	118

Oceans

	Names	*Area in Sq. Km*
1.	Pacific	166,240,000
2.	Atlantic	86,560,000
3.	Indian	73,430,000
4.	Arctic	13,230,000
5.	Other Seas	22,280,000
	Total :	361,740,000

Principal Waterfalls

	Name	*Location*
1.	Angel	Venezuela
2.	Tugela	South Africa
3.	Cuquenan	Venezuela
4.	Sutherland	New Zealand
5.	Takkakaw	Br. Columbia
6.	Ribbon	USA (California)
7.	Upper Yosemite	–do–
8.	Gavarine	France
9.	Vettisfoss	Norway
10.	Widow's Tears	USA (California)

Principal Natural Lakes

	Name	Area in sq. km
1.	Caspian Sea [Russia (CIS)]	394299
2.	Superior (N. Am)	82414
3.	Victoria (Africa)	69485
4.	Aral [Russia (CIS)]	66457
5.	Huron (N. Am)	59596
6.	Michigan (USA)	58016
7.	Tanganyika (Africa)	32893
8.	Baykal [Russia (CIS)]	31502
9.	Great Bear (Canada)	31080
10.	Nyasa (Africa)	30044

Principal Man-Made Lakes

	Name	Location
1.	Owen Falls	Uganda
2.	Kariba	Zimbabwe
3.	Bratsk	Russia (CIS)
4.	High Aswan	Egypt
5.	Akosombo	Ghana
6.	Daniel Johnson	Canada
7.	Guri	Venezuela
8.	Krasnoyarsk	Russia (CIS)
9.	Bennet W.A.C.	Canada
10.	Zeya .	Russia (CIS)

Principal Deserts

		Approximate Area (sq. km)
1.	Sahara	8,400,000
2.	Australian Desert	1,550,000
3.	Arabian Desert	1,300,000
4.	Gobi Desert	1,040,000
5.	Kalahari Desert	520,000
6.	Takli Makan Desert	320,000
7.	Thar Desert	260,000
8.	Atacama Desert	180,000

Source : U.N., its various Agencies and Associated Organisation.

PART-TWO

INDIA 1994-95 AND 1995-96

8

LAND AND ITS PEOPLE

India that is Bharat covering a land area 32,87,263 sq.km is the seventh largest and the second most populous country of the world. It stretches 3,214 km from North to South between the extreme latitudes and 2,933 km from East to West between the extreme longitudes. On this 2.4 per cent of earth's surface live 15 per cent (88 crore people) of world's population.

8.1 Population

Over 160 million people are added annually to our population (President's Republic day Speech, 25th January 1989). Since 1881, the Census in India has been taken reqularly aften ten years. According to 1991 Census, the total population of India (including the projected population of Jammu and Kashmir is 846,302,688. As compared 1981 census, it showed an increase of 23.85 per cent. According to 1991 Census, the growth of urban population in the country during the decade 1981-1991, slowed down by about ten per cent as compared to the earlier decade of 1971-1981. However, the number of cities and towns has been consistently increasing. The urban population at present in 25.72 per cent.

8.2 Density

The average population of density of per km^2 in 1991 was 267. It varies considerably from State to State.

8.3 Sex Ratio

According to 1991 Census (Provisional) there are 43.7 crore males and 40.6 crore females; thus for every 1,000 males India has 929 females. Only Kerala has more women than men, i.e., 1,040 per 1,000 men. The lowest female ratio among the State is in Haryana i.e. 874 for 1,000 men and the lowest female ratio among the Union Territories is in Chandigarh where it is 733 per thousand.

8.4 Literacy

According to 1991 Census, the literacy percentage is 52.21. Out of this 64.13 per cent of males and 39.29 per cent of females are literate.

8.5 Major Religions and Persuasions

TABLE 8.1 : Major religions and persuasions, 1991 and 1981 (excluding Assam)

Religion Community	*Population*		*Percentage of Total Population*	
	1991	*1981*	*1991*	*1981*
Hindus	67,20,00,000	54,97,24,517	82.41	82.63
Muslims	54,74,00,000	7,55,71,514	11.67	11.36
Christians	1,88,00,000	1,61,74,498	2.32	2.43
Sikhs	1,62,00,000	1,30,78,146	1.99	1.96
Buddhists	63,00,000	47,19,900	0.77	0.71
Jains	33,00,000	31,92,572	0.41	0.48
Other Persuasions	31,00,000	27,56,285	0.38	0.42
Religion not stated	4,00,000	60,217	0.05	0.01

8.6 Languages

The detailed data from the 1981 Census which were made available only in 1988, enumerate the main languages spoken in the household and not the mother tongue and groups related languages under a dominant language. By this count, 106 languages are separately recognised. Of these 94 are spoken by 10,000 or more people.

There were 1562 mother tongues, 10 writing system, and 76 languages as used in the school system out of 2000 codified languages.

Eighteen languages have been specified in the Eighth Schedule of the Constitution. These are: Assamesse, Bengali, Gujarati, Hindi, Kannada, Kashmiri, Konkani, Malayalam, Manipuri, Marathi, Nepali, Oriya, Punjabi, Sanskrit, Sindhi, Tamil, Telugu and Urdu.

8.7 National Flag

The National Flag is horizontally tricolour with deep saffron *(Kesari)* at the top, white in the middle and dark green at the bottom in equal proportion. The ratio of the width of the flag to its length is two to three. In the centre of the white band is a wheel, in navy blue, which represents the *Charkha*. Its design is that of the wheel *(Chakra)* which appears on the abacus of the Sarnath Lion Capital of Ashoka. It diameter approximates to the width of the white band and its has 24 spokes.

The design of the National flag was adopted by the Constituent Assembly of India on July 22, 1947. Its use and display are regulated by a code.

8.8 State Emblem

The State Emblem of India is an adaptation from the Sarnath Lion Capital of Ashoka as preserved in the Sarnath Museum. In the original, there are four lions, standing back to back, mounted on an abacus with a frieze carrying sculptures in high relief of an elephant, a galloping horse, a bull and a lion separated by intervening wheels (Chakras) over a bell-shaped lotus. Carved out of a single block of polished sandstone, the capital is crowned by the Wheel of the Law (Dharma Chakra).

In the State emblem adopted by the Government of India on January 26, 1950, only three lions are visible, the fourth being hidden from view. The wheel appears in relief in the centre of the abacus with a bull on the right and a horse on the left and the outlines of the other wheels in the extreme right and left. The bell-shaped lotus has been omitted. The words *Satyameva Jayate* from the *Mundaka Upanishad,* meaning *'Truth Alone Triumphs'* are inscribed below the abacus in Devanagri script.

8.9 National Anthem

The song *Jana-gana-mana,* composed by Rabindranath Tagore (1861-1941) was adopted by the Constituent Assembly as the National Anthem of India on January 24, 1950. It was first sung on Deember 27, 1911 at the Calcutta session of the Indian National Congress. The complete song consists of five stanzas. The first stanza constitutes the full version of the National Anthem. It reads:

Jana-gana-mana-adhinayaka, jaya he
Bharata-bhagya-vidhata
Punjab-Sindhu-Gujarata-Maratha-
Dravida-Utkala-Banga
Vindhya-Himachala-Yamuna-Ganga
Uchchala-jaladhi-taranga.
Tava shubha name jage,
tava shubha asisa mage,
gahe tava jaya-gatha,
Jana-gana-mangala-dayaka jaya he
Bharata-bhagya-vidhata.
Jaya he, jaya he, jaya he,
Jaya Jaya Jaya, Jaya he!

Playing time of the full version of the National Anthem is approximately 25 seconds. A short version consisting of the first and last lines of the stanza (playing time approximately 20 seconds) is also played on certain occasions.

The following is Tagore's English rendering of this stanza:

Thou art the ruler of the minds of all people,
dispenser of India's destiny.
Thy name rouses the hearts of Punjab, Sind, Gujarat and Maratha
Of the Dravida and Orissa and Bengal;
It echoes in the hills of the Vindhyas and Himalayas,
mingles in the music of Jamuna and Ganges
and is chanted by the waves of the Indian Sea.
They pray for thy blessings and sing thy praise.
The saving of all people waits in thy hand,
thou dispenser of India's destiny.
Victory, victory, victory of thee.

8.10 National Song

The song *Vande Mataram,* composed by Bankimchandra Chatterji (1838-1894), was a source of inspiration to the people in their struggle for freedom. It has an equal status with *Jana-gana-mana.* The first political occasion on which it was sung was the 1896 session of the Indian National Congress. The following is the text of its stanza :

Vande Mataram !
Sujalam, suphalam, malayaja shitalam,
Shasyashyamalam, Mataram !
Shubhrajyotsna pulakitayaminim,
Phullakusumita drumadala shobhinim,
Suhasinim sumadhura bhashinim,
Sukhadam, Varadam, Mataram!

The English translation of the stanza rendered by Sri Aurobindo (1872-1950) in prose[2] is:

I bow to thee, Mother,
richly-watered, richly-fruited,
cool with the winds of the south,
dark with the crops of the harvests,
the Mother!
Her nights rejoicing in the glory of the moonlight,
her lands clothed beautifully with her trees in flowering bloom,
sweet of laughter, sweet of speech,
the Mother, giver of boons, giver of bliss.

8.11 National Calendar

A uniform National Calendar based on the *Saka Era* with *Chaitra* as its first month and a normal year of 365 days was adopted from March 22, 1957 (along with the Gregorian calendar) for the following official purposes in particular :

(i) Gazétte of India
(ii) News broadcast by All India Radio and T.V.
(iii) Calendars issued by the government of India, and
(iv) Government communications addressed to members of the public.

The dates of the National Calendar have a permanent correspondence with the dates of the Gregorian calendar; *Chaitra 1* falling on March 22 normally and on March 21 in a leap year.

Chaitra 1 of *Saka Era* is the New Year Day. *Saka Era* was established in A.D. 78 by Emperor Kanishka of the Saka dynasty, who ruled in the North and North-Western India in the first century of the Christian era. The day, which has been chosen to become the first day of the New Year, is vemal equinox when the day and the night are of equal duration throughout the world. *Saka* calendar is based on *Solar Chaitra* and not on *Lunar Chaitra. Chaitra Shukla Partipada*

1. As published in *Sri Aurobindo Birth Centenary Library,* Popular edition, 1912, vol. 8: which is celebrated as New Year Day in many parts of the country, is called differently. It is *Gudi Padwa* in Maharashtra and *Yugadi* in Karnataka based on lunar calendar, etc. April 13, *Baisakhi* in Punjab, Pongal

on April 14 in Tamil Nadu and *Palia Baisakhi* in West Bengal are based on solar calendar. In solar calendar this discrepancy of 22 or 23 days (between March 22 and April 13/14) has been caused by an astronomical phenomenon called the precession of the equinoxes.

8.12 National Animal

The majestic tiger *[Panthera tigris* (Linnaeus)], the national animal of India for its rich colour, illusive design and formidable power, has always been held in high esteem in India. Among the carnivores, the tiger is very georgeous and attractive with roaring voice as symbol of power. Out of eight races of the species known the world over, the Indian race is the Royal Bengal Tiger. The Royal Bengal Tiger is found throughout the country expect the North-Western region and also in Nepal, Bhutan and Bangladesh. As shrinkage of habitat in India dwindled its population to only 1,827 in 1972, the Project Tiger was launched on April 1'st 1973. Since then there is a gradual increase in its population. The tiger population 4,430 of the country according to 1989 censes was 4,339. So far 19 tiger reserve have been established covering over 29,716 sq km forest area.

8.13 National Bird

The Indian peacock *[Pavo cristatus* (Linnaeus)], the national bird of India, is one of the most beautiful birds, particularly the males having the glistering blue neck and breast, fanshape crest and long magnificent tail. The courtship dance of the male by fanning out the tail before the female is most spectacular. From time immemorial, this bird has found a profound place in Indian literature, folkore and legends.

The Indian peafowl, as the peacock is called, is widely found in the country in south and east of Indus river, Jammu and Kashmir, east Assam, south of Mizoram and the whole of Indian peninsula. It is fully protected under the Indian Wild Life (Protection) Act, 1972.

(Source : India 1993).

8.14 Presidents of India

January 26, 1950 — May 13, 1962	Rajendra Prasad
May 13, 1962 — May 13, 1967	S.Radhakrishnan
May 13,1967 — May 3, 1969	Zakir Husain
May 3,1969 — July 20, 1969	V.V.Giri (Acting)
July 20, 1969 — August 21. 1969	M. Hidayatullah (Acting)
August 24, 1969 — August 24, 1974	V.V.Giri
August 24, 1974 — Febuary 11, 1977	Fakhruddin Ali Ahmed
February 11, 1977 — July 25 1977	B.D.Jatti (Acting)
July 25, 1977 — July 25, 1982	N.Sanjeeva Reddy
July 25, 1982 — July 25, 1987	Zail Singh
July 25, 1987 — July 25, 1992	R.Venkataraman
July 25, 1992 —	S.D.Sharma

8.15 Vice Presidents of India

1952-1962	S.Radhakrishnan
1962-1967	Zakir Husain

1967-1969	V.V.Giri
1969-1974	G.S.Pathak
1974-1079	B.D.Jatti
1979-1984	M.Hidayatullh
1984-1987	R.Venkataraman
1987-1992	S.D.Sharma
1993-	K.R.Narayanan

8.16 Prime Ministers of India

August 15, 1947 — May 27, 1964	Jawaharlal Nehru
May 27, 1964 — June 9, 1964	Guljari Lal Nanda (Acting)
June 9, 1964 — January 11, 1966	Lal Bahadur Shastri
January 11, 1966 — January 24, 1966	Guljari Lal Nanda (Acting)
January 24, 1966 — March 24, 1977	Indira Gandhi
March 24, 1977 — July 28. 1979	Morarji Desai
July 28, 1979 — January 14, 1980	Charan Singh
January 14, 1980 — October 31, 1984	Indira Gandhi
October 31, 1984 — December 1, 1989	Rajiv Gandhi
December 2, 1989 — November 10, 1990	V.P.Singh
November 10, 1990 — June 21, 1991	Chandra Shekhar
June 21, 1991 —	P.V.Narasimha Rao

8.17 Speakers of the Lok Sabha

1952-1956	G.V.Mavlankar
1965-1962	Ananthasayanam Ayyangar
1962-1967	S.Hukam Singh
1967-1969	N.Sanjieeva Reddy
1969-1975	G.S.Dhillon
1975-1977	B.R.Bhagat
March 1977 — July 1977	N.Sanjieeva Reddy
1977-1979	K.S.Hegde
1980-1989	Balram Jakhar
November 19, 1989 — June 1991	Rabi Ray
July 10, 1991 —	Shivraj Patil

8.18 Important Days

National Youth Day	January 12
Army Day	January 15
Republic Day	January 26
International Customs Day	January 26
Martyrs' Day	January 30
National Science Day	February 28
International Women's Day*	March 8
World Consumers Rights Day	March15
World Disabled Day	March (Third Sunday of March)
International Day for the Elimination of Racial Discrimination	March 21
World Forestry Day	March 21
World Meteorological Day	March 23
National Maritime Day	April 5

World Health Day*	April 7
May Day (Worker's Day International Labour Day)	May 1
World Red Cross Day	May 8
World Telecommunication Day*	May 17
World Day for Cultural Development*	May 21
Commonwealth Day	May 24
World No-Tobacco Day*	May 31
World Envirnoment Day*	June 5
International Day of Solidarity with the Struggling People of South Africa*	June 16
World Population Day*	July 11
Hiroshima Day	August 6
Quit India Day	August 9
Nagasaki Day	August 9
International Day of Solidarity with the Struggle of Women in South Africa*	August 9
Independence Day	August 15
Teacher's Day	September 5
International Literacy Day*	September 8
International Day of Peace	September (Third Tuesday of September)
World Tourism Day	September 27
International Day for the Elderly*	October 1
University Children's Day*	October (First Monday of October)
Mahatma Gandhi Birthday	October 2
World Habitat Day	October 5
Air Force Day	October 8
Universal Postal Union Day*	October 9
Day of Solidarity with South African Political Prisoners	Octocer 11
Post Office Day	October 19
World Standard Day	October 14
World Food Day*	October 16
United Nations Day	October 24
World Development Information Day*	October 24
National Re-Dedication Day	October 31
Children's Day	November 14
National Integration Day	November 19
International Day of Solidarity with the Palestinian People*	November 29
World AIDS Day*	December 1
International Day of Disabled Persons*	December 3
Navy Day	December 4
International Volunteer Day for Economic and Social Development	December 5
Flag Day	December 7
Human Rights Day*	December 10
Kisan Day	December 23

* Proclaimed by UN System/UNESCO Associated Schools

9

INDIA SINCE INDEPENDENCE

9.1 ACHIEVEMENTS

Going back, India that is Bharat was the richest and the most prosperous country in the world. It was then known as the *'Golden Sparrow'*. The standard of living of the common man was reasonably high. Articles of everyday needs were available in plenty. A common man could get easily things like milk, butter, ghee an foodgrains. Literally speaking 'Rivers of milk flowed'. Indain handicrafts and industrial products were known for their excellence of design and quality all over the world. From the richness of this land and from the labour and wisdom of its people had sprung great wealth, great ideas, great skills and arts. Naturally, therefore, foreigners were tempted to come to India for learning, as well as loot and plunder.

The well-knit economic organisation of the country received a serious set-back with the advent of invaders and especially with the British rulers who were primarily concerned with the governance of the country, not its growth. They wrer greatly interested in draining out wealth from India. Industrial crafts, industries and agriculture, all suffered heavily. As a result, India became a poor country. People remained underfed, ill-housed and scantily dressed.

The statement 'A rich country inhabited by the poor people' seems paradoxical and strange. But it is still true to a considerable extent though since independence we have made a spectacular progress in different fields. The giant *irrigation dams* at *Bhakra, Hirakud* and *Nagarjunasagar*, the huge steel millis at *Bhilai, Bokaro, Rourkela* and *Durgapur;* the fertilister factories at *Sindri* and *Nangal;* the 1000-tonne per day ammonia plant (said to be the largest in the world) at Tuticorin; the *aircraft factories at Bangalore, Hyderabad* and *Nasik;* the locomotive factory at Chittarajan; the atomic reactor at Trombay; the rocket launching station at Sriharikota; the ISRO's establishment like *Vikram Sarabhai Space Centre,* Trivandrum and Space Application Centre, Ahmedabad; launching of Indain Satellite *Bhaskara* and *Rohini;* three axis-stabilished Geostationary Communication Satellite; *APPLE (Ariane Passenger Payload Experiment),* establishment of *Indian National Satellite System (INSAT);* participation of an Indian Cosmonaut in a joint Indo-Soviet Flight; nuclear explosion of Pokaran, etc., are the prized possessions of the Indian Nation.

November 21, 1988 marked the 25th anniversary of Indian Space Programme. The Silver Jubilee Year saw the launching of three major programmes; IRS-1A, ASLV-02 and INSAT-1A (see relevant Chapter for details). Militarily we are among the first five countries in the world.

India is the sixth country to successfully detonate a nuclear device as part of its successful experiment for peace purposes.

We have the third largest reservoir of highly skilled scientific and technical manpower in the world.

India is the fifth nation to have its remote sensing satellite.

We have achieved self-sufficiency in foodgrains.

India is the third largest producer of books in English, next to the U.S.A and U.K.

The eradication of poverty problem of the masses became the first consideration of the government soon after we achieved independence. We decided to adopt the system of planned development for tackling our problem of poverty which was linked with rising prices, low production, unemployment and inequalities of income.

The frame a development plan for independent India, the *Planning Commission* was set up in March 1950, by a resolution of the Government of India. The aims of planning as defined by the resolution were, 'to promote a rapid rise in the standard of living of the people by efficient exploitation of the resources of the country, increasing production and offering opportunities to all for employment in the service of the community'.

The *First Five Year Plan* was initiated in April 1951. This covered the period 1951-1956. So far we have had seven Five Year Plans and Three Yearly Plan. The *Eighth Five-Year Plan,* covers the period 1992 to 1997.

The most important achievement of planning in the post-independence period is our self-sufficiency in foodgrains. Now we need not import foodgrains for domestic requirements as we did till a few years ago. The production was about 172 million tonnes in 1991-92 as against 51 million tonnes 1950-51.

As a result of many multipurpose projects, area under irrigation increased from 226 lakh hectares in 1950 to 860 lakh hectares in 1990-91.

Our industry has many strengths: a wide range of products, a demonstrable ability to absorb and operate high technology, a large entrepreneurial capability and ample managerial and technical skills.

During the Plans, industrial production has made rapid strides, both in terms of quality and quantity. As per the index of *industrial production,* the growth rates achieved in the industrial sector as a whole were 8.6 per cent in 1984-85, 8.7 per cent in 1985-86, 9.1 per cent in 1986-87, 7.3 per cent in 1987-88, 8.7 in 1988-89, 8.6 in 1989 and 8.1 in 1990-91. However, there was setback in 1991-92. There was a (–) 0.9 per cent decline (April-November).

In the year 1950-51, there were only two major units producing iron and steel. Now we have eleven relevant major steel plants. Steel production rose from about one million tonnes in 1950-51, to about 13.40 million tonnes in 1990-91.

Cotton textile industry holds the second place in the production of cloth in the world. At present there are about 700 textile mills in the country.

In 1951, we had 138 sugar mills in the country. This number increased to 351 in 1987. About half the mills are in the public sector.

The production of cement increased from 2.69 million tonnes in 1951 to 10.7 million tonnes in 1990-91 (provisional).

The generation of electric power registered a twenty-fold increase.

Public sector in the field of industries has witnessed a very significant rise. In 1951, we had only 5 public undertakings whereas there were 255 public undertakings in 1991, in the Central Sector.

The road network in the country has become very elaborate system of national highways, state and district roads, and rural roads totalling about 23 lakh kms. This is five and a half times the figure of 4 lakh km of roads in 1950-51.

Between 1950-51 and 1991-92, the number of trucks rose from 82,000 to 16,85,000 and busses from 34,000 to 3,70,000.

Per captia income increased from Rs. 246 in 1950-51 to about Rs. 4,254 in 1989-90 at current prices.

Prior to Independence, average life span of an Indian was 32 years. Today it has lengthened to 58 years.

Our Constitution can be described as a charter of freedom. It enshrines the supremacy of the will of the people and their resolve to secure for all citizens: justice, social, economic and political; Equity of status and opportunity, and to promote among them all Fraternity assuring the dignity of the individual and the unity of the nation. The will of the people is exercised through universal adult franchise and a parliamentary democracy. Election to Parliament and State legislature are open contests for all political parties, and independent candidated also enjoy full scope to express themsleves.

Notwithstanding various problems and the magnitude of the task of conducting elections, we have all *general elections* with significant success. Barring the period, March 1977 to July 15, 1979 and December 1989 to May 1991 when the Janata Party and National Front were in power at the Centre, the Congress had held the reigns of the Government since the first General Election in 1951-52.

Many political changes accompanied by government changes, especially in States have taken place in the country since Independence, through peaceful and constitutional means. Transfer of power from one party to another has taken place as a natural course and in an orderly manner.

Another historic step in the development of democracy in the country was the inauguration of *Panchayati Raj* in October 1950. The Panchayati Raj aims at giving full authority and responsibility to the village people and helping them paly an active role in local development through the Panchayats. There are over 228,500 Village Panchayats in the country covering partially the entire population of India.

With the Panchayati Raj, we now have parliamentary democracy in operation from the Gram Sabha to the Lok Sabha.

We have got an estalished judicial system.

9.2 PROGRESS MADE AND TASKS AHEAD

Excerpts from the text of President Shanker Dayal Sharma's address to the joint session of Parliament.

As I address you in the New Year, I sense that the country is today in a frame of mind different from the one it was in, this time last year. We faced many difficulties at the beginning of the year 1993 but our people displayed tremendous resilience as the year progressed and 1993 ended certainly on a note of optimism. There was steady progress on all fronst as evidenced from the improved law and order situation, a record foodgrain production, unprecedented levels of procurement, very high levels of foodgrains stocks, containment of the rate of inflation at a single digit level, comfortable foreign exchange reserves, considerable reduction in trade gap, buoyancy in exports, improved performance in certain essential areas of the infrastructure sector, and increased inflow of foreign investment both direct and portfolio. All these have symbolised and justified this emerging optimism. Clearly, we have regained our elan internally and our confidence globally. We have reason and justification to feel encouraged at the all round performance. But we still have a long way to go before we achieve the objectives we have set for ourselves in social and economic development. It is on this note of cautious optimism that government approaches its tasks in 1994.

There has been overall improvement in the law and order situation. The stituation in regard to insurgency in the north-east has shown improvement. The gains of last year in Punjab were consolidated. The elections to the assemblies in five States and the National Capital Territory of Delhi were peaceful. Government is determined to consolidate the gains of this improvement and address the areas of concern that still remain.

Around this time last year the Ayodhya issue had cast its long shadow on the national scene. There was a great deal of concern over the possible fall-out of the demolition and the riots that followed. Thanks to the inherent wisdom and sagacity of the Indian people, the grim predictions that were being made have been proved wrong. The atmosphere has improved considerably and we can hope for a lasting solution to the dispute. Proceedings are continuing in the Supreme Court on the reference made to it under the Constitution. Government will take appropriate measures in the light of the opinion of the Supreme Court.

The Ayodhya issue is the most convincing demonstration in recent times of the danger inherent in mixing communalism and politics. It is of utmost importance to correct this aberration and keep both religion and politics in their legitimate domains. Our secular State demands nothing less. The issue needs to be debated fully and effective measures evolved. The Government will welcome suggestions in this regard.

In Jammu and Kashmir, we pursue our policy of firm action against terrorism. The police and the security forces have gained considerable success during the year in their counter-terrorist operations. Steps have been taken to further improve their operational efficiency. Every effort is made to see that the maximum restraint is exercised in the use of force. The grave crisis that arose in the Hazratbal shrine was handled by the administration and the security forces in a commendable manner, with the cooperation of the people. The resolution of this crisis demonstrated the efficacy of Government's approach of restraint. Whenever there has been any incident suggesting excessive use of force, an inquiry has been promptly instituted and action taken. Action against the terrorists is continuing in order to restore law and order. At the same time appropriate measures are being taken to tone up the administration. Development and economic activity have been intensified to generate employment opportunities. We are deeply concerned about the difficulties of the common people and the grievance redressal mechanism has been strengthened. We are also pursuing steps to bring about effective involvement of the people in dealing with matters which concern them. Jammu and Kashmir is an inalienable part of India and we shall foil any attempt to destabilise it either from across the border or from any other quarter.

Human Rights

The National Commission on Human Rights has been set up with a former Chief Justice of India as its Chairman. Members of the Commission include a former justice of the Superme Court and one former Chief Justice of a High Court. The setting up of the Commission is indicative of our continuing determination to deal with questions of human rights with promptitude and transparency. The Commission has started its work in right earnest.

In order to strenghten the accountability of the executive of Parliament, 17 department-related standing committees of Parliament were constituted in April 1993 to make detailed examination of Bills, demands for grants, annual reports of the ministries and national basic long-term policy documents presented to the House. This will greatly facilitate the working of Parliament.

The country had its share of national calamities. However, the unprecedented scale of damage in the Maharashtra earthquake stands out among these. In all these instances, Government responded with commendable alertness and provided prompt relief. Governments of several other countries, the World Bank and other institutions promptly offered assistance and we are grateful to all of them. A massive reconstruction programme in the earthquake affected areas of Maharashtra is being taken up at an outlay of Rs. 1,000 crore. Non-governmental organisations are being appropriately associated with the reconstruction programme.

The economic reforms introduced in 1991 gained momentum last year and have been pursued consistently. Still much more needs to be done. Government is aware that the reform is an irreversible and continuous process and needs to be implemented with determination and foresight, keeping the responses and circumstances in the country constantly in view. As a result of this approach, the progress of implementation has been steady and firm and based on a general consensus. We shall hasten with care.

In drawing up the refrom package, stress has been laid by the Government on reforms in the financial sector. The financial institutions have necessarily to be restructured and strengthened to enable them to take on the new responsibility imposed by the expanded activity in the private sector. An important policy change was the unification of the exchange rate and the floating of the rupee in March 1993. The fact that the rupee has remained steady since it was floated is testimony to the good judgment of the Government in the matter.

The basic economic indicators show that although the year started in a difficult environment, the performance of the economy during 1993-94 has been satisfactory. In 1992-93, the gross domestic product (GDP) is estimated to have grown by four per cent. In 1993-94, the Government expects the rate of growth to be maintained at about the same level. The inflation rate touched a low of below six per cent for a short period during this year, the highest level being 8.4 per cent.

Global investors have shown growing confidence in the Indian market. Direct foreign investment approved since the inception of the new industrial policy till the end of 1993 is now approximately Rs. 13,000 crore in terms of equity. The total investment in these project is estimated to be of the order of Rs. 65,000 crore. The significant point of this investment is that the bulk of this, is proposed in sectors like power, oil refining, food processing, metallurgical industry, electrical equipment, chemicals, electronics and other priority areas. Only about seven per cent of the proposed investment will be for products which could be categorised as consumer goods. The investment inflow will be spread over a peroid of three to four years which is the gestation period of the mega projects.

Government continues to lay a great deal of emphasis on export promotion. The results of changes in the trade policy coupled with the floating of the exchange rate and the general liberalisation of the economy have yielded results and exports have shown good growth recording an increase of around 20 per cent in dollar terms during April-December, 1993 compared to a little over three per cent in the corresponding period in 1992.

Government attaches the highest priority to development of agriculture. The timely provision of adequate and reasonably priced inputs and the creation of a structure that provides for the timely announcement of prices which in turn promotes higher production so as to meet fully the domestic needs of the country as well as exports, are the major objectives of the Government. In keeping with the overall strategy, the Plan outlay for the Department of Agriculture and Cooperation has been raised by 26.6 per cent from Rs. 1,050 crore in 1992-93 to Rs. 1330 crore in 1993-94. The production of foodgrains during 1992-93 was 180 million tonnes which was more than the production in 1991-92 by 7.1 per cent. The kharif foodgrains production in 1993-94 is expected to be 99 million tonnes. The prospects for rabi are excellent.

As part of the agriculture policy, States have been advised to remove all intra and inter-State restrictions on the movement of foodgrains.

It is Government determination that no vulnerable section of the population - be it women, children, minorities, Scheduled Caste, Scheduled Tribes or backward classes - should remain outside the main-stream of development. In all areas of development of the poor, resource allocations were enhanced during 1993-94 compared to the previous year. The revised outlay for the Ministry of Rural Development went up by 56 per cent while the Plan outlay of the Welfare Ministry was raised from Rs. 820 crore to Rs. 980 crore. The Jawahar Rozgar Yojana has been strengthened in 120 most backward districts. The subsidies under the Integrated Rural Development Programme were enhanced by Rs. 1,000 per household. The improved tool kits to rural artisans programme started in 1992-93 was extended in 1993-94 to 100 more districts, thus covering in all 162 districts in the country benefiting 2,30,000 rural artisans. Comprehensive programmes for the welfare and development of the weavers were evolved. They include housing, work sheds, handloom development centres, quality dyeing units, training in improved practices and provision of working capital. These programmes with a total outlay of Rs. 1,372 crore were started during the year. The scheme for handloom development centres and quality dyeing units launched towards the end of 1993 seeks to merge and expand existing units and establish new ones. Against the 1993 target of 120 centres and 20 units, 213 centres and 94 units have been approved. Twenty-five centres and 25 units have already started operating.

New Schemes

Government has formulated three new and innovative schemes to benefit the poor, particularly rural women and urban youth.

The employment assurance scheme introduced in 1,752 of the most backward and remote blocks of the country, where seven crores of the country's poor people live, will provide assured wage employment for 100 days during the lean agaricultural season to the rural labour. This scheme thus expands rural employment of fuller levels.

The Mahila Samriddhi Yojana will empower rural women by enabling them to gain and exercise control over their own earnings and household resources. Already, more than 4 lakh women have opened accounts under this scheme in rural post offices. This scheme, along with the Rashtriya Mahila Kosh, would greatly enhance opportunities for self-employment among rural women.

To provide sustained employment to the educated urban youth in micro enterprises, a rozgar yojana has been launched. About 1,95,000 applications have been received so far from youth in different States. So far 41,275 applications have been processed and recommended to banks and about 2,000 of them have also been sanctioned. During the current year, the scheme will cover 40,000 beneficiaries and from 1994-95 onwards it is intended to cover 2.20 lakh beneficiaries every year, thus, covering in all 7 lakh beneficiaries during the rest of the 8th Plan period. The Reserve Bank of India has been instructed to support the programme fully. The scheme provides for 22.5 per cent reservation for the Scheduled Castes and Scheduled Tribes and 27 per cent for the other backward classes with preference for women.

Our relations with our neighbours continued to be cordial, and our interaction in various fields with Bangladesh, Bhutan, Maldives, Nepal and Sri Lanka recorded good progress during the year. In the case of Pakistan, however, its continuing support for terrorism and subversion in Jummu and Kashmir and anti-Indian activities world-wide seriously hampered our efforts at normalising relations. The Prime Minister offered Pakistan a dialogue aimed at establishing good-neighbourly relations as enshrined in the Shimla Agreement. Bilateral talks have since taken place, but the stridency of Pakistan's anti-Indian statements has grown, adversely affecting efforts at improving bilateral ties. There are no quarrels between us and the people of Pakistan. We feel that for good relatins between our countries the Government of Pakistan should give up its negative approach and reciprocate our desire to normalise India-Pakistan relations in accordance with the Shimla Agreement.

Our relations with China have improved markedly. The Prime Minister's visit to China in September 1993, and the signing of the agreement on the maintenance of peace and tranquility along the line of actual control have brought them to a new stage of development. The expert group set up under this agreement held its first meeting recently, reflecting the desire of both sides to maintain and continue the interaction on this complex issue.

India values SAARC as an innstrument of regional cooperation consistent with the objectives of its charter. The Prime Minister attended the SAARC summit in Dhaka last year. SAARC has recorded progress in dealing with certain important issues of common interest such as poverty, terrorism, population growth, problems relating to the status of women, children, youth and drugs and psychotropic sustenances. We continue to pay an active role in SAARC with a view to promoting its socio-economic and other objectives in accordance with the SAARC charter.

Our interaction with the United States has traditionally ranged over a number of areas from education and science and technology to culture and sports. We have also cooperated in the UN on issued relating to disarmament such as the comprehensive test ban treaty. The response from the United States to our economic liberalisation policies has been very positive and the US investments in India in the last two years were very substantial. We look forward to working with the United States towards mutual understanding, including on those issues on which such understanding needs enhancement. This will reflect the vibrant democratic and secular ideals of our two countries.

Relations with the Russian Federation,drawing upon rich traditions of our friendship of the past, continued with mutual understanding and cooperation. Despite certain difficulties the two countries face, cooperation in the political, economic, commercial and other areas was sought to be promoted by both sides. The goodwill and understanding that underpins our relations reinforce our joint efforts at identifying possibilities of further cooperation in various areas in today's changed context.

We welcome the signing of the declaration of principles on interim self-government arrangements between Israel and the PLO in September 1993 as a notable step towards peace and stability in West Asia and the restoration of the legitimate rights of the Palestinian people.

India continues to play an active role in shaping the global agenda on issued pertaining to political and security matters, economic and social development, human rights, environment and population.

I am confident your debates and deliberations in the course of this session and beyond will take the nation forward in fulfilling the aspirations of the people. I commend you to your talks and wish you all success.

(Source : Hindustan Times, February 22, 1993).

9.3 CONCLUDING OBSERVATIONS

A large part of our population still remains backward. There is a wide gulf between the rich and the poor. *Unemployment* is on the increase. National integration is our urgent need. Erosion in the standard of values, in fact is the topmost blockade, which requires to be checked and a crusade for 'Clean Life, Clean Poltics and Clean Administration' is to be given first priority.

India is on the move. The tasks before us are very challenging and tremendous. But there is no causes for despair. By harnessing all our resources and working unitedly and sincerely, we can usher in an era of peace, progress and prosperity.

The 21st century beckons up holding fourth new hopes. We, the people of India, must march ahead as an integrated resurgent.

As *Gurudev Rabindranath Tagore* would advise, we must "hold the faith firm", surely "the day will dawn".

10

EIGHTH FIVE YEAR PLAN (1992-97)

Introduction

Starting from the First Five Year Plan (April 1951 to March 1956), India has formulated and implemented seven Five Year Plans and three Annual Plans. Eighth Five Year Plan is in operation. These plans form a continuous process, both in terms of investments and benefits. They also represent a picture of evolution in basic socio-economic policies. Inevitably, these are important adaptations from one plan to another, reflecting, both changing conditions and new problems arising out of fresh experience and evolution.

Raising the standard of living of the people and also opening out to these new opportunities for a richer and varied life was sought to be achieved by planning for growth, modernisation, self-reliance and social justice. We have come a long way over the past 47 years. Yet a lot has to be achieved still.

Objectives of the Eighth Five Year Plan

1. Generation of adequate employment to achieve near full employment level by the turn of the century.
2. Containment of population growth through active people's cooperation and an effective scheme of incentive and disincentives.
3. Universalisation of elementary education and complete eradication of illiteracy among the people in the age group of 15 to 35 years.
4. Provision of safe drinking water and primary health care facilities, including immunisation, accessible to all the villages and the entire population, and complete elimination of scavenging.
5. Growth and diversification of agriculture to achieve self-sufficiency in food and generate surpluses for export.
6. Strengthening the infrastructure (energy, transport, communication, irrigation) in order to support the growth process on a sustainable basis.

The Eighth Plan to concentrate on these objectives keeping in view the need for, (a) continued reliance on domestic resources in financing investment (b) increasing the technical capabilities for the development of science and technology, (c) modernisation and competitive efficiency so that the Indian economy can keep pace with and take advantage of the global developments.

TABLE 10.1. Targets for Selected Commodities During the Eighth Plan

Commodity		*Unit*	*Position 1991-92*	*Target 1996-97*
Foodgrains		Mill. Tonnes		
	Production		172.50	210.00
	Export/Stock		(-)6.30	2.00
	Consumption		178.80	208.00
Oilseeds		Mill. Tonnes		
	Production		17.50	23.00
	Consumption		17.50	23.00
Sugarcane		Mill. Tonnes		
	Production		235.00	275.00
	Consumption		235.00	275.00
Cotton		Mill. Bales		
	Production		10.50	14.00
	Export		0.60	0.30
	Consumption		9.90	13.70
Milk		Mill. Tonnes		
	Production		57.50	70.00
	Consumption		57.50	70.00
Coal		Mill. Tonnes		
	Production		229.26	308.00
	Import		6.09	3.00
	Export		0.11	1.00
	Change in Stock		6.41	–
	Consumption		228.83	310.00
Crude Oil		Mill. Tonnes		
	Production		30.34	50.00
	Import		24.00	13.32
	Change in Stock		2.92	–
	Consumption		51.42	63.32
Iron Ore		Mill. Tonnes		
	Production		56.50	72.00
	Export		32.00	32.00
	Consumption		24.50	40.00
Sugar		Mill. Tonnes		
	Production		12.00	15.50
	Import			1.00
	Export		0.60	4.00
	Change in Stock			(-) 1.00 $
	Consumption		11.40	13.50
Cloth		Bill. Mtrs.		
	Production		18.26	24.70
	Export (Net)	Rs. crore	12000.00	28000.00
	Consumption	Bill. Mtrs.	16.68	22.80

(Contd.)

TABLE 10.1 *(Contd.)*

Commodity		*Unit*	*Position 1991-92*	*Target 1996-07*
Petroleum Products		Mill. Tonnes		
	Production		49.15*	61.57*
	Import		9.44	22.92
	Export		2.70	3.30
	Change in Stock		(-)0.77	–
	Consumption		56.66	81.19
Nitrogenous Fertilizers		Mill. Tonnes		
	Production		7.30	9.80
	Import		0.50	1.70
	Change in Stock		(-)0.70	–
	Consumption		8.50	11.50
Phosphatic Fertilizers		Mill. Tonnes		
	Production		2.50	3.00
	Import		0.90	–
	Change in Stock		(-)0.20	–
	Consumption		3.60	5.00
Potassic Fertilizers		Mill. Tonnes		
	Import		1.30	1.80
	Change in Stock		(-)0.10	–
	Consumption		1.40	1.80
Fertilisers (N+P+K)		Mill. Tonnes		
	Production		9.80	12.80
	Import		2.70	5.50
	Change in Stock		(-)1.00	–
	Consumption		13.50	18.30
Cement		Mill. Tonnes		
	Production		53.00	76.00
	Import			2.00
	Export		1.00	7.00
	Consumption		52.00	71.00
Finished Steel (main + main)		Mill. Tonnes		
	Production		14.50	22.80
	Import (canalised)		1.00	1.00
	Export		0.30	2.80
	Consumption		15.20	21.00
Aluminium		Th. Tonnes		
	Production		514.17	656.00
	Import		3.00	16.00
	Export		68.00	–
	Consumption		449.17	672.00

(Contd.)

TABLE 10.1 *(Contd.)*

Commodity		*Unit*	*Position 1991-92*	*Target 1996-97*
Copper		Th. Tonnes		
(refined)	Production		45.49	55.00
	Import (Incld. non-canalised)		104.51	145.00
	Consumption		150.00	200.00
Zinc		Th. Tonnes		
(Primary Metal)	Production		102.00	154.00
	Import		10.00	26.00
	Consumption		112.00**	180.00
Lead		Th. Tonnes		
(Primary Metal)	Production		48.39	96.00
	Import (Incl. non-canalised)		20.00	4.00
	Consumption		68.39	100.00
Electricity		Bill. KWH		
	Generation (incl. non-utilities)		311.21	448.00
	Import		1.43	2.00
	Consumption		312.64	450.00
Railways		Mill. Tonnes		
	(Originating traffic)		363.00	443.40

$ The closing stock of sugar as on 31.1.92 was 4.93 million tonnes.

* Includes production of LPG from natural gas 1 million tonnes and 2.05 mill. tonnes for 1991-92 and 1996-97 respectively.

** Abnormally Low Consumption.

Extracts from Chapter 3 of the 8th Plan "Macro-Economic Dimensions", Volume 1.

(*Note* : For achievements during the First to Seventh Plan, see chapter *'Indian Economy at a Glance'*.

TABLE 10.2. Eighth Plan Outlay by Heads of Development : Centre, States and Union Territories, 1992-97

		Amount (Rs. crore)					Percentage Distribution				
		Eighth Plan 1992-97	Annual Plan 1992-93 (Actual)	Annual Plan 1993-94 (Actual)	Annual Plan 1994-95 (RE)	Annual Plan 1995-96 (BE)	Eighth Plan 1992-97	Annual Plan 1992-93 (Actual)	Annual Plan 1993-94 (Actual)	Annual Plan 1994-95 (RE)	Annual Plan 1995-96 (BE)
1		2	3	4	5	6	7	8	9	10	11
I.	Agricultural & allied activities	22467.2	4215.6	4263.5	5677.5	6660.5	5.2	5.8	4.8	5.3	5.2
II.	Rural development	34425.4	5091.4	7033.3	8270.1	9922.7	7.9	7.0	8.0	7.8	7.7
III.	Special area programmes	6750.1	1283.8	1363.6	1465.7	1780.2	1.6	1.8	1.5	1.4	1.4
IV.	Irrigation and flood control	32525.3	4705.2	5370.5	5410.1	7472.9	7.5	6.5	6.1	5.1	5.8
V.	Energy	115561.1	20289.8	26909.0	29026.2	35236.7	26.6	27.9	30.6	27.3	27.4
	a. Power	79588.7	12157.4	14773.1	15671.8	19622.4	18.3	16.7	16.8	14.8	15.3
	b. Petroleum	24000.0	5698.5	9589.3	10509.5	11938.2	5.5	7.8	10.9	9.9	9.3
	c. Coal & lignite	10507.0	2276.5	2293.1	2539.7	3207.1	2.4	3.1	2.6	2.4	2.5
	d. Non-conventional sources of energy	1465.4	157.4	253.5	305.2	469.0	0.3	0.2	0.3	0.3	0.4
VI.	Industry and minerals	46921.7	7444.2	8481.1	10789.6	13877.5	10.8	10.2	9.6	10.2	10.8
	a. Village and small scale industries	6334.2	995.3	1152.2	1459.5	1867.4	1.5	1.4	1.3	1.4	1.5
	b. Other industries	40587.5	6448.9	7328.9	9330.1	12010.1	9.3	8.9	8.3	8.8	9.3

(Contd.)

TABLE 10.2 *(Contd.)*

1		2	3	4	5	6	7	8	9	10	11
VII.	Transport	55925.6	10662.7	11976.7	15211.9	18096.8	12.9	14.6	13.6	14.3	14.1
	a. Railways	27202.0	6162.0	5901.0	6889.0	7694.0	6.3	8.5	6.7	6.5	6.0
	b. Others	28723.6	4500.7	6075.7	8322.9	10402.8	6.6	6.2	6.9	7.8	8.1
VIII.	Communications	25110.0	5150.9	6201.6	7497.7	8321.2	5.8	7.1	7.0	7.1	6.5
IX.	Science, technology & environment	9041.7	929.9	1153.4	1473.5	1744.9	2.1	1.3	1.3	1.4	1.4
X.	General economic services	4549.5	1490.1	848.8	2193.5	1827.4	1.0	2.0	1.0	2.1	1.4
XI.	Social services	79011.9	11322.8	14016.6	18223.4	22401.9	18.2	15.5	15.9	17.2	17.4
	a. Education	19599.7	2619.4	3147.3	4282.3	5345.9	4.5	3.6	3.6	4.0	4.2
	b. Medical & public health	7575.9	1213.9	1300.4	1709.2	2173.2	1.7	1.7	1.5	1.6	1.7
	c. Family welfare	6500.0	1008.1	1312.6	1430.0	1581.0	1.5	1.4	1.5	1.3	1.2
	d. Housing	5273.0	650.6	1291.5	1359.0	1673.0	1.2	0.9	1.5	1.3	1.3
	e. Urban development	5277.0	791.3	855.8	1072.4	1956.1	1.2	1.1	1.0	1.0	1.5
	f. Other social services	34786.3	5039.5	6109.0	8370.5	9672.7	8.0	6.9	6.9	7.9	7.5
XII.	General services	1810.5	266.0	462.6	965.1	1247.3	0.4	0.4	0.5	0.9	1.0
XIII.	Total (I to XII)	434100.0	72852.4	88080.7	106204.3	128590.0	100.0	100.0	100.0	100.0	100.0
	(a) Central Plan	247865.0	43693.8	55215.9	68315.7	78848.9	57.1	60.0	62.7	64.3	61.3
	(b) State Plans	179985.0	27916.7	31500.6	35825.1	47440.0	41.5	38.3	35.8	33.7	36.9
	(c) Union Territory Plans	6250.0	1241.9	1364.2	2063.5	2301.1	1.4	1.7	1.5	1.9	1.8

Source : Planning Commission.

TABLE 10.3. Financing for Central and State Annual Plans, 1994-95 and 1995-96.

(Rs. crore)

	1994-95 Latest estimates			1995-96 Annual plan estimates		
	Centre and UTs	*States*	*Total*	*Centre and UTs*	*States*	*Total*
1	*2*	*3*	*4*	*5*	*6*	*7*
1. Domestic resources						
(a) Balance from current revenues (BCR incl. ARM)	-13370	-5722[a]	-19092	-14796	1642[a]	-13154
(b) Resources/contribution of public sector enterprises	28171	-1721	26450	35241	884	36125
(c) Issue of bonds/debentures by PSEs	7234	1461	8695	8354	2253	10607
(d) Market loans	3700	5123	8823	3700	5931	9631
(e) Long and medium term borrowing	17000	0	17000	19000	0	19000
(f) Small savings	14000	7342	21342	8000	8344	16344
(g) Provident funds	1900	4645	6545	2000	4937	6937
(h) Term loans from financial institutions/corporations	0	3261	3261	0	3123	3123
(i) Misc. capital receipts	14092	-4073	10019	19638	-4565	15073

(Contd.)

TABLE 10.3 : *(Contd.)*

1	2	3	4	5	6	7
(j) Opening balance and other resources	0	-1265	-1265	0	642	642
Total domestic resources	72727	9051	81778	81137	23191	104328
II. Net inflow from abroad	10100	0	10100	11870	0	11870
III. Budgetary deficit	6000	0	6000	5000	0	5000
IV. Aggregate resources (I to III)	88827	9051	97878	98007	23191	121198
V. Central assistance to States[b]	-17138	17822	684	-18378	20984	2606
VI. Plan grants to States under Article 275(1)	-2680	2666	-14	0	2058[c]	2058[c]
VII. Resources for the Plan[d]	69009 (69963)	29539[e]	98548	79629 (81150)	46233	125862

a Includes ARM committed at CMs level.

b The variation is due to difference in the allocation for States' EAPs by the Centre and States, non inclusion of outlays on Area Programmes in the funding of State Plans etc.

c Provisionally included; to be made up by the States as TFC did not recommend any such grant.

d Figures in brackets are inclusive of the full outlay for Union Territories.

e Gap in resources to be made up by States through better fiscal management.

Source : Planning Commission.

11

STATE OF INDIAN ECONOMY

Macroeconomic Overview

The reforms undertaken since 1991-92 have led to a revival of economic growth, expansion of productive employment, a reduction of poverty, a substantial boom in export and a marked decline in inflation. Growth of real GDP at factor cost, which had fallen to a mere 0.8 per cent in the crisis year of 1991-92, recovered within a year to reach 5.1 per cent in 1992-93. Fiscal and macroeconomic policies helped in maintaining a growth rate of 5.1 per cent in 1993-94, despite the disturbing events of late 1992-93. Overall economic growth accelerated significantly in 1994-95 to attain 6.3 per cent and is projected to record a similar high growth of 6.2 per cent in 1995-96.

The growth recovery has been accompanied by much lower current account deficits in the balance of payments, a drop in inflation below the historical average of around 8 per cent, a rise in the domestic saving rate to a record high level of 24.4 per cent of GDP and a reduction in the gross primary fiscal deficit to its lowest level in decades.

After declining by 6.2 per cent in the crisis year of 1991-92 the growth of real wages of unskilled agricultural labour has averaged 5.1 per cent per annum in the next three years. Provisional estimates by the Planning Commission indicate that in 1993-94 the incidence of poverty had declined to below 19 per cent of India's total population. The rate of poverty reduction, in terms of per cent of people below the poverty line, during 1987-88 to 1993-94 was the same as in the 1983-84 to 1987-88 period, despite the intervening crisis of 1991-92. After the crisis-induced low of 1991-92, annual economy-wide employment growth is estimated to have averaged 6.3 million jobs per year over 1992-93 to 1994-95, with 7.2 million additional employment in 1994-95.

Gross Domestic Savings

Gross domestic savings as a proportion of GDP, which averaged 21.3 per cent in 1992-93 to 1993-94 because of the poor performance of direct household savings in fixed assets, staged recovery in 1994-95. The gross domestic saving rate set a new record of 24.4 per cent, exceeding the recent peak of 23.6 per cent in 1990-91. Private saving also recorded its highest level, reaching 22.7 per cent of GDP, based both on a recovery of household saving rate to 18.9 per cent and a record corporate saving rate of 3.8 per cent of GDP.

Domestic Investment

The Economic Survey of 1994-95 had envisaged a sharp increase in gross domestic investment, based on available data on growth of capital goods production, new equity raised and long-term loans disbursed. This expectation has been confirmed by the rise in real gross capital formation to 24.9 per cent of GDP in constant prices. More importantly, real gross fixed capital formation as per cent of GDP at constant prices reached a record 22.2 per cent in 1994-95. This is substantially higher than the recent peak of 21.3 per cent of GDP in 1990-91. Real private fixed capital formation, which recovered as rapidly as GDP growth, had already reached a peak of 13 per cent of GDP (in constant prices) in 1992-93. After falling as a per cent of GDP in 1993-94 to 12.7, the pre-crisis peak level, it has set a new record of 13.7 per cent in 1994-95. Real private fixed capital formation has consequently averaged 13.1 per cent of GDP in the three years following the crisis.

Favourable Balance of Payment

Reforms of the external sector and the consequent achievements on the balance of payments front have played a key role in the turnaround in growth of GDP, employment and social indicators. After registering a decline in the dollar value of exports in 1991-92, the country has witnessed a three-year boom with annual export growth averaging 19 per cent in 1993-94 and 1994-95 and then accelerating to 24 per cent in the first 9 months of 1995-96. As a result, the ratio of exports to imports which averaged 62 per cent in 1985-86 to 1989-90, has ranged between 81 per cent and 95 per cent in the last four years. Despite the 29 per cent growth in imports during 1995-96 (nine months), fueled by high industrial growth, the export-import ratio in 1995-96 is likely to remain close to the average of 85 per cent for the last four years. The improvements in the trade account have been reinforced by favourable trends on invisible transactions. As a result, India's current account deficit in the balance of payments declined from 3.2 per cent of GDP in 1990-91 and, despite rapid import growth, is projected at a sustainable 1.5 per cent in the current year. Growth of foreign direct investment has averaged 100 per cent per annum over 1992-93 to 1994-95. The same rate of growth was maintained in the first eight months of 1995-96. These favourable trends in both current and capital accounts of the balance of payments have been reflected in foreign currency reserves. Reserves have risen rapidly from a low of one billion dollars in 1991, equivalent to hardly a fortnight's expenditure on imports, and stood at $ 16.3 billion on January 31, 1996, equivalent to about 5 months of import cover.

Improvement in External Debt Situation

The country's external debt situation has also improved markedly in the past few years. The growth of external debt between March 31, 1991 and September 30, 1995 averaged $ 2.2 billion per year, compared to the much higher average annual increase of $ 4.9 billion a year (even excluding Defence debt and short-term debt) between end-March 1986 to end-March 1991. The overall external debt to GDP ratio has fallen from a peak of 41 per cent in 1991-92 to 29 per cent in September 1995. The proportion of short-term debt in total external debt has declined from above 10 per cent in March 1991 to less than 5 per cent in September 1995. Correspondingly, debt service payments as a per cent of current receipts have declined from a peak of 35.3 per cent in 1990-91 to 26.6 per cent in 1994-95. In the first half of 1995-96, the level of external debt fell by about US$ 5.2 billion to $ 93.8 billion at the end-September, 1995. Two-thirds of the decline reflected strengthening of the US dollar in international markets relative to other major currencies in which India's external debt is denominated.

Downward Trend in Inflation

On the prices front, after a temporary setback in 1994-95, inflation has resumed its downtrend. The annual rate of inflation, as measured by the WPI, has dropped from a peak of nearly 17 per cent in August 1991 to a low of 5 per cent (provisional) on January 27, 1996. This is much below the historical average inflation rate of about 8 per cent and is the lowest rate attained since December, 1988. Furthermore, the price rise in essential commodities of wheat, edible oils and sugar has been even lower than the general inflation rate of 5 per cent.

Agricultural Production

After recording a decline in 1991-92, agricultural production has increased steadily since then at an average growth rate of above 4 per cent per annum. Foodgrains production, which had fallen by about 5 per cent of 168 million tonnes in 1991-92, touched a record level of 191.1 million tonnes in 1994-95. The output of foodgrains in 1995-96 may be marginally lower at 190 million tonnes because of some decline in rice output. Nevertheless, public food stocks soared to a record level of 36 million tonnes in July, 1995 and stood at 24.6 million tonnes at the beginning of 1996.

Industrial Production

The industrial sector has surged ahead, registering a growth of 8.6 per cent in 1994-95 and a still higher growth of 12.0 per cent during April-September 1995 (over corresponding period of last year). The capital goods sector has emerged as an important contributor to the industrial recovery, with a growth rate of 25 per ent during 1994-95, and 14.3 per cent in April-September 1995. Industiral recovery has been very broad based, and its width and depth has improved over these two years. In 1994-95, the growth of 8.6 per cent in the general index of industrial production (IIP) was due to a growth of 9 per cent in manufacturing, 8.5 per cent in electricity generation and 6.2 per cent in mining and quarrying. During April-September 1995 overall growth of 12 per cent was due to a growth of 12 per cent in manufacturing, 10.9 per cent in electricity, and 12.5 per cent in mining. A similar growth profile is mirrored in the "use-based classification", where this overall growth in 1995-96 has come from a 14.3 per cent growth in capital goods, 13.5 per cent growth in consumer goods, 12.5 per cent growth in basic goods and 6.3 per cent growth in intermediate goods. Of particular significance is the fact that small scale industrial sector has performed strongly in the post-reform period, growing faster than the overall industrial production in each of the last four year.

Performance of Infrastructure Sectors

The overall performance of the core, infrastructure sectors, which was quite satisfactory during 1994-95, has been sustained in 1995-96. The declining trend of crude oil production was arrested and reversed in 1994-95 due to creation of additional capacities. In 1995-96 (April-December) electricity, coal, salable steel, cement, crude oil and petroleum products, with a combined weight of 28.8 per cent in IIP, showed a growth rate of 8.2 per cent, compared with 8.0 per cent for April-December 1994. Electricity generation grew by 9.1 per cent, salable steel by 9.3 per cent, cement by 9.2 per cent and crude oil by 10.0 per cent. Coal, which had registered a growth rate of 3.2 per cent during April-December, 1994 has now shown an increase of 6.0 per cent during April-December, 1995. Infrastructure sectors not included in the IIP also show good performance during 1995-96. For example, new telephone connections grew by 29.3 per cent, cargo handled at major ports by 10.7 per cent and revenue generating traffic of the railways by 6.3 per cent during April-December, 1995.

Money and Prices

The point-to-point annual rate of inflation, based on movement of thc wholesale price index (WPI) touched a low ot 5 per cent (provisional) on January 27, 1996. This performance is better than earlier expectations of an inflation rate of 7 per cent to 8 per cent by the end of 1995-96. There has been a sharp deceleration in the growth of WPI during fiscal year 1995-96 (April-December) to 4.3 per cent as against 8.6 per cent during the same period of 1994-95. This subdued trend in the growth of WPI is likely to continue through the last quarter (January-March) of 1995-96, resulting in an inflation of 6 to 7 per cent (provisional) for the full year.

Monetary Management

Monetary management in 1995-96 was aimed at the twin objectives of reducing inflation and providing necessary credit support for production and investment. The sharp upward trend visible in the growth of money supply in the second half of 1994-95 was reversed in 1995-96. With money supply (M3) growing by only 7.4 per cent in 1995-96 up to January 5, 1996, the annual (point to point) growth of M3, dclined from 22.2 per cent on March 31, 1995 to 15.1 per cent on January 5, 1996.

Fiscal Developments

Over the past five budgets the fiscal deficit of the Central Government has declined as a proportion of GDP from 8.3 per cent in 1990-91 to a budgeted 5.5 per cent of GDP in 1995-96. This 2.8 per cent reduction has been brought about by an even sharper 3.8 per cent reduction in the primary deficit. The primary deficit at 0.5 per cent of GDP in 1995-96 (BE) is low than it has been since at least 1975-76.

Non-plan expenditures of the Central Government declined from 14.4 per cent of GDP in 1990-91 to 11.8 cent in 1995-96 (BE), while Plan expenditures went from 5.3 per cent of 4.6 per cent over the same period. Central Government debt, which reached a peak of 69.7 per cent of GDP in 1993-94, declined to 67.0 per cent in 1994-95 (RE). Gross dissavings of the Central Government show a modest decline to 1.7 per cent of GDP in 1995-96 (BE), from 2.0 per cent in 1990-91.

Reform of the tax system has been one of the key elements of the structural reforms undertaken since July 1991. The basic approach has been to move to a tax structure which is simple, relies on moderate tax rates with a wider base and better enforcement and serves the objectives of equity and efficiency. Substantial progress has been made in the five years. The maximum marginal rate of personal income tax was reduced from 56 per cent (inclusive of 12 per cent surcharge) to 40 per cent. The rates of corporate income tax (inclusive of 15 per cent surcharge), which were 51.75 per cent for publicly held companies and 57.5 per cent for closely held companies were unified and reduced to 46 per cent.

On the indirect tax side reforms have covered both customs and excise. Peak import duty rates which in several cases were around 300 per cent prior to reforms, were brought down in a phased manner to 50 per cent to reduce the input cost for producers in India and promote competition. The import duty on capital goods for general projects and machinery, which was 85 per cent prior to reforms, was brought down to 25 per cent in 1995 and unified for nearly four-fifths of machinery imports. The number of customs duty rates were sharply reduced to 12 and a large number of end-use exemptions were eliminated. The excise duty regime has been greatly improved with a significant switch over from specific to ad-valorem duties to ensure built in revenue elasticity.

As a result of the reforms revenues from direct taxes are budgeted to rise from 2.1 per cent of GDP in 1990-91 to 2.9 per cent in 1995-96 (BE), while customs revenues declined from 3.9 per cent of GDP to 2.8 per cent (BE) over the same period. As a consequence, the share of direct taxes in the gross tax revenue of the Centre is expected to rise from 19.1 per cent in 1990-91 to a budgeted 29.2 per cent in 1995-96 (BE), while that of customs revenue is expected to decline from 35.9 per cent to 28.4 per cent (BE) over the same period. The contribution of direct taxes could be even higher when revised estimates for 1995-96 become available.

Balance of Payments

The strength and resilience of India's balance of payments in recent years has been largely due to the robust export growth, measured in dollar terms, during the last three years. Compared to the negative growth of 1.5 per cent in 1991-92, exports recorded a growth rate of 20.0 per cent in 1993-94, 18.4 per cent in 1994-95 and 24.2 per cent during April-December of 1995-96. Imports, which remained subdued for the greater part of 1993-94, picked up towards the end of the year, in tandem with industrial recovery, ending with a growth of 6.5 per cent. Growth in imports in US dollar terms was 22.9 per cent during 1994-95, comapred to 12.7 per cent in 1991-92. During April-December 1995, imports grew at a much faster rate of 29.3 per cent. The trade deficit, measured on the basis of DGCI & S data, was US$ 1.07 billion in 1993-94 and rose to US$ 2.32 billion in 1994-95 and widened further to US$ 3.53 billion during April-December 1995.

Employment and Poverty Alleviation

The Government has accorded the highest priority to promoting sustainable, employment-intensive growth in its economic reform policies. As a result, total annual employment growth in the economy is estimated to have increased to about 7.2 million in 1994-95 as compared to only 3 million in the crisis year of 1991-92.

The proportion of people below the poverty line declined from 25.49 per cent in 1987-88 to 18.96 per cent in 1993-94, based on the provisional quinquennial data generated from the sub sample 1 for 50th round of the National Sample Survey. The lower incidence of poverty in 1993-94, despite the intervening crisis of 1991-92, suggests that the various policies and programmes adopted in the process of economic reforms have helped the poor in the country.

Several important new schemes for social uplift and poverty alleviation were launched during the recent years of reform.

— The Employment Assurance Scheme for providing 100 days of unskilled manual labour to rural poor in our 2475 backward blocks including those that are flood prone in the country;
— The Prime Minister's Rozgar Yojana aimed at providing employment to unemployed youth through the creation of micro-enterprises;
— The National Social Assistance Programme which encompasses old age pension, family benefits in case of death of the bread-earner and maternity benefits;
— The Rural Group Life Insurance Scheme, with a subsidised premium;
— The National Programme of Nutritional Support to Primary Education (also known as the Mid-Day Meal Scheme) aimed at providing a nutritious meal to children in primary school;
— The Mahila Samridhi Yojana to promote the savings habit among rural women; and
— The Indira Mahila Yojana aimed at more effective empowerment of women.

Foreign Investment

Our needs for external capital to fuel rapid economic development remain substantial. Greater access and use of foreign investment is necessary for promoting higher growth of output, exports and employment. Fifteen years ago when the East Asian Tigers (Korea, Taiwan, Singapore and Hongkong) were beginning to be recognised as successful cases of rapid economic development, there were few convincing examples of foreign direct investment (FDI) leading to or being associated with rapid economic growth. Today, this is one of the more important ingredients of the Asian Miracle in Malaysia, Thailand, China, and Indonesia. FDI has proved to be the most effective and rapid method of technology transfer (in the form of knowledge, technical and marketing skills, organisation and management systems, new material and products) and effective promotion of comparative advantage through exports. Even when it forms a small fraction of the total domestic investment, its catalytic role is out of proportion of its size. For India to aspire to sustained growth at 7 to 9 per cent over the next two decades, we have to be prepared to encouarge a rapid increase of FDI to levels comparable to China's $ 30 billion or more per year. This requires confidence in our own knowledge and capabilities, an open and competitive economy and public confidence in procedures for leasing out publicly owned resources (such as land, mines, electricity distribution networks, ports).

Fears of foreign investment swamping our domestic industry or creating unemployment are unfounded or grossly exaggerated. The experience of high growth East Asian economies highlights the potential of foreign investment for accelerating the growth of output, employment and exports. If China can absorb about $ 30 billion a year of foreign investment and become a powerful and independent-minded nation, we should not feel insecure about using foreign investments to augment the growth of output and jobs in our country.

TABLE 11.1. Selected Economic and Allied Indicators (1950-51 to 1994-95)

	1950-51	1960-61	1970-71	1980-81	1987-88	1988-89	1989-90	1990-91	1991-92	1992-93	1993-94	1994-95
1	2	3	4	5	6	7	8	9	10	11	12	13
Economic Indicators												
GDP at factor cost :												
(i) At current prices (Rs. crore)	8979	15254	39708	122427	294851	352706	408662	477814	552768	630182	723103	854103#
(ii) At 1980-81 prices (Rs. crore)	42871	62904	90426	122427	170322	188461	201453	212253	213983	224887	236064	251010#
Per capita net national product at (1980-81) prices (Rupees)	1127	1350	1520	1630	1901	2059	2157	2222	2175	2239	2292	2401#
Index of industrial production (Base : 1980-81)	18.3@	36.2	65.3	100.0	166.4	180.9	196.4	212.6	213.9	218.9	232.0	251.9(P)
Index of agricultural production (Base : triennium ending 1981-82)	46.2	68.8	85.9	102.1	115.3	140.0	143.0	148.4	145.5	151.5(P)	156.9(P)	164.1
Gross domestic capital formation (as per cent of GDP)	10.2	15.7	16.6	22.7	22.9	24.5	25.6	27.0	23.4	23.1	21.6	25.2#
Gross domestic savings (as per cent of GDP)	10.4	12.7	15.7	21.2	20.9	21.4	22.2	23.6	22.8	21.2	21.4	24.4#

(Contd.)

TABLE 11.1. *(Cont.)*

	1950-51	*1960-61*	*1970-71*	*1980-81*	*1987-88*	*1988-89*	*1989-90*	*1990-91*	*1991-92*	*1992-93*	*1993-94*	*1994-95*
1	*2*	*3*	*4*	*5*	*6*	*7*	*8*	*9*	*10*	*11*	*12*	*13*
Output												
(a) Foodgrains (million tonnes)	50.8	82.0	108.4	129.6	140.4	169.9	171.0	176.4	168.4	179.5	184.3(P)	191.1
(b) Finished Steel (million tonnes)	1.04	2.39	4.64	6.82	11.68	12.84	13.00	13.53	14.33	15.20	15.1	17.8
(c) Cement (million tonnes)	2.7	8.0	14.3	18.6	39.6	44.3	45.8	48.8	51.7	54.7	57.8	62.4
(d) Coal (including lignite) (million tonnes)	32.3	55.2	76.3	119.0	190.9	207.0	213.7	225.5	243.8	254.9	264.1	273.1
(e) Crude oil (million tonnes)	0.3	0.5	6.8	10.5	30.4	32.0	34.1	33.0	30.4	27.0	27.0	32.2
(f) Electricity generated (utilities only) (Billion KWH)	5.1	16.9	55.8	110.8	202.1	221.4	245.4	264.3	287.0	301.1	323.5	351.0
Wholesale price index* (Base : 1981-82)	16.9	19.6	35.5	91.1	143.6	154.3	165.7	182.7	207.8	228.7	247.8	274.7
Consumer price index (Base : 1982=100) @@	17	21	38	81	149	163	173	193	219	240	258	279
Plan outlay (Rs. crore)	260##	1117	2524	15023	44034	48645	55630	58369	64751	72852	88081	106204(RE)
Centre's budgetary deficit (Rs. crore)	(-)33##	(-)117	285	2576	5816	5642	10592	11347	6855	12312	10960	6000(RE)

TABLE 11.1. *(Cont.)*

	1950-51	*1960-61*	*1970-71*	*1980-81*	*1987-88*	*1988-89*	*1989-90*	*1990-91*	*1991-92*	*1992-93*	*1993-94*	*1994-95*
1	*2*	*3*	*4*	*5*	*6*	*7*	*8*	*9*	*10*	*11*	*12*	*13*
Foreign Trade												
(i) Exports												
Rs. crore	606	642	1535	6711	15674	20232	27658	32553	44041	53688	69751	82674
US $ million	1269	1346	2031	8486	12089	13970	16612	18143	17865	18537	22238	26330
(ii) Imports												
Rs. crore	608	1122	1634	12549	22244	28235	35328	43198	47851	63375	73101	89971
US $ million	1273	2353	2162	15869	17156	19497	21219	24075	19411	21882	23306	28654
Foreign exchange reserves (excluding gold and SDRs):												
Rs. crore	911	186	438	4822	7287	6605	5787	4388	14578	20140	47287	66006
US $ million	1914	390	584	5850	5618	4226	3368	2236	5631	6434	15068	20809
Social Indicators												
Population												
Population (million)[a]	361.1	439.2	548.2	683.3	795.1	811.3	827.4	846.3	862.5[b]	878.6[b]	894.6[b]	910.7[b]
Birth rate (per 1000)[c]	39.9	41.7	41.2	37.2	31.5	30.6	30.2	29.5	29.2	28.7	28.6P	..
Death rate (per 1000)[c]	27.4	22.8	19.0	15.0	11.0	10.3	9.7	9.8	10.1	9.3	9.2P	..

(Contd.)

TABLE 11.1. *(Cont.)*

	1950-51	1960-61	1970-71	1980-81	1987-88	1988-89	1989-90	1990-91	1991-92	1992-93	1993-94	1994-95
1	*2*	*3*	*4*	*5*	*6*	*7*	*8*	*9*	*10*	*11*	*12*	*13*
Life expectancy at birth (In years)												
(a) Male	32.4	41.9	46.4	50.9	..	57.7	58.1	58.6	..	60.4	..	..
(b) Female	31.7	40.6	44.7	50.0	..	58.1	58.6	59.0	..	61.2	..	..
Total	32.1	41.3	45.6	50.4	..	57.7	58.3	58.7	..	60.8	..	..
Education												
Literacy rate (percentage)[e]												
(a) Male	27.16	40.40	45.95	56.37	..	..	..	64.1	..	..	..	..
(b) Female	8.86	15.34	21.97	29.75	..	..	..	39.3	..	..	..	..
Total	18.33	28.31	34.45	43.56	..	..	..	52.2	..	..	..	..
Health & Family Welfare[f]												
Registered medical practitioners (RMP) (thousand)	61.8	83.7	151.1	268.7	335.6	368.6	381.9	394.0	410.8	..	..	..
RMP per 10,000 population	1.7	1.9	2.8	3.9	4.4	4.5	4.6	4.7	4.8	..	..	..
Beds (all types)** per 10,000	3.2	5.2	6.4	8.3	9.2	9.5	9.4	9.6	..	..	..	..

Notes of Table 11.1

@ Relates to the calendar year 1950.
@@ Figures for the period up to 1988-89 derived by converting indices on earlier bases into base 1982=100.
# Quick estimates.
Relates to 1951-52.
* Figures for the period up to 1980-81 derived by converting the indices on earlier bases into base 1980-81=100.
** Includes beds in hospitals, dispensaries, P.H.Cs, clinics, sanatoriums, etc.
RE Revised estimates.
.. Not available.
P Provisional.

Notes :

[a] As on March 1, 1951 and so on up to 1980-81 and 1990-91 as per Census of India. Figures for the period 1987 to 1990 are based on adjusted projections of the Standing Committee of Experts on Population Projections.

[b] Relate to March 1, 1992, 1993, 1994 and 1995 based on annual series of the Standing Committee of Experts on population projections and adjusted to confirm to 1991 census data.

[c] Data for 1950-51, 1960-61, 1970-71 and 1980-81 are census estimates and relate to decades 1941-50, 1951-60, 1961-70 and 1971-80 respectively. The estimates for 1987-88 onwards are based on the SRS.

[d] Data for 1950-51, 1960-61, 1970-71 and 1980-81 relate to the decades 1941-50, 1951-60, 1961-70 and 1971-80 respectively. centred at mid-point of the decade, i.e., 1946, 1956, 1966 and 1976. The estimates for 1988-89, 1989-90 and 1990-91 refer to the periods, 1986-90, 1987-91 and 1988-92 respectively. For 1992-93, it is based on the extrapolated values of the Standing Committee of Experts on Population Projections centred at June 1992.

[e] Data for 1950-51, 1960-61, 1970-71, 1980-81 and 1990-91 relate to the years 1951, 1961, 1971, 1981 and 1991 respectively. The figures for 1951, 1961 and 1971 relate to population aged 5 years and above and those for 1981 and 1991 relate to population aged 7 years and above. All India literacy rates exclude Assam for 1981 and J&K for 1991.

[f] Relate to calendar year e.g., 1950-51 pertains to December 1951 and so on.

12

BALANCE OF PAYMENT, EXTERNAL DEBT AND FOREIGN TRADE

Improvement in Balance of Payment

The improvement in India's balance of payments witnessed in 1993-94 was sustained in 1994-95. Exports showed a growth of 18.4 per cent in US dollar terms. There was a large increase in imports by 22.9 per cent in line with the expansion in industrial growth and investment activities. Invisible payments also rose considerably, reflecting the liberal policy regime for current payments. As a result, the current account deficit widened from the low level of US$ 315 million in 1993-94 to US$ 2315 million in 1994-95. At this level, the current account deficit was about 0.8 per cent of GDP which is modest. The rise in the current account deficit in 1994-95 was anticipated as the economy recovered and did not pose any financing problems. In fact, total capital flows in 1994-95 were much in excess of financing needs, reflecting the continuing reserve build up of about US$ 4.76 billion during 1994-95. Foreign currency assets of the Reserve Bank of India (RBI) increased from US$ 15.07 billion at the end of March 1994 to a peak of US$ 20.81 billion at the end of March 1995. Total foreign exchange reserves, including gold and Special Drawing Rights (SDRs), amounted to US$ 25.19 billion at the end of March 1995, equivalent to about ten months of imports in 1994-95.

The trade and payments position remained reasonably comfortable during 1995-96. For the third year in succession, export growth was robust, supported by a congenial domestic policy environment. Import growth was also high, reflecting good performance of the industrial sector. Net inflow of invisibles marked a sharp decline over the previous year, partly due to inflows of private transfers declining from the abnormally high level of 1993-94 to a level consistent with normal trends, and partly due to an increase in interest payments on foreign loans. Reflecting these developments on the trade and invisibles accounts, the current account deficit widened in 1995-96. But the level of the deficit was reasonable and sustainable. On the capital account, foreign investment flows were the major component, as in the two previous years. However, there was a significant deceleration in these flows, mainly because of the subdued trend in portfolio investments. Direct foreign investment flows, on the other hand, showed a considerable improvement. The residual financing need was met by drawing down foreign exchange reserves. Foreign currency assets of the RBI declined by US$ 4.48 billion, to a level of US$ 16.32 billion by the end of January 1996. The decline in reserves reflects the expansion in imports and greater investment absorption capacity of the economy in response to reform measures introduced since 1991.

External debt

India's external debt rose from US$ 92.70 billion at the end of March 1994 to US$ 99.04 billion at the end of March 1995. Of the US$ 6.34 billion increase in external debt during 1994-95, as much as US$ 5.61 billion, or 88% of the increase, was due to exchange rate changes alone. The increase in external debt at constant end March 1994 exchange rates was only US$ 794 million during 1994-95. Provisional estimates for the current financial year show that India's external debt has declined by US$ 5.20 billion during the first six months of US$ 93.84 billion at the end of September 1995. Two-thirds of the decline in external debt is accounted for the appreciation of the US dollar against major world currencies since March 1995. The long term debt has declined by US$ 5.43 billion and the short term debt has increased marginally by US$ 0.23 billion since end March 1995. As a percentage of GDP, India's external debt declined from the peak of 41.0 per cent in 1991-92 to 33.0 per cent in 1994-95. The external debt stock at the end of September 1995 worked out of about 29.4 per cent of the estimated GDP for 1995-96. Debt service payments as a percentage of current account receipts also declined markedly from 35.3 per cent in 1990-91 to 26.6 per cent in 1994-95 and it is expected to decline further in 1995-96.

Table 12.1 presents a summary view of India's balance of payments for the years 1990-91 through April-September of 1995-96. The developments in India's trade and payments over the past five years marked a noticeable structural change towards a more stable and sustainable balance of payments.

Structural Aspects of India's External Debt

— India's external debt amounted to US$ 92.70 billion at end March 94, US$ 99.04 billion at end March 95 and US$ 93.84 billion at end September 95. India's external debt increased by only $ 1.14 billion between end March 1994 and end September 1995.

— The growth of India's external debt has slowed down substantially to an average annual increase of only $ 2.2 billion between March 31, 1991 and September 30, 1995 compared to $ 4.9 billion (excluding defence and short term debts) between end March 1986 and end March 1991.

— As a per cent of GDP at current market prices, India's external debt declined from the peak of 41.0 per cent in 1991-92 to 33.0 per cent in 1994-95 and further to 29.4 per cent in end September 1995.

— Short term debt (debt of maturity upto one year) as a proportion of total external debt declined from 10.2 per cent at end March 1991 to 4.3 per cent at end March 1995. It was 4.8 per cent at end September 1995.

— A large part of the external debt, especially debt to multilateral (excluding the IMF) and bilateral agencies has high degree of concessionality, i.e. grant element of at least 25 per cent. The share of concessional debt in total debt is about 45 per cent.

— Debt in rupees owned to the former Soviet Union, rupee denominated Non-Resident deposits and debt due to Foreign Currency Convertible Bonds, moderate the degree of concern about the current level of external debt because of their special characteristics.

TABLE 12.1. Balance of Payments : Key Indicators

(In US$ million)

	1990-91 (P)	1991-92 (P)	1992-93 (P)	1993-94 (Q.E.)	1994-95 (Q.E.)	Apr-Sep (Q.E.) 1994-95	1995-96
1. Exports	18477	18266	18869	22700	26763	11853	14980
2. Imports	27914	21064	23237	23985	31269	13385	18165
Of which : POL	6028	5364	6100	5650	5882	2650	3113
3. Trade balance	-9437	-2798	-4368	-1285	-4506	-1532	-3185
4. Invisibles (net)	-243	1620	842	970	2191	1096	445
Non-factor services	979	1207	1128	777	-494	-659	-193
Investment income	-3752	-3830	-3422	-4002	-3905	-1938	-2112
Pvt. transfers	2069	3783	2773	3825	6200	3569	2600
Official Grants	461	460	363	370	390	124	150
5. Current Account Balance	-9680	-1178	-3526	-315	-2315	-436	-2740
6. External assistance (net)	2210	3037	1859	1700	1250	-55	-40
7. Commercial borrowings (net)[1]	2249	1456	-358	1252	1029	-73	25
8. IMF (net)	1214	786	1288	191	-1146	-1134	-839
9. NRI deposits (net)	1536	290	2001	940	847	621	59
10. Rupee debt service	-1193	-1240	-878	-745	-1050	-650	-300
11. Foreign investment	68	154	585	4110	4895	2586	1490
of which :							
(i) DFI	68	154	344	620	1314	466	856
(ii) FIIs	0	0	1	1665	1503	1017	533
(ii) Euro equities	0	0	240	1460	1839	903	46

(contd.,

TABLE 12.1 *(Contd.)*

	1990-91 (P)	1991-92 (P)	1992-93 (P)	1993-94 (Q.E.)	1994-95 (Q.E.)	Apr-Sep (Q.E.) 1994-95	Apr-Sep (Q.E.) 1995-96
12.Other flows[2]	2318	271	-243	1735	1247	2463	1056
13.Capital account total (net)	8402	4754	4254	9183	7072	3758	1451
14.Reserve use (-increase)	1278	-3576	-728	-8868	-4757	-3322	1289
Memo items :			*As per cent of GDP*				
Exports	6.2	7.3	7.8	8.9	8.9		
Imports	9.4	8.3	9.8	9.4	10.4		
Trade balance	-3.2	-1.1	2.0	-0.5	-1.5		
Invisibles balance	-0.1	0.7	0.2	0.4	0.7		
Current account balance	-3.2	-0.4	-1.8	-0.1	-0.8		

(P): Preliminary Actuals; Q.E. : Quick estimates

1 Figures include receipt on account of India Development Bonds in 1991-92 and related repayments, if any, in the subsequent years.

2 Include delayed exports receipts and errors & omissions. For the year 1992-93, it also includes errors & omissions arising out of dual exchange rates applicable under the Liberalised Exchange Rate Management System (LERMS).

TABLE 12.2. Ratios of selected items of the Balance of Payments

Item/Years	1980-81	1985-86	1989-90	1990-91	1991-92	1992-93	1993-94	1994-95	1995-96[1]
1. Exports/Imports (%)	52.4	54.7	69.5	66.2	86.7	81.2	94.6	85.6	86.6[2]
2. Current account/GDP (%)	-1.6	-2.3	-2.5	-3.2	-0.4	-1.8	-0.1	-0.8	-1.5
3. Current account deficit (US$ million)	2095	4845	6837	9680	1178	3526	315	2315	4800
4. ECB/TC (%)	10.9	22.2	34.4	26.8	30.6	-8.4	12.4	14.6	NA
5. NRI deposits/TC (%)	9.7	33.6	28.4	18.3	6.1	47.0	10.2	12.0	NA
6. External assistance/TC (%)	60.9	31.9	35.9	26.3	63.9	43.7	18.5	17.7	NA
7. Debt service payments as a % of current receipts	10.2	18.7	30.9	35.3	30.2	28.6	25.1	26.6	26.5

[1] Projections.

[2] Based on DGCI&S trade data for April-December 1995.

Notes : (i) TC : Total capital flows (net).

(ii) GDP : Gross domestic product at current market prices.

(iii) ECB : External Commercial Borrowings.

(iv) NA : Not Available.

(v) As total capital flows are netted after taking into account some capital outflows, the ratios against item no. 4, 5 and 6 may in some years add up to more than 100.

(vi) Debt service payments for the years 1980-81 and 1985-86 exclude debt.

TABLE 12.3. Foreign Exchange Reserves[1] : Historical Perspective

(US$ million)

Years	*Forex Reserves*[2]	*Import Cover (No. of Months)*[3]	*Current Payments Cover*[4] *(No. of Months)*[3]
1950-51	1914	16.8	14.6
1955-56	1648	12.2	10.6
1960-61	390	2.0	1.7
1965-66	383	1.6	1.3
1970-71	584	2.9	2.2
1975-76	1657	3.3	2.9
1980-81	5850	4.5	4.0
1985-86	5972	4.2	3.5
1990-91	2236	1.0	0.8
1991-92	5631	3.2	2.3
1992-93	6334	3.3	2.5
1993-94	15068	7.5	5.4
1994-95	20809	8.0	5.7
1995-96	16317[5]	5.0[6]	3.8[6]

Notes :

1. Excluding Gold and SDRs.
2. Year-end Level.
3. Based on foreign exchange reserves of respective year-end levels.
4. Current payments represent sum of merchandise imports and invisibles payments.
5. End-January 1996.
6. Estimates.

— The relatively high grant element in India's external debt translates into downsizing the nominal value of the debt by about one-third in present value (PV) terms. The PV of India's external debt at end March 1994 is estimated at US$ 60.52 billion or 24.6 per cent of GDP.

— Debt service payments as a percent of current receipts declined from the peak of 35.3 per cent in 1990-91 to 26.6 per cent in 1994-95 and it is estimated to decline further in 1995-96.

Recent Developments in the Exchange Rate of the Rupee

— In March 1993, India moved to a single, market-determined exchange rate system.

— The rupee-dollar rate remained steady at about Rs. 31.4 for over two years after March 1993.

— The stability vis-a-vis the US dollar resulted from buoyant inflows of capital which were sterilized by the Reserve Bank through intervention to prevent an appreciation that would have hurt the export recovery.

— These inflows slowed down in the last quarter of 1994-95, but the exchange rate of the rupee vis-a-vis the US dollar remained stable until August 1995 after which it depreciated against the US dollar to Rs. 37.0 as of February 9, 1996.

— The exchange rate developments need to be appropriately assessed with reference to rupee's movement against all the currencies of India's major trading partners and the inflation differential between India and her trading partners.
— The nominal effective exchange rate (NEER) of the rupee, which is a weighted average of exchange rates vis-a-vis the currencies of major trading partners, showed a depreciation of the rupee of about 8 per cent by August 1995 in nominal terms since 1993-94.
— However, the higher rate of inflation in India vis-a-vis the trading partners implied an appreciation of the rupee in real effective exchange rate (REER) terms by about 7 per cent during the period from 1993-94 to August 1995. The appreciation was 10.5 per cent as compared to March 1993.
— The period since the middle of September 1995 was characterised by the periodic speculative pressures on the exchange rate which were actively countered by the RBI.
— The movement in the rupee's exchange rate in recent months has brought the current external value of the rupee, in REER terms, back to approximately the level that prevailed in March 1993.

TABLE 12.4. Composition of India's Exports

(Percentage Shares)

Commodity Group	*1993-94*	*1994-95*	*Apr-Sept 1994-95*	*Apr-Sept 1995-96*
I. Agriculture & allied, of which	18.0	16.0	16.0	16.0
1. Tea	1.5	1.2	1.2	1.1
2. Coffee	0.8	1.3	1.6	1.6
3. Cereals	1.9	1.5	1.4	3.4
4. Unmanufactured tobacco	0.5	0.2	0.3	0.4
5. Spices	0.8	0.7	0.7	0.7
6. Cashew nuts	1.5	1.5	1.8	1.3
7. Oil meals	3.2	2.2	2.2	1.5
8. Fruits & vegetables	0.6	0.7	.06	.07
9. Marine products	3.7	4.3	3.8	2.8
10. Raw cotton	0.9	0.2	0.3	0.1
II. Ores and minerals, of which	4.0	3.8	3.6	4.0
11. Iron ore	2.0	1.6	1.6	1.8
12. Processed minerals	1.0	1.0	0.9	1.0
13. Other ores and minerals	0.9	1.0	1.0	1.2
III. Manufactured goods, of which	75.5	78.1	78.0	77.7
14. Leather & manufactures	3.8	4.0	4.1	3.7
15. Leather footwear	2.2	2.1	2.1	2.0
16. Gems & jewellary	18.0	17.1	17.4	16.8
17. Drugs, pharmaceutics & fine chemicals	2.9	3.0	3.0	3.0

(Contd.)

TABLE 12.4 : *(Contd.)*

Commodity Group	*1993-94*	*1994-95*	*Apr-Sept 1994-95*	*Apr-Sept 1995-96*
18. Dyes intmdtes & Coal tar chemicals	1.7	1.8	1.9	1.6
19. Manufactures of metals	2.8	2.7	2.6	2.6
20. Machinery and instruments	2.9	2.8	2.7	2.7
21. Transport equipment	2.7	2.9	2.9	2.9
22. Primary & semi-finished iron & steel	2.2	1.6	1.6	1.7
23. Electronic goods	1.4	1.6	1.5	2.0
24. Cotton yarn, fabrics, makeups etc.	7.0	8.5	8.7	8.2
25. Ready made garments	11.6	12.5	11.4	12.0
26. Handicrafts	4.2	3.9	4.2	3.8
IV. Crude & petroleum products	1.8	1.6	1.9	1.6
V. Others & unclassified items	0.7	0.6	0.5	0.7
Grand Total	100.0	100.0	100.0	100.0

Source : DGCI&S, Calcutta.

TABLE 12.5. Composition Of India's Exports

(Percentage Shares)

	1993-94	*1994-95*	*Apr-Sept 1994-95*	*Apr-Sept 1995-96*
I. Food and allied products, of which	2.4	5.1	6.4	3.7
1. Cereals	0.4	0.1	0.1	0.1
2. Pulses	0.8	0.7	0.7	0.5
3. Cashew nuts	0.7	0.8	0.9	0.5
4. Edible oils	0.7	0.8	0.9	0.5
II. Fuel, of which	26.7	23.2	24.1	21.5
5. Coal	2.0	2.5	2.6	2.3
6. POL	24.7	20.7	21.5	19.2
III. Fertilizers	3.5	3.7	3.1	4.9
IV. Paper board, manufactures & newsprint	1.0	0.9	0.8	1.4
V. Capital goods, of which	26.7	26.5	25.3	27.5
7. Machinery except elec & machine tools	8.1	9.5	8.9	10.4
8. Electrical machinery	4.8	5.2	4.2	5.5
9. Transport equipment	5.5	3.9	4.0	2.9
10. Project goods	7.0	6.5	6.6	7.0

(Contd.)

Table 12.5 . *(Contd.)*

	1993-94	*1994-95*	*Apr-Sept 1994-95*	*Apr-Sept 1995-96*
VI. Others, of which	26.8	24.0	23.9	24.3
11. Chemicals	8.5	10.3	10.1	10.5
12. Pearls precious semi precious stones	11.3	5.7	6.1	5.7
13. Iron & steel	3.2	3.8	3.6	3.5
14. Non-ferrous metals	2.0	2.5	2.4	2.6
15. Professional instruments, optical goods etc.	1.8	1.7	1.6	1.9
VII. Unclassified items	12.9	16.7	16.4	16.6
Grand Total	100.0	100.0	100.0	100.0

Source : DGCI&S, Calcutta.

Trade Policy Reforms

It is not widely acknowledged that major reforms in trade policy and procedures since the announcement in March 1992 of the EXIM Policy for 1992-97, have accelerated India's transition towards a globally oriented economy by stimulating exports and facilitating imports of essential inputs as well as capital goods.

One of the main objectives of the EXIM Policy 1992-97 and changes therein during the last four years was to phase out quantitative restrictions in the form of licensing and other discretionary controls. Thus :

— In 1991 imports were regulated by means of a positive list of freely importable items. Since 1992 imports are regulated through a limited negative list.

— Quantitative restrictions on imports of most intermediate inputs and capital goods have been eliminated.

— In July 1991 out of 5,021 Harmonised System (H.S.) tariff lines (6 digits), 80 per cent i.e., 4,000 lines were subject to import licensing restrictions. As of December, 1995 more than 3000 tariff lines covering raw materials, intermediates and capital goods are free of import licensing requirements.

— A large number of items covering 1,487 tariff lines whose import is otherwise restricted, are now allowed to be imported under freely tradable Special Import Licences, which are granted to the export houses/trading houses/star trading houses and super star trading houses.

— Through continuous review and revisions during the last four years, control on exports has been liberalised to the extent that now all goods may be exported without any restriction except the few items mentioned in the negative list of exports. The items in the negative list are regulated because of strategic considerations, environmental and ecological grounds, essential domestic requirements, employment generation, and on grounds of socio-cultural heritage.

TABLE 12.6. Direction of India's Trade

(Percentage Share)

Country	Exports				Imports			
	1993-94	*1994-95*	*1994-95*	*1995-96*	*1993-94*	*1994-95*	*1994-95*	*1995-96*
	(Apr-March)		*(Apr-Sept)*		*(Apr-March)*		*(Apr-Sept)*	
1 U.K.	6.2	6.4	6.5	6.5	6.6	5.4	5.6	5.1
2 Germany	6.9	6.6	6.7	6.5	7.7	7.6	7.3	8.6
3 Other EC	12.9	13.6	12.8	13.9	15.8	11.8	11.1	12.2
4 U.S.A.	18.0	19.1	19.8	18.5	11.7	10.1	10.0	11.1
5 Japan	7.8	7.7	7.7	6.7	6.5	7.1	7.3	7.6
6 Russia	2.9	3.1	3.0	3.4	1.1	1.8	1.3	2.5
7 Other East Europe	0.9	0.5	0.6	0.6	0.7	0.6	0.6	0.8
8 OPEC	10.7	9.2	9.5	8.9	22.4	21.1	21.1	20.6
9 Other LDCs	24.2	23.9	23.2	25.0	15.4	19.9	21.3	18.7
10 Others	9.4	9.8	10.2	10.2	12.1	14.6	14.6	12.7
	100.0	100.0	100.0	100.0	100.0	100.0	100.0	100.0

Source : DGCI&S, Calcutta

TABLE 12.7. Direction of India's Trade With Selected East Asian Countries

(Percentage Shares)

Country	*Exports*						*Imports*					
	1991-92	1992-93	1993-94	1994-95	1994-95	1995-96	1991-92	1992-93	1993-94	1994-95	1994-95	1995-96
			(April-March)		*(Apr-Sep.)*				*(April-March)*		*(Apr-Sep.)*	
1. Indonesia	0.8	0.7	1.1	1.1	0.9	1.6	0.3	0.3	0.5	1.1	1.1	1.2
2. Malaysia	1.1	1.0	1.1	1.1	1.0	1.2	2.0	1.9	1.1	1.7	2.2	2.6
3. Hongkong	3.4	4.1	5.6	5.8	5.4	6.0	0.6	0.8	0.8	1.0	0.8	1.0
4. South Korea	1.4	0.9	0.9	1.3	1.2	1.3	1.7	1.6	2.4	2.2	2.1	2.1
5. Singapore	2.2	3.2	3.4	2.9	2.9	2.6	3.6	2.9	2.7	3.1	2.8	3.2
6. Thailand	1.1	1.4	1.6	1.5	1.5	1.5	0.3	0.3	0.2	0.6	0.8	0.5
7. Chinese Taipei	1.0	1.0	1.2	1.0	1.1	1.0	1.5	1.0	0.8	1.0	0.9	1.0
Total (SEASC)	11.1	12.3	14.9	14.6	14.2	15.0	9.9	8.7	8.6	10.8	10.8	11.7

Source : DGCI&S, Calcutta.

13

FISCAL AND BUDGETARY DEVELOPMENTS

Further consolidation of fiscal balance, tax reform, social equity and poverty alleviation were some of the major considerations for the 1994-95 and 1995-96 budget of the Central Government. Over the five year period 1990-91 to 1995-96 (BE) the fiscal deficit was estimated to decline by 2.8 per cent of GDP. The contribution of the decline in Plan expenditure (0.7 per cent of GDP) was less than 2/7th the contribution of the decline in non-Plan expenditure (2.6 per cent of GDP). The primary deficit, which is a better measure of the effort made, declined by 3.8 per cent of GDP over the period.

Gross dissaving by the Central Government, which rose sharply in 1993-94 and then declined in 1994-95 (RE) was estimated to decline still further to 1.7 per cent of GDP in 1995-96 (BE). Total outstanding liabilities of the Central Government, after reaching a peak of 69.7 per cent of GDP in 1993-94 were on the decline. A substantial proportion of these liabilities were on behalf of the States, Union Territories and Public Sector Enterprises. Loans given to them constituted over 31 per cent of the total marketable outstanding liabilities, arrived after excluding borrowings from RBI, in 1994-95 (RE). The book value of the economic assets aggregated to another 26 per cent of these liabilities. Thus, only 43 per cent of the marketable outstanding liabilities were on account of social and administrative assets and expenditure.

The outlay for the Annual Plan 1995-96 for the Centre, States and Union Territories was estimated to increase by 21.1 per cent compared to the outlay in 1994-95 (RE). Financial performance of the Departmental Commercial Undertakings was estimated to improve in 1995-96 (BE). Postal deficit was estimated to decline from Rs. 352 crore in 1994-95 (RE) to Rs. 304 crore in 1995-96 (BE).

Reforms in the tax system has been one of the key elements of the structural reforms initiated since July 1991. These reforms have encompassed both direct and indirect taxes and have moved towards a tax structure which is simple, relies on moderate tax rates with a wider base and better enforcement and serves the objectives of equity and efficiency. Substantial progress has been made in the last five years. The maximum marginal rate of personal income tax was reduced from 56 per cent to 40 per cent and exemption limit raised from Rs. 22,000 in 1991 to Rs. 40,000 in 1995. The rates of corporate income tax, (inclusive of 15 per cent surcharge) which were 51.75 per cent for publicly held company and 57.5 per cent for closely held company were unified and reduced to 46 per cent. In the case of foreign companies the tax rate was brought down from 65 to 55 per cent. Peak import duty rates, which were in excess of 300 per cent prior to reforms were brought down in a phased manner to 50 per cent. Excise duty regime has been greatly improved with a significant switchover from specific to ad valorem duties to ensure built in revenue elasticity and a far reaching rationalisation of the rate structure. The ambit of MODVAT i.e., credit for taxes paid on inputs, was extended to cover capital goods, R & D equipment, POL etc. The number of ad valorem excise duty rates were brought down to 10 (including nil rate) and a large number of end use exemptions eliminated. The budget for 1995-96 continued the emphasis on strengthening the incentives for investment, simplification, lower rates and greater buoyancy. To facilitate expansion of quality infrastructure a five year tax holiday was provided to enterprises which provide certain facilities in the area of highways, bridges, etc.

Overall, tax reforms since July 1991 have helped in correcting the imbalance in the structure of revenue sources. Direct taxation is generally regarded a more equitable way of raising revenue. It is noteworthy that the share of direct taxes in GDP rose from 2.1 per cent in 1990-91 to an estimated 2.9 per cent in 1995-96. The latter could be even higher when revised estimates for 1995-96 become available. Besides, the share of direct taxes in the gross tax revenue of the centre rose from about 19 per cent in 1990-91 to an estimated 29 per cent in 1995-96. Another noteworthy dimension is the drop in the share of customs revenue in GDP from 3.9 per cent in 1990-91 to 2.8 per cent in 1995-96. Over the same period contribution of customs to the gross tax revenue of the Centre declined from almost 36 per cent to 28.4 per cent. These are healthy portents from the point of view of equity and efficiency.

Fiscal Deficit : 1990-91 to 1995-96

Between 1990-91 and the budget estimates of 1995-96, the fiscal deficit would have declined by 2.8 per cent of GDP. Reduction in the fiscal deficit was due to a 3.2 per cent decline in total expenditure, from 19.7 per cent of GDP in 1990-91 to 16.5 per cent in 1995-96 (BE). The decline in the fiscal deficit was lower than the decline in the total expenditure because revenue receipts including non-debt capital receipts declined by approximately 0.5 per cent of GDP over the same period. However, a better measure of success achieved in fiscal consolidation is the primary deficit which is the fiscal deficit net of interest payments, which are a committed liability for the past borrowings. The primary deficit declined from 4.3 per cent of GDP in 1990-91 to 0.5 per cent of GDP in 1995-96 (BE), a decline of 3.8 per cent of GDP (Table 13.1).

The finances of the Central Government, which had reached a critical stage in 1990-91, registered a substantial improvement. Total expenditure of the Central Government which was 19.7 per cent of GDP in 1990-91 declined to 17.2 per cent in 1994-95 (RE) and is estimated to decline further to 16.5 per cent in 1995-96 (BE). Thus, between 1990-91 and 1995-96 (BE), the expenditure would have declined by 3.2 per cent of GDP. Most of this, 2.6 per cent of GDP, decline was due to a decline in the non-plan expenditure which decline from 14.4 per cent of GDP in 1990-91 to 11.8 per cent in 1995-96 (BE). The decline

TABLE 13.1. Components of Gross Fiscal Deficit of the Central Government

(Rs. crore)

	1980-81	*1990-91*	*1991-92*	*1992-93*	*1993-94*	*1994-95 (R.E.)*	*1995-96 (B.E.)*
1. Fiscal Deficit	7733	44632	36323	40173	60257	61035	57634
1.1 Interest Payments	2604	21498	26596	31075	36741	44000	52000
1.2 Primary Deficit	5129	23134	9727	9098	23516	17035	5634
1.2.1 Primary Deficit Consumption	1310	6358	1306	979	11985	7588	3407
1.2.2 Primary Deficit Investment	3819	16776	8421	8119	11531	9447	2227
(As per cent of GDP)							
1. Fiscal Deficit	5.7	8.3	5.9	5.7	7.5	6.5	5.5
1.1 Interest Payments	1.9	4.0	4.3	4.4	4.6	4.7	5.0
1.2 Primary Deficit	3.8	4.3	1.6	1.3	2.9	1.8	0.5
1.2.1 Primary Deficit consumption	1.0	1.2	0.2	0.1	1.5	0.8	0.3
1.2.2 Primary Deficit Investment	2.8	3.1	1.4	1.2	1.4	1.0	0.2
Memorandum items							
(a) Interest Receipts	1795	8730	10933	12487	15062	16235	18420
(b) Dividend and Profit	82	564	708	993	948	1221	1446

Notes : 1. Primary deficit consumption = Revenue deficit-interest payments+interest receipts+dividend & profits

2. Primary deficit investment = Capital expenditure-interest receipts-dividend & profit-recovery of loans-other receipts

in the Plan expenditure was much lower, only 0.7 per cent of GDP, from 5.3 per cent in 1990-91 to 4.6 per cent in 1995-96 (BE). Revenue receipts declined from 10.3 per cent to 9.6 per cent over this period. However, the decline was offset to some extent by increase in the non-debt capital receipts by 0.2 per cent of GDP. Non-tax revenue also improved from 2.2 per cent of GDP in 1990-91 to 2.5 per cent in 1995-96 (BE).

In line with the policy of the Government to reduce the subsidies by targeting them in favour of the poor and needy, total subsidies declined from 2.3 per cent of GDP in 1990-91 to 1.2 per cent in 1995-96 (BE). There is some decline in the defence expenditure as well.

Central Public Sector Enterprises are now increasingly less dependent on the Government for financing their Plan outlays. Budget support declined from 24.4 of their Plan outlay in 1990-91 to 16.9 per cent in 1994-95 (RE) and is estimated to decline further to 12.3 per cent in 1995-96 (BE).

Internal liabilities of the Central Government are estimated to decline marginally from 52.9 per cent of GDP in 1990-91 to 52.1 per cent in 1995-96 (BE). External debt which was 12.4 per cent of GDP in 1990-91 and rose sharply in 1991-92 to 17.8 per cent, mainly due to the devaluation of rupee, has since then declined continuously. It was 14.1 per cent of GDP at the end of September, 1995, a decline of 3.7 per cent since 1991-92. However, compared to 1990-91, these is an increase of 1.7 per cent of GDP. Total liabilities which increased from 65.2 per cent of GDP in 1990-91 to 69.7 per cent in 1993-94 seem to have stabilized. There was a reduction to 67.0 per cent in 1994-95 (RE) and to 66.2 per cent in 1995-96 (BE).

Fiscal and Budgetary Developments in 1994-95

The declining trend of fiscal deficit which suffered a temporary reversal in 1993-94 was again restored and strengthened further. From 7.5 per cent of GDP in 1993-94, the fiscal deficit declined to 6.5 per cent in 1994-95 (RE). The fiscal deficit would have been still lower but for sudden surge in the collection from Small Savings and resultant increase in the loans to States and Union Territories. These loans are treated as expenditure of the Central Government and add to the fiscal deficit. If this expenditure, over which the Central Government had no control, was excluded, the fiscal deficit declined to 5.4 per cent of GDP.

Central Government

Revenue receipts of the Central Government which had registered a sharp decline in the year 1993-94, remained stable at 9.4 per cent of GDP as per the revised estimates of 1994-95. Non-tax revenue declined to 2.5 per cent of GDP from 2.7 per cent in 1993-94. However, the increase in the tax revenue offset the decline in the non-tax revenue. Tax revenue increased from 6.7 per cent of GDP in 1993-94 to 6.9 per cent of GDP in 1994-95 (RE).

Total expenditure declined from 17.7 per cent of GDP in 1993-94 to 17.2 per cent of GDP in 1994-95 (RE). There was no reduction in the capital expenditure which remained at 4.2 per cent of GDP. The entire decline was in the revenue expenditure which came down to 13.0 per cent of GDP from 13.5 per cent in 1993-94. This was despite the fact that interest payments continue to increase. There was further success in checking the growth of subsidies which declined from 1.6 per cent of GDP in 1993-94 to 1.4 per cent of GDP in 1994-95 (RE). Defence expenditure declined marginally but remained above its level in 1992-93. Non-plan expenditure declined from 12.4 per cent of GDP in 1993-94 to 12.0 per cent of GDP in 1994-95 (RE). Plan expenditure declined marginally to 5.2 per cent of GDP.

Savings and Capital Formation

Gross dissavings of the Central Government, which had shot up from 1.2 per cent of GDP in 1992-93 to 2.5 per cent of GDP in 1993-94 improved to 1.9 per cent of GDP in 1994-95 (RE). Further, as per the Economic and Functional Classification of the Central Government's Budget, consumption expenditure declined from 4.0 per cent of GDP in 1993-94 to 3.8 per cent in 1994-95 (RE). Transfer payments also declined by 0.2 per cent of GDP during this period. Gross capital formation out of budgetary resources consisting of physical and financial assets as a per cent of GDP increased by 0.2 points from 5.6 per cent in 1993-94 to 5.8 per cent in 1994-95 (RE).

Government Debt

Government debt, consisting of internal and external liabilities, fell from 69.7 per cent of GDP in 1993-94 to 67.0 per cent in 1994-95 (RE). Internal liabilities declined from the 53.8 per cent of GDP in 1993-94 to 51.9 per cent of GDP in 1994-95 (RE). The decline in internal liabilities was mainly because of the decrease in internal debt from 30.7 per cent of GDP in 1993-94 to 29.0 per cent in 1994-95 (RE). 'Other internal liabilities' consisting of Small Savings and Provident Funds etc. registered a smaller decrease from 23.1 per cent of GDP in 1993-94 to 22.9 per cent in 1994-95 (RE). The share of market borrowings in total internal liabilities, which was 32.4 per cent in 1980-81 and has been declining over the years because of a reduction in the Statutory Liquidity Ratio, reached 25.7 per cent in 1993-94. However, the share increased to 26.8 per cent during 1994-95 (RE) because of the incentive provided by market based interest rates on government securities.

Central Government Budget : 1995-96

Consolidation of fiscal balance, tax reform, social equity and poverty alleviation were the main considerations in the 1995-96 budget. The fiscal deficit was budgeted to decline to 5.5 per cent of GDP mainly through reduction in the total expenditure. A number of new schemes/programmes were introduced in the budget for the welfare of poor, especially for those in rural areas. The Central Government also decided to participate in the phased expansion of the schemes for providing mid-day meals for school children. National Social Assistance Scheme was introduced for providing old age pension, lump-sum survivor benefits to poor household on the death of primary bread winner and sustenance for pre-natal and post-natal maternity care to women belonging to poor households below thc poverty line. Establishment of a new Rural Infrastructure Development Fund, a Technology Development and Modernization Fund for the Small Scale Industries and exclusive line of credit to Cooperatives and Regional Rural Banks in predominately tribal districts for meeting the credit needs of Scheduled Tribes were some of the other schemes introduced in the budget for 1995-96.

Budget Deficit

The budget deficit, defined as receipts minus total expenditure, both revenue and capital, is estimated to decline from Rs. 6000 crore as per the revised estimates of 1994-95 to Rs. 5000 crore in 1995-96 (BE). The deficit which crossed the budget estimates in April, 1995 itself kept on rising and touched the peak of Rs. 21786 crore in the first week of August, 1995. Thereafter, it started declining till the end of September, 1995 when it was Rs. 12156 crore. After that the budget deficit started rising once again. At the end of December, 1995 the budget deficit was again low at Rs. 7064 crore. But within a week, it again increased to Rs. 14319 crore. The movement of budget deficit in 1995-96 was in contrast with its movement in 1994-95, when except for the three months period of May of July, the budget was in surplus. This was due to less borrowing from the market in 1995-96 compared to 1994-95. The budget was, however, again in deficit at the end of 1994-95.

The fiscal deficit, defined as the difference between the revenue receipts plus non-debt capital receipts and the total expenditure including loans, net of repayments has also been at higher levels during 1995-96. At the end of June, 1995, the fiscal deficit was Rs. 21156 crore against Rs. 16792 crore at the end of June, 1994. It increased further to Rs. 28297 crore at the end of September, 1995 against Rs. 23003 crore at the end of September, 1994.

TABLE 13.2. 1994-95 and 1995-96 Budgets at a Glance

(Rs. crore)

		1993-94 Actuals	*1994-95 Budget Estimates*	*1994-95 Revised Estimates*	*1995-96 Budget Estimates*
1.	Revenue Receipts	75,453	86,084	88,770	1,00,787
2.	Tax Revenue (Net to Centre)	53,449	62,742	64,988	74,374
3.	Non-Tax Revenue	22,004	23,342	23,782	26,413
4.	Capital Receipts	55,440	59,615	67,502	66,364
5.	Recoveries of Loans	6,191	6,700	6,700	6,730
6.	Other Receipts	–48	4,000	5,767	7,000
7.	Borrowings and other Liabilities	49,297	48,915	55,035	52,634
8.	Total Receipts (1+4)	1,30,893	1,45,699	15,6272	1,67,151

(Contd.)

TABLE 13.2 *(Contd.)*

		1993-94 Actuals	*1994-95 Budget Estimates*	*1994-95 Revised Estimates*	*1995-96 Budget Estimates*
9.	Non-Plan Expenditure	98,998	1,05,117	1,13,511	1,23,651
10.	On Revenue Account	83,545	90,749	93,965	1,06,998
11.	Interest Payments	36,695	46,000	44,000	52,000
12.	On Capital Account	15,453	14,368	19,546	16,653
13.	Plan Expenditure	42,855	46,582	48,761	48,500
14.	On Revenue Account	24,624	28,062	28,937	29,330
15.	On Capital Account	18,231	18,520	19,824	19,170
16.	Total Expenditure (9+13)	1,41,853	1,51,699	1,62,272	1,72,151
17.	Revenue Expenditure (10+14)	1,08,169	1,18,811	1,22,902	1,36,328
18.	Capital Expenditure (12+15)	33,684	32,888	39,370	35,823
19.	Revenue Deficit (1-17)	32,716	32,727	34,132	35,541
20.	Budgetary Deficit (8-16)	10,960	6,000	6,000	5,000
21.	Fiscal Deficit [(1+5+6)- 16-7+20]	60,257	54,915	61,035	57,634
22.	Fiscal Deficit adjusted for Small Savings Loans to State & Union Territory Governments	55,257	49,763	51,386	50,634
23.	Primary Deficit (21-11)	23,562	8,915	17,035	5,634

Notes :

Non-tax revenues—Interest receipts on loans to states, dividends and profits of Central PSUs, external grants and receipts of Union Territories.

Recoveries of loans—Recovery of loans to states.

Other receipts—Money raised through disinvestment of PSU stock.

Plan and non-plan expenditure—Plan expenditure for asset creation under the on-going five-year plan gives rise in non-plan expenditure in the form of maintenance of assets over the subsequent plan periods.

Non-Plan revenue and capital expenditure—Interest payments, defence expenditure and expenditure on social and economic infrastructure.

Plan revenue and capital expenditure—All central plans and plan assistance for States and Union territories.

Budget deficit—Difference between total revenues and total expenditure.

Revenue deficit—Difference between revenue receipts and revenue expenditure.

Fiscal deficit—Difference between all receipts except borrowings and total expenditure. Alternatively, total of budget deficit and borrowings.

Primary deficit—Difference between fiscal deficit and interest payments.

Budget estimates—Estimates presented at the beginning of the fiscal year.

Revised estimates—Presented at the end of a fiscal year, based on partly actual and partly estimated figures.

Actual—Figures are presented two years after the presentation of budget estimates.

Source : National Budget 1995-96.

TABLE 13.3. Central Plan Outlay 1995-96

(Rs. crore)

	1994-95 Budget Estimates	*1994-95 Revised Estimates*	*1995-96 Budget Estimates*
Budget Support	27,278	27,934	28,994
Internal and Extra Budgetary Resources of Public Enterprises etc.	42,863	40,382	49,855
Total-Central Plan Outlay	70,141	68,316	78,849
Central Plan Outlay by Sectors			
Agriculture	2,637	2,853	3,022
Rural Development	6,036	5,637	6,540
Irrigation and Flood Control	261	233	288
Energy	22,857	20,349	23,795
Industry and Minerals	10,394	8,872	11,598
Transport	11,344	11,668	14,088
Communications, Science, Technology & Environment	7,191	7,495	8,318
Environment	1,362	1,408	1,617
Social Services	7,381	8,251	8,839
Others	678	1,550	744
Total	70,141	68,316	78,849

Source: National Budget 1995-96.

TABLE 13.4. Plan Expenditure and Receipts

Expenditure *(Rs. crore)*

	1994-95 Budget Estimates	*1994-95 Revised Estimates*	*1995-96 Budget Estimates*
Plan Expenditure			
A. Revenue Expenditure			
1. Central Plan	18078	17796	19853
2. Central assistance for States & Union Territory Plans	9984	11141	9477
State Plan	9815	10931	9211
Union Territory Plan	169	210	266
Total—Revenue Plan Expenditure	28062	28937	29330
B. Capital Expenditure			
1. Central Plan	9200	10138	9141
2. Central assistance for States & Union Territory Plans	9320	9686	10029
State Plans	8296	9204	9515
Union Territory Plan	394	482	514

(Contd.)

TABLE 13.4 (*Contd.*)

	1994-95 Budget Estimates	*1994-95 Revised Estimates*	*1995-96 Budget Estimates*
Total—Capital Plan Expenditure	18520	19824	19170
Total—Plan Expenditure	66582	48761	48500
Total Central assistance for State & UT Plans	19304	20827	19506
Total—Expenditure**	151690	162272	172151
**(Excluding expenditure matched by receipts)			
Debt Servicing			
1. Repayment of debt*	63632	62258	70480
2. Total Interest Payments	46000	44000	52000
3. Total debt Servicing (1+2)	109632	106258	122480
4. Revenue Receipts	86084	88770	100787
5. Percentage of 2 to 4	53.4	49.5	51.5
* Excluding discharge of 91 days treasury bills, reserve funds and deposits not bearing interest and suspense transactions.			
Receipts			
1. Tax Revenue			
Gross Tax Revenue	87136	89831	103762
Corporation Tax	12480	13250	15500
Income Tax	10925	11000	15500
Interest Tax	1044	1000	1000
Expenditure Tax Act, 1987	210	170	175
Wealth Tax	125	80	90
Gift Tax	5	14	10
Customs	25200	26450	29500
Union Excise Duties	36700	36900	42780
Service Tax	–	375	600
Other Taxes and Duties	261	401	406
Taxes of Union Territories	186	191	201
Less States' Share	24394	24843	29388
Income Tax	8205	8560	9734
Union Excise Duties	16189	16283	19654
Less : Assignment of UT taxes to Local Bodies	–	–	–
Net Tax Revenue	62742	64988	74374
2. Non-Tax Revenue			
Interest Receipts	15978	16234	18419
Dividends and Profits	2793	2721	2946
External grants	1365	1176	1154
Other Non-Tax Revenue	3014	3467	3698
Receipts of Union Territories	192	184	196
Total-Non-Tax Revenue	23342	23782	26413
Total Revenue Receipts	86084	88770	100787

TABLE 13.5. Non Plan Expenditure and Receipts

Expenditure *(Rs. crore)*

Items	*Budget Estimates 1994-95*	*Revised Estimates 1994-95*	*Budget Estimates 1995-96*
Non-Plan Expenditure			
A. Revenue Expenditure			
1. Interest Payments	46000	44000	52000
2. Defence Revenue Expenditure	16169	16611	18146
3. Major Subsidies (Food, Fertilisers and Export promotion)	8300	10826	10965
4. Interest and Other Subsidies	1643	1436	–
5. Debt Relief to Farmers	341	341	–
6. Postal Deficit	125	313	287
7. Police	2623	2685	2837
8. Pensions	3604	3651	3851
9. Other General Services (Organs of State, tax collection, external affairs etc.)	3665	3939	4208
10. Social Services (Education, Health, Broadcasting etc.)	2613	2722	2750
11. Economic Services (Agriculture, Industry, Power, Transport, Communications, Science and Technology etc.)	3181	4204	3720
12. Grants to States and U.T. Govts.	2334	2327	6016
13. Expenditure of Union Territories without Legislature	523	550	577
14. Grants to Foreign Governments	187	153	205
Total-Revenue Expenditure			
B. Capital Expenditure			
1. Defence Capital	6831	6933	7354
2. Other Non-Plan Capital Outlay	1402	1664	1485
3. Loans to Public Enterprises	637	911	439
4. Loans to State and U.T. Governments	5228	9739	7073
5. Loans to Foreign Governments	89	77	100
6. Other Non-Plan Loans	210	251	231
7. Expenditure of Union Territories without Legislature	(-)29	(-)29	(-)29
Total Non-Plan Expenditure	105117	113511	123651

(Contd.)

TABLE 13.5 (*Contd.*)

Items	*Budget Estimates 1994-95*	*Revised Estimates 1994-95*	*Budget Estimates 1995-96*
Total-Capital Expenditure	14368	19546	16653
Defence Expenditure (Revenue and Capital)	23000	23544	25500
Receipts			
Capital Receipts @			
Recoveries of Loans[1]	6700	6700	6730
Market Borrowings	3700	3700	3700
Other Medium & Long term Loans #	11000	17000	19000
Short term Loans #	12000	3340	4387
Gold Bonds 1998	1225	1100	65
External Assistance	4279	3947	4456
Disinvestment of equity holding in Public sector enterprises	4000	5237	7000
Issue of bonus shares*	–	530	–
Small Savings, PPF and Deposit Scheme for Retiring Government Servants*	6000	14000	8000
State Provident Funds	1800	1000	2000
Special Deposits	8100	8900	8964
Others	811	1148	2062
Total-Capital Receipts	59615	67502	65364
Total Receipts[2]	145699	156272	167151
1. Excluding recoveries of short-term loans and advances from States and Loans to Government servants, etc.	1131	1131	1132
2. Excluding receipts offset by matching expenditure (Details in Annexure 12 to Receipts Budget, 1995-96)			
* Less-Share of States	-5152	-9649	-7000
Net to Centre	848	4351	1000

@ The receipts (other than recoveries of loans) are net receipts, gross receipts minus repayments.

These include Zero Coupon Bonds and loans in conversion of maturing Treasury Bills.

These include 364 days Treasury Bills.

* Contra adjustments on the receipt side offsetting acquisition of Bonus Shares shown as expenditure in the Expenditure Budget.

TABLE.13.6. Interest as Per cent of Total Expenditure of the Central Government

Year	*Interest as % of Expenditure*
1990-91	20%
1991-92	24%
1992-93	25%
1993-94	26%
1994-95	27%
1995-96 (Estimate)	30%

Tax Reforms 1991-92 to 1995-96

Direct Taxes

* Initial exemption limit for levy of income tax was raised from Rs. 22,000 in 1991 to Rs, 40,000 in 1995. The number of slabs were reduced from 4 to 3. The maximum marginal rate of personal income tax was reduced from 56 per cent, inclusive of surcharge, to 40 per cent.
* Introduction of presumptive tax (lump-sum) for small traders, retailers and small road transport operators.
* A number of provisions were introduced to widen the tax base. These include presumptive taxation for small business, estimated income scheme for persons engaged in the business of civil construction, plying, leasing or hiring of trucks; tax deduction at source introduced on interest income on term deposits, income in respect of units of mutual funds, professional fees and host of contracts.
* The incentive structure for savings in the form of financial asset has been strengthened. The wealth tax, which was earlier applicable to all personal assets, has been modified to exempt all productive assets including financial assets such as bank deposits, shares and other securities. The threshold limit for levy of wealth tax was raised to Rs. 15 lakhs.
* The rates of corporate income tax, which were 51.75 per cent for a widely held company and 57.5 per cent for a closely held company have been unified and reduced to 46 per cent. All these rates are inclusive of a 15 per cent surcharge. Surcharge is leviable only in case of companies having income above Rs. 75000. Without the 15 per cent surcharge, the rate of corporate tax would be 40 per cent which is the same as the maximum marginal rate on personal taxation. Long term capital gains tax on domestic companies was reduced from 40 to 30 per cent.
* Tax rate on foreign companies (branches) was reduced from 65 to 55 per cent. There is no surcharge on foreign companies.
* Five year tax holiday for investments in infrastructure facilities (high ways, bridges, airports, ports and mass repaid transport), power generation and distribution, in backward States and electronics hardware and software parks.

Indirect Taxes

Customs duties

* Import duties were inordinately high and, in several cases more than 300 per cent prior to reform. A phased reduction in the peak rate of customs duty was undertaken in each of the five budgets since 1991, 110 per cent in 1992, 85 per cent in 1993, 65 per cent in 1994 and to 50 per cent in 1995 with the exception of passenger baggage, alcoholic beverages, dried grapes, almonds and ball and roller bearings.
* The import duty on capital goods for general projects and machinery which was 85 per cent prior to reforms was brought down and unified for nearby 80 per cent of machinery, at 25 per cent in 1995. Reduction in customs duty on power projects and related machinery to 20 per cent and for fertiliser projects to nil. This was accompanied by lowering of duties on ferrous and non ferrous metals to 35/40 per cent in 1995.
* The number of duty rates have been brought down to 12 (Including nil rate) at present.

Excise taxes

* Switchover from a system where excise duties were specific and numerous and varying in nature with a large number of exemptions to one largely based on ad valorem basis with fewer duty rates and exemptions.
* Ambit of MODVAT (tax credit for taxes paid on inputs) extended to capital goods, specified quality control, testing, pollution control and R & D equipment, POL and spun yarn made from fibres.
* Switchover from specific to uniform ad valorem rates of 10 per cent on all petroleum products with the exception of motor spirit.
* The number of duty rates have been brought down to 10 (including nil rate) at present.

Service tax

* Introduction of service tax by imposition of a 5 per cent tax on amount of telephone bills, premium payments for non life insurance and on commission/brokerage charged by the stock brokers.

Import Duties

In the area of customs duty the objective was to reduce the high rates of import duty gradually, so as to lower costs of production and improve competitiveness of user industries while allowing domestic producers facing competition from imported goods reasonable time to adjust. The acceleration in the industrial growth in 1995-96 on the top of robust trends in 1994-95, demonstrates conclusively that customs duty reforms have succeeded in imparting the necessary dynamism to industrial production. In addition, the acceleration in exports reflects enhanced competitive strength of our industry. However, customs duties, though lowered in the past five budgets, still remain much above the levels of our competitor countries.

The thrust of import tariff reforms in the budget for 1995-96 was to further reduce the cost of inputs to domestic producers, promote competition and efficiency and lower prices paid by Indian consumers and thereby check the potential for inflation. Towards this end, the peak rate of customs duty was further brought down from 65 to 50 per cent accompanied with significant decreases in duty rates on key intermediates and capital goods to promote investment. In addition, attempt was made to reduce dispersion in tariff rates and minimize anomalies.

14

INFLATION, PRICES AND PUBLIC DISTRIBUTION SYSTEM

Inflationary pressures which had resurfaced from mid-October 1994 started decelerating after January 1995, when the annual inflation rate had peaked at 12 per cent. By mid April, it had declined to single digit level and, at the close of 1995, it decelerated steeply to touch a low of 6 per cent. January 1996 saw the inflation rate decline further to 5 per cent (provisional). Reasonably good rainfall and comfortable food stock situation together with liberal imports of some essential commodities to make up for the shortfall in domestic supply aroused expectations of a declining trend in the prices. But these expectations were sustained largely by the sharp drop in monetary growth which curbed excessive demand side pressures on inflation.

The movement of wholesale prices during the past five years 1991-92 to 1995-96, throws up three phases of very distinct growth paths. The first phase represented escalating inflationary path with annual inflation rate attaining a peak level of over 16 per cent in September, 1991, that is just about the time the new economic reform policies became operational. The next phase saw a gradually decelerating growth path with inflation rate touching a low of 6.9 per cent in April-May 1993. The third phase (1994-95) exhibited again an uptrend in growth of prices, but the inflationary undercurrent was not as strong as it was in the first phase (1991-92) and it peaked at about 12 per cent by January 1995. At the beginning of fourth phase inflation rate decelerated to about 5 per cent level in January 1996.

The most remarkable phenomenon during 1995 was that growth in prices of primary articles was only 4.4 per cent (December 1995/December 1994) as against 14.4 per cent in the same period of preceding year. The fuel, power, light sub-sector representing mostly energy products whose prices are still administered, recorded a modest growth of just 1.1 per cent at the end of 1995 (December 1995 over December 1994) thus contributing very little to current year's inflation.

The manufactured sector recorded an inflation rate of 8 per cent by the end of December 1995 over December 1994 as against 10.8 per cent in the corresponding period of previous year. Primary articles contributed 24.5 per cent to the annual growth of prices (6 per cent) whereas manufactured products group contributed a disproportionately large share of about 74 per cent, solely because this group registered 8 per cent growth in prices compared to only 4.4 per cent growth in primary articles. Thus this year's sharp deceleration in the annual inflation rate should therefore be seen more as a result of stronger influence of much slower growth of prices in primary articles.

Among primary articles major part of the annual growth has been contributed by food articles (14.2 per cent) attributed to the sharp rise in the prices of fruits and vegetables. Among manufactured products the key products that recorded a higher annual rise than last year and contributed the major proportion in the annual growth of prices in manufacturing sector were textiles (27.3 per cent), paper and paper products (6.8 per cent), rubber and plastic products (3.7 per cent), non-metallic mineral products (6.3 per cent) and transport equipment and parts (2.6 per cent).

Financial year changes in WPI in 1995-96

The 4.3 per cent growth in prices in the first three quarters (April-December) of this financial year, was almost half of the growth registered in the corresponding period of last year. From 3 per cent growth recorded in the WPI in the first quarter, the second quarter (July-September 1995) growth was only 1.5 per cent. Thus the cumulative rise in wholesale prices of 4.5 per cent in the first-half of 1995-96 was much lower than 6.1 per cent rise in the first half of the last year, thus confirming the effectiveness of supply and demand management policies adopted in early 1995-96. In the third-quarter prices decelerated further and actually declined by 0.2 per cent. The cumulative growth in prices was thus 4.3 per cent during April-December, which was half of the price rise in the same period of last financial year.

Primary Articles

The wholesale prices of primary articles increased by 4.2 per cent in the first three quarters of the financial year, which is about one-third of the rise (12.6 per cent) in the corresponding period last year. In the first quarter (April-June) of 1995-96 the rise in wholesale prices was only 3.7 per cent compared to the rise of 6.9 per cent in the first quarter of last year. This modest rise indicated strong disinflationary trend in the current year even though major part of the rise during the quarter was contributed by the food articles where the escalation in the prices of foodgrains, fruits and vegetables and tea was larger than last year. This trend persisted through the third quarter and hence foodgrains, fruits and vegetables and tea remained the major contributors to the rise in the prices of primary group of articles. Prices of food articles—gram, eggs, fish and meat and coffee-registered negative growth during the current financial year. Contrary to this, non-food articles which include cotton, registered negative growth of 1.7 per cent in the first quarter but rose in the second quarter, through marginally, and through the year registered a rise of only 0.3 per cent which was largely due to the escalation in the prices of oilseeds. This was a very modest rise compared to the rise of 11.2 per cent in the last financial year. Prices of minerals, the third constituent of the primary articles sub-group, rose by 5.1 per cent which is only marginally lower than the rise of 5.7 per cent in the same period last year.

Manufactured products

During the current year prices of manufactured products registered a rise of 5.2 per cent which is a lower rise as against the rise of 7.8 per cent in the preceding year. Rise of 3.2 per cent in the first quarter (April-June), was almost same as the rise in the corresponding period last year. By the end of second quarter (July-September) the rise of 4.8 per cent was a subdued rise compared to the rise of 6.1 per cent registered last year. The price rise was lower in cement (4.8 per cent), chemicals and chemical products (3 per cent) and machinery and machine tools (3.3 per cent). But other manufactured items showed a sharper rise than last year. These are textiles (7.9 per cent), paper (10.5 per cent), rubber and plastic products (7.8 per cent), metals and transport equipment (over 4 per cent).

Essential Commodities

The wholesale price of 30 essential commodities recorded a rise of 5.3 per cent during the current year upto December, 1995 as against last year's rise of 10.4 per cent. The contribution of this group to current year's inflation was nearly 27 per cent, and like last year, was disproportionate to its weight in WPI.

Consumer Price Index Movement

The movement in retail prices as measured by various Consumer Price Index Number series, namely (1) Industrial Workers (CPI-IW), (2) Urban Non-Manual Employees (CPI-UNME), and (3) Agricultural Labours (CPI-AL), indicate that inflationary undercurrent in retail prices moved in tandem with wholesale prices recording a peak rise in July 1994 (11.1 per cent in CPI-IW and 13.4 per cent in CPI-AL). But in CPI-UNME which had a slower rise, the peak rise was reached late in October, 1994. The distinctive feature of the CPI series this year is that even when there was a gradual deceleration in the growth of wholesale prices, the point-to-point annual inflation based on CPI has stayed at two-digit level through November 1995. This indicates that deceleration in retail prices is slower so far compared to wholesale prices since May, 1995. This is apparently so because the consumer price series assign higher weightage to food items than the wholesale price series and since inflation rate based on WPI was still over 8 per cent upto end of November 1995, the sharp fall recorded in December 1995 to 6 per cent would get reflected in CPI series only thereafter. Already in December 1995, it had declined to 9.7 per cent.

The CPI-IW, the most common and widely used series indicates that by October 1995 in the current financial year the retail prices registers a growth rate of 8.9 per cent as against 8.2 per cent in the corresponding month last year. The higher rate of growth is mainly ascribed to the uptrend seen in the group of essential commodities (which have a weight of 49 per cent in CPI-IW series) whose prices were higher by 10.2 per cent in October 1995. Apparently, vegetables especially potatoes, onions, arhar amongst pulses and edible oils were the major contributors to the uptrend in prices at retail level.

Steps taken to Control Inflation

Supply side measures

- Continuation of FCI's open market sale of rice and wheat through 1995-96 to check market price. By November, 1995, 7.09 lakh tonnes of rice and 30.10 lakh tonnes of wheat had been sold/lifted.

* Allowing import of edible oils (except coconut oil) under OGL at a reduced duty of 30 per cent.
* Importing 1.5 lakh tonnes of palmolein at concessional duty of 20 per cent for supply through PDS.
* Continuing OGL import policy for sugar and allowing import of 2 lakh tonnes for augmenting PDS stocks.
* Increase by 5 per cent allocation of levy sugar for PDS effective August, 1995.
* Pulses import under OGL with duty reduced to 5 per cent.
* Adjustment in trade and tariff policies in the Budget for current year to ensure that domestic prices of industrial products remain competitive.
* Substantial reduction in excise duties on a number of items expected to accelerate the pace of industrial revival and raise industrial growth.
* Strengthening of public distribution system and its expansion in RPDS areas.

Demand side measures

* Reduction of fiscal deficit in the budget proposals for current financial year to 5.5 per cent of GDP as against 6.7 per cent in the last financial year.
* Placing a cap on Central Government's borrowings from the RBI through the issue of ad-hoc Treasury Bills and containing monetary growth through a series of measures including raising of CRR and sale of Government securities by the RBI.

Public Distribution System (PDS)

Availability of foodgrains-mainly rice and wheat, sugar, edible oils and kerosene is ensured through a net work of fair price shops (FPSs) where each such shop is envisaged to serve a population of 2000. From over 4 lakhs in March, 1992 the number of FPSs rose to over 4.33 lakhs as on 31 March, 1995, of which the number operating in rural areas rose from 3.05 lakhs to 3.30 lakhs. In urban areas their number rose from 94 thousand to 1.02 lakhs. For the tribal, hill and arid area populations remotely located and having poor infrastructure, additional items like tea, soap, pulses and iodised salt are made available under the scheme known as Revamped Public Distribution Scheme (RPDS). This scheme, started in June, 1992 in 1700 blocks, is now operating in 1775 blocks. Additional quantity of 3.1 lakh tonnes of foodgrains of rice and wheat are envisaged to be distributed in these areas. By December 1995, the number of fair price shops operating in RPDS areas is reported to be 102264 out of which, 54500 fair price shops had been brought under the door step delivery scheme. It has now been decided that the geographical coverage of RPDS would be extended to all the 2446 Employment Assurance Scheme (EAS) Blocks. Foodgrains—rice and wheat—are allocated to States/UTs for RPDS blocks at prices lower by Rs. 50 per quintal than the issue price for normal PDS and, it is ensured further, that the retail price at RPDS shops is not higher than CIP by more than 25 paise/kg.

Supply of sugar for PDS was maintained at a level of 3.36 to 3.88 lakh tonnes per month during 1995-96. Allocations were raised to 4.02 lakh tonnes in October and 3.60 lakh tonnes in November 1995 to meet the festival season requirement. During 1994-95, the Government imported 9.77 lakh tonnes and in 1995-96 about 2 lakh tonnes of sugar exclusively for augmenting PDS stocks. Government also arranged import of 1.5 lakh tonnes of edible oil (palmolein) at concessional duty of 20 per cent, well in advance of the festival season for distribution in States so as to check speculative price spurt in edible oils.

Foodgrains: Central Government's food stocks have three important functional components—food security reserve, operational stocks and market intervention stocks. Stocks are released each month for distribution to the State Governments for supply through the PDS. Each State is allocated a prescribed quantity based on past demand, off-take trends, relative need and other related factors besides adhering to the norm of maintaining the prescribed minimum buffer stock for meeting food security needs. Stocks are also released for open sale to augment supplies and help moderate the open market prices.

Foodgrains Allocation and Off-take : Allocation of 11-12 million tonnes of rice and 9-10 million tonnes of wheat to States for distribution through PDS has generally been the norm in the past few years. However, the actual off take by the States in three successive years, 1992-93 to 1994-95, has been much lower, reflecting perhaps better free market access and narrowing down of price differential between PDS retail price and the free market price. The off-take had particularly dropped more in case of wheat. During 1995-96 (till November 95), the off-take of wheat has been only 3.17 million tonnes, a little more than the corresponding period last year. As for rice, the annual allocation has continuously increased from 9.61 million tonnes in 1990-91 to 13.32 million tonnes in 1994-95. As against these allocations the annual off-take of rice which was 9.95 million tonnes in 1991-92, dropped to 8.88 million tonnes in 1993-94 and further down to 7.98 million tonnes in 1994-95. In 1995-96, however, rice off-take was 6.21 million tonnes till November 1995 which is higher than the off-take of 5.20 million tonnes in the corresponding period last year.

New Schemes for Utilisation of Surplus Food Stocks

The Prime Minister in his Independence Day Speech on 15th August 1994, announced New Schemes for utilisation of surplus public stocks of foodgrains for the benefit of the economically and socially weaker sections of the society. The Schemes now under operation are :

Release of Subsidised Wheat to MFIL and its Franchised Units

A quantity of 1.87 lakh tonnes of wheat was earmarked for supply to the Modern Food Industries India Ltd. (MFIL) during 1994-95 priced at Rs. 3020 per tonne, which was Rs. 1,000 per tonne lower than the Central Issue Price for PDS. Out of 1.87 lakh tonnes, 1.5 lakh tonnes was meant for bread manufacturing and the remaining 0.37 lakh tonnes for production of energy foods. The supply of low priced wheat was to ensure reduction in the prices of bread by 50 paise for 800 gms. loaf and 25 paise for 400 gms. loaf and keeping the price of energy foods frozen during the period of supply of wheat at concessional rate. Subsequently, it was decided to release 2358 tonnes wheat per month from March 1995 to the 'franchised units' of MFIL for bread manufacturing at par with MFIL and subject to same terms and conditions.

Supply of Subsidised Foodgrains to SC/ST/OBC Hostels

This Scheme was launched in October, 1994. A quantity of 1.68 lakh tonnes of foodgrains (rice and wheat) per annum was earmarked to be issued to Hostels having at least two-third inmates belonging to SC/ST/OBC categories, at a price which is Rs. 500 per tonne lower than the Central Issue Prices for PDS.

Employment Generation Scheme

An annual quantity of 5 lakh tonnes of foodgrains (rice and wheat) for a period of 5 years, was allocated at concessional price which was Rs. 1,000 per tonne lower than the Central Issue Prices for PDS, for Employment Generation through manufacture of food products by families falling below poverty line. Out of this allocation, 3.5 lakh tonnes was for rural areas and the balance 1.5 lakh tonnes for urban areas.

Mid-Day Meals Scheme

The Ministry of Human Resource Development launched on 15 August 1995 the Mid-Day Meals Scheme for the benefit of students enrolled in Primary Schools in 2368 RPDS/EAS Blocks. The foodgrains for the Scheme are supplied to States/UTs free of cost. In addition, handling/transport charges were also be reimbursed to States by the Ministry of HRD (Department of Education) subject to a maximum ceiling of Rs. 25 per quintal. The FCI would, however, charge economic cost of the foodgrains (rice and wheat) supplied by it to States/UTs under this scheme from the Ministry of HRD. The Ministry of HRD have placed a revolving fund of Rs. 150 crore at the disposal of FCI for implementation of the scheme. The scheme is to be extended to all other Low Female Literacy (LFL) Blocks (2005) during 1996-97 and to all Primary Schools in the country, 828 Blocks and 3,000 Nagar Palikas during 1997-98.

Open Market Sale of Foodgrains by FCI

Food Corporation of India (FCI) was authorised to sell wheat and rice in the open market to serve the twin objective of disposing of some of its surplus stock and to check the rise in their market prices as a part of its market intervention function to moderate supply side effects on inflation. It sold 79.47 lakh tonnes of wheat from October, 1993 to March, 1995.

15

MONETARY POLICY

A number of monetary policy measures were taken by Reserve Bank of India to contain the growth of money supply, namely, (1) increase of Cash Reserve Ratio (CRR) from 14 to 15 per cent; (2) imposition of CRRs on FCNR(B) and Non Resident Non Repatriate (NRNR) accounts; (3) lowering of interest rate on NRE accounts; (4) phasing out of exchange guarantee by Government under the FCNR scheme to moderate the foreign exchange inflow through Non-Resident deposits; and (5) a hike in ceiling interest rate on domestic term deposits by one percentage point. Apart from efforts to contain demand side pressures, supply side policy was geared to ensure availability of key commodities in short supply like cotton, sugar and edible oils through import, besides vigorous open market sale from central food stocks which helped dampen further price escalation in foodgrains.

Financial Sector Policy and System Reforms : 1991-92 to 1995-96

- Statutory Liquidity Ratio (SLR) on incremental net domestic demand and time liabilities (NDTL) reduced from 38.5 per cent in 1991-92 to 25 per cent.
- SLR securities to be continuously valued on same basis, as valued for the purpose of balance sheet of banks.
- Incremental Cash Reserve Ratio (CRR) of 10 per cent removed.
- Average CRR on net demand and time liabilities reduced from 15 tc 14 per cent. CRR removed from FCNR(B) and NRNR accounts. CRR on NRE deposits outstanding as on October 27, 1995 reduced from 14 per cent to 10 per cent. CRR on increase in NRE deposits removed.
- The prime lending rate of SBI and most other banks on general advances of over Rs. 2 lakh has come down by 2.5 percentage points to 16.5 per cent between 1991-92 and 1995-96.
- Interest rates on deposits and advances of all co-operative banks (except urban co-operative banks) deregulated, subject to a minimum lending rate of 12 per cent. Subsequently, interest rates on advances of primary co-operative banks were also deregulated subject to a minimum lending rate of 13 per cent.
- Bank Interest rate on loans above Rs. 2 lakh fully decontrolled. The number of administered interest rates on bank advances reduced from more than 20 in 1989-90 to 2 in 1994-95.
- Interest rate on domestic term deposits above two years and on NRNR accounts decontrolled.
- The State Bank of India Act 1955 amended effective October 15, 1993 to enable the bank to access the capital market and allow 10 per cent

voting rights to share holders. SBI raised over Rs. 3200 crore by public issue of equity shares and bonds. The RBI shareholding reduced from 99 per cent to 66 per cent.

- Nationalised banks enabled to access the capital market for debt and equity, through an amendment of The Banking Companies (Acquisition and Transfer of Undertakings) Act, 1970/1980. Oriental Bank of Commerce raised Rs. 387.24 crore through its first issue.
- Prudential norms for income recognition, classification of assets and provisioning for bad debts introduced for the first time. Provisioning requirement for non-performing advances of less than Rs. 25,000 raised to 10 per cent in 1995-96.
- As on March 31, 1995, 13 public sector banks have attained a capital to risk weighted assets ratio of 8 per cent. Full norm of 8 per cent already attained by foreign banks in India and by some Indian banks. All Indian Banks are to attain the norm by end March 1996.
- Recapitalisation of less strong public sector banks through budgetary support of Rs. 14987 crore till 1994-95. These banks simultaneously agreed with RBI to strengthen bank management and improve efficiency.
- Nine new private banks have already started functioning. 'In principle' approval given to two other proposals. Banks allowed to raise capital contribution from foreign financial institutions/banks upto 20 per cent and from Non-resident Indians, OCBs upto 40 per cent.
- Banks given freedom to open new branches and upgrade extension counters on attaining capital adequacy norms and prudential accounting standards. Subsequent to the review of the above policy, it has been decided that those banks which achieved 8 per cent CRAR, net profits for last 3 consecutive years, NPAs less than 15 per cent of total outstanding loans and minimum owned funds of Rs. 100 crore will be free open branches on their own as per a plan of action drawn up by the concerned individual banks and duly approved by the banks' board of directors. They are permitted to close non-viable branches other than in rural and semi-urban areas.
- A Board of Financial Supervision has been set up with an Advisory Council to strengthen the supervisory system of banks and financial institutions. An independent Department of Supervision also established in RBI in December 1993 for assisting the Board.
- Recovery of debts due to Banks and Financial Institutions Act, 1993, passed to set up Special Recovery Tribunals to facilitate quicker recoveries of loan arrears. Five tribunals started functioning and an Appellate Tribunal set up at Bombay.
- Banking Regulation Act, 1949, amended to enable a banking company to have a non-executive Chairman, upto three directors from among the directors of promoting institutions, to raise the ceiling for the exercise of voting rights for a shareholder to 10 per cent, and to raise the penalties for contravention of the Act.
- Union agreement in October 1993 paved way for faster computerisation in banks.

- Under Banking Ombudsmen Scheme 1995, eight Ombudsmen already appointed by RBI out of a total of 15 to look into and resolve customers' grievances in a Quick and inexpensive way.
- IFCI converted into a company and its maiden public issue raised over Rs. 600 crore as equity (including premium). IDBI act amended to broad base its ownership pattern IDBI raised capital through its maiden public issue.
- Capital adequacy norms for financial institutions' introduced.
- Prudential norms have been introduced for RRBs in a phased manner. Substantial equity support given to select banks to offset losses.

Financial Sector Operational Reforms : 1991-92 to 1995-96

- Bank lending norms liberalised and banks given freedom to decide levels of holding of individual items of inventories and receivables.
- Ceiling on term loans raised to Rs. 1000 crore for projects involving expansion/modernisation of power generation capacities.
- Scope of mandatory consortium arrangement narrowed to 76 large borrowal accounts in place of 934 accounts hitherto. As per the latest data of May 1995, the number of such borrowal accounts are 207. Borrowers allowed to induct new banks into a consortium and banks permitted to leave consortium after two years.
- Loan system introduced for delivery of bank credit. Banks required to bifurcate the maximum permissible bank finance of Rs. 20 crore and above into loan component of 40 per cent (short term working capital loan) and cash credit component of 60 per cent by December 31, 1995.
- Banks allowed to set their own interest rate on Post-shipment export credit in Rupees for over 90 days. The interest rate on loans over Rs. 2 lakh and that on deposits of maturities above 2 years deregulated.
- The banks were asked to maintain 85 per cent of amount of CRR required to be maintained during a reporting Fortnight from first working to the last but one working day.
- Minimum period of ready forward transactions (repose) in government and other approved securities by banks fixed at three days.
- Banks allowed to reduce their paid up capital at a time upto 25 per cent.
- Banks freed to fix its own foreign exchange open position limit subject to RBI approval.
- Guidelines issued to banks to ensure qualitative improvement in their customer service as a follow-up on the recommendations of the Committee on Customer Service in Banks.
- Convertibility clause no longer obligatory for assistance sanctioned by term lending institutions.
- Floating interest rate on financial assistance (linked to interest rate on 364 day treasury bills) introduced by some all India development banks.

Monetary Policy and Credit Control Measures 1995-96

- Money supply (M3) growth target of 15.5 per cent in 1995-96.

- The ceiling interest rate on term deposits of 46 days to 2 years prescribed at 12 per cent, and that on Non-Resident External (Rupee) Accounts deposits also raised to 12 per cent.
- Decontrol of interest rates for scheduled commercial banks' term domestic deposits of over two years.
- Interest rate on Post-shipment export credit in Rupees for over 90 days deregulated.
- Export Credit (Rupee) Refinance by RBI to scheduled commercial banks, to be 100 per cent of the increase in export credit over the monthly average level of 1992-93.
- Interest Rate on post-shipment export credit in US Dollars (PSCFC) upto 90 days raised to 7.5 per cent and that on such credit beyond 90 days and upto six months from the date of shipment raised to 9.5 per cent. Banks permitted to fix their own interest rates on PSCFC above 90 days and export credit not otherwise specified for PSCFC. The PSCFC scheme was later abolished with effect from February 8, 1996.
- The interest rate on refinance against such credit also raised to 6.5 per cent. Refinance limit reduced from 80 to 70 per cent of the outstanding PSCFC credit.
- Effective from October 31, 1995 a 15 per cent interest surcharge imposed on the outstandings under the import credit sub-limit. It was later raised to 25 per cent in February 1996.
- "Loan System" introduced in April 1995. Cash credit component restricted to 75 per cent of the maximum permissible bank finance (MPBF) for borrowers with assessed MPBF to Rs. 20 crore and above. The balance 25 per cent to be sanctioned by way of a short term loan for working capital purposes.
- Cash Credit component reduced to 60 per cent in September 1995, with bifurcation to be completed latest by December 31, 1995.
- The overall limit for lending by banks/financial institutions to non-banking finance companies (NBFCs) reduced : to three times the net owned funds (NOF) of equipment leasing/hire purchase companies with not less than 75 per cent of their assets (gross income) in equipment leasing and hire purchase : to two times the NOF of other equipment leasing/hire purchase companies and equal to NOF of other non-banking finance companies.
- Bridge loans by banks and financial institutions banned.
- Effective from April 29, 1995 rediscounting of commercial bills and derivative usance promissory notes required to be for a minimum period of 15 days.
- Private mutual funds approved by SEBI permitted to enter call/notice money/bill rediscounting market as lenders.
- Effective September 30, 1995 refinance limits against government and other approved securities raised from 0.5 per cent to 1 per cent of fortnightly average outstanding aggregate deposits in 1994-95 (April-March).

- Rate of interest on bank advances of over Rs. 2 lakh to depositors against term deposits deregulated.
- Daily minimum 85 per cent CRR requirement liberalised to be maintained only from the first working day of the reporting fortnight and not to apply on the last working day of the fortnight.
- Effective October 18, 1995 CRR on increase in NRER deposits, over level as on October 27, 1995 eliminated.
- The average CRR reduced from 15 per cent of 14.5 per cent effective from fortnight of November 11, 1995 and to 14 per cent effective from fortnight of December 9, 1995 and that on CRR on NRER deposits up to the level outstandings as on October 27, 1995 reduced to 10 per cent effective from the fortnight beginning January 6, 1996. From the same fortnight CRR on FCNR (B) and NRNR deposits removed.
- Scheduled commercial banks (including RRB's) required to adopt the same system of valuations of securities for SLR as for their balance sheets.
- Effective September 30, 1995 the minimum period for ready forward transactions (Repos) fixed at three days.
- Each scheduled commercial bank allowed to fix its own overnight open exchange position limit subject to approval by RBI. New limits of 16 banks approved.

16

POVERTY ALLEVIATION AND EMPLOYMENT

Budget provisions as shown in Table 16.1 were enhanced for poverty alleviation and employment generation. The Central Plan outlay for Rural Development, which encompasses the major programmes for poverty alleviation and employment generation, was raised by 148 per cent over the past three years to a level of Rs. 7700 crore in 1995-96 (BE). Five new schemes, namely, the National Social Assistance Programme (NSAP), the Mid-Day Meal Programme, the Rural Group Life Insurance Scheme (RGLIS), the Indira Mahila Yojana (IMY) and the Prime Minister's Integrated Urban Poverty Eradication Programme (PMIUPEP) were launched in 1995-96.

The Government has also accorded the highest priority to promoting sustainable, employment-intensive growth in its economic reform policies. As a result, the annual increment in total economy-wide employment per year in the economy, as estimated by the Planning Commission has increased to over 7 million in 1994-95 as compared to only 3 million in the crisis year of 1991-92.

The Planning Commission estimates the incidence of poverty in rural and urban areas of the country using the quinquennial survey data on household consumption expenditure released by the National Sample Survey Organisation (NSSO), coupled with the poverty lines as set out in the Report of The Task Force on Projection of Minimum Needs and Effective Consumption Demand, constituted by the Planning Commission in 1979. In view of the recent revisions in the aggregate private consumption expenditure made by CSO and the population data derived from census results, the poverty estimates for 1987-88 have been revised. Preliminary estimates have also become available for 1993-94, based on sub-sample 1 of the data on household consumption expenditure compiled by the NSSO in its 50th Round (1993-94); sub-sample 1 pertains to almost half of the total sample size of the survey. These estimates indicate that the percentage of India's population below the poverty line has declined from 25.49 per cent in 1987-88 to 18.96 per cent in 1993-94 (Table 16.2). This significant decline in the poverty ratio has occurred despite the major economic crisis of 1991-92.

TABLE 16.1. Central Plan Outlay for Major Schemes on Poverty Alleviation and Employment

(Rs. crore)

Ministry/Department/Scheme	*1992-93*		*1993-94*		*1994-95*		*1995-96*	*Per cent change over BEs*		
	(BE)	*(Actual)*	*(BE)*	*(Actual)*	*(BE)*	*(BE)*		*1995-96/ 1994-95*	*1995-96/ 1993-94*	*1995-96/ 1992-93*
1. *Rural Development* of which	3100	3596	5010	5437	7010	7320	7700	9.8	53.7	148.4
(a) Jawahar Rozgar Yojana (JRY)	2046	2545	3306	3306	3855	3535	3862	0.2	16.8	88.8
(b) Employment Assurance Scheme (EAS)	—	—	—	438	1200	1140	1570	30.8	—	—
(c) Integrated Rural Development Programme*	390	394	654	657	675	675	656	-2.8	0.3	68.2
(d) Rural Water Supply and Sanitation	480	481	770	770	950	870	1170	23.2	51.9	143.8
2. *Other Programmes*										
(a) Nehru Rozgar Yojana (NRY)	71	71	75	75	70	70	71	1.4	-5.3	—
(b) Scheme for Self Employment for Educated Unemployed Youth (SEEUY)	45	40	40	38	*	—	—	—	—	—
(c) Prime Minister's Rozgar Yojana (PMRY)	—	—	—	35	145	125	145	—	—	—
Total (including other Sectors)	48407		63936		70141		78849	12.4	23.3	62.9

* BE as per the Department of Rural Development and Planning Commission. It was revised upward within total BE for the Deptt. of Rural Development. In the Budget Papers BE were Rs. 375 crore, Rs. 630 crore, Rs. 624 crore and Rs. 640 crore for the years 1992-93, 1993-94, 1994-95 and 1995-96 respectively.

— Not available.

TABLE 16.2. Number and Percentage of Population below the Poverty line-All India

item	*1987-88 (Revised)*	*1993-94 (Preliminary)*
Rural		
Number of poor (million)	168.30	141.05
Percentage below poverty line	28.37	21.68
Urban		
Number of poor (million)	33.11	27.52
Percentage below poverty line	16.82	11.55
Combined		
Number of poor (million)	201.41	168.57
Percentage below poverty line	25.49	18.96

Notes : (i) The estimates for 1987-88 based on National Sample Survey on Consumer Expenditure of the 43rd round (July 1987-June 1988) have been revised recently on account of revision in the estimate of aggregate private consumption expenditure at the all India level made by the Central Statistical Organisation and the population data derived from the Census results.

(ii) The estimates for 1987-88 are derived by using the poverty line at Rs. 132.0 per capita per month for rural areas and Rs. 152.3 per capita per month for urban areas at 1987-88 prices, corresponding to the poverty lines of Rs. 49.1 and Rs. 56.6, respectively, for 1973-74.

(iii) The estimates for 1993-94 are derived by using the poverty line of Rs. 228.9 per capita per month for rural areas and Rs. 264.1 per capita per month for urban areas at 1993-94 prices, corresponding to the poverty lines of Rs. 49.1 and Rs. 56.6 respectively, for 1973-74.

(iv) The estimates for 1993-94 are based on sub-sample 1 of the household consumer expenditure collected in the survey of NSS 50th Round. Since sub-sample 1 pertains to almost half of the total sample size of the survey, they are subject to revision once the full sample data become available and as such they may be treated as preliminary.

(v) The number of persons below poverty line relates to the population as on 1st October 1987 and 1st October 1993 for 1987-88 and 1993-94 respectively.

(vi) The difference between the aggregate all India private consumption expenditure estimated by the Central Statistical Organisation in its National Accounts Statistics and that derived from the NSSO data has been adjusted prorata among the different expenditure groups of the population, in the absence of any other information to allocate them.

Labour and Employment

By according the highest priority to labour intensive growth in its economic reform policies, the additional employment increased from 3.00 million in 1991-

92 to 7.18 million in 1994-95 (Table 16.3). Additional employment opportunities of the order of 18.78 million are estimated to have been generated during 1992-93 to 1994-95. This implies an average rate of employment growth at 2.03 per cent per annum, which is higher than the average annual rate of employment growth of 1.78 per cent during the preceding seven years (1985-92). These trends are reassuring that the employment content of growth has increased in the process of economic reforms.

TABLE 16.3. Estimates of Employment

Year	*Total Employment (million)*	*Annual percentage increase in total employment*	*Additional Employment Generated (million)*
1989-90	292.89	-	-
1990-91	298.73	1.99	5.84
1991-92	301.73	1.00	3.00
1992-93	308.31	2.18	6.58
1993-94	313.33	1.63	5.02
1994-95	320.51	2.29	7.18

Source : Planning Commission

In order to protect the workers against loss of income due to retirement, about 7 lakh additional employees have been brought under the Provident Fund scheme by the end of 1994-95 by launching special drive.

The Employees' Provident Fund and Miscellaneous Provisions (Amendment) Act was also amended and a Pension Scheme was framed for provident fund subscribers. The scheme as notified on 16.11.1995 has provision for the payment of monthly pension in contingencies like Superannuation on attaining the age of 58 years, retirement, permanent total disablement, death during service, death after retirement etc. It also provides for Children Pension & Orphan Pension. It is expected that about 18 million provident fund subscribers would be benefited from this scheme.

The eligibility ceiling of wages for coverage under the Employees's Provident Fund and Miscellaneous Provisions Act was also enhanced from Rs. 3,500 to Rs. 5,000 with effect from 1st October 1994. It is estimated that this would benefit about 10 lakh employees.

The Government also issued two Ordinances, viz. (a) The Building and Other Construction Workers (Regulation of Employment & Conditions of Services) Ordinance, 1995; and (b) The Building and Other Construction Workers Welfare (Cess) Ordinance, 1995. The Ordinances are expected to benefit a substantial number of the 8.5 million construction workers in the country.

The Maternity Benefit Act was also amended. The amendment provides for six weeks' leave with wages in cased of medical termination of pregnancy; two weeks' leave with wages to women employees who undergo tubectomy operation; and leave with wages for a maximum period of one month in case of illness arising out of medical termination of pregnancy or tubectomy.

The Payment of Bonus Act was amended in August 1995 raising the eligibility to Rs. 3,500 from the existing level of Rs. 2,500 and calculation ceiling from Rs. 1600 to Rs. 2500. The benefit on account of this measure is estimated at Rs. 845 crore with additional beneficiaries of about 24 lakh workers.

For the elimination of child labour from hazardous employment, 63 National Child Labour Projects with an annual expenditure of Rs. 40.50 crore benefiting a total of 1.20 lakh children in child labour endemic districts were sanctioned.

Maintenance of industrial peace and harmony is vital for sustained growth and continued productive employment for workers. The industrial relations scene continued to improve during the year. The total number of strikes and lockouts in the Central and State sphere, public and private sectors declined from 1810 in 1991 to 1201 in 1994.

Special Employment and Poverty Alleviation Programmes

Poverty alleviation programmes comprising wage employment and credit linked self employment packages continued to be at the top of the agenda. The strategy adopted has been a vigorous frontal attack on rural and urban poverty.

Special employment and anti-poverty programmes like Integrated Rural Development Programme (IRDP), Training of Rural Youth for Self Employment (TRYSEM), Jawahar Rozgar Yojana (JRY), Nehru Rozgar Yojana (NRY), Prime Minister's Integrated Urban Poverty Eradication Programme (PMIUPEP) and Prime Minister's Rozgar Yojana (PMRY) have been a central feature of India's development strategy.

Several social welfare schemes aimed at eradicating poverty and illiteracy besides providing succor to the aged and families below the poverty line were announced on 15th August 1995. The multi-dimensional National Social Assistance Programme (NSAP) for the poor encompasses old age pension, family benefit in case of death of the bread-winner and maternity benefits. The NSAP is a centrally sponsored programme with 100 per cent central funding and it is intended to ensure that social protection to the beneficiaries throughout the country is uninformally available without interruption. The NSAP consists of the following three components :

(a) National Old Age Pension Scheme (NOAPS)
Providing a pension of Rs. 75 per month to destitute and above 65 years of age.

(b) National Family Benefit Scheme (NFBS)
Rs. 5000 in case of death due to natural causes and Rs. 10,000 in case of accidental death of the primary bread-winner to the bereaved household.

(c) National Maternity Benefit Scheme (NMBS)
Rs. 300 per pregnancy upto the first two live births. The programme involves an expenditure of Rs. 867 crore in a full year. An outlay of Rs. 515 crore has been provided during 1995-96.

The Government launched Rural Group Life Insurance Scheme (RGLIS) on 15th August, 1995. The objective of the Scheme is to promote social insurance in the rural areas with the active involvement of the Panchayats and to partly alleviate the distress caused by the death of the bread-winner among the rural poor. The Scheme is being administered by Life Insurance Corporation (LIC) of India and implemented by the Panchayats in the Rural areas for the age group of 20-60 years. Under this new Scheme a life cover of Rs. 5,000 is provided to the Rural population for an annual premium of Rs. 60-70 depending upon the age of entry in the Scheme. As on December 31, 1995, the Scheme had been implemented in 12 States and Union Territories and 50,312 persons under 897 Panchayats have been covered under the Scheme.

The main objective of JRY is to generate additional gainful employment for the unemployment and underemployed in rural areas for the people below the poverty line. Since 1993-94, the JRY has been made more target oriented and expanded substantially through increased budgetary allocations. It has been divided into three streams viz. (i) JRY—1st stream with 84 per cent of total allocation; (ii) JRY—2nd stream with 10 per cent of total allocation for 120 selected backward districts of which 12 districts are such where there is concentration of unemployment and under employment; and (iii) JRY—3rd stream for innovative projects, aimed at prevention of migration of labourers, enhancing women's employment, special programmes through voluntary organisations and those aimed at drought proofing and watershed development. Under the 3rd stream, a total of 28 projects were cleared during 1993-94 and 35 during 1994-95. A sum of Rs. 25.38 crore was released during 1993-94 and Rs. 42.61 crore during 1994-95. During 1995-96, five projects have been cleared so far and Rs. 10.31 crore have been released.

The Employment Assurance Scheme (EAS) is implemented in 2475 backward blocks including those that are flood prone in the country. It aims at providing 100 days of unskilled manual work up to two members of a family in the age group of 18 to 60 years normally residing in villages within the blocks covered under EAS. Over 180 million persons have been registered under this programme as on end November 1995. It is a need-based programme; hence no target of employment generation has been fixed.

The objective of IRDP is to enable identified poor families to augment their income and cross the poverty line through acquisition of credit based productive assets which would provide self-employment on sustained basis. There is reservation for SC/ST up to 50 per cent of total families assisted. Forty per cent is reserved for women and 3 per cent for those who are physically handicapped.

The targets and achievements of the special programmes are given in Table 16.4.

The Prime Minister's Rozgar Yojana was launched on 2nd October, 1993. The Prime Minister's Rozgar Yojana is a scheme aimed at helping educated unemployed youth in establishing self-employment ventures. The scheme was in operation in urban areas in 1993-94 and was thereafter extended to also cover rural areas. For the years 1993-94 and 1994-95 as many as 2.28 lakh cases were sanctioned. For the year 1995-96 a target of 2.60 lakh micro-

TABLE 16.4. Performance of Special Employment and Poverty Alleviation Programme

(In lakh)

Programme	*1992-93*		*1993-94*		*1994-95*		*1995-96*	
	Target	*Achievement*	*Target*	*Achievement*	*Target*	*Achievement (P)*	*Target*	*Achievement (up to Nov. 95)*
A. *Programmes in Rural Areas*								
1. JRY—Mandays of employment generated	7557.95	7821.02	10383.26	10258.40	9865.45	9517.07	9054.75	3616.86
2. EAS*—Mandays of employment generated	—	—	**	494.74	**	2739.56	**	1632.66
3. IRDP—Families assisted	18.75	20.69	25.70	25.39	21.15	21.82	Not fixed	9.01
4. TRYSEM—Youths Trained	3.00	2.76	3.50	3.04	3.18	2.82	2.76	0.62
5. DWCRA—(a) Groups formed	0.08	0.09	0.11	0.15	0.18	0.38	—	0.12
(b) Membership	—	1.29	—	2.69	—	5.92	—	2.50
B. *Programmes in Urban Areas*								
6. NRY—(a) Families assisted	0.92	2.37	1.25	1.52	1.02	1.25	1.17	0.87$
(b) Mandays of employment generated	158.20	140.49	143.23	123.67	106.12	63.96	114.48	56.25$
(c) Persons trained	0.48	0.60	0.58	0.48	0.49	0.37	0.55	0.31$

(Contd.)

TABLE 16.4. *(Contd.)*

Programme	*1992-93*		*1993-94*		*1994-95*		*1995-96*	
	Target	*Achievement*	*Target*	*Achievement*	*Target*	*Achievement (P)*	*Target*	*Achievement (up to Nov. 95)*
C. *Other Programmes*								
7. SEEUY—Beneficiaries	1.00	0.73	1.26	0.56	@	—	—	—
8. PMRY*—(a) Micro-enterprises	—	—	0.40	0.32	2.20	1.96	2.60+	1.01
(B) Employment generated @ @	—	—	0.80	0.45	4.40	2.71	5.20	0.67

P Provisional.
* EAS and PMRY were launched on October 2, 1993.
** Targets are not fixed as it is need based.
@ Integrated with PMRY.
@ @ Estimated @ 2 per case disbursed for the concerned programme year.
$ As on 31.12.95.
\+ Including backlog.
— Not available.

enterprises (inclusive of backlog) has been fixed to generate about 5.20 lakh employment opportunities.

Under JRY, about fifty per cent employment generation during 1994-95 came from the SC/ST group. The coverage of SC/ST under IRDP during 1994-95 was about 50 per cent of total families assisted. The coverage of women was 34 per cent, as against the target of 40 per cent.

Nehru Rozgar Yojana (NRY) consists of the following three sub-schemes, which are meant for the benefit of the urban poor;

(i) Scheme of Urban Micro Enterprises (SUME).
(ii) Scheme of Urban Wage Employment (SUWE).
(ii) Scheme of Housing and Shelter Upgradation (SHASO).

The Prime Minister's Integrated Urban Poverty Eradication Programme (PMIUPEP) was launched during 1995-96 with the specific objective of effective achievement of social sector goals, community empowerment, employment generation and skill upgradation, shelter upgradation and environmental improvement with a multi-pronged and long-term strategy. The Programme will cover 5 million urban poor living in 345 class II Urban Agglomerations with a population of 50,000 to 1,00,000 each. There would be a provision of Rs. 800 crore as central share for the entire Programme period of 5 years.

Effective involvement of the Panchayati Raj Institutions (PRIs) and non-governmental organisations for the better implementation of employment generation and poverty alleviation programmes is being emphasised. In view of widespread unemployment and poverty, the programmes are especially focussed on disadvantaged sections of population and the disadvantaged areas of the country. The programmes are being dovetailed with sectoral and area development programmes. Proper planning, identification of thrust areas at grass root level, viable projects within the management capacities of poor families, and effective tying up of forward and backward linkages, credit and marketing, are also being increasingly emphasised with a view to bringing about qualitative improvements.

TABLE 16.5. Major Employment

('000 persons)

	1990	*1991*	*1992*	*1993(P)*	*1994(P)*
1. Public Sector	18772	19057	19210	19326	–
(a) Central Govt.	3397	3410	3428	3383	–
(b) State Govt.	6979	7113	7190	7293	–
(c) Quasi Govt. (Central)	3523	3564	3554	3592	–
(d) Quasi Govt. (State)	2650	2658	2839	2898	–
(e) Local Bodies	2223	2313	2198	2160	–
2. Private Sector	7582	7676	7846	7851	–

(*Contd.*)

TABLE 16.5 *(Contd.)*

	1990	*1991*	*1992*	*1993(P)*	*1994(P)*
3. Employment in Factories	8445	8548	8620	8928	–
4. Employment in Mines	765	790	791	779	–
5. Employment in Plantations	1084	1106	1088	1080	–
6. Employment in Railways	1647	1651	1654	1649	1620
7. Employment in Posts	585	592	596	596	598
8. Employment in Telecommunication	370	375	373	385	395
9. Employment in Banks	1015	1023	1048	1054	1059
10. Employment in Shops and Establishments	4153	5140	4966	4122	5032
11. Employment in Motor Transport undertaking	709	651	712	362	583

(P) : Provisional – Not available
Source : Labour Bureau Chandigarh/Shimla.

TABLE 16.6. Employment Services

	1990	*1991*	*1992*	*1993(P)*	*1994(P)*
1. No. of Exchanges	769	772	773	804	803
2. Registrations ('000)	6541	6236	5301	5532	5125
3. Vacancies Notified ('000)	491	459	420	385	292
4. Placements ('000)	264	253	239	231	188
5. Applicants on Live Register ('000)	34632	36300	36758	36276	32751
6. S.C. Applicants ('000)	4453	4720	–	–	–
7. S.T. Applicants ('000)	1149	1185	–	–	–

– Not available

N.B. Data in respect of No. of Exchanges, vacancies Notified and Applicants on Live Register are not available since November. 1994 from DGE&T.

Source : Labour Bureau Shimla/Chandigarh.

17

AGRICULTURE INCLUDING RURAL DEVELOPMENT

1995 was again a good year for agriculture, facilitated by a favourable Monsoon whose coverage across the country was fairly good. It was the eighth successive normal Monsoon year. The country's granaries were full and the initial estimates indicated that the current year might record 190 million tonnes output of foodgrains; a little lower than the record output of 191 million tonnes in 1994-95. Production of oilseeds was likely to be marginally better. Sugar production reached all time high of 146 lakh tonnes during 1994-95 (October-September) because of substantial increase in sugarcane availability. Among plantation crops tea output was expected to be higher than last year. The overall growth in agriculture production in 1994-95 was about 5 per cent as against 3.4 per cent in 1993-94.

Performance of agricultural production during the last few years and the likely out turn in 1995-96 is shown in Table 17.1.

Wheat : Uttar Pradesh, Punjab, Haryana, Madhya Pradesh, Bihar, Gujarat and Rajasthan are the major wheat growing states. In 1994-95, country's total wheat output was 65.5 million tonnes, which was 9.5 per cent higher than 1993-94. In 1995-96, the prospect of production is quite good and expected production is likely to be close to the level of last year. It is interesting to observe that since late sixties when the effect of the green revolution was first felt most in wheat output, the ratio of wheat to rice has steadily increased from one third in 1950-51 to over four fifth in 1994-95, (see Table 17.2.)

Rice : Rice production of 81.1 million tonnes in 1994-95 was a new record but in 1995-96, some decline in production in Haryana, Punjab and Andhra Pradesh was expected due to the adverse weather conditions (such as floods). Therefore, in 1995-96 total rice production was expected to be about 80 million tonnes.

Course Cereals : Jowar, bajra, ragi, maize and small millets constitute course cereals. Course grains have a strong supplemental influence on the food economy of the country. These are grown mostly by small and marginal farmers in areas characterised by low and often erratic rainfall. The major producing states are Rajasthan, Gujarat, Maharashtra, Karnataka, Andhra Pradesh, Tamil Nadu, Madhya Pradesh, Uttar Pradesh and Bihar. The likely production of course cereals during 1995-96 was reported to be at the same level of 30 million tonnes as achieved in 1994-95.

TABLE 17.1. Production of Principal Crops

(Million Tonnes)

Crop	1990-91	1991-92	1992-93	1993-94 (Revised)	1994-95 Target	1994-95 Final	1995-96 Target	1995-96 Likely
Rice	74.3	74.7	72.9	80.3	78.5	81.1	80.0	80.0
Wheat	55.1	55.7	57.2	59.8	58.5	65.5	60.0	65.2
Coarse Cereals	32.7	26.0	36.6	30.8	36.5	30.4	36.5	30.0
Pulses	14.3	12.0	12.8	13.3	15.5	14.1	15.5	14.8
Total Foodgrains	176.4	168.4	179.5	184.3	189.0	191.1	192.0	190.0
Kharif	99.4	91.6	101.5	100.4	106.3	100.6	107.5	100.0
Rabi	77.0	76.8	78.0	83.9	82.7	90.5	84.5	90.0
Oilseeds	18.6	18.6	20.1	21.5	22.0	21.4	22.5	22.0
Sugarcane	241.0	254.0	228.0	229.7	250.0	271.2	255.0	265.0
Cotton @	9.8	9.7	11.4	10.7	12.5	12.1	13.0	12.3
Jute & mesta $	9.2	10.3	8.6	8.4	9.3	9.5	9.3	9.4
(Percentage variation in production over the previous year)								
Rice	1.0	0.5	-2.4	10.2		1.0		-1.4
Wheat	10.6	1.1	2.7	4.5		9.5		-0.5
Course Cereals	-6.0	-20.5	40.8	-15.8		-1.3		-1.3
Pulses	10.9	-16.1	6.7	3.9		6.0		5.0
Total Foodgrains	3.2	-4.5	6.6	2.7		3.7		-0.6
Kharif	-1.6	-7.8	10.8	-1.1		0.2		-0.6
Rabi	10.0	-0.3	1.6	7.5		8.0		-0.6
Oilseeds	10.1	0.0	8.1	7.0		-0.5		2.8
Sugarcane	6.8	5.4	-10.2	0.7		18.1		-2.3
Cotton @	-14.0	-1.0	17.5	-6.1		13.1		1.7
Jute & mesta $	10.8	12.0	-16.5	-2.3		13.1		-1.1

@ Million Bales of 170 kg each.
$ Million Bales of 180 kg each.

TABLE 17.2. Production of Rice and Wheat

(Million Tonnes)

Year	*Rice*	*Wheat*	*Percentage of Wheat to Rice*
1950-51	20.58	6.46	31.39
1960-61	34.58	11.00	31.81
1970-71	42.22	23.83	56.44
1980-81	53.63	36.31	67.70
1990-91	74.29	55.14	74.22
1994-95	81.10	65.50	80.76

Pulses : Per capita daily availability of pulses came down significantly from 69 grams in 1961 to about 37 grams in 1995. This was due to stagnation in the production of pulses over the last three decades. The pulses production was 14.1 million tonnes in 1994-95, an increase of about 6.1 per cent over 1993-94. Production in 1995-96 was anticipated at 14.8 million tonnes. The main constraints in raising productivity levels in pulses is that pulse crops are largely grown on marginal lands, mostly in rainfed areas and there is virtually no break-through in developing improved and high yield seed varieties.

Growth in Foodgrains Production : Table 17.3 lists compound and annual growth rate in production of foodgrains. Lower productivity in pulses remains the only area of concern in the overall foodgrains economy of the country.

TABLE 17.3. Annual Growth Rate in Production of Foodgrains

(Per cent)

Year	*Rice*	*Wheat*	*Pulses*	*Foodgrains*
Compound growth Rate*				
1967-68 to 1994-95	2.91	4.80	1.04	2.67
1980-81 to 1994-95	3.48	3.70	1.67	2.89
Annual (Year to Year)				
1990-91	1.01	10.59	10.54	3.30
1991-92	0.54	1.02	-15.59	-4.24
1992-93	-2.46	2.72	6.66	4.87
1993-94	10.24	4.62	3.56	4.09
1994-95	1.05	9.41	5.65	3.40
1995-96	-1.41	-0.41	5.32	-0.46

*Based on the Index numbers, base triennium ending 1981-82=100

Oilseeds : With about 21.4 million tonnes production estimated in 1994-95, the production of nine oilseeds (groundnut, rapeseed mustard, soybean, sunflower, sesamum, castor seed, safflower, nigerseed and linseed) increased substantially from 10.83 million tonnes in 1985-86. Groundnut is by far the dominant oilseeds crop accounting for 38.56 per cent of total output of nine oilseeds (in 1994-95) followed by rapeseed/mustard which accounts for 27.45 per cent. Therefore, the two oil-seeds together (accounting for 66.01 per cent of production of nine oilseeds) dominate the edible oil economy in the country. The contribution of other oils, though significantly supplemental, play a relatively lesser role except that soybean oil and sunflower oil have of late emerged as the major potential growth areas. Production of soybean may soon outrank rapeseed/mustard and thus occupy second position after groundnut. Trend of production of oilseeds from 1987-88 to 1994-95 and the likely production during 1995-96 alongwith the targets are listed in Table 17.4.

Sugarcane : Sugarcane production shows an uptrend since 1985-86 except, in 1992-93 and 1993-94, when it suffered some marginal decline. In 1994-95, the cane production was 271.2 million tonnes. The likely production during 1995-96 would be around 265 million tonnes.

Cotton : In 1995-96, cotton production was expected to be 123 lakh bales against 121 lakh bales produced last year (an increase of 1.7 per cent). Apparently there have been significant gains in cotton productivity trends thus offsetting the decline in area under cotton from 80.6 lakh hectares in 1981-82 to 73.2 lakh hectares in 1993-94. Consumption of cotton has also continuously increased from 75.9 lakh bales in 1981-82 to 128 lakh bales in 1993-94, outpacing the increase in domestic cotton output, thus necessitating imports in some years. Future increase in raw cotton demand is likely to put further pressure on cotton prices.

Jute and Mesta : The combined production of Jute and Mesta in 1985-86 reached a peak level of 12.6 million bales (of 180 kgs. each), thereafter it fell in successive years to a level ranging between 8.4 to 10.3 million bales. Production in 1994-95 was 9.5 million bales. In 1995-96 the production of jute and mesta was likely to be around 9.4 million bales as against the target of 9.3 million bales.

Tea : Tea industry provides gainful direct employment to more than one million workers mainly drawn from the backward and socially weaker sections of the society. It is also a substantial foreign exchange earner (with negligible import content) and provides significant contribution to the State and Central exchequer. Tea plantations in India are mainly located in rural hill and backward areas of North Eastern and Southern States.

The production of tea in the country has grown steadily from 561 million kgs in 1982-83 to estimated 737.39 million kgs in 1994-95. However, the domestic demand for tea has risen at a faster pace, thereby, creating pressure on the exportable surplus which is close to about 200 million kgs. The Government have taken a number of steps to stimulate its production so as to meet the growing domestic and international demand for tea. In this context a perspective plan for achieving production target of 1000 million kgs by 2000 AD has been drawn up by the Tea Board. Quantity exported during 1993-94 was 154.55 million kgs. valued at Rs. 1062.03 crore and, during 1994-95, 149.76 million kgs. valued at Rs. 924.08 crore. The decline in exports in recent years was mainly due to lower off-take of Indian tea by Russia.

TABLE 17.4. Production of Oilseeds

(Million Tonnes)

Oilseeds	*1987-88*	*1988-89*	*1989-90*	*1990-91*	*1991-92*	*1992-93*	*1993-94**	*1994-95***	*1995-96*	
									Target	*Likely*
Groundnut	5.85	9.66	8.10	7.51	7.09	8.56	7.83	8.26	8.40	7.07
Kharif	4.18	7.49	6.10	5.12	4.99	6.66	5.71	6.22	6.20	4.87
Rabi	1.67	2.17	2.00	2.39	2.10	1.90	2.12	2.04	2.20	2.20
Castorseed	0.20	0.41	0.52	0.72	0.58	0.62	0.63	0.85	0.70	0.93
Sesamum	0.58	0.68	0.74	0.84	0.71	0.76	0.56	0.62	0.90	0.93
Rapeseed & Mustard	3.46	4.38	4.12	5.23	5.87	4.80	5.33	5.88	5.70	5.80
Linseed	0.39	0.36	0.33	0.33	0.29	0.28	0.33	0.32	0.35	0.35
Nigerseed	0.18	0.18	0.19	0.19	0.19	0.16	0.20	0.20	0.20	0.23
Safflower	0.46	0.44	0.49	0.32	0.20	0.34	0.52	0.42	0.45	0.50
Sunflower										
Kharif	0.38	0.22	0.27	0.33	0.36	0.43	0.50	0.32	0.60	0.45
Rabi	0.25	0.15	0.36	0.54	0.83	0.75	0.85	0.88	0.90	0.90
Soyabeen	0.90	1.55	1.80	2.60	2.49	3.39	4.75	3.67	4.30	4.85
Total	**12.65**	**18.03**	**16.92**	**18.61**	**18.60**	**20.11**	**21.50**	**21.42**	**22.50**	**22.01**
Kharif	6.42	10.53	9.62	9.80	9.31	12.03	12.35	11.88	12.90	12.26
Rabi	6.23	7.50	7.30	8.81	9.29	8.08	9.15	9.54	9.60	9.75

* Revised

** Final

A production target of 780 million kgs and an export target of 170 million kgs had been fixed for 1995-96. Upto October 1995, production of tea was estimated to be 625.38 million kgs as against 649.72 million kgs during the corresponding period of last year. During April-October 1995, 93.42 million kgs valued at Rs. 659.95 crore was exported as compared to 80.43 million kgs valued at Rs. 478.24 crore during the corresponding period of last year.

Coffee : Robusta and Arabica are the two main varieties grown in the country. India accounts for nearly 3.2 per cent of the total world production of coffee. The domestic demand for coffee hovers around 60,000 tonnes annually which constitutes nearly one-third of total production. Remaining two-third of output is available for exports.

In 1994-95 production of coffee was 1.8 lakh tonnes which is likely to have increased to an estimated 2.24 lakh tonnes in 1995-96. Large variation in coffee production (Table 17.5) in some years is due to seasonal factors as coffee is extremely sensitive to changes in weather conditions.

TABLE 17.5. Coffee Production

(Lakh Tonnes)

Year/Season	*Production*
1987-88	1.22
1988-89	2.15
1989-90	1.18
1990-91	1.70
1991-92	1.80
1992-93	1.69
1993-94	2.08
1994-95	1.80
1995-96*	2.24

* (Estimated)

In 1994-95 India's share in world exports is estimated to be around 3 per cent. Export during 1992-93 was 1,13,602 tonnes valued at Rs. 381.3 crore. However, in 1993-94, the exports rose to 1,36,690 tonnes and export realisation rose to Rs. 586.99 crore. In 1994-95, the exports reached 1,36,404 tonnes for a value of Rs. 1086.89 crore, the higher unit realisation being mainly due to high global prices.

Natural Rubber : Natural rubber is a vital raw material for the rubber manufacturing industry which in turn produces a variety of products indispensable in modern life. Currently about 96 per cent of the natural rubber demand in the country is met by indigenous production and the deficit is met by imports. Rubber production has shown a significant uptrend in recent years. From 3.3 lakh tonnes in 1990-91, it has increased to 4.72 lakh tonnes in 1994-95. Area under rubber has also gone up from 4.75 lakh hectares in 1990-91 to an estimated 5.15 lakh hectares in 1994-95. Kerala continues to be the major rubber producing state accounting for 86 per cent of the total area and contributing more than three-fourth of the total production. Most rubber plantations are small and the average size of holding is 0.5 hectares. As against production of 4.72 lakh tonnes and consumption of 4.86 lakh tonnes in 1994-95, the estimated production and consumption during 1995-96 is 5.11 lakh tonnes and 5.30 lakh tonnes respectively. Import of natural rubber from time to time continues to bridge the gap between demand and supply. Annual production and consumption of natural rubber during the past 5 years is listed in Table 17.6.

TABLE 17.6. Production and Consumption of Rubber

(Tonnes)

Year	*Production*	*Consumption*
1991-92	366745	380150
1992-93	393490	414105
1993-94	435160	450180
1994-95	472000	486000
1995-96*	511000	530000

* (Estimated)

Horticultural Crops : India produces a large variety of horticultural crops like fruits, coconuts, vegetables, cashewnuts, spices and plantation crops and diverse range of medicinal and aromatic plants, mushroom, floriculture, betelvine, root and tuber crops etc.

India ranked first in production of fruits during 1993, overtaking Brazil which held this distinction hitherto. India also occupies the first position in global production of mangoes and bananas and is amongst the top ten in apple and pineapple production. India holds the first position in global production of cauliflower, and is amongst the first ten countries leading in the production of green peas, onion, potato and tomato.

India, with a production level of 11375 million nuts in 1992-93, has moved to second position in the global production of coconuts (in terms of number of nuts) after staying at the third position for the last two decades.

Cashewnut is a prime cash crop and a key export commodity. India has the distinction of being world's largest producer of cashewnut with annual output of 3.5 lakh tonnes. Various programmes for increasing the overall productivity are being implemented so as to achieve a production target of 4.7 lakh tonnes of raw cashewnuts by the end of 1997.

Production of spices during 1994-95 was expected to be maintained at 2.2 million tonnes. Fifteen major spice crops out of a large number of spice crops, have been singled out for intensive development. Of these, black pepper occupies the most prominent place for domestic consumption and for exports. Better processing and quality control would help increase India's share in the expanding global export market.

Irrigation

A highly efficient and irrigated cropping system alone can sustain India's ever expanding population. The creation of irrigation potential and its optimum utilisation, therefore, continues to receive a high priority.

The country's Irrigation Potential Created (IPC) area has increased from 22.6 million hectares in the pre-plan period (1950-51) to about 87.06 million hectares at the end of 1994-95 comprising 32.27 million hectares under major and medium irrigation projects and 54.79 million hectares in minor irrigation schemes. The anticipated irrigated potential created by the end of 1995-96 is 89.42 million hectares comprising 33.04 million hectares under major and medium projects and 56.38 million hectares under minor irrigation schemes.

Under-utilisation of irrigation potential, particularly under major and medium irrigation projects continues to persist. At the end of 1994-95, the likely utilisation was 77.86 million hectares against the created potential of 87.06 million hectares.

Command Area Development Programme (CAD) has been under implementation since 1974-75 with the basic objective of reducing the gap between potential created and potential utilised. Up to March 1995 about Rs. 4322 crore were spent on the programme, of which the Central assistance amounted to Rs. 1426 crore and the balance of Rs. 2896 crore was met under the State sector schemes. The programme envisages execution of on-farm development works like construction of field channels, land levelling, contouring and shaping, implementation of 'warabandi' for rotational supply of water and construction of field drains.

Minor irrigation schemes include ground water and surface water schemes. While ground water schemes include dugwells, shallow tubewells and pumpsets, the surface water schemes include tanks and reservoir diversion schemes, lift irrigation from rivers and streams. These schemes have been accorded special attention under the Special Foodgrains Production Programme. At the end of 1994-95, irrigation potential created and its utilisation through Minor irrigation schemes was estimated at 54.79 million hectares and 50.22 million hectares respectively. For 1995-96 the targets for creation and utilisation of additional irrigation potential are 1.59 million hectares and 1.29 million hectares respectively. Because of shorter gestation period and relatively lower investment levels, added emphasis is being laid on undertaking and completion of minor irrigation schemes covering both surface and ground water. Because of comparatively advantageous water table levels, the eastern sector is being accorded special attention for development of minor irrigation during the Eighth Five Year Plan (1992-97). The progress of development of irrigation potential and its utilisation is listed in Table 17.7.

Strengthening of irrigation infrastructure is one of the main objectives in irrigation supply management. At the commencement of the Eighth Plan in 1992, there were 158 major, 226 medium and 95 Extension, Renovation and Modernisation (ERM) projects carried forward from the previous plans. The total spill over cost of these projects has been estimated at about Rs. 40,563 crore. Therefore, the Eighth Plan accorded high priority to completion of the on going projects. The other major elements of the strategy include ensuring of speedy transition to irrigated agriculture and optimum use of water through Command Area Development (CAD) programme, installation of sprinkler and drip irrigation systems in water scarce and drought prone areas and encouragement to surface water and lift irrigation.

TABLE 17.7. Development of Irrigation Potential and its Utilisation

(Million Hectares)

Irrigation Schemes	*At the end of Seventh Plan*	*During 1990-92*	*At the end of 1991-92*	*1993-94 actuals*	*1994-95 (Likely)*	*1995-96 (Targets)*
1. Major & medium irrigation						
Potential	29.9	0.8	30.7	0.5	0.7	0.8
Utilisation	25.5	0.8	26.3	0.5	0.6	0.8
2. Minor Irrigation						
Potential	46.6	3.8	50.4	1.4	1.5	1.6
Utilisation	43.1	3.4	46.5	1.2	1.1	1.3
3. Total						
Potential	76.5	4.6	81.1	1.9	2.2	2.4
Utilisation	69.6	4.2	72.8	1.7	1.7	2.1

Note : Irrigation projects with a Cumulative Command Area (CCA) of more than 10000 hectares are classified as major projects and projects with CCA of more than 2000 hectares and up to 10000 hectares as medium projects

Seeds : Seed quality is the basic and crucial input for attaining sustained growth in agricultural production. Seed is the carrier of new technology for crop production, propagation and multiplication. Distribution of assured quality seeds is fundamental to attain higher crop yields. Policy initiatives taken by Government of India during 1960's and 1970's for generating quality seed production and distribution of new improved plant varieties, identified by the scientists, is the main reason for country's current self-sufficiency in foodgrains. Indian seed industry has shown impressive growth and should continue to provide further potential for growth in agricultural production. The role of seed industry is not only to produce adequate quantity of seeds of good quality but also to achieve diversity in varietal distribution. Towards achieving this objective the principal players are the two national level organisations National Seed Corporation (NSC) and State Farms Corporation of India (SFCI), 13 State Seeds Corporations, and about 100 private seed organisations. Apart from this, there are 19 State Seed Certification Agencies and 86 State Seed Testing Laboratories to ensure-check the quality of seeds.

Major achievement in the seeds development sector has been the systematic release/notification of new varieties of agricultural and horticultural crops through Central Seed Committee. Since 1969, till date, 1898 varieties of agricultural and 340 of horticultural crops respectively have been notified. Out of this, 137 varieties of agricultural crops and 21 varieties of horticultural crops have been notified during last two years. Another major achievement has been the implementation of Seed Control Order, 1983 issued under the provisions of the Essential Commodities Act, 1955 with effect from July, 1994. It seeks to regulate supply, distribution and trade in seeds. Seeds Act 1966 and Seed

TABLE 17.8. Area under High-Yielding Varieties of Seeds

(Million Hectares)

Crop	*1966-67*	*1989-90*	*1990-91*	*1991-92*	*1992-93*	*1993-94*	*1994-95**	*1995-96* (Targets)
Paddy	0.9	26.2	27.4	28.0	27.5	28.9	31.0	31.2
Wheat	0.5	20.3	21.0	20.5	21.7	22.0	23.3	23.3
Jowar	0.2	6.9	7.1	6.8	6.9	6.8	7.1	9.0
Bajra	0.1	5.6	5.7	5.4	5.6	5.1	5.4	6.9
Maize	0.2	2.3	2.6	2.8	2.6	2.7	3.4	3.5
Ragi	-	-	1.2	1.2	1.1	1.2	1.1	1.1
Total	1.9	61.2	65.0	64.7	65.4	66.7	71.3	75.0
(Percentage of HYV area to Total Area under the crop)							-	
Paddy	2.6	62.1	64.2	65.7	65.9	68.8	74.6	
Wheat	3.9	86.4	86.9	88.1	88.2	88.4	90.7	
Jowar	1.1	46.6	49.4	55.0	53.1	52.7	60.2	
Bajra	0.8	51.4	54.4	53.8	52.8	53.7	53.4	
Maize	3.9	39.0	44.1	47.8	43.6	45.1	54.9	
Ragi	-	-	55.3	56.3	57.6	62.8	58.4	

* Revised

Rules, 1968 promulgated in 1968 have been instrumental in bringing about overall improvement in seed quality as per prescribed minimum seed certification standards.

National Seeds Project—a World Bank assisted project-provides assistance to NSC, SFCI, State Seed Corporation and State Seed Certification Agencies for their restructuring. As a result of these efforts 65 lakh quintals of certified/quality seed distribution during 1994-95 was achieved, which in 1995-96 is estimated to further improve to 68.8 lakh quintals. It is likely that the annual target of 70 lakh quintals by the end of Eighth Plan (1992-97) would be achieved. The progress of area covered under HYV seeds under different crops and their share in the total area is shown in Table 17.8.

Fertilizers : Use of chemical fertilisers continues to be one of the principal inputs for enhancing crop yields. The consumption of chemical fertilizers, which was only 0.13 million tonnes in nutrient terms in 1955-56, increased to 13.56 million tonnes in 1994-95. The overall increase in fertiliser consumption during 1994-95 over 1993-94 was 9.7 per cent. While the increase in potash consumption was 23.9 per cent during 1994-95 over the previous year, the consumption of nitrogenous and phosphatic fertilisers increased by 8.2 and 9.9 per cent respectively during 1994-95. The progress of fertiliser consumption since 1987-88 is shown in Table 17.9.

TABLE 17.9. Chemical Fertilizers-Consumption

(Million Tonnes of Nutrients)

Year	*Nitrogen (N)*	*Phosphate (P)*	*Potash (K)*	*Total NPK*
1987-88	5.7	2.2	0.9	8.8
1988-89	7.3	2.7	1.1	11.1
1989-90	7.4	3.0	1.2	11.6
1990-91	8.0	3.2	1.3	12.5
1991-92	8.0	3.3	1.4	12.7
1992-93	8.4	2.9	0.9	12.2
1993-94	8.8	2.7	0.9	12.4
1994-95	9.5	2.9	1.1	13.5
1995-96*	10.8	3.6	1.3	15.7

* Estimated.

The production of nitrogenous and phosphatic fertilizers during 1994-95 stood at about 9.05 million tonnes, recording an increase of about 15.4 per cent over 1993-94. In 1995-96, the production of nitrogenous and phosphatic fertilizers is expected to further increase to over 11.3 million tonnes (86.33 lakh tonnes of nitrogen and 26.67 lakh tonnes of phosphate). Production, imports and subsidy since 1987-88 are listed in Table 17.10.

The fertilizer subsidy budget of1995-96 was likely to come under pressure mainly on account of fluctuations in exchange rate and increase in the international price of urea.

TABLE 17.10. Fertilizer Production, Imports and Subsidies

Year	*Production (N+P) (000 Tons)*	*Imports (N+P+K) (000 Tons)*	*Subsidy (Rs. crore)* Imported Fertilizers	Domestic Fertilizers	Total
1987-88	7131	984	114	2050	2164
1988-89	8964	1608	201	3000	3201
1989-90	8543	3114	771	3771	4542
1990-91	9045	2758	659	3730	4389
1991-92	9863	2769	1300	3500	4800
1992-93	9736	2988	996	4800	5796
1993-94	9047	3166	600	3800	4400
1994-95	10438	2965	1166	4075	5241
1995-96 (Budgeted)	11300	–	1650	3750	5400*

* Incorporates import of Urea, in nutrient terms, the only controlled fertilizer imported on government account.

Agricultural Credit : Timely and adequate credit to farmers is vital for increasing agricultural production and productivity. Providing access to institutional credit for small and marginal farmers and other weaker sections to enable them to adopt modern technology and improved agricultural practices has been the major objective of the credit policy.

Loans are disbursed through a multi-agency network consisting of Commercial Banks, Regional Rural Banks (RRBs) and Cooperatives. The total agricultural credit from various institutional sources has increased from Rs. 9785 crore in 1988-89 to Rs. 21113 crore in 1994-95. The target for credit disbursement for 1995-96 is Rs. 26450 crore. Agency-wise disbursement of agricultural credit from 1991-92 to 1995-96 are indicated in the Table 17.11.

TABLE 17.11. Disbursement of Agricultural Credit

(Rs. Crore)

Item	*1991-92*	*1992-93*	*1993-94*	*1994-95*	*1995-96 (Target)*
Cooperative					
Short-term	4403	7170	7839	9462	9966
Medium-term	570				
Long-term	827	2208	2278	2454	2800
Sub-total	5800	9378	101171	1916	12766
Commercial and Regional Rural Banks					
Short-term & term loans	5402	5791	6377	9197	13684
Grand Total	11202	15169	16494	21113	26450

Crop Insurance : From Kharif 1985 to the end of Rabi 1994-95 season, 467 lakh farmers have been covered under Comprehensive Crop Insurance Scheme (CCIS) covering an area of 802 lakh hectares insuring a sum of Rs. 11846 crore. Claims amount to Rs. 1178.76 crore were paid to the farmers (of which, Gujarat alone accounted for more than half of the amount) till end of September, 1995 against a premium income of Rs. 195.55 crore.

Animal Husbandry and Dairy Development

Animal Husbandry and Dairying is estimated to account for 26 per cent of the total value of agricultural output.

Milk production was estimated at 63.1 million tonnes in 1994-95, about 4.3 per cent higher over 1993-94. India ranks perhaps second in the world milk production. About 70000 Dairy Cooperative Societies have been organised in 170 'milk sheds' involving about 9 million farmer members so far. The export earnings from the livestock sector and related products rose from Rs. 792 crore in 1988-89 to Rs. 1672 crore in 1994-95.

Poultry : Poultry production in the country has made significant progress over the years due to the research and development thrust of the Government and organised private sector. The egg production is expected to have increased to the level of 24.7 billion and broiler production to 300 million during 1994-95 compared to 8 billion eggs and 4 million broilers two decades ago.

Fisheries and Aquaculture : Fisheries and aquaculture play an important role in augmenting the country's food supply, raising nutritional levels, generating employment and earnings through exports. According to quick estimates of the Central Statistical Organisation, the contribution of fisheries sector to the net domestic product has increased from Rs. 1478 crore in 1984-85 to Rs. 6753 crore in 1993-94 at current prices.

Fish production in the country increased from 7.5 lakh tonnes in 1950-51 to 47.89 lakh tonnes during 1994-95. The average annual growth rate in fish production during the period 1984-85 to 1994-95 is 5.6 per cent. The growth rates in the marine and inland fisheries have been 5 per cent and 6.7 per cent per annum during this period. The export of marine products has recorded a significant increase and, for the first time, crossed 1 billion US dollars during 1994-95. The trend of fish production and export is listed in Table 17.11. The target for fish production in 1995-96 is 49.50 lakh tonnes comprising 28.25 lakh tonnes from marine sources and 21.25 lakh tonnes from inland waters.

Agricultural Marketing : The number of regulated markets in the country in March, 1995 was 6836. In the markets and also for setting up of rural godowns. To facilitate grading, standards have been laid down for 151 agricultural and allied commodities under the Agricultural Produce (Grading and Marking) Act, 1937. There were 3167 licensed cold storages with an installed capacity of 8.577 million tonnes as on March 31, 1995. To promote setting up of cold storage under the cooperative sector, the National Cooperative Development Corporation (NCDC) has provided Rs. 77.16 crore for setting up of 247 cold storages with an installed capacity of 7.33 lakh tonnes till the end of March, 1995.

TABLE 17.12. Marine and Inland Fish Production and Export of Marine Products

Year	*Fish production (Lakh tonnes)*			*Export of Marine products*	
	Marine	*Inland*	*Total*	*Quantity (Lakh Tonnes)*	*Value (Rs. Crore)*
1989-90	22.75	14.02	36.77	1.11	634.99
1990-91	23.00	15.36	38.36	1.39	893.37
1991-92	24.47	17.10	41.56	1.72	1375.89
1992-93	25.76	17.89	43.65	2.09	1767.43
1993-94	26.49	19.95	46.44	2.44	2503.62
1994-95(P)	26.92	20.97	47.89	3.07	3575.27
1995-96(T)	28.25	21.25	49.50	—	—

P : Provisional

T : Target

A number of organisations and institutions function currently to deal with product and area specific problems that have a bearing on production, pricing, and marketing of agricultural products. The most important of these institutions are the Commission for Agricultural Costs and Prices, the Food Corporation of India, the Cotton Corporation of India, the Jute Corporation of India and the Commodity Boards.

NAFED is a central nodal agency for undertaking price support operations for pulses and oilseeds and market intervention operation for horticultural items like kinoo/malta, onion, potato, grapes, black pepper and red chillies etc. During 1994-95 NAFED's turnover was Rs. 718.77 crore and the turnover target for 1995-96 is Rs. 874.92 crore. A few other organisations in the cooperative sector are the National Cooperative Tobacco Growers' Federation Ltd., the National Consumers' Cooperative Federation and the Tribal Cooperative Marketing Development Federation of India Ltd. (TRIFED) which attends specifically to the marketing problems of the tribal areas. However, the share of cooperatives in the total marketing of agricultural commodities is rather small.

Agricultural Research and Extension : As an apex scientific organisation at national level, the Indian Council of Agricultural Research (ICAR) plays as crucial role in promoting and augmenting science and technology programmes relating to agricultural research, education and demonstration of new technologies.

Agricultural Education Programmes are, by and large, carried out by 27 State Agricultural Universities (SAUs) of the country covering 16 major states. One Central Agricultural University (CAU) for North East Hill (NEH) Region has been established at Imphal to help and support the human resource development needs of the region. In addition to these, 4 National Institutes of the Council viz. Indian Agricultural Research Institute (IARI), Indian Veterinary Research Institute (IVRI), National Dairy Research Institute (NDRI) and Central Institute of Fisheries Education (CIFE) have been granted the status of deemed universities. These institutes offer post graduate degree programmes in addition to undertaking researches in their respective areas.

Export of Agricultural Products : In almost all the non-oil producing developing countries, agricultural commodities or value added products from agriculture account for a major portion of their export earnings. In India, share of agricultural exports to total exports was only 8.56 per cent in 1994-95. The total exports of agricultural products (excluding tea, coffee, marine products and raw cotton) during 1992-93, 1993-94 and 1994-95 were Rs. 5686.81 crore, Rs. 7532.99 crore and Rs. 7049.05 crore respectively. Important items of agricultural exports are rice, cashewnuts, horticulture and floriculture products, coffee, tea etc.

India's share in the world trade in agricultural commodities is less than 1 per cent.

18

DEFENCE

18.1 NATIONAL SECURITY ENVIRONMENT

Five years after the end of the Cold War, the global strategic environment continues to be in a state of transition. Its benefits have yet to become apparent globally. In Asia, East Europe and Africa, the post Cold War scenario is still characterised by instability, uncertainty and unpredictability. Instead of peace and tranquility, and a new world order, we are witnessing today new forms of conflict and continuing disorder. It is not so much inter-state wars as intra-state violence, internatinal terrorism and proxy wars by external powers that characterise the global security environment at present.

Within this environment, there are both positive and negative factors. On the one hand, there are attempts at confidence building, resolution of some of the more intractable problems of the past, and the formation of regional security structures. On the other hand, there are moves towards revival of hegemonic aspirations, ethnic assertions and religious fundamentalism leading to heightened tension in many areas of the globe.

Simultaneously, new sources of tension and potential conflict are emerging in today's world involving availability of resources such as oil, gas, food and water. There are anxieties regarding population migration, new concerns over ecological degradation and its effect on health and quality of life, the peddling of drugs and its links with terrorism, and the proliferation of small arms and their linkages with both state and non-state actors. All these lead to new challenges that confront nations today. Many of these are to be found in India's neighbourhood.

The post-Cold War world is not a more stable world. It has ended the possibility of conflict only in one dimension, that of the two contending ideologies centred mainly in Europe. In other parts of the world, conflicts continue. In Africa, Asia and Eastern Europe, these have actually increased and taken new forms. At one end of the spectrum are ethnic and tribal clashes within nations. At the other end, inter-state wars, supported by outside powers, take place. The latter have tended to become proxy wars, and have often take the form of subversion, insurgency and terrorism with enormous potential for violence. There is a resurgence of inter-state wars with the covert support of external powers as the principal means of conflict. At the same time, the process of new peace initiatives is also continuing which has shown positive indications towards establishment of peace. As a consequence, while new instabilities are emerging in some areas, some old ones are disappearing.

The United Nations has acquired a greater salience after the Cold War and emerged with a larger role in peace-keeping and providing humanitarian support. The Security Council has played a dominant role in this endeavour. This is all the more reason for the UN to be democratised and for the Security Council to be restructured to reflect contemporary realities. There is no agreement as yet regarding the actual nature of peace-keeping. A debate is currently on to clearly differentiate between peace-enforcement, peace-keeping and peace-making, and the nature of efforts and structures required for each. It is important that these issues are resolved through dialogue and discussions among countries. India has consistently participated in UN peace-keeping operations. As a major nation of the world and in line with its international obligations, India will continue to do so in the future, examining each case on its merit. We also believe that the underlying economic and social factors that ignite conflict need to be addressed more forcefully by the UN.

Various countries have called for an indefinite extension of the NPT while India's clearly articulated policy is one of opposition to such discriminatory treaties. Human rights have been raised by certain quarters in the West as an issue to scrutinise India's domestic affairs, in spite of our very good track record in this area. Members of the Missile Technology Control Regime continue to deny important technologies to India in an arbitrary manner under their national regulations. The COCOM provisions have expired but new regulations are being put in their place to target some nations including India. These factors seriously impinge on India's quest for self-reliance and defence preparedness. There are, however, several positive elements such as the agreement in principle in the Joint Statement issued at the end of Prime Minister P.V. Narasimha Rao's visit to the USA that the ultimate goal of non proliferation should be a nuclear weapon free world.

The issue of nuclear non-proliferation figures prominently on the internatinoal and regional disarmament agenda, and is likely to remain a high priority in view of the forthcoming NPT Review Conference scheduled to be held in New York in April 1995. India's position on this issue has been reiterated at the highest political levels in different fora. At the UN Security Council summit level meeting in January 1992. Prime Minister stated that the Council should deal with threats to peace emanating from proliferation of nuclear weapons only within the framework of the new international consensus, based upon a universal, comprehensive and non-discriminatory regime linked to the goal of complete elimination of nuclear weapons. India makes a distinction between the NPT and non-proliferation. While maintaining reservations on the former, India is fully committed to the goal of curbing nuclear proliferation. Merely preventive or punitive actions on a selective basis cannot be expected to achieve the desired results.

On the international front, there have been some positive developments in two areas relating to nuclear disarmament issues—progress in negotiations on a comprehensive test ban treaty and a Convention on a cut-off in the production of fissile materials for weapons purposes. It is hoped that multilateral negotiations on these agenda items will result in universal and non-discriminatory Conventions. Both these elements are part of the Nuclear Freeze proposal co-sponsored by India since 1982 and the Action Plan for Disarmament tabled by India at the UN in 1988.

India's relations with the USA have improved significantly in the last one year. Prime Minister Narasimha Rao's visit to the USA in May, 1994 was a major turning point. India has been identified by the USa sa one of the ten big emerging markets in the world and is attracting considerable interest in US economic circles. Commonalities of experience—as democracies, as multi-cultural societies based on the rule of law, as secular States with a free press and an independent judiciary—provide the two countries with a sound basis to strengthen bilateral cooperation. Greater interaction amongst the armed forces of the two countries has, meanwhile, been taking place. Joint exercises and common sports and training activities are being conducted. These meetings are leading to a better understanding of each other's security concerns.

India's relations with Russia continue to be excellent. PM's visit to the Russian Federation in June-July 1994 and the signing by PM and President Yeltsin of the landmark Moscow Declaration on the Protection of the Interests of Pluralistic States has testified to Indo-Russian understanding on issues of vital concern to both countries. The earlier problems of supply of military spares have been resolved. Russia continues to be a dependable source for India's military modernisation at affordable costs.

The disintegration of the USSR has unleashed forces which could change the geo-strategic equation in Central Asia and the rest of the former Soviet Union. The Central Asian Republics are attempting to restructure their economies and stop the decline in their GDP. This is a formidable task. Though the political situation in the region continues to be stable, changes due to economic and other factors cannot be ruled out. Presently, these countries cooperate with Russia in regard to their security as in the case of the Tajikstan-Afghanistan border. Pakistan's efforts at playing a major role in Central Asia have not been successful so far. But the possibility of Islamabad attempting to meddle in the region remains, especially if opportunities present themselves. Developments in the Central Asian Republic will deserve to be closely monitored from the point of view of India's national security.

Immediately to our East, the Southeast Asian scene is characterised by stability and economic development. There is much greater understanding between the ASEAN and Indochina, with Vietnam about to become the seventh member of the organisation. All these countries are experiencing high GNP growth. Enhanced economic potential, combined with the apprehension of a possible American withdrawal from the region, is leading to the building up of increased defence capabilities in these countries. Defence budgets are rising significantly. The armies are reorganising for a conventional war capability. The air forces and navies are acquiring state-of-the art equipment, though in limited numbers.

India's relations with all countries in Southeast Asia continue to be good. Regular visits and dialogues have helped in building cooperative relationships. Joint naval exercises with regional navies and military visits have removed earlier suspicions and strengthened mutual confidence. India is interested in furthering these developments.

The formation of the ASEAN Regional Forum (ARF) in July this year was a notable attempt at constituting a security structure in the Asia—Pacific region.

There are compelling reasons for this. With conflicting claims over the Spratly Islands in the South China Sea, anxiety over US withdrawal from the region, and awareness of Chinese and Japanese military capabilities, there are concerns amongst member countries. This Forum has the potential to play an important role in the future.

Our relations with China received a further boost with the Prime Minister's visit to Beijing in 1993. Since then there have been other high level contacts at the political level and between the armed forces. The Deputy Chief of the General Staff Department of the PLA visited India in January 1994. This was followed by the visit of the Indian Chief of the Army Staff of China in June. The Chinese Defence Minister visited India in August 1994. There have been 3 meetings : 2 at the expert level, 1 of the joint working group. These discussions have proved to be very positive in furthering relations between the two countries. Additional confidence building measures are being discussed with a view to removing tensions. It is important that both these go hand in hand. Both our nations are concentrating on economic development; hence, peace and tranquility on our common borders is important for both.

Some relevant factors also deserve mention. Beijing is engaged in building strategic road links from its border towns to rail-heads and sea ports of Myanmar. It is helping to develop these ports. China has also been rapidly modernising its armed forces and equipping them with sophisticated aircraft, airdefence weapons and enhancing its blue-water capabilities. China also continues to carry out nuclear tests.

Pakistan's unrelenting material and other forms of support to Kashmiri terrorists and separatist militants have highlighted the security needs in India's western flank. Pakistan's low-cost proxy war through a sustained propaganda offensive, as well as its attempts to internationalise the Kashmir issue by focusing on alleged human rights violations, is a function of its domestic political instability and ulterior political/territorial objectives vis-a-vis India.

Pakistan continues to maintain close lies with China. The latter is a major source of weapons, particularly of combat aircraft, missiles and tanks. The sale to Pakistan of M-11 missiles and allied technology by China is a cause of concern. Lately, Pakistan's effort to improve bilateral relations with Russia and other CIS countries is noteworthy. Russia's response to Pakistan's overtures, especially in regard to supply of weapons, has so far been subdued.

The revelation by Nawaz Sharif, the former Prime Minister of Pakistan, that Pakistan possesses a nuclear bomb, has added a new dimension to security in the region. Equally distressing has been his other disclosure implicating the Pakistan Army and the ISI in funding covert military operations against India through illegal narcotics trade.

Pakistan's support to subversive and terrorist elements directed against India is the root cause of tension in our bilateral relations. It has been breeding, abetting and extending support to terrorism in J&K and Punjab through organising training camps in Pakistan/POK. Pakistan has also been extending support to subversive elements in the North Eastern States of India through its Inter Services Intelligence (ISI). Investigations connected with Bombay blasts in March 1993, indicate Pakistan's organised support and involvement in the planning and execution of these terrorist acts.

In Kashmir, a sustained drive by the security forces has resulted in the elimination of a large number of hard core militants and foreign mercenaries. This has lowered the morale of the terrorists and their foreign masters. A perceptible change is coming about in the attitude of the people of Kashmir. The growing inter-gang rivalries among militants and their apparently sagging morale has also led Pakistan to increasingly take resort to infiltration of mercenaries. While there is no let up in vigilance on the borders and effective operations against the militants in the hinter-land, Government are also attempting the acceleration of the political and developmental processes in the State.

In the wake of Foreign Secretary level talks in early January 1994, the Government of India handed over six non-papers to Pakistan on January 24, containing specific and constructive proposals for confidence building and security. Our proposals related to Siachen, Sir Creek, measures to maintain peace and tranquility along the Line of Control, Tulbul navigation project, no first use of nuclear capabilities and non-attack on population centres, and constituting an India-Pakistan Joint Commission. Pakistan's response to these has not been constructive.

The continuing instability and civil war in Afghanistan is a source of anxiety. It is not in India's Interest that a neighbouring state should have prolonged instability. India stands for a peaceful negotiated settlement among the warring groups in Afghanistan.

India attaches considerable importance to cordial and cooperative relations with all its South Asian neighbours. Existing close and friendly relations with Sri Lanka have been further consolidated and reinforced. Both countries are committed to securing further expansion and diversification of their relations for mutual benefit. With the installation of a new Government in Nepal, India expects to continue the traditional good relations with that country in all spheres.

Indian insurgent groups in the North-Eastern states continue to use the border areas of Myanmar for sanctuary, training and import of arms. During the course of last two years, our relations with Myanmar have improved significantly. The two Governments have agreed to discuss ways and means to ensure better border management with a view to maintaining peace and tranquillity on the Indo-Myanmar border. This will naturally depend on the effective control of the Government of Myanmar on its western border areas.

India and Bangladesh are close neighbours with common historical and cultural links. India remains interested in, and active in pursuit of, settling all outstanding issues with Bangladesh, including illegal immigration from Bangladesh to India, the river waters issue and the completion of the repatriation of Chakma refugees.

The security environment in Asia, though much improved in recent years, still has the potential for turbulence. Sudden developments and unforeseen consequences can upset this stability and result in adverse consequences to our neighbourhood. India is determined to do all it can to help ensure a secure environment in Asia which will allow its economic development to proceed unimpeded. At the same time, it will have to remain prepared to counter developments adverse to its own security and development. For this, it is essential that India maintains a sufficiently strong defence capability to safeguard its national interests.

On the global front, India continues to contribute to peace processes designed to end conflicts in different parts of the world. India supports UN efforts in this direction and cooperates with all countries in the global endeavour to strengthen the forces of peace and development.

18.2 ARMY

The role of the Army is to safeguard the territorial integrity of the nation against external threats. Besides, whenever the situation so demands, the Army has also to discharge the additional responsibility of rendering assistance to the civil administration by helping it maintain internal security and restore alw and order. Furthermore, in the event of natural calamities, the Army is called upon to participation, or even spearhead, relief operations. Accordingly, the Army's force levels are structured to carry out its main role of defence preparedness, including occasional participation in counter-insurgency operations and matters relating to internal security.

Modernisation

The Army cannot afford merely to react to external impetus, the challenges posed by increasing force levels, and the induction of state-of-the-art weapon systems by our potential adversaries. As a dynamic and pro-active organisation, it is imperative for the Army to continuously modernise itself and simultaneously update its human and material resources. This is not only to keep pace with changing threat perception and the consequent evolving geo-political environment, but also, at the same time to familiarise itself with the rapid advancement of technology and the changing social milieu. With the spirit of liberalisation now permeating various sectors of economic activity and the rapid changes ensuing from it having gathered momentum, a commensurate pace of modernisation is required of the Army as well. The structural adjustment policies being implemented for the last three years in all the sectors of government expenditure require much greater emphasis on finding the most cost-effective means of ensuring a high level of operational preparedness. Therefore, our efforts to emphasise modernisation are based on a critical scrutiny of all areas of expenditure, which would result in bringing about cost efficiency in the Army's consumption of ammunition and energy, pattern of training and human resources. These developments, which had been initiated in the recent past, continued last year as well.

Weapons and Equipment Modernisation

Efforts towards the maintenance of ammunition reserves at the desired level, upgradation of critical weapon systems through refurbishment and technological updates and selective introduction of strategically improved force multipliers, are continuing. The effort to indigenise Extreme Cold Weather Clothing Systems and other equipment and Nuclear, Biological and Chemical (NBC) protection equipment, have shown very encouraging results. The setting up of production facilities for these items is being accelerated.

Armour

Efforts to enhance the fire power, night vision capability, mobility, and protection parameters of the tank fleet are continuing, primarily with indigenous technology. User trials of MBT Arjun are progressing on schedule and the modifications/ improvements suggested on the basis of trial results are being incorporated so that this latest state-of-the-art Main Battle Tank can be introduced into service on schedule.

18.3 NAVY

The Indian Navy is charged with the responsibility of defending the nation's maritime interests, which include the 7600 Kms coastline, outlying island territories, the Exclusive Economic Zone (EEZ) of 2.2 million Sq. Kms., offshore oil and seabed resources, sea lanes of communication, fishing interests, ports and harbours, shipbuilding industry and infrastructure to sustain the mercantile marine.

Being a maritime nation, India's natural outlet is to the sea, through which approximately 97% of our trade passes. Our sea lanes serve as vital trade routes through the Indian Ocean, and the country's economic well being is closely linked to our ability to keep these sea lanes free and open at all times.

Operations and Exercises

During the year under review, the naval forces have been on continuous patrol and surveillance tasks, off the coast of Tamil Nadu, in particular, the Palk Bay/ Gulf of Mannar areas in the Bay of Bengal, and off the coasts of Maharashtra and Saurashtra in the Arabian Sea against arm/explosive smuggling; besides off the Andaman and Nicobar Islands and Bay of Bengal areas.

Regular tactical exercises including Amphibious Exercises, involving the three Services, were conducted during the year to keep the Naval Fleet at optimum levels of operational readiness.

Indigenous Construction Programme

The indigenous path continues to be the mainstay of the Navy's acquisition programme and the blue print for development of the Navy has, therefore, been firmly anchored on its ability to indigenously design and construct modern warships and submarines. Indigenous warship construction capability not only makes one self-reliant but also saves precious foreign exchange. In addition, the Navy has instituted several measures to reduce the cost of ship production. Cost Accountants from the Department of Expenditure of the Ministry of Finance closely monitor expenditure on the indigenous ship construction programme in our shipyards.

As a part of the on-going indigenous construction programme, destroyer 'Bombay' has been launched at Mazagon Docks, and the frigate 'Beas' has been launched at GRSE, Calcutta during the year.

The second indigenously constructed submarine, 'INS Shankul' has been commissioned in May, 1994, making India a member of a select club of countries which possess the frontline technology for submarine construction. A state-of-the-art research vessel, INS Sagardhwani, which has been indigenously constructed at GRSE Calcutta has also been commissioned into the Navy.

Infrastructure Facilities

The Navy is an equipment intensive service but is conscious of the need for economy. Accordingly, the Navy has ensured the setting up of exclusive facilities for repair and maintenance of indigenously manufactured equipment, and major overhauls of equipment that is being presently imported.

The third & fourth line overhaul and maintenance facilities for the Sea Harrier aircraft engines and air frames are being set up at Cochin and Bangalore.

18.4 AIR FORCE

The Indian Air Force has completed 62 years of dedicated service of the nation. Though the youngest of the three Services, it has already rendered noteworthy service both in combat and in peace-time air support. It has maintained a balance in its air defence, air interdiction, reconnaissance, and offensive air support capabilities. As a part of its commitment to provide aid to civil authorities during natural calamities, the Indian Air Force was instrumental in providing prompt and expeditious logistic support and helping in search, rescue and relief operations during floods. The valiant men in their flying machines have become indispensable to the troops and the civilians in remote and inaccessible areas. Regular exercises and training have ensured that the men and their machines are in perfect harmony with each other so as to provide effective security and defence to our frontiers.

Operational Preparedness

A classic demonstration of the strength of air power during the Gulf War (1990-92) displayed that the battle in the air has to be won first before land and sea battles can be fought. The Indian sub-continent has a vast airspace stretching from the Himalayas to the Indian ocean. Guarding the air frontiers both at sea and over land is the avowed duty of the Indian Air Force. It has acquitted itself with honour and displayed a very high standard of operational preparedness and alertness at all times. The IAF maintains constant round-the-clock vigil of our borders. This warrants a high state of preparedness to scramble and intercept any violators of Indian air space. The IAF operates an efficient and well-planned air defence network comprising a sophisticated range of frontline aircraft, missiles, and radar systems which provide protective air cover to vital civilian and military installations.

The Indian Air Force has established an efficient and streamlined system of ensuring reliable maintenance and overhaul facilities for its aircraft and ground systems. It is progressively becoming self-sufficient in the overhaul and maintenance of its entire fleet of sophisticated aircraft. The vast infrastructure that the Air Force has been able to establish for such support is also now being utilised by other countries. The human resource endowment of IAF personnel is being constantly updated by on the job training programmes within the country and outside it. In fact, the training facilities established by the Indian Air Force have acquired widespread acclaim, and personnel from other air forces are now being deputed in increasingly large numbers for training in Indian Air Force establishments.

Modernisation and Resource Constraints

The field of aviation has witnessed tremendous technological advancement in recent years. Air warfare now involves an effective integration of excellent avionics and lethal armaments. Sophisticated, state-of-the-art weapons and platforms are being added to the arsenal of our adversaries. The Indian Air Force too has to be dynamic and to continuously upgrade its technology. Modernisation of the fleet and the addition of force multipliers in the present environment are essential to maintain fighting fitness and combat superiority. The aviation industry within the country has been making rapid advances, ensuring that our technology remains abreast of the latest that is being introduced in other countries.

Resource constraints in the recent past have compelled the IAF to evolve plans which are more resource driven, instead of being programme oriented. Even now the armed forces in general, and the Indian Air Force in particular, face severe resource constraints, which are further accentuated by the need for replacement of a large number of weapon systems. Budgetary support being restricted, it has become imperative to initiate innovative strategies.

Under these conditions, the Government's endeavour would be to ensure that existing resources are optimally utilised by serving the dual purposes of conserving and prolonging the period of effective utilisation of such systems without compromising the operational capability of the Service. Within resource constraints, the Government is committed to the IAF's all-round professional growth. The present thrust, therefore, is towards modernisation of the Service in select areas.

With this objective in view, the Government has adopted the undermentioned multipronged strategy :

(i) Undertaking mid-life upgradation of various aircraft in a phased manner.

(ii) Initiating the process of indigenising critically required items to ensure better serviceability of IAF fleet and establishing indigenous repair/overhaul facilites, wherever establishment of such facilities is economically viable or essential from operational point of view.

(iii) To effect economies in expenditure after carrying out a critical review of the competing requirements and also by initiating measures that would help in economising without affecting the operational effectiveness of the IAF. Brief details of the measures proposed to be taken for translating the strategy into concrete action are given in the succeeding paragraphs.

Upgradation of Aircraft

The cost of acquiring a new fighter aircraft with state-of-the-art technology is enormous and given the resource constraints, the need to undertake selective upgradation/modernisation of various combat aircraft in the IAF fleet has been identified as a priority requirement by the Government. The current trend all over the world is to commission such mid-life upgradations to ensure optimal utilisation. In fact, to prolong the usefulness of the existing aircraft, certain measures when undertaken judiciously by incurring considerably smaller expenditure for integrating state-of-the-art weapons and avionics enable the existing aircraft to be upgraded and made capable of meeting contemporary and future requirements.

The Government has, keeping in view the factors enumerated in the preceding para, approved the upgradation of the MiG-021 BIS aircraft in association with the concerned Russian agencies. The upgradation package would consist of new avionics and weapons systems to be installed on the aircraft. The upgraded MiG-21 BIS aircraft, which is expected to be available by 2000 AD, would be capable of meeting the requirements of the IAF for a much longer period and would also obviate the need for immediate replacement of the aircraft. This would, thus, not only help in conserving limited funds but would also ensure utilisation of the amount so conserved for meeting other critical requirements of the IAF. The life extension of this aircraft upto 4,000 hours is also envisaged as part of the upgradation/modernisation package.

The technical details of the proposed upgradation have been discussed with the Russian agencies and also with the Western companies who would be supplying certain of the sub-systems for the project. The indigenous equipment/ systems proposed to be installed on the upgraded aircraft have also been identified. The design and development of the upgraded package is being undertaken by the Mikoyan Design Bureau, Russia while the upgradation of the aircraft would be undertaken at HAL.

Future upgrading programmes of other aircraft in the IAF inventory will depend on the success of the MiG-21 BIS upgradation project.

Indigenisation and Other Measures

Indigenisation of the vast range of equipment in service in the IAF with complex and sophisticated technology should be awarded importance whilst ensuring uncompromising quality standards and stringent performance criteria.

18.5 DEFENCE PUBLIC SECTOR UNDERTAKINGS

The defence public sector undertakings (DPSUs) were structured with a flexible form of operation, decentralised management and adequate operational autonomy so as to utilise the defence technological base to a wide and diversified range of application, in addition to the basic task of catering to the needs of the armed forces. Eight defence PSUs currently function under the administrative control of this department.

The capabilities of the defence PSUs encompass design, development and manufacture of a large variety of sophisticated military hardware comprising aircraft, warships, electronic equipment, earthmoving equipment, missiles, aeronautical grade super alloys etc. The aggregate value of production in defence PSUs is likely to increase by about 5 per cent in 1994-95, as compared to the previous year. The defence PSUs are likely to earn about Rs. 248.53 crore as profit before tax during 1994-95.

18.6 RECRUITMENT AND TRAINING

Sainik Schools

The scheme to establish Sainik Schools was introduced in the year 1961 to remove regional imbalance in the officers cadre of the Defence Services. The aim of the Sainik Schools is to prepare boys academically, physically and mentally for entry into the National Defence Academy. Through these schools Public School education is brought within the reach of the common man.

At present there are 18 Sainik Schools in the country. There is one school in almost every major State. Boys from States and Union Territories which do not have a Sainik School are accommodated in the schools located in the adjoining State.

The Sainik Schools are managed by the Sainik Schools Society which is registered under the Societies Registration Act. The overall administration, supervision and control of Sainik Schools Society vests with the body called the Board of Governors headed by the Raksha Mantri. An Executive Committee under the Chairmanship of the Defence Secretary controls and supervises the functioning of Sainik Schools. An officer not below the rank of Deputy Secretary in the Ministry of Defence is appointed as the Honorary Secretary by the Chairman of Board of Governors.

Each Sainik School has a Local Board of Administration headed by General Officer Commanding in Chief of the Command, or a senior officer, not below the rank of Major General nominated by him, in which the school is located. The local Member of Parliament is also a member of the Local Board of Administration, besides State Government officials. Three Defence Service Officers are posted as Principal, Headmaster and Registrar in each Sainik School.

Sainik Schools admists boys in Class VI and IX on the basis of an All India Sainik School Entrance Examination followed by an interview-cum-medical examination of those who are in the merit list. 15%, 7.5% and 25% seats are reserved for sons of Scheduled Castes, Scheduled Tribes, Serving personnel and ex-Servicemen, respectively.

Resources of Sainik Schools are mainly from school fess which is Rs. 11,000/- per annum. In the majority of cases, the fee is being reimbursed by the State Governments, and the Ministry of Defence, by way of scholarships to the students.

Great emphasis is laid on physical and mental health to promote all round personality of the cadets in Sainik Schools. Sainik School cadets actively participate in several co-curricular activities, community service, adventure sports like mountaineering, trekking and cycle expeditions, and protection of environment and ecology programmes. Participation in NCC is compulsory for all cadets.

Since the inception of Sainik Schools, at total 4647 cadets have entered the portals of the National Defence Academy. The average pass percentage of Classes X and XII in Central Board of Secondary Education examination for the academic session 1993-94 have been 99 and 91 respectively. 27 cadets have won laurels by securing positions in top 0.1% of total qualified candidates in various subjects in the Board Examinations.

A painting done by a cadet during "On the Spot Painting Competition" was selected for the exhibition organised in Yokohama, Japan, in May 1994. Another cadet has brought laurels by winning the coveted "Sword of Honour" at the National Defence Academy passing out parade in June 1994.

Two teachers of Sainik Schools were conferred with National Award by Hon'ble President of India on September 5, 1994, for their valuable contribution in Sainik Schools.

19

EDUCATION AND CULTURE

Education

Education for All

The Education For All (EFA) Summit of Nine High Population Countries held in New Delhi on 16th December, 1993 culminated in a policy declaration and framework of strategies for its implementation. The policy declaration calls for providing basic education facilities for every child and consolidating efforts towards basic education for children, youth and adults. In the context of an integrated strategy of basic education for all people, literacy and adult education programme are to be improved and extended, eliminating disparities of access, improving the quality and relevance of basic education. Human Development is to be accorded the highest priority ensuring that a growing share of national and community resources is dedicated to basic education.

Developing a collaborative mechanism for distance education, periodic consultations and sharing experiences among the nine countries; Decentralized management of structure in education making the school more accountable to the community for its performance, development of performance norms and code of conduct for teachers and development of districts specific programmes are some of the steps taken in this direction.

The NPE 1986 and POA 1992 while resolving to ensure free and compulsory education of satisfactory quality to all upto 14 years of age before 21st Century adumbrate the policy statement made at the EFA Summit. Consequently the intensification of NPE/POA programmes with new initiatives and priorities is also an attempt towards commitment made during EFA Summit.

Elementary Education

The elementary education system in India is the second largest in the world with 149 million children enrolled in 1994-95 in the age group of 6-14 years covering about 82% of the children in this age group. Of these, 109 million children were enrolled in 581,305 primary schools and another 40 million in 163,605 upper primary schools. There are 2.8 million teachers -1.7 million employed in primary schools and 1.1 million in upper primary schools. 94.5% of the rural population living in 8.26 lakh habitations have a school within a walking distance of 1 km. and 83.98% have upper primary schooling facilities within a walking distance of 3 kms. The percentage of girls enrolled at primary stage stands at 42.8%. A study conducted by National Council of Applied Economic Research (NCAER) in 1993 indicates significant decline in the proportion of never enrolled children (boys as well as girls) in all States. The retention rate has also shown improvement and it is 62% at primary stage and 47% at upper primary stage.

Universal access, universal retention and universal achievement are broad parameters to achieve UEE. The focus was on school dropouts, working children, girls who cannot attend formal schools, particularly, belonging to SCs/STs and disadvantaged groups. Special focus has been given on removal of regional and gender disparities.

The major initiatives in the form of Operation Blackboard, Non-formal Education Programme and Teacher Education through mass orientation of teachers and District Institutes of Education and Training (DIETs) have continued to be accorded priority.

Strategy for achieving Universalisation of Elementary Education and Universal Adult literacy is being adopted through desegregated approach, with the focus on district-specific, population-specific plans both in Primary Education and in Adult Education Sectors.

District Primary Education Programme (DPEP)

In keeping with NPE 1986 and POA 1992 a new initiative to achieve UEE—'District Primary Education Programme' has been formulated. The programme takes a holistic view of primary education and to operationalise the strategy for UEE through district specific planning and disaggregated target setting. The programme lays great emphasis on participatory processes for planning and management, has marked gender focus and seeks to enhance school effectiveness through inputs in teachers training and decentralised management. The programme emphasizes capacity building at all levels and seeks to evolve strategies which are replicable and sustainable.

DPEP is a beachhead for effecting improvements and full-scale development of the entire elementary education sector. The overall goal of the programme is the reconstruction of primary education as a whole in the districts instead of the piecemeal implementation of schemes. The DPEP is not to be seen as an enclave project; it is a major and multi-faceted programme seeking to overhaul the primary education system in the country.

As of now the DPEP has been launched in 42 districts in the States of Madhya Pradesh, Assam, Haryana, Maharashtra, Karnataka, Tamil Nadu and Kerala. The Planning process has been initiated in five districts each in Andhra Pradesh and West Bengal where it would be funded by ODA. 19 districts of Madhya Pradesh are funded by European Community's programme assistance to DPEP while the remaining 23 districts are funded by IDA.

The emphasis has been shifted from enrolment per se to enrolment as well as retention and achievement. Micro planning will provide frame-work of universal access and universal participation. The targets for VIIIth plan include : (i) Universal enrolment of all children including girls and persons belonging to SC/ST; (ii) provision of Primary School for all children within one km. distance for habitation with a population of 200 and/or facility of non-formal education for school drop outs, working children and girls who cannot attend school; (iii) improvement of ratio of primary schools to upper primary schools from existing 4:1 to 2:1; (iv) reduction of drop out rates; (v) improvement of infrastructure facilities including upper primary level; (vi) achievement of MLL at primary and upper primary stage; (vii) quality of academic contents to be improved and NFE curriculum to be relevant to the specific needs of the target group; (viii) to facilitate lateral entry of NEE beneficiaries into formal system.

NCERT

NCERT has been providing resource support in crucial areas of School education and presently conducting Sixth All-India Educational Survey to assess the present status and facilities of school education in the country. Scheme of Science Education, Environment Education, CLASS project etc. have been revised to improve the quality of school education. Teacher Education has also been restructured and re-organized to upgrade the competency level at various stages. While Kendriya Vidyalayas and Navodaya Vidyalayas are promoting education with national identify, National Open School has been promoting distance education and is reaching out to deprived and Socio-economically backward sections of society in the remote parts of the country.

Scheme of Nutrition Support to Primary Education : A nation-wide Mid-day Meal programme was launched from 15th August, 1995 to give boost to UEE, improve enrolment, retention and attendance in primary schools and also to improve nutritional status of children. This scheme is expected to hasten the country's march towards the goal of UEE. Over a period of three years all the Government run/aided Schools are to be covered benefiting 12 crore children. During 1995-96, 378 districts, 2499 blocks, 2.25 lakhs schools and 3.35 crore children had been covered. The central support under this programme is on the following :

(i) Provision of foodgrains free to cost to the implementing agencies;
(ii) Reimbursement of transportation cost to District authorities for moving of foodgrains from Food Corporation of India godowns to schools/ villages.
(iii) Besides, remuneration for conversion of foodgrains into cooked food as well as expenditure on construction of kitchen sheds, will be eligible for coverage under the Poverty Alleviation Schemes being administered by the Ministry of Rural Development.

The expenditure towards the cost of foodgrains (payable to Food Corporation of India) and reimbursement of transportation cost will be incurred by the Ministry of HRD (Department of Education).

The Programme has commenced in all the States/UTs. Seven States namely, Gujarat, Haryana, Jammu & Kashmir, Kerala, Madhya Pradesh, Orissa and Tamil Nadu and U.T. of Pondicherry are serving cooked meal. In Delhi processed food is being served. In rest of the States/UTs, foodgrains are being distributed. The number of beneficiaries is about 3.34 crores.

Vocationalisation of Secondary Education : The main objective of the scheme of vocationalisation of Secondary Education at plus two level is to provide diversification of educational opportunities so as to enhance individual employability. The scheme covers vocational courses in the areas of business and commerce, agriculture, engineering and technology, Health and paramedical, Home Science and Humanities. The Vocational courses are also being offered to impart training in simple marketable skills and to develop vocational interests in students. 35 Vocational courses identified by UGC are being introduced at under graduate level.

Girls and Women Education : NPE has accorded highest priority to women's education and envisages the entire eudcational system to have built in provisions for women's empowerment. Enrolment and retention of girl child in formal and non-formal Schooling is emphasized. There is stress on removal of gender bias in curriculum. Recruitment of rural women as teachers is emphasized in various schemes. Free education is provided to girls upto Class VIII by various State Govts./UTs while education is free for girls upto Class XII in Kendriya and Navodaya Vidyalayas. Vocational programme with emphasis on entrepreneurship are being designed for girl drop outs. In major thrust areas-DPEP and TLC, Women are a special focus. Steps are being taken to increase women's participation in educational process, nation wide gender sensitization programme of educational personnel and parental awareness programmes for generating a positive climate for girl's education. The Mahila Samakhya project seeks to bring about a change in women's perception about themselves and that of Society in regard to women's 'traditional roles'. In Higher and Technical Education there have been significant expansion of educational opportunities for women.

Education of Minorities: An Area Intensive Programme has been launched to provide basic facilities to educationally backward minorities, who have remained deprived of educational and development opportunities.

Adult Education

The National Literacy Mission represent a national and political commitment on the need to harness all social forces to achieve the objective of effecting a qualitative change in the lives of the people. It has made it possible for the country to adopt a systematically planned approach which envisages coverage of the entire adult population by literacy of well defined level through instructions. The current rate of adult literacy as per 1991 census is 52.21% for the entire country (39.29% for females and 64.13% for males).

The Total Literacy Campaigns (TLCs), the major programme for universalising adult literacy, are now operational in 379 districts, either partially or fully, in the State of Andhra Pradesh, Bihar, Delhi, Goa, Gujarat, Haryana, Himachal Pradesh, Jammu & Kashmir, Karnataka, Kerala, Maharashtra, Madhya Pradesh, Manipur, Meghalaya, Orissa, Punjab, Rajasthan, Tamil Nadu, Tripura, Uttar Pradesh, West Bengal and UTs of Chandigarh, Dadra & Nagar Haveli, Daman & Diu and Pondicherry. Currently, approximately 62.36 million people in the 9-35 age group are learning with the help of about 6 million volunteers. They are in different stages of learning, but it is estimated that about 34 million of them have already acquired the threshold level of literacy and numeracy. The objective is to make 100 million people functionally literate.

Secondary Education

National Policy on Education places special emphasis on qualitative improvement and development of national curriculum and to improve the teaching of Languages, Mathematics, Science, Social Sciences, Vocational Education and Work experience, Art Education, Health and Physical Education alongwith Values in Education and Population Education. A number of Programmes have been formulated for enrolment of girls, SCs/STs and disabled children.

Vocationalisation of Secondary Education : With a view to make education work oriented, a Centrally Sponsored Scheme of vocationalisation of Secondary Education was introduced in February, 1988. The main objectives of the scheme are to enhance individual employability, reduce the mismatch between the demand and supply of skilled manpower and to provide an alternative for those pursuing higher education without particular interest or purpose. A Centrally Sponsored Scheme of Pre-Vocational Education at Lower Secondary Stage has also been introduced from the year 1993-94 primarily to impart training in simple marketable skills to the students of classes IX and X, to develop vocational interests and to facilitate students in making a choice of vocational courses at the higher secondary level. The target laid down in the revised National Policy on Education is to divert 10% of higher secondary students to the vocational stream by 1995 and 25% and 2000 A.D.

In order to provide expert inputs in policy formulation and implementation on a continuing basis, a Joint Council of Vocational Education (JCVE) has been set up at the national level under the chairmanship of Minister of Human Resource Development, with counterpart organisations at the State level. To ensure that the tasks laid down by JCVE are performed effectively, a Standing Committee of JCVE has been constituted under the chairmanship of Education Secretary. While the JCVE is to meet at least once a year, the Standing Committing meets more frequently.

A Central Institute of Vocational Education, named as "Pt. Sunderlal Sharma Central Institute of Vocational Education" (PSSCIVE) was set up at Bhopal on July Ist, 1993 under the overall umbrella of NCERT. The Institute acts as an apex level research and development organisation in the field of vocational education and provides technical and academic input to the programme. PSSCIVE has developed 82 competency-based curricula in 6 major areas which can be adopted by States/UTs with modifications based on the need and relevance of those courses in that particular area. The CIVE has now been entrusted with the task of standardising the curricula/textbook/ instructional material for vocational courses. The CIVE is also inter alia engaged in conducting programmes for training of teachers and orientation of key functionaries.

The scheme at +2 stage is implemented through the State Governments/ UT Administrations. So far all the States/UTs, except Lakshadweep, have joined the programme. Up to the end of 1994-95, 18055 vocational sections had been approved in 6280 schools, creating capacity for diversion of 9 lakh students to the vocational stream at the +2 stage. The actual enrolments, however, likely to be less, as optimum utilisation of facilities created may not be achieved. During the current year, i.e. 1995-96 main emphasis is, therefore, on consolidation and qualitative improvement of the programme.

TABLE 19.1 : Sexwise Enrolment at the High/Hr. Secondary Stage (1993-94 and 1994-95)

(In Million)

	1993-94	*1994-95*
Boys	15.3	16.0
Girls	8.0	8.4
Total	23.3	24.4

(Provisional)

Table 19.2 : Girls Enrolment : Percentage to Total Enrolment at the High/ Seċ.Hr.Sec./Inter Stage (1993-94 and 1994-95)

Year	*% to Total Enrolment (Provisional)*
1993-94	34.3
1994-95	34.4

University and Higher Education

Expansion of higher education : At the beginning of the year 1995-96, the total student enrolment in universities and colleges was 61.14 lakh. The enrolment in the University Departments was 10.14 lakh and that in the affiliated colleges was 51.0 lakh.

Out of ten students in higher education, four were in the Faculty of Arts, enrolled for courses in social sciences and humanities which include History and Culture and Languages. Three, out of ten students, were enrolled for courses in Science, Engineering, Medicine, Agriculture and related disciplines. The faculty of commerce enrolled two out of 10 students. Enrolment at the first degree level was 53.86 lakh (88.1%); at the post-graduate level 5.82 lakh (9.5%); at the research level 0.67 lakh (1.1%); and at the diploma and certificate level 0.79 lakh (1.3%). The total number of teachers increased to 3.01 lakh during the year. Of these, 0.69 lakh were in the University Departments/ University Colleges and the rest in the affiliated colleges. Of the 69283 teachers in the Universities, 8868 are Professors, 18152 are Readers, 39492 are Lecturers and 2771 are Tutors/Demonstrators. In the affiliated colleges, the number of senior teachers was 32,180; the number of Lecturers was 1,89,144 and that of Tutors/Demonstrators was 10,186.

Upto March 1996, the total number of Universities in the country was 167 and the total number of Institutions deemed to be universities was 36.

Higher Education among Women : The enrolment of women students at the beginning of the year 1995-96 was 20.65 lakh. At the postgraduate level, the enrolment of women was 35.6% of the total enrolment. The enrolment of women students was the highest in Kerala (52.0%), followed by Goa and Punjab (50.9% each), Pondicherry (45.1%), Delhi (44.2%), Manipur (42.4%), Meghalaya and Nagaland (39.5%) each and Jammu & Kashmir (39.3%). The enrolment of women was the lowest in Bihar (18.4%).

Programmes and Activities of the UGC Commission: Some of the major thrust areas pursued during the year were : Human Resource Development, Research and Studies in Emerging and Inter-disciplinary areas, Environment Education, Vocationalisation of Education at the first degree level, Academic Staff Colleges for Orientation of teachers, Eligibility test for recruitment of lecturers, Inter-University Centres and Consortium, Distance Education, COSIST, Adult Education and National Literacy Mission, Spread of Mass Communication and Educational Technology Network, Computer Education, Education for Scheduled Castes and Scheduled Tribes and for the minorities and weaker sections among the minority communities, Education for Women and the Handicapped and Population Education.

TABLE 19.3 : Educational Institutions (1993-94 and 1994-95)

	Type	*1993-94*	*1994-95*
1.	Pre-Primary Schools	17172	41487
2.	Primary Schools	572932	581305
3.	Middle Schools	155707	163605
4.	High Schools	65255	68065
5.	Hr. Sec. Schools (New Pattern-10+2)	20167	21125
6.	Inter/Jr./Pre-Degree Colleges	2989	3062
7.	Arts/Science/Commerce Colleges	5639	6089
8.	Engineering/Technical Colleges (Degree and Above level)	308	341
9.	Medical Colleges (Allopathy/ Ayurvedic)	233	303
10.	Teacher Training Colleges	584	586
11.	Teacher Training Schools		1179
12.	Polytechnics	1021	1107
13.	Universities (Including Deemed to be Universities and Institutions of National Importance	213	219
14.	Technical, Industrial Arts and Craft Schools	3861	3835

Culture

Archaeological Survey of India

The Archaeological Survey of India, at present has 3562 centrally protected monuments declared to be of national importance which include 16 World Heritage Monuments. Some of the important conservation work carried out by the Survey during the year are Taj Mahal Complex, Agra Fort Complex, Agra.

Ajanta caves Jalgaon, Elephanta caves Thane, Jagannath temple Puri, Sun temple Puri, Maharshi Bhawan Jorasanko, Metacalfe Hall Calcutta, etc. In addition the Survey has also undertaken conservation works of unprotected monuments like Jama Masjid, Delhi and Tawang Monastery Tawang as a special case. The science branch of the A.S.I. has carried out the chemical cleaning, consolidation and preservation works on some of the most important monuments like Golkonda Fort, Hyderabad Swarga Brahma temple, Alampur, etc. In the field of exploration a large number of sites and remains ranging from pre historic to the medieval times has been discovered in different parts of the country and exploration surveys arc continued. In the field of excavation, work at various places continued including the excavation work at Maheth (Sravasti, UP) which brought to light a big complex of early Gupta period, excavation at Khalkatapatnam, Distt Puri, Orissa revealed a single culture habitation.

Museum : During 1995-96, the National Museum organised three international exhibitions viz (i) "Buddha in India-Early Indian Sculptures"—in Vienna, Austria. (ii) "Feminine ideal in Indian Art"—in Paris in collaboration with the Crafts Museum, New Delhi. (iii) "International Buddhist Culture" at Seoul, South Korea. Under Cultural Exchange Programme it organised two international exhibitions (i) "Alankara : 5000 Years of India" in Singapore and (ii) "Vision of king : Art and Experience in India" at Canberra, Australia. Five international exhibitions entitled "Italy : Past and Present" under Indo-Italy Cultural Exchange Programme have been organised in the National Museum.

The Salarjung Museum organised an exhibition "Engravings of Indian Monuments by English Artists" which remained opened for 35 days. A mobile exhibition on theme "World Heritage monuments of India, select monuments of A.P and Game of Chess" covered 99 educational institutions including Nehru Zoological Park and Public Garden. Besides the Museum organised 5 gallery talks and 42 film shows. The Indian Museum, under Cultural Exchange Progamme took part in an exhibition on "Buddha on Early Indian Sculptures" in Vienna, Austria. A Week long Film Festival was organised entitled "Art and Artists of Bengal". A new galley entitled 'Earth' and 'Meteorite' was thrown open to public. The mass education programme has been further augmented. The Musco Bus held its guided tour and mobile exhibition in three districts of West-Bengal. The Allahabad Museum organised a seminar on "Literature and Social Change" jointly with the G.B. Social Science Institute, Jhusi, Allahabad. Another seminar was organised on "Sanskrit Kavya mein Jeevan Dàrshan". It also organised a workshop on printing, in batches. Four batches have completed the course till October, 1995. The National Council of Science Museum mounted an excellent mobile exhibition, "The Dinosaur Alive" which was a unique exhibition. The exhibition drew more then 89 lakhs visitors from all walks of life. Apart from these several new galleries and facilities were completed during the period under review in different science centres under NCSM. The Museum has been entrusted with a project for development of science centre in Mouritius, namely, the Rajiv Gandhi Science Centre. Work on the project is in progress.

The National Archives of India (NAI) an attached office of the Department of Culture houses Central Government records of permanent value for preservation and use by administration and scholars. During the years under report the holding of the Department was further enriched by acquisition of more than 500 Government files and many private papers of importance. The School of Archival Studies continued to conduct one year diploma course in Archival Studies as also various short-term courses of eight and four weeks duration. 8 trainees successfully completed one year Diploma Course in Archival Studies. To mark the conclusion of the year long celebrations on the 75th anniversary of Jallianwala Bagh episode of 1919, a function was organised during the year, in the Annexe of the Department where the Minister for Human Resource Development released a commemorative volume "Lahuluhan Baisakhi" which is a compilation of Urdu poems drawn from the prescribed literature available in the National Archives of India.

The Asiatic Society: The Asiatic Society has made considerable progress in the project 'Oriental Studies' which includes Indo-Arab relations and Indias concept of nature and concern for environment in the medieval period. The society has taken up a scheme for publishing a nine volume "Encyclopaedia Asiatica", this means covering all the aspects of the way of life of the people of Asia, starting from the physical condition in which they have lived, the history they have made the institution and arts and literature they have created etc. Each volume is being processed by an Expert Committee. Besides these, a number of cultural agreements for exchange of scholars, holding of joint international seminars and exchange of publications have been signed with foreign countries and institutions which have identified the Asiatic Society, Calcutta as the counterpart organisation in this country in respect of oriental studies.

The National Library : The National Library is the biggest library in the country with a collection of 2.4 million volumes. The Library renders service through its Reading Rooms and Lending Sections. The Library has on its roll over 16000 readers as Reading Room Members' and the Lending Section deals with more than 68000 registered borrowers both local and outstation. It also functions as the National Centre for International loan. The Central Reference Library Calcutta has published the cumulated volume of Index Indiana for the year 1986-88. Besides, monthly issues of the Indian National Bibliography has been published for the year 1993 upto April. The Central Secretariat Library, New Delhi, which is the second largest Central Government Library, after the National Library, enhanced its resources by acquiring 58,000 documents, which include 32,000 Indian Official documents, 25,000 foreign official documents, including Micro-film and Micro-fiche and monographs in English, Hindi and regional languages. The Khuda Baksh Oriental Public Library has acquired 1,100 books by purchase/gift/exchange. The Library has also instituted an Award to be given to scholars for outstanding research contribution in the Library's special fields of Arabic/Persian Urdu Islamic studies, Tibo, South Asian studies etc. The first Khuda Baksh Award has already been conferred. The second and third Award, earmarked for National integration and Ganga Jamuna Composite Culture of India is to be conferred shortly. The Raja Rammohun Roy Library foundation, is operating two types of schemes of assistance—Matching and Non-matching. Matching schemes are operated from the matching fund created with State Governments contribution and equal share from Foundation where as Non-matching schemes are operated fully from Foundation Fund. The Foundation has also initiated a number of promotional activities to promote library movement in the country.

Anthropological Survey of India : In the field of Anthropology, the Anthropological Survey of India, a scientific research organisation completed its 50 years of dedicated service to the nation on 1st December 1995. The Survey is the nodal organisation of anthropological research in the country. During the year it continued with all its ongoing programmes of collection documentation, research and dissemination. As regard the project "People of India" the scholars were engaged in various activities relating to checking and verification of data, collection of fresh information, revision of papers, proof reading etc. of two national volumes and 14 State/Union Territory volumes. Out of these, 2 national volumes and 5 state volumes were taken up for printing. In addition, the survey paid adequate attention towards the execution of Non-Plan projects. Collection of data and their analysis are under process in respect of these projects.

The Indira Gandhi Rashtriya Manav Sangrahalaya : Bhopal added a new exhibition—a dwelling complex of the Santhal tribe of Bihar to "Tribal Habitat" the open air exhibition of the Sangrahalaya. A special exhibition mounted by the Museum "The family"—was organised in collaboration with the UNESCO, the Anthropological Survey of India & National Council of Science Museums. Another exhibition "Pravaha" on the theme "Environment, Heritage and Community" was organised as part of World Environment Day in June 1995. Collection in the Sangrahalaya is a regular activity. The Museum organised several artists camps in the it's premises for this purpose. About 450 specimens were collected from among the tribal population of Toda, Kota, Irula etc. residing in various part of the country. Besides, the following programmes were organised towards dissemination of information, they were (i) "Do and learn" Education programme on Muria woodcraft. (ii) 3 week long programme featuring demonstration-cum-practical training on Shola crafts of Assam. (iii) Ten-day long workshop on painted pottery of Kutch region. (iv) 3 week long training camp on Madhubani painting of Mithila region of Bihar.

Academies : The Sangeet Natak Academi during the period about 650 Black and white photographs, 950 colour photographs 425 slides, 45 hours of video recordings were added to the archives of the Academi. The first workshop, under scheme Playwrights Workshops in Indian Languages was held in Tamil Nadu. Two Tamil plays were produced during this workshop. It has brought out a special issue of the quarterly journal Sangeet Natak devoted to Theatre criticism. *The Sahitya Akademi* has a big publication programme and some of the major publication projects which are continuing are publications of series of Makers of Indian literature—series histories of Indian literature, publication of bi-monthly journals entitled "Indian Literature"—in English and "Samakaleena Bharatiya Sahitya" in Hindi and a half yearly journal entitled "Sanskrit Pratibha" in Sanskrit. The six volumes "Encyclopaedia of Indian Literature" have been published, other projects of reference works like Bibliographics are in progress.

The Lalit Kala Akademi has been serving the cause of art and artists for the last 40 years. The Akademi conducted a few programmes with a new projection which are "Paricharcha and Dialogue" programme where eminent artists are invited to speak on their works through slides. Along with regular activities of the Akademi, the Akademi organised new programmes "Camp and workshop for young artists in different Regional Centres". In addition to the Commaraswamy Memorial lecture, lectures in honour of distinguished personalities in the field of art were held in Bhubaneshwar and Calcutta. The National School of Drama, one of the foremost theatre training institutions in the world and the only one of its kind in India continued with its activities. During the period under review many plays were produced by the students of the school which include Manoj Mitra's "Bagiya Bacharam Ki" Eduardo De 2 Filippo's "Rani Sethami" Harishankar Parsai's "Ladi Nazariya" etc. The Repertory Company of NSD started a new activity of presentation of FRINGE performances consisting of dramatic readings of World classics as well as new plays. The new production of the company are : (i) Ant Anant, (ii) Tamancha Khan Ki Gazab Dastan, (iii) Raste. In the Rangyatra exhibition the work of NSD Repertory Company since its inception is depicted through photographs, models, jewelry, costumes etc.

20

ENERGY (COAL, ELECTRICITY AND PETROLEUM)

The overall performance of infrastructural sectors has been quite satisfactory during 1994-95. The declining trend of crude oil production was arrested and reversed due to creation of additional capacities. The year 1995-96 has also shown a promising performance in infrastructural sectors. During April-November 1995-96, electricity generation increased by 9.9 per cent, crude oil by 11.6 per cent. Six infrastructural industries viz. electricity, coal, steel, cement, crude oil and petroleum products with a combined weight of 28.8 per cent in the Index of Industrial Production (IIP) recorded a growth rate of 8.9 per cent in April-November, 1995 compared with 7.4 per cent in April-November, 1994.

20.1 COAL

Coal is one of the primary sources of energy, accounting for about 67 per cent of total energy consumption in the country. Coal production at 253.8 million tonnes in 1994-95 represented a growth of 3.2 per cent over 1993-94. Non-coking coal production, contributing about 83 per cent to total coal output, increased by 4.3 per cent, whereas coking coal production declined by 1.8 per cent. Coal production during April-November, 1995 increased by 6.4 per cent (Table 20.1), but it fell short of the target fixed for the period by 4.1 per cent. The underground mines registered a growth of 0.6 per cent while the Opencast mines showed a growth of 8.8 per cent during April-November 1995 and continued to account for the major share in coal production.

Coking coal producing at 13.2 million tonnes during April-November, 1995 was 7.2 per cent less than that in April-November, 1994. Imports of coal have been consistently increasing and reached a level of 8.5 million tonnes in 1994-95.

Total despatches of coal in 1994-95 at 248.3 million tonnes increased by 2.4 per cent, but increased substantially by 6.4 per cent in April-November 1995. The total pithead stocks of coal declined from 46.4 million tonnes as on March 31, 1995, to 34.2 million tonnes as on November 30, 1995.

One of the major constraints on the profitability of the coal sector is low productivity in underground mines. This has stagnated at an output per man shift (OMS) of 0.55 tonnes for the last two decades, despite massive investments made in mechanisation of underground mines. The underground mines employ 80 per cent of manpower, but contribute only 30 per cent of total output. Productivity levels can be improved through better utilisation of existing stocks of machinery and equipment, greater flexibility in manpower deployment and rationalisation of the work force.

TABLE 20.1. Trends in the Coal Sector

	1993-94	1994-95*	April-November* 1994	April-November* 1995	Change over previous year 1994-95	Change over previous year 1995-96 @
			(Million tonnes)		(per cent)	
1. *Production*						
(a) Opencast	169.6	178.6	102.9	111.9	5.3	8.8
(b) Underground	76.4	75.2	42.9	43.2	-1.6	0.6
Total	246.0	253.8	145.8	155.1	3.2	6.4
2. Production (By coal grades)						
(a) Coking coal	45.1	44.3	14.2	13.2	-1.8	-7.2
(b) Non-coking coal	201.0	209.6	131.6	141.9	4.3	7.8
(c) Washed coal	12.2	11.8	6.0	6.1	-3.8	2.3
(d) Middlings	5.2	6.3	3.3	3.3	22.2	1.2
3. Pithead stocks (year-end)	50.7	46.4	34.0	34.2	-8.4	0.5
4. Despatches	242.6	248.3	155.3	165.3	2.4	6.4
5. Lignite production	18.1	19.3	9.1$	11.3$	6.6	23.7
6. Output per man-shift (OMS)						
(i) CIL	1.5	1.6	1.4	1.5	7.2	10.0
(ii) SCCL	1.1	1.1	0.9	1.1	2.9	17.1

* Provisional. @ April-November. $ By NLC only.

Indian coal has high ash content and low calorific value. The ash content varies from 20 to 30 per cent and sometimes exceeds 40 per cent. The transportation of such a non beneficiated coal, carrying inert material over long distances, not only leads to wastage of transport capacity and energy, but also results in low efficiency of coal based thermal power plants and adds to air pollution through higher emission and ash disposal. Distant thermal power stations are now being encouraged to use beneficiated coal. Two non-coking coal washeries with a capacity of 11 million tonnes per annum are likely to be commissioned in 1996. Four more washeries with a capacity of about 21 million tonnes per annum are to be set up by CIL under Build-Own-Operate (BOO) Scheme during the Ninth Five Year Plan. Given our large coal reserves and high import prices of alternative fuel, it is imperative to assess the status of advanced coal utilisation techniques to minimise environmental damage.

In order to encourage private sector investment in the coal sector, the Coal Mines (Nationalisation) Act, 1973 was amended with effect from June 9, 1993 for operation of captive coal mines by companies engaged in the production of iron and steel, power generation and washing of coal in the private sector. Imports of coking coal under Open General Licence (OGL) are being allowed and the import tariff has been slashed from 85 per cent to 35 per cent. Captive coal mining blocks have been identified for thirteen power generating companies/Electricity Boards and for our companies in the iron and steel sector.

As on September 30, 1995, out of 76 projects under implementation in the coal sector, 22 projects are bedevilled by time and cost overruns. On an average, the cost overrun per project is about Rs. 65 crore and the time overrun per project is about 35 months. There is urgent need to improve project implementation in the coal sector.

The borrowings of Coal India Limited (CIL) from the Central Government as on March 31, 1995, were Rs. 3814 crore. With the reduction in budgetary support public sector coal companies are required to approach external, domestic and international sources for medium and long term credit to finance their planned increases in production. The cash and carry scheme implemented by CIL from October 1, 1992, enabled the company to slow down the growth of arrears, but the company is required to take steps to realise the large outstanding undisputed sales dues.

Power

Power generation in 1994-95 at 351.02 billion kwh. recorded a growth of 8.5 per cent over 1993-94 but fell short of the target for the year by 0.3 per cent. Thermal, hydro and nuclear generation went up by 6.1 per cent, 17.3 and 3.7 per cent respectively, in comparison to the generation during the year 1993-94 (Table 20.2).

TABLE 20.2. Trends in the Power Sector (utilities only)

	1993-94	1994-95*	April-November* 1994	April-November* 1995	Change over previous year 1994-95	Change over previous year 1995-96@
	(Billion KWH)				(per cent)	
1. Power generation	323.5	351.0	226.2	248.7	8.5	9.9
(i) Hydro-electric	70.4	82.5	58.3	52.9	17.3	-9.3
(ii) Thermal	247.8	262.9	164.6	190.6	6.1	15.8
(iii) Nuclear	5.4	5.6	3.3	5.2	3.7	58.4
2. Plant load factor of thermal plants (per cent)	61.0	60.0	56.6	60.5		

* Provisional. @ April-November.

Total generation of power in April-November, 1995 was 248.7 billion kwh, compared to 226.2 billion kwh during April-November, 1994, showing a growth of 9.9 per cent. While thermal and nuclear generation went up by 15.8 per cent and 58.4 per cent respectively, hydro generation declined by 9.3 per cent.

Thermal plants accounted for 74 per cent of total power generation and hydro electricity plants for 24 per cent, with the balance 2 per cent being generated by nuclear plants. The installed capacity of power generation as on March 31, 1995, was 81,164 MW. The total installed capacity increased by 3537 MW in 1992-93, (79 per cent of the target), 4539 MW in 1993-94 (102 per cent of the target), and by 4599 MW in 1994-95 (95 per cent of the target). Thus in the first three years of the Eighth Plan, capacity addition has been 12675 MW, as against the Eighth Plan target of 30858 MW. About 13 per cent of the total capacity addition during the first three years was accounted for by hydel and the remaining by thermal units. Nearly half of the addition in capacity occurred in the Central sector, 44 per cent in the State sector and the rest in the private sector. The Central sector achieved 49.5 per cent of the Eighth Plan target in the first three years of the plan. The corresponding figures for the State and private sectors are 37.8 per cent and 24.2 per cent respectively. Against the target of 1234.25 MW set for April-December 1995-96, the actual additions have been 510.25 MW during this period. (Table 20.3)

TABLE 20.3. Addition to Generating Capacity

(MW)

Sector	1993-94 Target	1993-94 Actual	1994-95 Target	1994-95 Actual	April-December 1995* Target	April-December 1995* Actual
Thermal	3265.0	3742.0	4125.5	3928.5	1170.0	503.5
Hydro	954.0	797.0	473.3	450.0	64.3	6.8
Nuclear	220.0	—	220.0	220.0	—	—
Total	4439.0	4539.0	4818.8	4598.5	1234.3	510.3

* Provisional.

The Plant Load Factor (PLF) is an important indicator of operational efficiency of thermal power plants. The average PLF in 1994-95 and in April-November 1995 in Central PSUs was appreciably higher than that achieved by State Electricity Boards (SEBs) (Table 20.4). The low capacity utilisation of thermal power plants of the SEBs is largely due to deficiencies in management and operation, lack of proper maintenance and non-availability of coal of appropriate quality. There are wide inter state variations in the average PLF of thermal plants. The average PLF in the case of Eastern and North Eastern regions continued to be much lower than the all India average, which was 60.5 per cent during April-November 1995.

TABLE 20.4. Thermal Plant Load Factor

	1991-92	1992-93	1993-94	1994-95*	*April- November** 1994	1995	1995 Target
			(per cent)				
I. Ownership							
State	50.6	54.1	56.6	55.0	51.1	51.7	55.4
Central Sector	64.5	62.7	69.8	69.2	64.0	65.0	67.7
Private Sector	55.3	58.3	56.6	65.9	66.1	66.4	78.3
II. Region							
Northern	58.8	62.0	64.0	59.3	55.3	55.8	60.0
Western	59.6	59.7	63.4	63.8	57.8	60.1	65.5
Southern	60.8	62.6	68.3	69.0	65.6	63.8	71.0
Eastern	37.3	39.8	44.8	43.7	43.3	43.1	40.9
North Eastern	24.6	24.3	19.9	26.8	22.4	24.5	29.4
All India	55.3	57.1	61.0	60.0	55.9	56.6	60.5

* Provisional.

The critical problem area in the power sector continued to be the poor performance of SEBs, which generate and distribute power, set tariffs and collect revenues. Agriculture and industry continued to be the two most important categories of consumers in terms of their relative shares, with SEB electricity charges set at much below cost for the agricultural sector and above unit cost for the industrial sector (Table 20.5). Unit revenue realisation from the agricultural sector in none of the SEBs covers a reasonable fraction of the unit average cost for the SEB, leading to heavy financial losses. The commercial losses of SEBs in absolute terms which were little over Rs. 7500 crore in 1995-96 (RE) are projected to increase further to about Rs. 10,096 crore in 1996-97. The hidden subsidy for agriculture and domestic sectors increased from Rs. 7439 crore in 1992-93 to Rs. 13,589 crore in 1995-96 (RE) and is projected to further go up to Rs. 15,349 crore in 1996-97 (Table 20.6).

TABLE 20.5. Consumer Categorywise Sale of Electricity and Average Tariff

Consumer	*1993-94*		*1994-95*		*1995-96@*	
	Sale (%)	*Tariff (paise/ kwh)*	*Sale (%)*	*Tariff (paise/ kwh)*	*Sale (%)*	*Tariff (paise/ kwh)*
Domestic	16.5	85.0	16.6	93.0	16.9	91.8
Commercial	4.7	134.3	4.5	203.4	4.6	208.1
Agriculture	28.4	20.1	28.9	21.8	28.0	24.5
Industrial	37.3	185.8	35.8	211.6	36.1	218.4
Rly. Traction	2.1	227.8	2.0	248.6	2.0	254.5
Outside state	1.5	77.9	1.6	104.5	1.8	112.4
Overall	9.5	120.7	10.6	132.9	10.6	140.7
All Consumer	100.0	112.7	100.0	127.4	100.0	132.8

@ Projection.

In addition, the SEBs have continued to suffer from high transmission and distribution (T & D) losses.

Restoration of financial health of SEBs and improvement in their operational performance continue to remain the most crucial issues in the power sector.

A process of restructuring of SEBs was initiated in several States, namely, Orissa, Haryana, Uttar Pradesh, Rajasthan, Bihar and Andhra Pradesh.

The net budgetary support to Central PSUs under the Ministry of Power as compared to the approved plan outlay has been declining steadily over the years and stood at about Rs. 689 crore (9.9 per cent) in 1995-96. Because of the decline in budgetary support from year to year, Central PSUs have to mobilise resources through internal and extra budgetary resources (IEBR). During 1994-95, the PSUs were able to mobilise resources amounting to Rs. 3375 crore (79 per cent), as against the approved allocation of Rs. 4276.2 crore under IEBR. During 1995-96 IEBR component constituted Rs. 4327 crore (62 per cent) of the total approved plan outlay of Rs. 6923.5 crore. The actual realisation against the total plan outlay till November 1995 was of the order of Rs. 2671 crore, out of which the actuals against IEBR is Rs. 1952.3 crore.

Petroleum Oil and Lubricants

The production of crude oil during 1994-95 at 32.24 million tones was close to the target of 32.28 million tonnes, and much higher than the production of 27.03 million tonnes achieved during 1993-94. Oil and Natural Gas Corporation Limited (ONGC) produced 91 per cent of total crude oil in 1994-95, while the rest was produced by Oil India Limited (OIL). Against the annual target of 37.24 million tonnes of crude oil production for the year 1995-96, the production of crude oil during April-November 1995 at 23.41 million tonnes was 97 per cent of the target set for the period and 11.6 per cent higher than the output during the corresponding period in 1994-95. (Table 20.7)

TABLE 20.6. Financial Performance of the State Power Sector

	1991-92	*1992-93*	*1993-94 (Pre-Actual)*	*1994-95 (RE)*	*1995-96 (RE)*	*1996-97 (AP)*
			(Rs. Crore)			
A. Gross Subsidy involved						
(i) On account of sale of Electricity to :						
(a) Agriculture	5938	7205	8888	10113	12364	13770
(b) Domestic	1310	1919	2420	2963	3158	3875
(c) Inter-State Sales	201	226	138	232	238	288
Total	7449	9350	11446	13308	15760	17933
(ii) Subscriptions Received from State Governments	2045	1911	2068	1831	2171	2584
(iii) Net Subsidy	5404	7439	9378	11477	13589	15349
(iv) Surplus Generated by sale to other sectors $	2173	3312	3502	5308	6294	5764
(v) Uncovered Subsidy	3231	4127	5876	6169	7295	9585
B. Commercial Losses @	4117	4358	4995	6332	7557	10096
C. Revenue Mobilisation						
(i) Rate of Return (ROR)#	-12.7	-11.8	-12.2	-13.5	-14.6	-18.2
(ii) Additional Revenue Mobilisable from Achieving						
(a) 3 per cent ROR	4959	5462	6221	7737	9106	11763
(b) From Introducing 50 paise/ unit from Agriculture/ Irrigation	2176	2159	2223	2017	2275	2339

Source : Planning Commission

RE : Revised Estimates. AP-Annual Plan Projections.

@ Commercial losses are different from uncovered subsidy because they include financial result of other activities undertaken by the SEBs.

\# in per cent

Note : Information in Item (A) and (C) (ii) (b) is excluding Delhi Electricity Supply Undertaking (DESU).

The total refinery crude throughout during 1994-95 at 56.34 million tonnes, compared to 54.3 million tonnes achieved in 1993-94 was 106.3 per cent of the target of 53.02 million tonnes set for the year. The average capacity utilisation of the 13 refineries was 106 per cent in 1994-95, compared to 102.5

per cent achieved in 1993-94. The total refinery crude throughout during April-November 1995 at 38.9 million tonnes was 22.1 per cent higher than the target of 31.7 million tonnes set for this period.

TABLE 20.7. Trends in the Petroleum Sector

			*April-November**		*Change over previous year*	
	1993-94	*1994-95**	*1994*	*1995*	*1994-95*	*1995-96@*
		(Million tonnes)				*(per cent)*
1. Crude oil production	27.0	32.2	21.0	23.4	19.3	11.6
(i) Onshore	11.7	12.0	8.0	8.0	3.1	0.0
(a) ONGC	8.8	9.1	6.0	6.1	3.3	0.3
(b) OIL	2.8	2.9	2.0	1.9	2.5	-1.0
(ii) Offshore (ONGC)	15.4	20.2	13.0	15.4	31.5	18.7
2. Refinery throughput	54.3	56.3	37.8	38.9	3.8	3.0
3. Production of petroleum products $	51.1	52.9	35.1	36.3	3.6	3.5
		(Billion cubic meters)				
4. Natural gas production	18.3	19.4	13.1	14.6	5.7	11.8

* Provisional. @ April-November.

$ Does not include LPG Production from fractionator.

The production of natural gas in 1994-95 at 19.4 billion cubic metres (BCM) was higher by 5.7 per cent than 1993-94. The utilisation of natural gas during 1994-95 was 18.3 BCM, compared to 16.3 BCM in 1993-94. The production of natural gas during April-November 1995 at 14.6 BCM was 11.8 per cent higher than that in April-November 1994.

The refining capacity in the country was 53.4 million metric tonnes per annum (MMTPA) at the end of 1994-95, which has increased to 57.4 MMTPA till December, 1995. Considering the proposed expansion of existing refineries and based on the Letters of Intent issued till December 1995 to various parties, the refining capacity is expected to increase to 135 MMTPA for meeting the estimated demand of 102 MMTPA of petroleum products by 2001-02. As a part of a liberalisation programme in the hydrocarbon sector, Government has issued Letters of Intent (LOI) to 11 private sector parties for a total refining capacity of 60 MMTPA of which six LOIs with a total refining capacity of 23.3 MMTPA are of Export Oriented Units. These LOIs are in addition to the expansion in the existing refineries or the joint venture companies that are being put up by Public Sector.

During 1994-95, the consumption of petroleum products was 65.5 million tonnes, showing a growth of 7.7 per cent over the previous year. Though the overall consumption of petroleum products witnessed moderate growth during 1994-95 the consumption of LPG, MS, HSD and FO showed substantially higher growth rates. During April-November 1995, the consumption of petroleum products grew by 9.5 per cent over April-November 1994 (Table 20.8). The gross imports of crude oil and petroleum products at 41.3 million tonnes in 1994-95 was 3.7 per cent lower than in 1993-94. The value of POL imports during 1994-95 was Rs. 17,838 crore as against Rs. 17,730 crore during 1993-94. The gross imports of POL during April-November 1995 was 29.73 million tonnes, valued at Rs. 13879 crore as against the import of 27.31 million tonnes, costing Rs. 11,592 crore during April-November 1994.

TABLE 20.8. Consumption of Petroleum Products**

			*April-November**		*Change over previous year*	
	1993-94	*1994-95**	*1994*	*1995*	*1994-95*	*1995-96@*
			(Million tonnes)		*(per cent)*	
1. Light distillates of which	10.6	11.6	7.4	8.4	10.1	13.4
(a) Naphtha	3.2	3.4	2.1	2.4	6.6	13.2
(b) LPG	3.1	3.4	2.2	2.4	10.3	10.5
(c) Mogas	3.8	4.1	2.7	3.1	8.1	12.9
2. Middle distillates of which	38.2	41.0	26.6	29.1	7.4	9.4
(a) Kerosene	8.7	9.0	5.9	6.1	3.0	3.4
(b) Diesel Oil	25.9	28.3	18.3	20.6	9.2	12.6
3. Heavy ends of which	12.1	12.9	8.4	8.9	6.5	6.3
(a) Fuel oil	9.2	9.9	6.5	7.0	7.6	6.8
Total	60.8	65.5	42.4	46.5	7.7	9.5

* Provisional.
@ April-November.
** Excluding Refinery Boiler Fuel (RBF).

The Government announced a reduction in import duties on LPG in January 1994 from 85 per cent to 25 per cent, to facilitate the operations of the PMS. This duty was further modified to 15 per cent, with a 10 per cent countervailing duty in the budget for 1994-95.

In order to make policies in the energy sector environmentally benign, a number of steps have been taken. The Government has formulated a plan for supply of unleaded/lowlead petrol throughout the country in phased manner. Government has introduced unleaded petrol from April 1995 in four metropolitan cities and at selected highways to mitigate the pollution menace for cars fitted with catalytic converters. It has further been decided to introduced unleaded petrol in all State capitals/UTs by the year 1998, and throughout the country by the year 2000. Unleaded petrol has also been introduced in the Taj Trapezium Area.

A number of steps have been taken for promoting the conservation of petroleum products. These include improving energy efficiency of refineries, increasing fuel efficiency in the transport sector, introduction of Compressed

Natural Gas (CNG) as fuel in the road transport sector, upgradation of lubricants, replacement of inefficient boilers and furnaces and promotion of fuel efficient equipment and practices in the industrial sector, rectification of irrigation pumpsets in the agriculture sector, development and promotion of fuel efficient kerosene and LPG stoves and hurricane lanterns in the domestic sector, and launching of multi-media awareness campaigns and imparting of education and training to various target groups of oil users.

Renewable Sources of Energy

Until the end of March 1995, a capacity of about 350 MW through wind power generation had been established, including private sector projects.

A capacity of 119 MW of small hydro power projects had been commissioned upto March 1995. The target for the year 1995-96 was for initiating additional Small Hydro Power Projects with aggregate capacity of 25 MW. Projects with a total capacity of 2.5 MW had been commissioned by October 1995.

In order to tap the potential of 3500 MW of surplus power from bagasse in 420 sugar mills in the country a programme on bagasse based co-generation has been launched under which 12 demonstration projects are being set up with partial budgetary support. An interest subsidy scheme has been launched during 1995-96 to cover large number of sugar mills under which 2 per cent interest subsidy is provided.

Special emphasis is being given to rural energy programmes particularly for setting up of Biogas Plants and Improved Chullahs in rural areas. Over 21.88 lakh biogas plants had been set up in the country till the end of March 1995 under the National Project of Biogas Development (NPBD). The target for 1995-96 had been fixed at 1.60 lakh plants, of which over 47,000 plants had been installed upto November 1995. Under Improved Chullah Programme, 196 lakh improved chullahs were installed till March 1995. Against the target of installing 25 lakh improved chullahs during 1995-96, 6.43 lakh have been installed till November 1995.

In the areas of Solar Photovoltaics, solar lights, Solar Photovoltaic pumps, village level power packs and Solar Photovoltaic Lanterns are being promoted. Over 29000 Solar Domestic lights, 36,000 Solar Lanterns, 30,000 Solar Street Lights and 141 Solar Power Packs have already been installed till March 1995.

21

INDUSTRY

The industrial sector registered a growth of 12 per cent in April-September 1995 following growth of 8.6 per cent in 1994-95. The capital goods sector emerged as an important contributor to the recent industrial recovery, with a growth rate of 27.4 per cent during April-September 1994 and 14.3 per cent in April-September 1995. Consumer durables also performed well with a growth of 28.1 per cent during April-September 1995. Within the broad group of manufacturing sector—food products, basic metals and alloys, metal products and parts, non-electrical machinery and transport equipment did well. Within individual industries—sugar, commercial vehicles, ship building (including repairs), iron ore, penicillin—showed a robust growth.

Industrial Policy Reforms

The major policy changes initiated in the industrial sector since July 1991 included removal of entry barriers, reduction of areas reserved exclusively for public sector, rationalisation of the approach towards monopolistic and restrictive practices, liberalization of foreign investment policy, far reaching liberalization of import policy with respect to intermediate and capital goods, measures to bring about regional balance, especially the development of backward areas and encouraging the growth of employment intensive small and tiny sector.

Following were the major reforms in the industrial sector :

— The number of items, in respect of which industrial licensing remains, reduced to 15. These industries account for only 15 per cent value added in manufacturing sector.

— The number of industries reserved for the public sector reduced to 6, viz. defence products, atomic energy, coal and lignite, mineral oils, railway transport, minerals specified in the schedule to the Atomic Energy Order 1953. Private participation in some of these sectors is also permitted on a case by case basis.

— More and more private initiative encouraged in the development of infrastructure like power, roadways, telecommunication, shipping and ports, airports and civil aviation etc.

— The manufacture of readymade garments—an item reserved for exclusive manufacture by the ancillary/small scale industrial undertakings opened to large scale undertakings, subject to an export obligation of 50 per cent and investment limit of Rs. 3 crore.

— Automatic approval of foreign investment upto 51 per cent and foreign technology agreements permitted for 35 priority industries which account for about 50 per cent value added in the manufacturing sector.

— Foreign investment has also been liberalized in many other sectors.

Pattern of Industrial Growth

Table 21.1 shows trends in growth rates of overall Index of Industrial Production (IIP) and its three major components viz. Mining, Manufacturing and Electricity Generation. In the second half of eighties both Electricity Generation and Mining tended to show a slower growth, with mining indicating a more pronounced decline. The manufacturing sector on the other hand witnessed an upward trend in growth rates, registering growth rates of 8-9 per cent in the second half of eighties. In the nineties, the period immediately following in reforms was marked by low growth rates and even stagnation in the major industrial sectors. However, the growth rates quickly recovered and the IIP increased by 6.0 per cent and manufacturing sector by 6.1 per cent in 1993-94. Electricity generation has tended to maintain high growth rates throughout the period. The industrial sector is now growing at rates similar to the high growth rates of 1980s.

Similarly, among sectors by use based classification, it was the capital goods to first surge ahead, registering a growth rate of 25 per cent in 1994-95. This is followed by an excellent performance by consumer durables. (Table 21.1.)

TABLE 21.1. Annual Growth Rates in Major Sectors of Industry

(*per cent*)

Period (Weights)	*Mining (11.46)*	*Manufacturing (77.11)*	*Electricity (11.43)*	*General (100)*
1981-82	17.7	7.9	10.2	9.3
1982-83	12.4	1.4	5.7	3.2
1983-84	11.7	5.7	7.6	6.7
1984-85	8.9	8.0	12.0	8.6
1985-86	4.1	9.7	8.5	8.7
1986-87	6.2	9.3	10.3	9.1
1987-88	3.8	7.9	7.7	7.3
1988-89	7.9	8.7	9.5	8.7
1989-90	6.3	8.6	10.8	8.6
1990-91	4.5	9.0	7.8	8.2
Average from 1981-82 to 1990-91	8.4	7.6	9.0	7.8
1991-92	0.6	-0.8	8.5	0.6
1992-93	0.6	2.2	5.0	2.3
1993-94	3.5	6.1	7.5	6.0
1994-95	6.2	9.0	8.5	8.6
April-Sep.				
1993-94	3.4	3.2	8.6	4.0
1994-95	4.5	9.8	7.0	8.8
1995-96	12.5	12.0	10.9	12.0

The general IIP has registered a growth of 13.6 per cent in September 1995, aided by a growth of 6.4 per cent, 15.8 per cent and 7.4 per cent in mining, manufacturing and electricity generation respectively. The overall growth in industrial production in April-September 1995 was 12.0 per cent supported by a growth of 12.5 per cent in mining, 12.0 per cent in manufacturing and 10.9 per cent in electricity. Analysing growth trends by use based classification also brings out an excellent performance during 1995-96. It is observed from the Table 21.2 that all the use based sectors performed well during April-September 1995 with consumer durables registering a growth of 28.1 per cent. However, the growth rate of intermediate products at 6.3 per cent during the period was low compared to rates achieved by other sectors.

TABLE 21.2. Growth Rates in Industrial Production by use-based Classification

Sectors	*(Weight)*	*91-92*	*92-93*	*93-94*	*94-95*	*Sept. '95*	*April—Sep.*	
							1994	*1995*
Basic Goods	(39.4)	6.2	2.6	9.5	3.8	13.3	3.9	12.5
Capital Goods	(16.4)	-12.8	-0.1	-4.2	25.0	17.6	27.4	14.3
Intermediate Goods	(20.5)	-0.7	5.3	11.8	3.9	10.4	4.6	6.3
Consumer Goods	(23.6)	-1.8	1.9	3.9	8.5	12.3	7.3	13.5
Consumer Durables	(2.6)	-12.5	-0.7	16.1	9.8	42.4	11.6	28.1
Consumer Non-Durables	(21.0)	1.2	2.5	1.3	8.2	4.7	6.3	9.8

The general IIP recorded a growth of 8.6 per cent during 1994-95 aided by a growth of 6.2 per cent in mining and quarrying, 9.0 per cent in manufacturing and 8.5 per cent in electricity generation.

In 1994-95 capital goods registered a growth of 25.0% and the consumer goods 8.5%, while the performance of the Intermediate goods (3.9%) and basic goods (3.8%) was below the expectations.

Composition of Growth : The recovery of growth was well spread out. Many of the seventeen sectors, among manufacturing, after showing a sluggish growth in the period immediately following the reforms, registered high growth rates. These rates were comparable to growth rates achieved in the preceding decade.

Of the 17 sub-sectors within manufacturing, nine sectors registered growth rates of 12 per cent of more during April-September 1995. These sectors were food products (28.2%), Wood and Wood products (12.5%), paper & paper products (13.6%), non-metallic min. products (15.8%), basic metal and alloy industries (12.5%), metal products & parts (16.6%), non-electric machinery (20.7%), electrical machinery (12.7%), and transport equipment (20.9%). None of the sub-sectors within manufacturing showed a decline during April-September 1995. (Table 21.3)

A similar trend was seen in 1994-95 for growth rates of sub-sectors of manufacturing. Four groups viz., beverages and tobacco, cotton textiles, jute textiles, basic metals and alloys, with a combined weight of 25.7 per cent, of these 17 major industry groups recorded negative growth rates during 1994-95. On the other hand, Electrical Machinery, Appliances and Parts registered the highest growth rate of 32.4 per cent, while Metal Products & Parts (18.2%),

TABLE 21.3. Growth Rates of Industrial Production by Broad Groups of Manufacturing

Code	Sectors	Weights	1992-93	1993-94	1994-95	Apr-95	May-95	June-95	July-95	Aug.-95	Sept.-95	April-Sept. 1994	April-Sept. 1995
20-21	Food Products	5.3	-1.6	-8.7	13.6	54.5	50.9	25.0	11.3	9.9	9.7	2.9	28.2
22	Beverages & Tobacco	1.6	5.9	21.3	-2.5	-9.4	17.7	-7.0	37.2	7.4	36.7	8.4	11.0
23	Cotton Textiles	12.3	8.0	6.9	-2.9	3.2	4.4	-1.3	0.5	2.7	1.8	-2.4	1.9
25	Jute, Hemp and Mesta Textiles	2.0	-4.2	18.7	-10.5	7.1	14.0	4.2	4.8	7.9	17.1	-20.1	9.1
26	Textile Products	0.8	-22.0	-3.2	6.8	9.4	3.0	2.2	9.1	8.3	12.2	17.2	7.4
27	Wood and wood products	0.5	3.0	4.6	1.9	-2.2	17.0	10.2	11.8	26.7	12.4	1.6	12.5
28	Paper & paper products	3.2	3.9	6.6	14.5	17.9	15.3	12.0	10.4	13.4	13.0	14.6	13.6
29	Leather and Leather & fur products	0.5	3.5	8.8	3.3	6.1	-10.3	-2.5	4.1	1.4	37.8	4.6	4.5
30	Rubber, Plastic, Petroleum and Coal Products	4.0	1.5	1.0	3.1	12.7	8.4	5.7	3.0	0.0	12.1	4.3	6.8
31	Chemicals and Chemical Products	12.5	6.0	7.6	10.0	11.6	5.5	6.1	9.6	6.1	10.6	9.1	8.2
32	Non-metalic mineral products	3.0	1.8	4.6	7.0	9.5	9.6	12.7	25.6	16.5	22.3	6.5	15.8

(Contd.)

TABLE 21.3. (*Contd.*)

Code	Sectors	Weights	1992-93	1993-94	1994-95	Apr-95	May-95	June-95	July-95	Aug.-95	Sept.-95	April-Sept. 1994	April-Sept. 1995
33	Basic Metals and alloys Industries	9.8	0.4	33.1	-10.7	16.8	20.2	-1.2	9.3	9.8	22.6	-4.9	12.5
34	Metal Products & parts	2.3	-6.4	1.6	18.2	22.3	17.5	15.9	11.7	12.7	20.4	15.4	16.6
35	Machinery, Machine Tools and Parts	6.2	-1.2	4.4	9.7	17.6	12.9	0.1	27.2	31.2	36.2	3.0	20.7
36	Electrical machinery,	5.8	-2.0	-4.9	32.4	33.7	33.2	8.8	-8.8	8.2	14.1	40.2	12.7
37	Transport equipment and Parts	6.4	5.0	5.3	13.2	14.7	17.8	19.9	19.5	25.7	27.0	18.6	20.9
38	Other manufacturing industries	0.9	4.2	-5.1	0.3	6.4	15.3	5.3	11.1	7.5	10.4	-10.8	9.3

Paper and Paper Products (14.5%), Food products (13.6%), Transport Equipment (13.2%), and Chemical and Chemical Products (10%) recorded growth rates exceeding 10 per cent.

Investment Scenario and Trends : The investment scenario showed and upward swing. The number of industrial entrepreneurs memorandum (IEMs) and Letters of Intent (LOIs) filed from 1991 to October 1995 totalled 24, 667 with overall investment intention of Rs. 505,290 crore and estimated employment of 4.6 million. (Table 21.4)

TABLE 21.4. Industrial Investment Intention through IEMs Filed and LOIs

Year	*Numbers*	*Proposed Investment (Rs. crore)*	*Proposed Employment ('000)*
1991	3279	78,381	803
1992	5480	129,866	1020
1993	4984	76,821	804
1994	5210	106,708	959
1995 (Jan-Oct)	5714	121,029	1010
Total	24667	505290	4596

Transnational corporations and foreign firms also expressed keen interest in investing in India. The total number of FDI proposals approved between August 1991 to September 1995 was 3716 with a proposed total investment of Rs. 33060 crore (Table 21.5). More than 80 per cent of these approvals were in high priority sectors such as power generation, oil refinery, electrical equipment, chemicals and export related sectors. Even in areas still reserved for the public sector (such as hydrocarbons, coal, railways and postal services) and in infrastructure sectors (roads, highways, bridges, ports, telecommunications) the government has adopted a more liberal approach towards private investment including foreign investments.

TABLE 21.5. Total Foreign Direct Investment Approvals and Investment Inflows

Year	*No. of approvals*	*Amount (Rs. crore)*	*Actual inflow (Rs. crore)*
1991	289	534	351
1992	692	3888	675
1993	785	8859	1786
1994	1040	8947(*)	2970
1995 (Jan-Sept)	975	10820 (*)	4729
Total (Post Policy)	3716	33060	10513

* Excludes 24 approvals of GDRs involving Rs. 5940 crore

Reforms in Public Sector Enterprises : The Industrial Policy Statement announced by Government in July 1991 envisaged disinvestment of a part of Government holdings in the share capital of selected Public Sector Enterprises (PSEs) in order to provide market discipline and to improve the performance of public enterprises. A total amount of around Rs. 10,500 crore has already been disinvested to the public sector financial institutions, mutual funds and general public.

To protect the interests of workers, and provide a social safety net for labour a National Renewal Fund (NRF) was set up in February 1992 and schemes were proposed to assist the employees in re-training, redeployment and counselling. Provision of funds through NRF also exist for cases where workers retire voluntarily or are declared surplus. To implement the NRF schemes an empowered authority was created. An amount of Rs. 542.29 crore was released from NRF during 1993-94 and Rs. 261.13 crore during 1994-95. An estimated 75000 workers had opted for voluntary retirement under the scheme. A major portion of the amount has been utilised in the textiles sector.

The provisions of SICA (Sick Industrial Act) was extended to public sector undertakings in December, 1992. Consequently, upto end of December 1995, 59 cases of Central Public Sector Undertakings and 79 cases of State Public Sector Undertakings had been registered with Board for Industrial and Financial Reconstruction. 26 cases out of the above were dismissed as non-maintainable. In 29 cases rehabilitation proposals were sanctioned and two cases in Central and one in State PSU were declared 'no longer sick'.

Performance of Selected Public Sector Undertakings : 99 PSEs had signed MOUs for the year 1994-95. For 1994-95 self evaluations had been received for 95 PSEs. After these were examined by Department of Public Enterprises, of the 95 PSEs, 39 were rated as excellent, 26 very good and only 2 rated as poor. Evaluation for 16 was pending. It was awaited for 4. The financial performance of these enterprises was better than what had been targeted for in the MOUs. The gross margin during 1994-95 was Rs. 26,137 crore as against the target of Rs. 24, 106 crore. Thus the target for gross margin was exceeded by 8 per cent.

Performance of Selected Industries : Steel : The production of various categories of steel, after being sluggish in the last 2/3 years, picked up significantly in 1994-95. The production of finished steel increased by 17.2 per cent in 1994-95. The peak rate of duty on import of steel was reduced from 50 per cent to 40 per cent and the duty on HR coils from 40 per cent to 30 per cent in the Budget for 1995-96.

The production of finished steel at 12.86 million tonnes increased by 12.6 per cent in April-November, 1995, with secondary producers registering an increase of 15.7 per cent. Production of saleable pig iron has shown a mixed trend with main producers registering a decline and secondary producers registering an increase. (Table 21.6)

TABLE 21.6. Output of Iron & Steel

(Million tonnes)

	1994-95	*1994-95*	*1995-96*
		(April—November)	
Saleable Steel			
SAIL & VSP	10.51	6.50	7.02
	(6.9)		(8.0)
Total			
Main Producers	12.96	8.20	9.01
	(8.2)		(9.9)
Finished Steel			
Main Producers	9.57	6.12	6.71
	(9.1)		(9.9)
Secondary			
Producers	8.25	5.32	6.15
	(28.3)		(15.7)
Total	17.82	11.44	12.86
	(17.2)		(12.6)
Saleable Pig Iron			
Main Producers	2.00	1.36	1.13
	(1.0)		(-17.3)
Secondary			
Producers	0.76	0.48	0.62
	(180.0)		(28.9)

Note : Figures in brackets indicate percentage change over the same period of the previous year.

There was an increase of 10 per cent in exports of iron and steel during April-September 1995, compared with a decline of 19.8 per cent in 1994-95. Imports, had increased by 68 per cent during 1994-95, mainly of HR coils, CR coils and semis.

Fertilizers : Policy initiatives to overcome difficulties in fertilizer sector included continuation of concessions for decontrolled fertilizers with some modifications, decanalistion of the imports of Muriate of Potash (MOP), Mono Ammonium Phosphate (MAP) and Sulphate of Potash (SOP). Only urea was covered under the statutory price and movement controls.

During 1994-95, the production of nitrogenous and phosphatic fertilizers reached a record level of 104.3 lakh tonnes representing an increase of 9.9 per cent for nitrogen and 37.3 per cent for phosphate. During April-December, 1995, fertilizer production increased by 10.6 per cent for nitrogen and 6.7 per cent for phosphate as compared to April-December 1994. The production target for 1995-96 was fixed at 86.3 lakh tonnes of nitrogen and 26.7 lakh tonnes of phosphate, representing a growth rate of 8.6 per cent in nitrogen and 7.2 per cent in phosphate for the year 1995-96.

As on 1.4.1995, the total installed capacity of fertilizer production in the country was 89.72 lakh tonnes of nitrogen and 28.22 lakh tonnes of phosphate.

Sugar : Sugar production showed a substantial increase during 1994-95 season and reached a record level of about 146 lakh tonnes in the year. This represented a sharp recovery from the low level of production of 98 lakh tonnes in 1993-94 season. The sugar industry continued to remain under a compulsory licensing regime and almost all aspects of industry from entry to exports were regulated. There was a statutory minimum price (SMP) fixed by the Central Government and State Advised Prices (SAP), for sugarcane. The SMP for sugarcane for 1994-95 season was Rs. 39.10/quintal and advance SMP for 1995-96 season was Rs. 42.50 per quintal.

A certain portion (normally 40 per cent with lower rates for new units) of sugar production was allotted to the State/UT Governments as levy. This was used for distribution through the Public Distribution System (PDS). Prices of levy sugar are fixed zonewise, on the basis of SMP of sugarcane plus conversion costs as recommended by the Bureau of Industrial Costs and Prices (BICP).

In April 1995, stock holding limits and turnover periods of sugar and khandsari dealers were doubled and licensing of wholesalers had been abolished in the hill districts of Uttar Pradesh. The Gur (control) Order 1994 was rescinded.

Automobiles : Automobiles has been one of the very fast growing industries in recent years. Its turnover was over Rs. 22,000 crore during 1994-95. The sales of automotive vehicles rose from 18.91 lakh in 1992-93 to 28.51 lakh during 1994-95 registering a growth of around 25% both during 1993-94 and 1994-95. The industry was expecting to maintain the same or even a higher growth level during 1995-96. The production of vehicles during the first 6 months of 1995-96 was reported to be 16.48 lakh as against 12.97 lakh during the corresponding period of the previous year, recording a growth rate of around 27 per cent. Similarly, the production of auto components in value terms went up from Rs. 5204 crore in 1993-94 to Rs. 6700 crore in 1994-95 and is expected to be over Rs. 8,500 crore during 1995-96.

Exports of the automotive industry also showed a consistently high growth. Exports of vehicles rose from Rs. 305 crore during 1991 to Rs. 1348 crore during 1994-95. Similarly, exports of auto components went up from Rs. 234 crore in 1990-91 to Rs. 730 crore in 1994-95. The exports of vehicles as well as auto components were expected to go up further during the current year (1995-96).

Electronics : Indian Electronics industry continued its upward trend in 1994-95 witnessing a growth of about 17 per cent. The TV and component industry, showed excellent performance during the year (Table 21.7).

TABLE 21.7. Production of Electronics (Sectoral Break-up) 1992-93 to 1994-95

(*Rs. crore*)

	1992-93	*1993-94*	*1994-95*
1. Consumer Electronics	3300	4050	4525
2. Industrial Electronics	1700	1750	2080
3. Computer Systems	1040	1050	1350
4. Communication & Broadcasting Equipment	2800	3150	3250
5. Strategic Electronics	385	500	600
6. Components	2200	2600	3050
7. Free Trade zones (Hardware)	350	550	771
8. Software for Exports (including EPZ, 100% EOU)	575	1020	1474
Total	12350	14670	17100

Exports of the electronics sector increased steadily from Rs. 910 crore in 1990-91 to Rs. 2,981 crore in 1994-95. One of the areas of focus for exports is computer software.

Textiles : The textile industry continue to be the largest industry in our country. It accounts for 20 per cent of total industrial output, provides employment to 20 million people and contributes nearly 38 per cent to the total value of exports.

In line with the general policy of liberalization, several measures were undertaken to eliminate/reduce controls and bring about greater transparency in the textile sector. The textile industry has been delicensed as per the Textiles (Development and Regulation) Order 1993. The Agreement on Textiles and Clothing (ATC) included as part of the Final Act of GATT, provides for a dismantling of the discriminatory quota regime practised under the Multi Fibre Agreement (MFA), within a definite time span of 10 years. In the wake of the coming into force of ATC, the current Export Entitlement Distribution Policy (known as Quota Policy) effective from January 1994 to December 1996 was formulated to enable the industry to meet the emerging challenges in the international market.

The Indian textiles industry continues to be predominantly cotton based, with about 65 per cent of raw materials consumed being cotton. As per estimate made by the Cotton Advisory Board at its meeting held on 5.6.95, the cotton production during the cotton season 1994-95 (September, 1994 to August, 1994) was 130.00 lakh bales of 170 kgs each (provisional) against the production of 121.50 lakh bales of 170 kgs each during the cotton season 1993-94, registering a growth rate of 7.00 per cent. During 1994-95, cotton prices showed mixed trend. Government took several steps like permitting import of 29104 MT of Viscose Staple Fibre (VSF), a near substitute to cotton at zero/concessional rate of duty, keeping Import of cotton under OGL at zero rate of duty and tightening of Selective Credit Control measures for cotton. All these helped to contain the rise in prices of cotton. Looking to the supply and demand situation in the country, the Government had released an export quota of 1.856 lakh bales of various varieties of cotton during the cotton season 1994-95, out of which 1.08 lakh bales of cotton valued at Rs. 83.39 crore were exported during that year.

Fabrics production recorded an increasing trend over the years, except for a marginal setback in 1991-92. Total fabric production in 1994-95 was higher by 1.8 per cent than in 1993-94. Production of fabrics during April-October 1995 increased by 5.4 per cent over April-October, 1994. Production of spun yarn war almost entirely in the organised sector and showed a steadily increasing trend over the years, except for a marginal setback in 1991-92. Production of spun yarn increased by 1.1 per cent in 1994-95 and by 11.1 per cent in April-October 1995. The production of spun yarn by small scale units at 110 million kgs. during 1994-95 now forms a significant part of total production.

The production of man-made fibres at 478.6 million kgs. registered an increase of 5.6 per cent in 1994-95. Production during April-October, 1995 was 283.5 million kgs. as against 267.9 million kgs. in April-October 1994, recording an increase of 5.8 per cent. (Table 21.8)

TABLE 21.8. Production of Fabrics

Million Sq. Metrs.

Sector	*1990-91*	*1991-92*	*1992-93*	*1993-94*	*1994-95*	*April-October*	
						94-95	*95-96 (P)*
Mills	2589	2376	2000	1990	1779	1060	942
Powerlooms	16044	16089	17826	19631	20016	11535	12194
Handlooms	4295	4123	5219	5851	6180	3589	3919
Total	22928	22588	25045	27472	27975	16184	17055
			Share in Output (per cent)				
Mills	11.20	10.52	7.98	7.24	6.35	6.54	5.52
Powerlooms	69.98	71.23	71.18	71.46	71.55	71.28	71.50
Handlooms	18.73	18.25	20.84	21.30	22.10	22.18	22.98
Total	100.00	100.00	100.00	100.00	100.00	100.00	100.00

(P) : Provisional including hosiery.

The export of textiles has been increasing at a fast rate during the last few years. During 1994-95, total exports of textiles (including coir, jute and handicraft) was estimated at Rs. 31336 crore, registering an increase of 25.3 per cent over 1993-94. Among the various items of textiles, ready-made garments achieved a growth rate of 19.51 per cent, cotton textiles (mill made, powerlooms and handlooms) 38.7 per cent, silk textiles 18.8 per cent, man-made fibre textiles 33.6 per cent, woollen textiles—11.2 per cent, handicrafts 23.5 per cent, jute goods 25.2 per cent and coir goods 31 per cent.

Food Processing : The food processing industry encompasses industries like fruit & vegetable processing, milk, fish, and meat. The industry has a tremendous potential for increasing agricultural productivity, providing significant and wide spread employment and contributing significantly to exports. And all this, using relatively simpler technology.

To encourage private sector initiative in food processing, the Government has taken several steps. Union excise duty on fruit and vegetable products was withdrawn in the 1991-92 Budget. Foreign equity participation up to 51 per cent and foreign technology agreements are provided automatically. There are no entry barriers in the food processing industry. Changes in Export Import Policy and the liberalized exchange rate have also helped the sector.

Recent trends of production and exports of various segments of the industry show an impressive performance. This is largely the outcome of policy initiatives undertaken for the sector.

Small Scale Sector: The number, employment, output and exports in the small scale sector as estimated by the Office of the Development Commissioner, Small Scale Industries, are given in Table 21.9.

TABLE 21.9. Overall Performance of SSI Sector

Year	*No. of units (In lakh) as on 31st December*	*Output At current prices (Rs. crore)*	*Employment (lakh Nos.)*	*Export (In Rs. crore)*
1991-92	20.82 (6.9)	1,78,699 (15.0)	129.80	12,883
1992-93	22.46 (7.9)	2,09,300 (17.1)	134.06 (3.3)	17,785 (28.1)
1993-94	23.84 (6.1)	2,41,648 (15.5)	139.38 (4.0)	25,307 (42.3)
1994-95 (P)	25.71 (7.8)	2,93,990 (21.7)	146.56 (5.2)	28,000* (10.6)

* Quick Estimate. P Provisional
(figures in the brackets give the increase over previous year).

In real terms, the small scale sector recorded a growth rate of 10.1 per cent in 1994-95, as against 7.1 per cent in 1993-94 and 5.6 per cent in 1992-93. These rates were significantly higher than the growth rates achieved by the industrial sector as a whole.

The small scale sector contributes around 40 per cent to the gross turnover in the manufacturing sector and about 34 per cent of total exports.

Incentives and Facilities for Small Scale Industries

Fiscal incentives

- Excise concessions available for both registered and unregistered units on a graded scale depending on turnover upto Rs. 300 lakh.
- A scheme of Integrated Infrastructure Development was launched in March, 1994 to strengthen infrastructural facilities in rural and backward areas. 15 projects have been sanctioned so far.

- Quality Certification Scheme launched to improve SSI product quality. Financial support to acquire ISO 9000. Till date, 46 units approved for reimbursement.
- Seven Point Action Plan has been initiated to improve credit flow to SSI sector. 51 specialised SSI branches have been opened up to October, 1995.
- Scope of National Equity Fund scheme enlarged to cover the whole country except metropolitan areas to support expansion, modernisation & technology upgradation. Under the scheme Rs. 187 lakh released during April-December 1995.
- Technology Development & Modernisation Fund scheme launched for modernisation and adoption of improved and updated technology. During first 7 months of 1995-96, SIDBI has assisted 43 units and sanctioned Rs. 1549.47 lakh under this scheme.
- A scheme for creation of Technology Development Fund in the States launched with the involvement of State Government and Industry Associations.

Credit Policies

- Priority sector lending.
- 40% of advances to SSI sector reserved for tiny sector and village & cottage industries.
- Refinance facilities and special schemes of SIDBI.
- Concessional/fixed rates of interest for loans up to Rs. 2 lakhs (2 slabs).
- Single Window Scheme of SIDBI for project outlays up to Rs. 50 lakh.
- Under Prime Minister's Rozgar Yozana, loans in respect of 31971 micro enterprises were sanctioned in 1993-94, 196,133 enterprises in 1994-95 and 101,321 enterprises in April-November, 1995.

Other incentives

- Reservation of products for exclusive manufacture (836 products at present).
- Purchase and price preference.
- Infrastructural support to Entrepreneurship Development Institutes to augment their training capacities.
- Entrepreneurship Development Institute set up in Guwahati, Assam for improving the entrepreneurial base for the North Eastern Region.
- Joint programme with the State Bank of India and Small Industries Development Bank Of India (SIDBI) for modernisation and technology upgradation of industry clusters.
- Assistance to industrial associations/voluntary agencies to set up testing centres.
- Special programmes on vendor development, quality awareness and pollution control.

22

POLITY

Summoning and Prorogation of both Houses of Parliament Article 85(1) of the Constitution empowers the President to summon each House of Parliament to meet at such time and place as he thinks fit. Clause (2) thereof states that the President may from time to time prorogue the Houses or either House or dissolve the House of the People (Lok Sabha). The Allocation of Business Rules framed under Article 77(3) of the Constitution assign this function to the Ministry of Parliamentary Affairs. After assessing the time likely to be required for transaction of Government Business and for discussion on topics of public interest as may be demanded from time to time by Members of Parliament, a note is placed before the Cabinet Committee on Parliamentary Affairs for making a recommendation as to the date of commencement of a session of Parliament and its likely duration. The recommendation, if agreed to by the Prime Minister, is submitted to the President for his approval of the date(s) of commencement of the session. After his approval, the date(s) of commencement and duration are conveyed to the Secretariats of Lok Sabha and Rajya Sabha for issuing of summons to Members of Parliament.

During the period from 1.1.95 to 31.3.1996, four Session each of the Lok Sabha and the Rajya Sabha were held.

TABLE 22.1 : Details of Sessions

Sessions	*Duration*	*Sittings*	*Days*
	Tenth Lok Sabha		
	1995		
13th	February 13 to June 3	42	111
14th	July 31 to August 26	16	27
15th	November 27 to December 22	20	26
	1996		
16th	February 26 to March 12	10	16
		88	180
	Rajya Sabha		
	1995		
173rd	February 13 to June 2	41	110
174th	July 31 to August 26	16	27
175th	November 27 to December 22	20	26
	1996		
176th	February 26 to March 12	10	16
		87	179

After obtaining the approval of the Cabinet Committee on Parliamentary Affairs to prorogue the Houses, the Government's decision is conveyed to the two Secretariats of Parliament to issue the order of the President and to notify the same in the Gazette of India.

TABLE : 22.2 : Dates of Adjournment sine-die and the Prorogation by President

	Dates of	
Sessions	*Adjournment Sine-die*	*Prorogation*
	Tenth Lok Sabha	
	1995	
13th	June 3	June 15
14th	August 26	September 6
15th	December 22	January 2, 1996
	1996	
16th	March 12	March 14, 1996
	Rajya Sabha	
	1995	
173rd	June 2	June 15
174th	August 26	September 6
175th	December 22	December 29
	1996	
176th	March 12	March 14, 1996

Leader of the Lok Sabha : Shri P.V. Narasimha Rao, Prime Minister is the Leader of the Lok Sabha with effect from 6 December, 1991.

Leader of the Rajya Sabha : Shri S.B. Chavan, Minister of Home Affairs has been functioning as the Leader of the Rajya Sabha with effect from 2 July, 1991.

Leader of Opposition in the Lok Sabha : Shri Atal Bihari Vajpayee, Leader of the Bharatiya Janata Party in the Lok Sabha, is the Leader of Opposition with effect from 26 July, 1993.

Leader of Opposition in the Rajya Sabha : Shri Sikander Bakht, Leader of the Bharatiya Janata Party in the Rajya Sabha is the Leader of Opposition in the Rajya Sabha with effect from 7 July 1992.

TABLE : 22.3 : Number of Sittings of Parliament From 1952 to 31st March, 1996

Year	*Number of Sittings*		*Year*	*Number of Sittings*	
	Lok Sabha	*Rajya Sabha*		*Lok Sabha*	*Rajya Sabha*
1952	103	60	1953	137	100
1954	137	103	1955	139	111
1956	151	113	1957	104	78
1958	125	91	1959	123	87
1960	121	87	1961	102	75
1962	116	91	1963	122	100
1964	122	97	1965	113	96
1966	119	109	1967	110	91
1968	120	103	1969	120	102
1970	119	107	1971	102	89
1972	111	99	1973	120	105
1974	119	109	1975	63	58
1976	98	84	1977	86	70
1978	115	97	1979	66	54
1980	96	90	1981	105	89
1982	92	82	1983	93	77
1984	77	63	1985	109	89
1986	98	86	1987	102	89
1988	102	89	1989	83	71
1990	81	66	1991	90	82
1992	98	90	1993	89	79
1994	77	75	1995	78	77
1996 (upto 31.3.96)	10	10			

Salary and Allowances of Members of Parliament : The Ministry is responsible for the administration of the following Acts of Parliament :—

1. The Salary, Allowances and Pension of Members of Parliament Act, 1954;
2. The Salaries and Allowances of Officers of Parliament Act, 1953; and
3. The Salary and Allowances of Leaders of Opposition in Parliament Act, 1977.

Under Section 9 of the Salary, Allowances and Pension of Members of Parliament Act, 1954 a Joint Committee of both Houses of Parliament has been constituted to make rules on manners specified under sub-section (3) thereof. Recommendations of the Joint Committee are processed in the Ministry in consultation with the Lok/Rajya Sabha Secretariats, and the concerned Ministries/ Departments. Action is taken to bring forward legislation, wherever necessary.

TABLE 22.4 : Dates of Poll, Constitution, First Sitting, Expiration of the Term and Dissolution of Lok Sabha (First to Tenth Lok Sabha)

Lok Sabha	*Last date of Poll*	*Date of the Constitution*	*Date of the first sitting*	*Date of the expiration of the term*	*Date of Dissolution*
1	*2*	*3*	*4*	*5*	*6*
First	21.2.52	2.4.52	13.5.52	12.5.57	4.4.57
Second	15.3.57	5.4.57	10.5.57	9.5.62	31.3.62
Third	25.2.62	2.4.62	16.4.62	15.4.67	3.3.67
Fourth	21.2.67	4.3.67	16.3.71	15.3.77	27.12.70*
Fifth	10.3.71	15.3.71	19.3.71	18.3.77	18.1.77*
Sixth	20.3.77	23.3.77	25.3.77	24.3.82	22.8.79*
Seventh	6.1.80	10.1.80	21.1.80	20.1.85	31.12.84
Eighth	28.12.84	31.12.84	15.1.85	14.1.90	27.11.89
Ninth	26.11.89	2.12.89	18.12.89	17.12.94	13.3.91*
Tenth	15.6.91	20.6.91	9.7.91	8.7.96	10.5.96

* Mid-term Polls were held. Dissolution took place even before the elections.

Note: Last dates of Poll in column (2) are based on reports of Election Commission.

The Salary, Allowances and Pension of Members of Parliament (Amendment) Bill, 1995 was introduced in the Lok Sabha on 30.3.1995. The Bill was considered and passed by the Lok Sabha on 30.3.1995 and was also considered and passed by the Rajya Sabha on 30.3.1995. The Bill came into force with effect from 1.4.1995 and contained provisions entitling Members of Parliament to payment of air fare for every air journey performed for visiting any place in India during the interval not exceeding 7 days between two sittings of a Department related Standing Committee during the recess of the Budget Session only. In addition to the air fare, Members will also get incidental charges limited to the daily allowances for the days of their absence for such journeys.

The Joint Committee on Salaries and Allowances of Members of Parliament constituted under Section 9 of the Salary, Allowances and Pension of Members of Parliament Act, 1954 and the Joint Parliamentary Committee under the Chairmanship of Shri A.R. Antulay, MP set up to suggest Facilities and Remuneration for Members of Parliament had made a number of recommendations for increasing the allowances and facilities of Members of Parliament. After carefully considering these recommendations from the administrative, financial and legal feasibilities, some of these recommendations were accepted by the Government and in order to implement them, a Bill, namely the Salary, Allowances and Pension of Members of Parliament (Second Amendment) Bill, 1995 was introduced in the Lok Sabha on 25.8.1995. The Bill contained provisions to provide for:

(i) secretarial allowance of Rs. 2,500 per month in lieu of the existing Office Expense Allowance of Rs. 1,000 per month;

(ii) free postage stamps of Rs. 6,000 per annum to each Member of Parliament;

(iii) (a) proportionate pension to ex-Members of Parliament who have served as Members between two and four years at the rate of Rs. 350 per month for each completed year which will comprise of the period more than six months;

(b) increase in the amount of pension from Rs. 500 per month to Rs.1,000 per month for a period of 5 years to a spouse or dependent of a Member of Parliament who dies during his term of office; and

(iv) to enable a Member of Parliament to claim daily allowance if he has participated in the proceedings of the House but has not signed the register, if the Presiding Officer condones his not signing the register.

The Bill came up for consideration in the House on 26.8.1995 and the Hon'ble Speaker announced that it would be referred to the Standing Committee. Accordingly, the Bill was referred to the Standing Committee on Finance.

23

RADIO, DOORDARSHAN AND MEDIA POLICY

Objectives of AIR

— Upholding unity and integrity of the country and democratic values enshrined in the Constitution.
— Fair and balanced flow of information of national, regional, local and international interest without any ideological orientation.
— Projecting the composite culture of India.
— Informing, enlightening, educating, entertaining and enriching all sections of the society.
— Projecting the developmental activities of the nation in all their facets including agriculture, education, health and family welfare and science and technology.
— Serving the rural illiterate, under-privileged and handicapped sections of the society, apart from minorities and tribal populations.
— Promotion and projection of equity and social justice.

Present Position : Network

Presently AIR is utilising INSAT-ID and 2A for distribution of radio programmes throughout the country. Seven radio networking (RN) carriers are operational with INSAT-ID in CXS band. Uplink stations for these RN carriers are : (a) Delhi—four channels, (b) Mumbai, Calcutta—one channel each and (c) Madras. Four RN channels are uplinked from Broadcasting House, Delhi Earth Station with INSAT-2A in C-Band and these programmes are being received by Mumbai, Chinsurah, Nagpur, Ahmedabad, Bhopal, Guwahati, Hyderabad, Rajkot, Madraś, Bangalore, SPT Bangalore, Aligarh, Gorakhpur, Dharwar, Alleppy and Cuttack AIR stations.

With the availability of INSAT-2 additional 23 RN channels in CXS-1 of INSAT-2A have been operationalised. The distribution of uplinks for these channels are : Delhi seven, Mumbai two (VB), Srinagar, Ahmedabad, Bangalore, Jaipur, Shimla, Lucknow and Itanagar one each.

Doordarshan

As on 31 March 1996, 40 Programme Production Centres are in operation in various parts of the country. In addition, a Central Production Centre comprising two large studies equipped with modern and sophisticated technical facilities is in operation at Delhi. This centre caters to high quality programme production. Also there is a production centre at Guwahati equipped with modern equipment

TABLE 23.1. Growth of AIR

	1990-91	*1995-96*	*Growth (%)*
No. of stations	108	185	71
No. of transmitters	197	293	49
Radio coverage (area) (%)	84.6	90.6	06
Radio coverage (population) (%)	95.4	97.3	02
Broadcast duration on FM metro channel (in hours)	05.5	24	
Commercial revenue (Rs. in crore)	35	64	83
Budget (Rs. in crore)	355.58	511.79	43.93

which produces programmes for being relayed by various TV stations in the North Eastern part of the country.

Fifteen colour outdoor broadcast (OB) vans each equipped with four cameras and other associated equipment and a large OB van equipped with six cameras and nine electronic field production (EFP) and 12 Mini Vans are available in the network. Besides, Electronic News Gathering (ENG) equipment is available at all the programme producing stations for coverage of outdoor activities.

Development Programme : For the purpose of expansion of coverage (DD-I) about 500 Transmitter Projects are presently under implementation/ envisaged to be set up. With the commissioning of above transmitting, over 92 per cent population of the country is expected to be brought under TV coverage as against 85.8 per cent population covered at present. Also, there would be improvement in coverage in the areas presently served. To extend reach of DD-II channel programmes, additional Low Power Transmitters are envisaged to be commissioned in big cities. At Bangalore and Hyderabad, High Power Transmitters are envisaged to be set up in replacement of the existing Low Power Transmitters.

TABLE 23.2. Progress of Doordarshan (1990 to 1995-96)

		Years	
		1990	*1995-96*
Programme Production Centres	(Nos.)	18	38
Programme Output	(Hours per week)	300	1300
Transmitters	(Nos.)	519	772
Transmission	(Hours per week)	11	1021
Satellite Channels	(Nos.) (Only two terrestrial channels)	Nil	19
Regional Networks	(Nos.)	20	34
Primary Viewers	(In millions)	150	250
Area covered	(Percentage)	54.5	68.4
Population covered	(Percentage)	76.3	85.4
Commercial earnings	(Rs. in crore)	254	398
Budget	(Rs. in crore)	602	1513

Media Policy

Paswan Committee on Media Policy

The Sub-Committee of the Parliamentary Consultative Committee of the Ministry of Information and Broadcasting, constituted under the Chairmanship of Shri Ram Vilas Paswan, Member of Parliament (Lok Sabha) presented its report to the Ministry on March 29,1996.

Paswan Committee's Recommendations on National Media Policy

— There should be a regulatory body to oversee both public and private telecasting/broadcasting. In this connection, the Sub-Committee noted that the provisions of the Prasar Bharati Act, which was unanimously passed by Parliament in 1990 should be kept in mind while framing the regulatory mechanism which should be an independent autonomous authority. The Sub-Committee is of confirmed opinion that no recourse should be taken by the Government to dilute the provision of the Prasar Bharati Act, 1990. This regulatory body may be set up to ensure adherence to the programmes/advertisement codes and other stipulations. This body or similar independent bodies may also develop an effective mechanism for public grievance redressal as well as implementation of its recommendations in respect of such grievances.

— Adequate care should be taken to enable the setting up of non-commercial broadcasting stations to be run by universities, educational institutions, panchayats/local bodies, State Governments, etc.

— The Sub-Committee recognises that for public broadcasting, adequate funding in the form of state support is necessary. The content of programmes or software is often dictated by the funding and therefore, the Sub-Committee strongly recommends that this aspect should receive the attention of the government and an institutionalised system be worked out.

— The national broadcasters—Akashvani and Doordarshan—should bear the responsibility to offer a high quality public service broadcasting that informs, educates and entertains the people and also provide coverage to national events like the Republic Day Parade. Taking into account the reach of the national broadcasters, primary and exclusive responsibility should be provided to them in the matter of coverage of national events like Republic Day Parade, Independence Day, the President's Address to both the Houses of Parliament, etc.

— The rights/obligations and exclusivity of the national broadcasters should be codified through law.

— Whereas the broad policy approach should be the same for radio and television, minor variations/differences can be made in view of the difference in reach and impact of the two media. Programme/advertisement codes should be similar, if not, same. The viewer/listener interest should be kept in mind while spacing the advertisements. A new production style, which is people-oriented should be developed.

- In tune with the policy framework suggested here, the Indian private sector/State Government/NGOs/Local Self Government should be allowed to enter the field of broadcasting/telecasting.
- Appropriate provisions must be made to ensure that the control of private broadcasting does not fall in the hands of companies having major stake in the print medium or vice-versa. Cross-media ownership restrictions must, therefore, be considered.
- Direct or indirect foreign equity participation in companies entering the field of private broadcasting should not be permitted.
- Access on the private channel should be available to the common man through appropriate provisions in the law.
- In view of the Supreme Court's Judgement on airwaves, an independent authority must be set up to control and regulate the use of airwaves. The Sub-Committee felt that the integrity of the Indian Skies is as important as her territorial integrity. This regulatory authority must be set up through a law enacted by the Parliament at the earliest. This Body can combine the functions of the regulatory body or can be a separate body exclusively for controlling the sky waves under the regulatory body.
- The apex regulatory body should be an independent autonomous public authority representative of all sections and interests in the society and should control and regulate the use of air waves in the interests of the public and to prevent invasion of their rights.
- The foreign satellite channels must also be brought within the ambit of the said regulatory body in order to make them amenable to the Indian laws.
- The Sub-Committee felt that in the case of skywaves, efforts should be made to develop an international convention to forge multilateral/regional agreements with countries especially in regard to software.
- The Sub-Committee noted that it will be difficult to pre-censor programmes aired on television in view of vast structure such a step would call for. By bringing in the private broadcasting/foreign channels within the purview of the Indian legal system, much of laissez-faire that exists can be curbed.
- The Sub-Committee felt that the present programming in electronic media, especially television, needs to be more decentralised to meet the regional/local aspirations. In this connection, the Verghese Committee recommendations regarding decentralised programming, programme autonomy and constitution of five zones for this purpose (viz. South, West, Central, Eastern and North) should be considered by the Government.
- Care should be taken that no monopoly is developed by the private broadcasters, by restructuring the number of channels, especially 'several interest' channels owned by them.
- The Sub-Committee agrees with the broad objectives of national film policy set out by the Working Group on National Film Policy, and we

reiterate the same. As a formal declaration of the national film policy would be useful, the Sub-Committee recommends that the Government should formalise the same as early as possible.

— Since the Estimates Committee and the Standing Committee have examined in detail the working of the CBFC as mentioned above, we have nothing further to add except to reiterate their recommendations. These recommendations are discussed elsewhere. The Sub-Committee wishes to add that Government should amend the guidelines for certification of films to curb the distortion of image of eminent leaders in films.

— The production of good short films, both by Films Division and independent producers, needs to be actively encouraged. The Films Division should make efforts to improve the quality of its documentaries and made them more interesting. The Sub-Committee recommends that Government should encourage the growth of Indian documentary film movement. The Sub-Committee suggests in this regard that the Films Division should farm out more and more films to independent producers on its panel. Further, Doordarshan should commission production of documentaries through the Films Division and other agencies.

— It has been stated that it would be very difficult to find sponsors for telecasting documentaries on Doordarshan. The Sub-Committee recommends that the Doordarshan should allot time-slots for at least half-an-hour every day on prime time for documentaries, even if there are no sponsors.

— The Sub-Committee also recommends that the feasibility of showing documentary films in various educational institutions, schools, colleges and universities should be examined. The Ministry of Human Resource Development should consider the allocation of funds for the purpose.

— With a view to encourage children's films, the Sub-Committee recommends that more infrastructural facilities should be developed for production of animation films.

— The Sub-Committee also recommends that more avenues for exhibition of children's films in each district of the country should be identified.

— During meetings, representatives of the film industry pointed out that though Government called for recommendations from the Film Federation of India for the Dadasaheb Phalke Award, it did not normally accept their recommendation. The Sub-Committee is informed that Government gets recommendations for the Award. To give more creditability to the Government's decision, the Sub-Committee would recommend that a small Committee consisting of eminent persons including those from Film World should be appointed by Government to consider all names received and recommend the name of the person who should be honoured with the Dadasaheb Phalke Award.

— The National Film Awards were instituted in 1953 to provide for a special impetus to regional cinema and to encourage the production of films of aesthetic excellence and social relevance. The Sub-Committee also recommends that the award winning films should be screened at various

State capitals and other large towns so that the people in the regional centres may get an opportunity to see them. The Central Government should provide funds to the State Governments to organise such festivals of award-winning films.

— A number of witnesses before the Sub-Committee represented for the full implementation of the recommendations of the High-Power Committee (1990). The Sub-Committee would suggest that the matter should be taken up with the various State Governments/Union Territory Administrations again.

— The Sub-Committee recommends that the State Governments/Union Territory Administrations should be persuaded to rationalise the rates of Entertainment Tax to help the film industry.

— During discussions some of the film industry representatives represented to the Sub-Committee that in view of high cost of imported raw stock, the customs countervailing duty may be reduced if not abolished. The Sub-Committee recommends that the countervailing duty on raw stock may be abolished in view of the fact that there are no facilities to manufacture the raw stock in the country.

— Some of the witnesses before the Sub-Committee expressed concern about the shortage of theatres as well as the closure of cinema houses due to the advent of television and video. To overcome the shortage of exhibition facilities, the Sub-Committee suggests that wherever cinema theatres are being converted into commercial complexes, the local authorities should ensure that in the complex coming up at the site at least one mini theatre is provided in the complex. The Sub-Committee would also recommend that more multiplex theatrical complexes should be encouraged.

— The Sub-Committee recommends that the National Film Development Corporation and other agencies should encourage construction of theatres with 400 to 500 capacity instead of very large theatres.

— During meetings the representatives of the cine workers pleaded for the declaration of the film industry as an "Industry" so that the workers of the industry are not exploited by the producers. The Sub-Committee feels that introduction of labour welfare measures to film industry workers will go a long way in improving their conditions. The Sub-Committee, therefore, recommends that the film industry may be declared as an industry not only for the purpose of institutional finance but also for application of labour legislation relating to welfare of labour.

— The National Film Archive of India is charged with the responsibility of preservation of cinema. There have been press reports about the damage and loss of important films. The Sub-Committee suggests that the Archive should take immediate steps to acquire all film classics and preserve them properly for posterity.

— The Sub-Committee also suggests that the National Film Archive of India should take over the old documentaries from the Film Division for restoration and preservation.

— Nowadays film appreciation courses have been started in various universities and new film societies are coming up. However, Government gives only Rs. 3 lakh per year to the Federation of Film Societies of India for its activities. This is awfully inadequate. The Sub-Committee recommends that Government should encourage film society movement by giving all facilities including finance. The grant-in-aid to the Federation of Film Societies of India should be augmented suitably.

— Some of the witnesses informed the Sub-Committee that Akashvani's royalty rate for film songs which are broadcast, is Rs. 2 per song and was fixed a long time ago. Considering the time lapse and increase in the cost of picturising film songs, the Sub-Committee recommends that this should be suitably revised upwards by Akashvani.

— With respect to the suggestions regarding evolving a code of conduct for the journalists and for vesting the Press Council of India with more powers, the Sub-Committee felt that the matter may be left to the Press Council for suitable decisions. However, the Press Council should consider arming itself with adequate powers to deal with habitual offences with respect to communalism, threats to national security and other undesirable activities.

— The language Press and the small and medium newspapers should continue to grow. Therefore, the Sub-Committee recommends that the Government must endeavour to create a suitable environment by helping in the modernisation of these sections of the Press.

— Though the financial viability of a newspaper depends to a larger extent on the advertisement revenue which it is able to attract, Government's advertising policy and rate structure should be rational and uniform, evolved with a view to eliminate the possible use of advertisements as a lever to influence the press and thereby affecting its freedom.

— Even though the import of newsprint has been put under OGL, there is a need for a nodal agency to import newsprint on behalf of small and medium newspapers as they do not have the necessary infrastructure and the bargaining power for such imports.

— The training requirements of the journalists is yet another aspect which needs immediate attention. The press over the years has to become increasingly professional in nature. With a view to ensure that the press as a whole is capable of reporting and explaining and interpreting in their proper perspective various developments taking place, it is imperative that additional facilities are created to enable journalists to have a broad educational preparation and specific training in journalism.

— Indian news agencies have not been able to operate effectively in the sphere of dissemination of national news abroad, and the gathering of foreign news for dissemination within the country. Foreign news agencies still dominate international news sections in leading newspapers. It should be the endeavour of the Government to permit and strengthen the news agencies to become self-sufficient in these spheres. In this connection, renewed efforts should be made in revitalising the efforts taken in the wake of Non-Aligned Conference, 1976 which lead to the establishment of Newspool for exchange of news among the third world countries.

- To strength the Indian news agencies, the Sub-Committee recommends that corporatisation of these news agencies with adequate equity base, as was suggested by the First Press Commission, should be seriously considered.
- Freedom of the editors, and editorial contents, insulated from the business and other interests of the owners, should be ensured through a proper institutional mechanism or guidelines to be evolved by the press themselves or by the Press Council of India. The issue of division of funds from the newspaper industry to other industries may be examined.
- The Sub-Committee feels that towards professionalisation of the print media, adequate institutional finance should be made available to the journalists etc., through cooperatives on easy terms.

Prasar Bharati Act, 1990 : A Chronology (1990 to 1995)

1990 The Act received assent of the President and is yet to come into force as the requisite notification has not been issued.

The Act essentially envisages functioning of All India Radio/ Doordarshan as two Wings of a single Corporation which is operationally outside the purview of the Government.

1991 The Act was reviewed within the Ministry. The review suggested amendments, primarily, of administrative nature.

1992-93 The amendments suggested by the Ministry were discussed with various political parties.

1994 After the discussions with the political parties, a Note for the Cabinet for the review of the Act and its amendments was done in 1994.

1995 A presentation on the same was made to the Prime Minister in January, 1995.

After the presentation before the Prime Minister, it was decided to further review it in the light of changes in the telecasting scenario in Asia due to the advent of international satellite broadcasting.

A landmark judgement of Supreme Court delivered for establishment of an independent autonomous public authority to regulate the use of airways which in turn, required the regulatory provisions in Prasar Bharati to be deleted since Prasar Bharati would be only one of the users of the airwaves which were declared as public property.

High Court of Calcutta gave a direction to the Central Government to take appropriate steps to give shape to the objectives and ideals of the Prasar Bharati Act and, if necessary, by fresh legislation before 31 December 1995. Since it was not feasible to adhere to the deadline, extension of the deadline was sought by and was given upto 30 June 1996.

Expert Group under the Chairmanship of Shri Nitish Sengupta has been constituted to review the provisions of the Prasar Bharati Act and answer some of the very basic questions, such as mode of financing. This Expert Group was notified on 28 December 1995 and its report is expected by 31 July 1996.

24

SCIENCE AND TECHNOLOGY

24.1 RESEARCH AND DEVELOPMENT (R & D)

Major Role for R & D in Ninth Plan

Prime Minister H.D. Deve Gowda called upon the industry and the business community to invest in the research and development to build a strong technological base enabling the country to lead the world by 2020 AD. The Prime Minister also announced that science and technology would be integrated into the planning process beginning with the Ninth Plan. The Prime Minister's call came while unveiling the blueprint for a resurgent new India, 'Technology Vision 2020', in New Delhi on Aug. 2. The report prepared in combination with a number of departments is aimed ensuring a better quality of life for the people, a globally competitive products through the development of a scientific approach and building up of a vibrant economy. The blueprint has taken into consideration the impact of the multinational corporations on technology development and is drawing up a framework for IPR-related issues in the post-GATT scenario.

It has suggested massive technology upgradation in all key areas. In the case of internal security, for example, the plan demands a shift from the traditional intensive manpower approach to technically trained personnel. Mr. Gowda said that there was a major programme to network the scientific laboratories and transfer the R&D developed by them for a faster economic growth. He hoped various social sciences would integrate their work with the scientist community to make the R&D realistic and not a mere 'lab to lab' experiment. The blueprint visualises the future for such critical areas as health care, biotechnology, security, agriculture, telecommunications, engineering and power. It aims at involving groups outside the Government and especially the business community to create a wider base. The vision hopes that instead of exercising controls and curbs, the Government would function by regulation and adopt a promotional role with bureaucrats acting as facilitators rather than as administrators.

Drawn up by the Technology Information, Forecasting and Assessment Council (TIFAC), led by its Chairman and Scientific Adviser to the Defence Minister, P.J. Abdul Kalam, the plan sees India switching to a technology-driven mode.

Decline in Contribution to Scientific Research

India's contribution to world scientific research has declined by as much as 32 per cent in the past 15 years, pushing it to the 13th rank from its earlier 8th position, according to a leading science journal. The study, in "Nature", reveals that between 1981 and 1995 Indian research publications in the world science literature have plummeted by 32 per cent. While the country's ranking in terms of quantity declined from eighth position in 1980 to 13th in 1995, the decline in its quality ranking hit 81st position in 1989—"and probably further since then"—from the 57th in 1985, the study points out. "This indicates that India is losing out not only in terms of quantity but also in quality." The study points out that "even at 17 per cent, not other country suffered such a massive decline except the Commonwealth of independent States" revealing that India's decline is worse than sub-Saharan Africa.

Basing their findings on Science Citation Index (SCI), an international database, N. Raghuram and Y. Madhavi have pointed out the absence of long-term monitoring of publishing trends as an input to policy and planning. Emphasising that the decline cannot be only explained by a publishing bias against developing countries in inernational journals, the study says "other such countries (especially in South-East Asia and China) improved their world share tremendously during 1982-93 and there is not enough evidence to suggest any specific anti-India bias." Whereas the share of South-Asia shot up by 312 per cent. China registered a growth of 247 per cent. Scientific output is measured in terms of quantity and quality of research publications in leading journals. While quantity is defined by the number of research papers, the quality is defined by the frequency with which these are quoted by other scientists. Attributing the decline mainly to the "brain drain", declining government funding, the "ageing" of scientific institutions, "lack of motivation" and 'a feudal work culture', the authors underline the need "for an in-depth analysis of science management."

24.2 ATOMIC ENERGY

AEC Needs Funds for Expansion

India should look at all aspects of the proposed global treaty to ban production of fissile material for weapons, the Chairman of the Atomic Energy Commission, Dr. R. Chidambaram has said. "The fissile material cut-off treaty, as far as we know, will suggest a date from when all production of material for weapons purpose will halt. It is for the Government to take into consideration the terms of it. The treaty is non-discriminatory also", Dr. Chidambaram said in response to a question at a Press conference in Narora. The cash strapped Atomic Energy Department is also bidding for more funds for its expansion. Around Rs. 1000 crore per year, over three times the current level, will be needed for it to grow, the head of the Nuclear Power Corporation of India Limited (NPCIL), Mr. Y.S.R. Prasad, also present at the Press conference, said "(We will) require around Rs. 1000 crore funding per year if we want to grow. This will mean 20,000 mw of nuclear power supply by the year 2020. The current level of funding, however, is sufficient to sustain the existing infrastructure", he said.

Nuclear power plants today have an installed capacity of 1,720 mw, contributing around three per cent to the national requirements. Of this, 320 mw are generated by boiling water reactors. Seven pressurised heavy water Reactors can put out another 1,400 mw. According to a Parliamentary panel report, restrictions in funding has led to a drastic slashing of power generation targets. Under revised plans, a generating capacity of 2820 mw by 1997 is intended, an over three times cut in the goal fixed for the year 2000 in 1984. The past practice of sharing half of the funds required for power plants by the Government should be restored. Mr. Prasad said, "The government's equity participation with the NPC was in the ratio of 1:1. Unfortunately it has now become 1:2. There should be a mechanism to finance basic industries like nuclear power production that require long term investment", he said.

PEC Power Generation

The Nuclear Power Corporation's six operating plants have recorded a total generation of 900 million units during October 1996. While two units each—the Madras Atomic Power Station (MAPS) and the Kakrapar Atomic Power Station (KAPS)—operated at 100 per cent capacity utilisation, Narora Unit-2 had 91 per cent capacity utilisation. The availability factors of KAPS Unit-1, which has been operating for more than 97 days, has been 100 per cent. While the availability factor for TAPS Unit-2 also was 100 per cent, for Unit-2 of NAPS and MAPS, it was 93 per cent during September 1996. The actual generation for the financial year 1996-97 upto October 31, 1996, was 4,605 m units, which is 761 m units above the MoU target.

According to Health Society Director G.R. Srinivasan, the NPC's outage planning and major job execution has also shown improved performance both at the operating stations and at the Units 3 and 4 of the Kaiga and Rajasthan construction projects. He said that for the first time in India, the removal of the Coolant channel at the RAPS Unit-2 was done in a record time and seven months ahead of schedule. This is the first time that such a complex job is undertaken by NPC engineers in any country outside Canada. It was done with indigenously developed tools and methods at a lower collective radiation exposure. The NPC would now install state-of-the-art Zircalloy-Niobium coolant channels with four tight garter springs. At the Tarapur Atomic Power Station, the core shroud inspection of Unit-1 is in the final stages of completion and to date no cracks have been observed.

24.3 TECHNOLOGY

Technology Fund Being Set Up

A new Rs. 100-crore fund is being created by the Centre to develop technology and put in into operation in the industry. Its basic aim is to bring scientists and industrialists together so that the benefits of the latest technology can flow right up to the grassroots level, without being siphoned off on the way. Under the changed scenario, industry is becoming competitive. Scientists also have to tread the same path. The new fund will be utilised exclusively to facilitate the technology transfer to actual users. It will be created out of the cess levied on payments made for importing technology. It was announced at the ongoing Indian Science Congress in Patiala on Jan. 4 that the President has given his assent to a Bill with regard to the creation of a technology development board in the Department of Science and Technology, which will operate the fund.

The experience so far has been that the money earmarked for research and development get misused. The earlier scheme to give incentives to R&D in the industry is likely to be discarded because there was no suitable mechanism to monitor the utilisation. Under the new plan, the technology development board will be a partner in the R&D work. While the theme of the present Congress is to use science and technology for food, economic and health security, the focus of the previous Congress, help in Calcutta in January, 1995, ws on using science for industrial development. Prof. V.S. Ramamurthy, Secretary, Science and Technology, presented the report of the inter-ministerial task force on the recommendations of the previous session at the Science Auditorium of Punjabi University. Prof. U.R. Rao, general president of the Congress, presided. One of the most significant developments is that the Council of Scientific and Industrial Research (CSIR) has signed several MoUs with industry associations for strengthening the linkages between government R&D system and industry and enhancing investments in R&D by the industry.

As many 536 polytechnics of the country will be upgraded under a World Bank-supported project of the Department of Education. A participant in the session suggested that the government should explore the possibility of setting up polytechnics in jails also. Prof. Ramamurthy welcomed the suggestion and promised to act on it. A group has been identified for promoting close interaction between oil and mineral based industries and research institutes and universities. The VLSI (Very Large Scale Integration) wafer fabrication facility at the Semiconductor Complex Ltd (at Mohali) is being rebuilt to have a capacity of 20,000 six-inch wafers per annum at a technology level of 1.2 micron. The seismological network will be upgraded to cover the entire country, including the north-eastern region. In his presidential remark, Prof. Rao, who released the report, pointed out that the least expensive technology was at times the most effective, especially in a country like India.

Critical Defence Technology

The much-awaited Technology Vision 2020 document aims at India building military and commercial aircraft on a design-driven programme, achieving top place in agricultural productivity, a leading exporter of machine tools and a force to reckon with in the field of genetic engineering. The document, evolved by country's top-notch think tanks comprising ten industrialists, industrial associations, experts from R&D institutions, the Government and academia, is due for release in May, says Prof. A.P.J. Abdul Kalam. The paper also envisages deployment of cost effective and affordable therapeutic intervention. Prof. Kalam who was speaking at the inaugural function of the workshop on institutionalisation of responsive R&D and industry partnership in New Delhi said as per the document India was planning to build light combat aircraft (LCA) and even commercial aeroplanes not on fabrication and licence production norms but on an indigenous design and development programme.

The workshop was organised by Federation of Indian Chamber of Commerce and Industry (FICCI) and National Institute of Science, Technology and Development Studies (NISTADS). Prof. Kalam, who discussed the main highlights of the paper said a review meeting of seven task forces and 11 panels, the authors of the paper, is scheduled for tomorrow. The document was initiated in November 1993 by the Technology Information Forecasting and Assessment Council (TIFAC). On the issue of agricultural productivity, Prof. Kalam said the paper aims at being the world leaders from the present ranking of being 54th. In case of capital goods industry, India should be transformed into a leading exporter of machine tools. The document also envisages breakthroughs in life sciences and biotechnology. Regarding navigation, Prof. Kalam informed that the document has laid emphasis on making navigation possible throughout the year, at least 18 hours per day from the present 12 hours per day. Prof. Kalam said that the Technology Vision also aims at cost effective and affordable therapeutic intervention. In this refard, he said that more than a quarter of the health burden is due to infectious diseases, such as AIDS, TB and acute respiratory infections.

Agricultural Technology

The Prime Miniser, Mr. P.V. Narasimha Rao, on Jan. 3 called upon the scientific community to help increase the productivity of Indian agriculture from the present level of 1.6 tonnes per hectare to the world average of 2.6 tonnes. Pointing out that India still ranked way down in the average yields of rice, wheat, cereals and soyabeans, he urged the scientists, who had gathered in Patiala for the 83rd Indian Science Congress, to concentrate on developing quality seeds of improved varieties and hybirds of different crops and on improved nutrient availability to plants, better pest and weed control methods and better water management. A judicious mix of high technologies such as new materials, and sensors, and fertiliser and pesticide delivery systems with traditional practices could help considerably even in relatively small plots, he said, in his inaugural speech for the Congress (which was read in absentia by the Indian Science Congress Association's Headquarters Secretary, Prof. S.P. Mukherjee. Mr. Rao's visit to Patiala to inaugurate the Science Congress was cancelled because of thick fog which did not lift even by noon. Consequently the function had to proceed without the customary inaugural address by the Prime Minister).

The Prime Minister also called for special attention for the promotion of natural pesticides like neem and insect growth regulators and integrated farm practices, including rearing of domesticated animals, poultry and fishery. Besides, he wanted greater attention towards the development of cost-effective and appropriate technology for value addition of agriculture and horticultural produces through processing, packaging, storage and marketing and pointed out that a major study had indicated that there was a need for relatively simple processing technologies like pre-cooling units, packaging, controlled atmosphere storage and transport containers. He also called for increasing focus on conservation of soil and water resources at the watershed level, and acceleration of the pace of plant breeding, and identification of new sources of food and new technology for its retrieval. Referring to the patent scenario, he said it was unfortunate that more than 70 per cent of the patent applications were being filed in the country by foreigners, and the average number of patents published in the country annually was as low as 2,050 of which 75 per cent were held by foreigners. This issue must be collectively addressed by R&D institutions, industry and the Government.

PSLV-D3 Satellite Put Into Orbit

India on March 21 became a force to reckon with in the global satellite launch vehicle market with the successful launch of PSLV-D3, the country's third and last developmental polar satellite launch vehicle from the Sriharikota Range (SHAR) in Andhra Pradesh. The 44m tall, 283 tonne vehicle, which blasted off from the country's 'spaceport' at 10-23 a.m., the appointed time, traced the predetermined trajectory with absolute precision and injected IRS-P3, a 922-kg remote sensing satellite into a polar sun-synchronous orbit after 17 minutes. This is the second successful launch of the PSLV in a row. "We have done it again", said a visibly moved Dr. K. Kasturirangan, Chairman, Indian Space Research Organisation (ISRO), immediately after the deployment of the satellite. "It is a perfect launch", and a precise flight not only in the country, but anywhere else in the world, he said. "We are on the threshold of the operationalisation of the vehicle". It was a significant milestone in the country's space programme, he added.

Immediately after the launch, Dr. Kasturirangan spoke to the Prime Minister, Mr. P.V. Narasimha Rao, and conveyed the news of success of the Rs. 90-crore mission to him. "His reaction was instant and enthusiastic", the Chairman said. The solar panels of the satellite were deployed 70 seconds after its injection into orbit. The satellite has been switched to an 'inert' mode till it starts receiving commands from March 22. After about three weeks it is expected to become operational. Accordingly to Mr. P.V. Pernumal, Mission Director, all systems on board the vehicle worked exactly the way they were planned. Once the Rs. 35-crore satellite containing four payloads was pushed into orbit, it was time for restrained celebration at the emotionally surcharged Mission Control Centre which issues the final authorisation for the launch. Top ISRO officials, including Dr. Kasturirangan, Dr. S. Vasantha, Director, SHAR; Mr. K. Thyagarajan, Project Director, IRS-P3, Dr. S. Srinivasan, Director, VSSC, Trivandrum Mr. Madhavan Nair, Director, LPSC, Trivandrum, and Mr. S. Ramakrishna, Vehicle Director, were seen congratulating and hugging one another. Some of the dignitaries who witnessed the launch included Dr. U.R. Rao, Space Commission member, and Dr. A.P.J. Abdul Kalam, Advisor to the Defence Minister.

Prithvi Successfully Testfired

India on Jan. 27 successfully test-fired the 250-km "extended range" version of the lethal Prithvi missile, now being developed for the Air Force, from the Interim Test Range (ITR) at Chandipur-on-sea in Orissa. "All mission objectives were fuly met", said a Defence Ministry spokesman after the missile was flight tested at 2-25 pm. The test heralded an important milestone for the Prithvi project under the country's Integrated Guided Missile Development Programme (IGMDP), with the missile achieving the 250 km range. Prithvi-I, with a range of 150 km, has been already successfully developed for the Indian Army.

Today's flight by Prithvi II was tracked by a network of three radars, three optical tracking telescopes, three telemetry stations and a naval ship located at the down range, closer to the impact point.

The naval ship, monitoring the terminal trajectory of the missile, confirmed the splashdown at the predicted impact point located 250 km from the launch pad, the spokesman said. Minutes after the successful missile test, an elated Dr. A.P.J. Abdul Kalam, Scientific Adviser to the Defence Minister, said at the launch pad : "It was an excellent flight following the predicted trajectory in a text-book manner and the Prithvi impacted at the exact point." Besides, Dr. Kalam, senior officials of the Army and the Air Force and scientists of the Defence Research and Development Organisation (DRDO) participated in today's launch. Powered by liquid propellant, the state-of-the-art Prithvi has the latest on-board computers as well as an advanced inertia and navigation system. The 8.55 metre missile with a 1000 kg payload is capable of hitting a target at a distance of 150 km.

25

SOCIAL WELFARE (INCLUDING, CHILD AND WOMEN DEVELOPMENT)

25.1 WELFARE OF SCHEDULED CASTES, SCHEDULED TRIBES, MINORITIES AND THE DISABLED

Scheduled Castes Development

National Commission for Safai Karamchari : National Commission for Safai Karamcharis has been set up w.e.f. 12.8.94 to look into the specific problems of Safai Karamcharis.

Special Central Assistance : An indepth review of the utilisation of Special Central Assistance for SCs by the States/UTs was done through regional meetings that were covered by the Ministry. An amount of Rs. 267.41 crores has been released to the States/UTs upto Jan. 1995 and it is expected that 28.78 lakhs families will be benefited during the current year.

Scheduled Castes Development Corporation : Under the Centrally Sponsored Scheme of Assistance to Scheduled Castes Development Corporations, the Central Government is participating in the share capital investment of SCDCs to the extent of 49% as against 51% of the State share. The Government has recently modified the scheme to the extent that :

(i) Central share will be released directly to the SCDCs instead of through State Governments;

(ii) The optimum unit cost of Rs. 35,000 fixed earlier has been removed and the State Governments and SCDCs can evolve their own coast norms; and

(iii) The subsidy component would now be on IRDP pattern and therefore, subsidy has been raised from Rs. 5000 to Rs. 6000.

An amount of Rs. 21.65 crores has been released upto Jan. 1995 under the scheme.

National SCs and STs Finance & Development Corporation : NSFDC is a 100% Government of India own no profit no loss Corporation to channelise loan from the SCDCs to develop entrepreneurial and skilled abilities in Scheduled Castes and Scheduled Tribes. The Government has raised the share capital of NSFDC from Rs. 125 crores, Rs. 300 crores. NSFDC has sanctioned cumulative of 633 schemes with total project cost of Rs. 494.65 crores with its own commitment Rs. 254.44 crores as on date. 1,79,000 members of SCs/STs will be benefited on completion of these schemes.

National Scheme of Liberation & Rehabilitation of Scavengers : Survey of Scavengers has been completed except in the States of Bihar and West Bengal,

7.76 lakh scavengers have been identified so far. During the last three years 34,492 beneficiaries have been trained in various trades and 6406 beneficiaries have been rehabilitated. During the year 1995-96 another 1 lakh scavengers were like to the trained and rehabilitated. Rs. 73 crores have been provided under the scheme during 1994-95 Rs. 182 crores were also released to the States UTs during 1991-92 to 1993-94.

Pre-Matric Scholarships : The Centrally Sponsored Scheme of Pre-Matric Scholarships for children of those engaged unclean occupations i.e. scavenging. Tanning and Flaying has been modified to the effect that the children shall also be eligible for the Scholarship of Classes-I to VIII (except that if a third subsequent child is born after 1.4.93, only two children would be eligible) and two children in respect of classes IX and X (Earlier, Scholarship was restricted to one child per family). It is expected that 2.05 lakh students would be awarded scholarships.

Post-Matric Scholarships : The Centrally Sponsored Scheme of Post-Matric Scholarship for SC and ST students provides for payment of maintenance allowance and reimbursement of all non-refundable compulsory fees charged by the educational institutions. During the year 1994-95, 18.43 lakh students are expected to be benefitted.

Hostels for SC Boys & Girls : With a view to facilitate the States to construct Boys and Girls Hostels for SCs in a larger number, the Ministry of Welfare has revised the guidelines to an extent that the State Governments may get their construction proposals formulated on the basis of schedule of rates as prescribed by the CPWD/PWD in their respective States. It is expected that 168 hostels would be constructed to accommodate 8,400 inmates during the current financial year.

Book Banks for SC/ST students : Under this scheme, book banks are set up for SC/ST students studying in Medical/Engineering/Veterinary/Agriculture and Polytechnic courses. One set of text books is to be shared by two students. It is expected that the scheme would cover an additional 20,000 students.

Coaching & Allied Scheme : Centres spread across the country provide pre-examination coaching for Civil Services, State Services, Medical, Engineering and other entrance examinations. Reputed Private Coaching Institutes such as Rao's study circle also impart training to SC/ST students free of cost. The scheme was revised during 1995-96 to include more private coaching institutes as also other professional courses like CA, MBA and Hotel Management. About 11,000 students would avail of the training facilities during the current year.

Implementation of the PCR Act, 1995 and the SCs and STs (Prevention of Atrocities) Act, 1989 : In the Misc. Petition No. 798 of 1992 (Shri K.P. Jaiswal Vs. Union of India and others) filed in the Hon'ble High Court of Madhya Pradesh at Jabalpur, the High Court has by order dated 25.3.94 upheld the constitutional validity of the Act except Section 18 which barred applicability of Section 438 of the Criminal Procedure Code, 1973. It has been held by the Hon'ble High Court that Section 18 of the SCs and STs (Prevention of Atrocities) Act, 1989 is unreasonable and violates article 14 and 21 of the Constitution. The State Govt. of Madhya Pradesh filed a SLP in the Supreme Court who have upheld the section 18 of the SCs and STs (Prevention of Atrocities) Act, 1989 in their judgement delivered on 6.2.1995.

As these two Acts are very important for the protection of Scheduled Castes and Scheduled Tribes, Ministry of Welfare proposes to include the two Acts in the IX Schedule of the Constitution so that adequate measures to guard the Acts are taken.

Tribal Development

20-Point Programme: Under point 11 (b) of the 20 point Programme 10.42 lakh Scheduled Tribe families have been assisted during 1993-94.

Tribal Cooperative Marketing Development Federation: The Authorised Share Capital of the Tribal Cooperative Marketing Development Federation of India (TRIFED) is Rs. 100.00 crores and the paid up capital is Rs. 49.23 crores of which Rs. 49.00 crores is the contribution given by the Government of India. During 1994-95, the Grant-in-aid to TRIFED has been merged with the share capital contribution of TRIFED. There was a substantial increase in the turnover of TRIFED from Rs. 86.00 crores in 1992-93 to about Rs. 106.55 crores during 1993-94. For the current financial year (1994-95) the turnover has reached Rs. 173.27 crores (upto December, 1994).

Backward Classes Development

Lists of OBCs: On 19th of October, 1994 the Government notified the OBC lists for the purpose of reservation in Civil posts and services under the Government of India, in respect of 4 States and 3 Union Territories, namely, Rajasthan, Orissa, Tripura, West Bengal, Daman & Diu, Dadar and Nagar Haveli and Pondicherry. Earlier such lists for 14 States, viz. Andhra Pradesh, Assam, Bihar, Goa, Gujarat, Haryana, Himachal Pradesh, Karnataka, Kerala, Madhya Pradesh, Maharashtra, Punjab, Tamil Nadu and Uttar Pradesh had already been notified on 10.9.93. Action in regard to notification of lists of OBCs in respect of the remaining States/UTs except those where the population is mainly tribal is at different stages of completion.

National Commission for Backward Classes : The National Commission for Backward Classes which was constituted on the 14th of August 1993, received 347 representations from castes/communities all over the country for inclusion and 8 representations for exclusion from the Central list of OBCs ending November,1994.

Relaxed Standard given to OBCs : In order to ensure full utilisation of the reservation quota for OBCs, the Government through an order issued on 13 October 1994, provided OBC candidates, the benefit of relaxed standards in respect of written examinations and interviews as in the case of SC/ST candidates Government of India have also allowed age relaxation of 3 years and three additional attempts for OBC candidates in the Civil Services Examinations conducted by the UPSC.

Development of the Minorities

National Minorities Development & Finance Corporation : A National Development & Finance Corporation was set up and registered on 30th

September, 1994 as a company under section 25 of the companies act, 1956 with an authorised share capital of 500.00 crores. The main aim of the Corporation is to promote economic and developmental activities for the benefit of backward sections amongst the minorities preference being given to occupational groups and women.

Wakf Bill, 1993: The Wakf Bill, 1993 was deliberated upon in depth by the Parliamentary Standing Committee on Labour & Welfare. The Standing Committee has since concluded its deliberations and presented its Report to Parliament on 20.12.1994.

Grant to Central Wakf Council: The amount give by the Government as grant-in-aid to the Central Wakf Council for development of Urban Wakf properties totals to Rs. 1143.94 lakhs as on 31st December, 1994.

Maulana Azad Education Foundation: At the meeting of its General Body, held on 15th January, 1994, the Foundation resolved to amend its Memorandum of Association, Rules and Regulations so as to enable it to function as an independent entity with a view to enable it to achieve its objectives more effectively.

Welfare of the Disabled

Draft Bill for the welfare of the handicapped: To protect the rights of the persons with disabilities, to ensure equality of opportunity and full participation in national life, a Legislation called Persons with Disabilities (Equal Opportunities, Protection of Rights & Full Participation) Bill, 1995 has been drafted. The proposed legislation covers areas like constitution of Central and State Coordination Committees, prevention, early detection, intervention, education, employment vocational training, non-discrimination, social security, affirmative action, etc.

SAARC Workshop : A 5 day SAARC Workshop on Rehabilitation Techniques for Disabled was held at Hyderabad from 28th November to 2nd December, 1994 which was attended by members of SAARC courtries, resource persons, directors of National Institutes, some NGOs and officers from the Central Government.

Special Olympic Games for Mentally Retarded Children: Special Olympic Games for Mentally Retarded Children were organised by the National Institute for the Mentally Handicapped at Hyderabad from 7-11 January, 1995.

World Congress on Mental Retardation : A World Congress on Mental Retardation was organised by the International League of Societies on Mental Handicap (ILSMH) in collaboration with Thakur Hari Prasad Institute of Mental Retardation, Secunderabad from 20-27 November, 1994 in Vigyan Bhawan, New Delhi to discuss early identification, intervention and rehabilitation of the mentally handicapped. The Congress was attended by delegates/countries from different international organisations, eminent NGOs in the field, experts and officials from the concerned Ministries.

Social Defence

Observance of 1994 as International Year of the Family : United Nations had declared 1994 as the 'International Year of the Family'. Ministry of Welfare performed the role of nodal agency for its observance. A National Action Programme was drawn for creating awareness about the importance of family as a unit. The major activities undertaken included : (i) holding of a National Seminar; (ii) release of a book; (iii) release of posters and press advertisements; (iv) special commemorative stamp; and (v) special commemorative coin on the subject.

25.2 CHILD DEVELOPMENT

Our Commitment Towards Children

Constitutional Provisions

The Constitution of India both in the Directive Principles of State Policy and as a part of the Fundamental Rights, has laid down that the State shall direct its policy towards securing that the health and strength of workers, men and women, and the tender age of children are not abused, and that citizens are not forced by economic necessity to enter avocations unsuited to their age or strength and that particularly children are given opportunities and facilities to develop in a healthy manner, and in conditions of freedom and dignity. Childhood and youth are to be protected against exploitation, and against moral and material abandonment.

The Constitution presents an impressive list of rights for children, some of them not even available to adults.

While the right of "equality before the law and the equal protection of the laws" is available to any person, including children, *Article 15(3)* empowers the State to have special laws for children.

Article 23 of the Constitution has put a total ab on forced labour and made such practices punishable under law.

The Constitution in *Article 24* has prohibited the employment of children below the age of 14 years in any factory, mine or in any hazardous activity.

Besides all the seven sets of Fundamental Rights in the Constitution are available to children with such authority and accessibility as that with adult citizens.

The special provisions enumerated in the Directive Principles of State Policy of the Constitution which promotes child rights are—

Article 39 : The State shall, in particular, direct its policy towards securing—

(e) that the health and strength of workers and the tender age of children are not abused and that citizens are not involved by economic necessity to enter avocations unsuited to their age or strength;

(f) that children are given opportunities and facilities to develop in a healthy manner and in conditions of freedom and dignity and that childhood and youth are protected against exploitation and against moral and material abandonment.

Article 42 : The states shall make provisions for securing just and humane conditions of work and for maternity relief.

Article 45 : The State shall endeavour to provide, within a period of ten years from the commencement of this Constitution, for free and compulsory education for all children until they complete the age of fourteen years.
Article 47 : The State shall regard the raising of the level of nutrition and the standard of living of its people and the improvement of public health as among its primary duties and, in particular, the State shall endeavour to bring about prohibition of the consumption except for medicinal purposes of intoxicating drinks and of drugs which are injurious to health.

Major legislations pertaining to children are—

- The Apprentices Act, 1961
- The Guardian and Wards Act, 1890
- The Reformatory Schools Act, 1897
- The Child Marriage (Restraint) Act, 1929
- The Children (Pledging of Labour) Act, 1993
- The Young Persons (Harmful Publications) Act, 1993
- The Immoral Traffic (Prevention) Act, 1956
- The Hindu Minority and Guardianship Act, 1956
- The Hindu Adoption and Maintenance Act, 1956
- The Women's and Children's Institutions (Licensing) Act, 1956
- The Probation of Offenders Act, 1958
- The Orphanages and Other Charitable Homes (Supervision and Control) Act, 1960
- The Juvenile Justice Act, 1986
- The Infant Milk Substitutes Feeding Bottles and Infant Foods (Regulation of Production, Supply and Distribution) Act, 1992
- The Prenatal Diagnostic Technique (Regulation, Prevention and Misuse) Act, 1994
- The Persons with Disabilities (Equal Opportunities, Protection of Rights and Full Participation) Act, 1995

There are also a lot of related welfare and criminal laws which have beneficial provisions for the care and protection of children.

There are several central statutes which have been adopted by most States, some with local modification.

The Women and Child Department's recent initiative has been aimed at reviewing the existing laws and legislations to bring it in line with the various provisions of the UN Convention on the Rights of Children, which has been ratified by India on 2nd December 1992. An inter-departmental committee has been set up for this purpose in the Department.

Integrated Child Development Services (ICDS)

The Integrated Child Development Services was universalised by sanctioning *1705* new ICDS Projects to extend the outreach to the uncovered CD Blocks and urban slums, extending integrated package of services to *182.29* lakh children and *38.07* lakh mothers living in backward rural/tribal areas and urban slums.

Interventions for the hitherto neglected Adolescent Girls in the age group 11-18 years aiming to meet their special needs in the areas of nutrition, health, education and skill development were extended to 3.50 lakh girls through 507 ICDS blocks.

The World Bank Assisted multistate ICDS Projects continued to be implemented in the predominantly tribal areas of Andhra Pradesh (191 blocks), Orissa (110 blocks) Bihar (210 blocks) and Madhya Pradesh (244 blocks). These Projects provided for income generation activities for women, interventions for adolescent girls, nutritional rehabilitation of severely malnourished in addition to normal ICDS Services.

Early Childhood Education

The programme of Early Childhood Education (ECE) extended pre-school education to over one lakh children through 4365 ECE centres run by the voluntary organisations in the nine educationally backward states of Andhra Pradesh, Assam, Bihar, Jammu & Kashmir, Madhya Pradesh, Orissa, Rajasthan, Uttar Pradesh and West Bengal.

Creches

12470 creches continued to be run throughout the country by voluntary organisations for the children of poor working mothers, providing day care services, supplementary nutrition, immunization, medical and health care and recreation facilities.

The National Creche Fund was set up in March 1993 in response to the demand for more creches with a Corpus Fund of Rs. 19.90 crores. From the fund, upto 31 March 1996, 1243 additional creches were sanctioned.

Thus, presently there are *13713* creches providing day care services to *3.43* lakh children.

Balwadi Nutrition Programme

5641 balwadis are providing supplementary nutrition and catering to the social & emotional development of 2.25 lakh children of the age group 3-5 years.

National Nutrition Policy

The National Nutrition Policy, adopted in 1993, spelt out direct nutrition interventions for vulnerable groups, duly inculcating nutrition concerns across different sectors. A National Nutrition Council under the Chairmanship of the Prime Minister was set up to monitor the implementation of the policy.

National Plans of Action (NPAs)

Two National Plans of Action (NPAs)—one for the children other exclusively for the girl child to achieve the goals set in the World Declaration on survival, protection and development of children were drawn up. Based on the National Plans of Action, the State Governments have also formulated State Plans of Action. Coordination Committees have been set up for strict monitoring of the implementation of the Action Plans.

Objectives of National Plans of Action for Children

A. Child Health

— Eradication of Poliomyelitis by the year 2000

— Elimination of neonatal tetanus by 1995

— Reduction by 95 per cent in measles deaths and reduction by 90 per cent of measles cases compared to pre-immunisation levels by 1995.

— Achievement and maintenance of high level of immunisation coverage at a level of 100 per cent for infants and against tetanus for women of child bearing age.

— Reduction by 50 per cent in deaths due to diarrhoea in children under the age of five years and 25 per cent of diarrhoea in incidence rate.

— Reduction in mortality rates due to ARI among children under five by 40 per cent by 2000 A.D., from the present level.

B. Maternal Health

— Special attention to health and nutrition of the female child and to pregnant and lactating women.

— Access by all couples to information and services to prevent pregnancies that are too early, too closely spaced, too late or too many.

— Access by all pregnant women to prenatal care, trained attendants during child birth and referral facilities for high risk pregnancies and obstetric emergencies.

— Universal access to primary education with special emphasis for girls and accelerated literacy programmes for women.

Nutrition

— Reduction in severe as well as moderate malnutrition among under five children by half of 1990 levels.

— Reduction in incidence of low birth weight (2.5 kg. or less) babies.

— Reduction of iron deficiency anemia in women.

— Control of iodine deficiency disorders.

— Control of vitamin A deficiency and its consequences, including blindness.

— Empowerment of all women to breast feed their children exclusively for four to six months and to continue breast-feeding with complementary food, well into the second year.

— Growth promotion and its regular monitoring to be institutionalised by the end of the 1990s.

— Dissemination of knowledge and supporting services to increase food production to ensure household food security.

Water and Sanitation

— To provide the entire rural population with potable water supplied @ 40 lpcd.

— To cover 10 per cent population with sanitary facilities by the year 1997.
— To eradicate guineaworm disease by 1995.
— To provide safe water with fluoride content within tolerable limits by the year 2000 A.D.

Education

— Universal enrolment of all children including girls, using both full time formal schools and part time non-formal arrangements.
— Reduction of drop-out rate between class I and V and I to VIII from the existing 45 per cent and 60 per cent to 20 per cent and 40 per cent respectively.
— Achievement of minimum levels of learning by approximately all children at the primary level and introduction of this concept at the upper primary state on large scale.
— Reduction in disparities by emphasis on girls' education and special measures for children belonging to Scheduled Castes/Scheduled Tribes.
— Universalisation of effective access to schooling.

Early Childhood Education

— Expansion of early childhood development activities including appropriate low cost family and community based interventions.
— Children in Especially Difficult Circumstances.
— Provision of protection of children in especially difficult circumstances and tackle the root cause leading to such situations.

Girl Child

— To remove the gender bias and to improve the status of the girl child in society, so as to provide her with equal opportunities for her survival and development to her full potential.

Adolescent Girls

— Programmes for the adolescent girls should embrace a whole range of activities, such as nutrition, health, education, health and nutrition education, recreation, upgradation of home-based skills and promotion of her decision making capability as adolescent girls who are one of the most critical human resources, particularly at the village level.

Children and the Environment

— To conserve and protect environment so that it is conducive to the health and well being of the children.

25.3 WOMEN

Rashtriya Mahila Kosh: The Rashtriya Mahila Kosh was set up in March 1993 as a national instrument for extending credit to poor and needy women. It

Mahila Samriddhi Yojana : The Mahila Samriddhi Yojana, launched in October 1993, to promote thrift among women and empower them with control over an asset in terms of a Post Office Account, has entitled 169.06 lakh account holders. The total amount deposited is Rs. 172.42 crores.

Indira Mahila Yojana (IMY) : This scheme was launched on August 20, 1995 in 200 blocks throughout the country with a view to primarily coordinate and integrate components of all sectoral programmes and to facilitate their convergence to benefit women. The three basic constituents of the scheme are: (1) convergence of inter-sectoral services, (2) Income generation activities and (3) A sustained process of awareness generation/education.

National Commission for Women

Organisation of the Commission: The National Commission for Women (NCW) was set up as a National Apex Statutory Body in 1992 in accordance with the National Commission for Women Act, 1990. The composition of the Commission as per the Act provides for a Chairperson committed to the cause of women and five members nominated by the Government from amongst social scientists, experts in legislation, trade union movement, industrial management, administration, socio-economic development, etc., and a Member Secretary. The terms of Chairperson and Members (except one Member) expired on 30 January 1995. The new Chairperson and Members were nominated by the Government for another term of three years on 21 July 1995. The composition of this Commission is as follows :

Ms. Mohini Giri	Chairperson
Ms. Ganga Potai	Member
Ms. Kailash Pati	Member
Ms. Manorama Singh	Member
Ms. Kokila Vyas	Member
Ms. Padma Seth	Member (nominated on 18.1.96)

Ms. Ganga Potai and Ms. Manorama Singh, National Commission for Women resigned from the Commission with effect from 26.3.1996 and 31.3.1996 (A/N) respectively.

Functions of the Commission : investigate and examine the legal safeguards provided for women under the Constitution and other laws and to recommend measures to Government for their effective implementation;

— review the existing provisions of the Constitution and other laws affecting women and recommend amendments to meet any lacunae, inadequacies or shortcomings in these laws;
— look into complaints and take suo moto notice of matters relating to deprivation of women's rights and take up the issues with appropriate authorities;
— take up studies/research, etc. on socio-economic issues;
— participate and advise on the planning process of socio-economic development of women and evaluate the progress made;

— inspect jails, remand homes etc., where women are kept under custody and seek remedial action where necessary.

While investigating cases of violation of safeguards for women and complaints relating to deprivation of women's rights, the Commission has the power of a Civil Court trying a suit. The Commission can summon any person and examine the person on oath. It can requisition documents and receive evidence on affidavits. Section 16 of the Act makes it obligatory on the part of the Central Government to consult the Commission on all major policy matters affecting women.

To assist the Commission in discharging its functions, a number of expert Committees have been set up to tender advise on various subjects dealt in the Commission. These Committees work on the issues of "social security".

4th World Conference at Beijing (September 1995) and *National Policy for The Empowerment of Women* (1996).

Introduction : As a follow up action of the Beijing Conference, the Department of Women and Child Development, Ministry of Human Resource Development, Government of India prepared the final draft of the National Policy in 1996.

National Policy for the Empowerment of women—1996 (Final Draft)

Introduction

The principle of gender equality is enshrined in the Indian Constitution in its Preamble, Fundamental Rights, Fundamental Duties and Directive Principles.

Within the framework of a democratic polity, out laws, development policies, plans and programmes have aimed at women's advancement in different spheres. From the Fifth Five Year Plan (1974-78) onwards, there has been a marked shift in the approach to women's issues from welfare to development. In recent years, the empowerment of women has been recognised as the central issue in determining the status of women. The National Commission for Women was set up by an Act of Parliament in 1990 to safeguard the rights and legal entitlements of women. The 73rd and 74th Amendments (1993) to the Constitution of India have provided for reservation of seats in the local bodies of Panchayats and Municipalities for women, laying a strong foundation for their participation in decision making at the local levels.

India has also ratified various international conventions and human rights instruments committing to secure equal rights for women. Key among them is ratification of the Convention on the Elimination of All Forms of Discrimination Against Women (CEDAW-1979) in 1993.

The Mexico Plan of Action (1975), the Nairobi Forward Looking Strategies (1985), the Beijing Declaration as well as the Platform for Action (1995), have been unreservedly endorsed by India for appropriate follow up.

The women's movement with a wide-spread net work of non-Government Organisations which have strong grass-roots presence and deep insight into womens' concerns has inspired many initiatives for the empowerment of women.

However, there still exists a wide gap between the goals enunciated in the Constitution, legislation, policies, plans, programmes, and related mechanisms on the one hand and the situational reality of the status of women in India, on the other. This has been analysed extensively in the Report of the Committee on the Status of Women in India, "Towards Equality" (1974), and highlighted in the National Perspective Plan for Women (1988-2000) and the Shramshakti Report (1988).

Gender disparity manifest itself in various forms, the most obvious being the trend of continuously declining female ratio in the population last few decades. Social stereotyping and violence at the domestic and societal levels are some of the other manifestations. Discrimination against girl children, adolescent girls and women still persists.

Consequently, the access of women—majority of whom are in the rural areas and in the informal, unorganised sector—to education health and productive resources, among others, is inadequate. Therefore, they remain largely marginalised, poor and socially excluded.

In this background, having taken stock of national and international developments and after a series of consultations with Members of Parliament, State Governments, non-Governmental Organisations, Women's Organisations, social activists, researchers and other experts in the country, this Policy has been drawn up.

The goal of this Policy is to bring about the advancement, development and empowerment of women. This is to be achieved by changing societal attitudes and elimination of all forms of gender based discrimination, active participation of women in all spheres of life, incorporation of gender perspectives, translation of de jure equality of women into de facto equality and affirmative action, wherever necessary.

The positive features of India culture and tradition which reiterate the dignity of and respect for women, will be reinforced in the endeavour to achieve social harmony. Through appropriate programmes, women and men will be made aware of their social responsibilities as change agents. Their role as promoters of progressive values and respect for humanity will be emphasised therein.

1. The Policy will be widely disseminated so that a meaningful partnership is established with all sections of civil society, to achieve its goals.

2. *Human Rights and Fundamental Freedoms* : The dejure and de facto enjoyment of all Human Rights and Fundamental Freedoms by women on an equal basis with men shall be ensured both in letter and in spirit and all factors which impede the realization of such rights and freedoms eliminated.

3. *Elimination of Violence against Women* : All forms of violence against women, physical and mental, whether at domestic or societal levels, particularly sexual abuse and violence, including through recourse to customs, traditions or practices, shall be eliminated. Mechanisms/schemes for assistance will be created and strengthened for the rehabilitation of the victims of violence. Institutions and mechanisms responsible for elimination of violence against women and taking action against the perpetrators of such violence, will be strengthened.

4. *Ending Discrimination Against Women* : Recognising the equal entitlement of women and men to human rights and fundamental freedoms in all spheres, political, economic, social, cultural, civil etc., no discrimination shall be allowed in law or practice against women. Equal rights for women will be ensured in respect of access to health care and quality education at all levels, career and vocational guidance, employment, equal remuneration, occupational health and safety, social security, health care and public office.

5. *Elimination of Discrimination Against and Violation of the Rights of The Girl Child* : All forms of discrimination against the girl child and violation of her rights shall be eliminated by undertaking strong measures including punitive ones. These relate to strict enforcement of laws against pre-natal sex selection and foeticide, female infanticide, child marriage, child abuse and child prostitution. Removal of discrimination in the treatment of the girl child in the family and outside and projection of a positive image of the girl child will be actively fostered. There will be special emphasis on the needs of the girl child and earmaking of substantial investments in the areas relating to food and nutrition, health and education, including vocational education. In implementing programmes for eliminating child labour, there will be a special focus on the girl children.

6. *Empowerment of Women* : A synergy of development measures will be effected and affirmative action designed for the holistic empowerment of women. Women will be given complete and equal access to and control over factors contributing to such empowerment, particularly, health, education, information, life long learning for self-development, vocational skills, employment and income earning opportunities, technical services, land and other forms of property, including through inheritance, common property resources, credit, technology and markets, etc.

7. *Women in Decision Making* : Women's equality in power sharing and active participation in decision making, including political decision making at all levels and in all processes will be ensured for the achievement of the goal of empowerment. All measures will be taken to guarantee women equal access to and full participation in all decision making bodies at every level, in the private and public sectors, including the legislative, executive, judicial, local, corporate, statutory bodies, as also advisory Commissions, Committees, Boards, Trusts etc. Affirmative action, such as reservation/quotas including in higher legislative bodies, will be considered whenever necessary, on a time bound basis.

8. *Women and the Developmental Process* : Policies, programmes and systems will be established to ensure mainstreaming of women's perspectives in all developmental processes, as catalysts, participants and recipients. Co-ordinating and monitoring mechanisms will be devised to assess from time to time the progress of such mainstreaming. Women's issues and concerns will as a result be specially addressed and reflected in all concerned laws, sectoral policies, plans and programmes of action.

9. *Sensitization to Women's Issues* : Specially planned and well funded sensitization programmes will be conducted on a regular basis for all sections of society. There will be special focus on functionaries of the State in the Executive, Legislative and Judicial Wings and in all developmental agencies,

governmental and non-governmental. These programmes will be, in a phased manner, integrated as part of all on-going training programmes, both in the public and the private sectors.

10. *Women and Mass Media* : Media will be used to portray a positive image of girls and women. It will strive to remove demeaning, degrading and negative, conventional stereotypical images of women and violence against women. Legislation, media policies and regulatory mechanisms, including codes of conduct etc., will be put in place to address these aspects.

11. *Eradicating Poverty and Ensuring Provision of Women's Basic Needs :*

11.1 *Poverty Eradication* : Since women comprise the majority of people below the poverty line and are very often in situations of extreme poverty, given the harsh realities of intra-household and social discrimination, macro economic policies and poverty eradication programmes will specifically address the needs and problems of such women. There will be improved implementation of such programmes as are already women oriented or have special targets for women. New programmes will be devised, based on mobilization of poor women and convergence of services, by offering them a range of economic and social options, alongwith necessary support services to enhance their capabilities.

11.2 *Food Security* : In order to satisfactorily cater to the nutritional needs and requirements of households, the Public Distribution System will be strengthened. Intra-household discrimination in this regard vis-a-vis girls and women will be sought to be ended through appropriate strategies. Women's participation will be ensured in the planning, superintendence and delivery of the system.

11.3 *Housing and Shelter* : Women's perspectives will be included in housing policies, planning of housing colonies and provision of shelter both in rural and urban areas. Special attention will be given for providing adequate and safe housing and accommodation for women including single women, heads of households, working women, students, apprentices and trainees. This will be in the form of special facilities such as hostels, dormitories, short stay homes and reservation in housing colonies and townships etc.

11.4 *Education* : Equal access to education for women and girls will be ensured. Measures will be taken to eliminate discrimination, universalise education illiteracy, create a gender—sensitive educational system, increase enrolment and retention rates of girls and improve the quality of education to facilitate life-long learnings as well as development of occupation/vocation/technical skills by women. Sectoral time targets in existing policies will be achieved with a special focus on girls and women.

11.5 *Health* : A holistic approach to women's health will be adopted and special attention will be given throughout their lives, including in terms of nutrition and basic services during infancy, childhood, adolescence, reproductive years and services during old age. Sectoral time targets in existing policies will be achieved with a special focus on girls and women.

11.6 *Women and the Economy* : Women's perspectives will be included in designing and implementing macro-economic and social policies by institutionalizing their participation in such processes.

Women's contribution to socio-economic development as producers and workers will be recognised in the formal and informal, sectors and appropriate policies related to employment and other working conditions will be drawn up.

There will be reinterpretation and redefinition of conventional concepts of work wherever necessary e.g. in the Census records, to reflect women's contribution as producers and workers.

Satellite Accounts will be prepared by Government, consistent with National Accounts to highlight women's work. This will be done by the development of appropriate methodologies.

11.7 *Support Services* : Support services for women, like child care facilities, including creches at work places and educational institutions, homes for the aged and the disabled will be expanded and improved. Women-friendly personnel policies will also be drawn up to encourage women to participate effectively in the developmental process.

11.8 *Drinking Water and Sanitation* : Special attention will be given to the needs of women in the provision of safe drinkingwater, sewage disposal, toilet facilities and sanitation within accessible reach of house-holds. Women's participation will be ensured in the planning, delivery and maintenance of such services.

12. *Women and Environment* : Women will be involved and their perspectives reflected in the policies and programmes for eco-systems management. Considering the impact of environmental factors on their livelihoods and the distribution of labour and time within households, in connection with the collection of fuel and fodder, women's participation will be ensured in the conservation of the environment and control of environmental degradation.

13. *Women and Science* : Programmes will be strengthened to bring about a greater involvement of women in science and technology. These will include measures to motivate girls to take up science and technology for higher education and also ensure that development projects with scientific and technical inputs involve women fully. Efforts to develop a scientific temper and awareness will also be stepped up.

14. *Needs of Specially Disadvantaged Women* : In recognition of the diversity of women's situations and in acknowledgement of the needs of specially disadvantaged groups, measures and programmes will be established to provide them with special assistance. These groups include women in extreme poverty, women in conflict situations, women affected by natural calamities, women in less developed regions, dalits, tribals, minorities, the disabled, widows, elderly women, single women in difficult circumstances, women heading house-holds, those displaced from employment, migrants, the internally displaced and prostitutes etc.

15. *Resources* : Additional resources for expanding and strengthening the existing institutions/mechanisms for women's development and empowerment will be provided. There will be an enhancement in the budget for the Department of Women and Child Development and earmarking of funds for women in the budgets of Ministries/Departments implementing development programmes in different sectors like education, health, welfare, rural

development, urban development, labour, agriculture, industry, science and technology etc.

A synergistic modality of resource mobilisation will be effected to ensure flow of funds and related services from banking/financial institutions, corporate bodies and community organisations at the grass-roots level.

16. *Involvement of NGOs* : The involvement of voluntary organizations, associations, federations, trade unions and other non-governmental organisations, women's organisations, as well as institutions dealing with education, training and research, will be ensured in formulation, implementation, monitoring and review of all policies and programmes affecting women. Towards this end, they will be provided with support related to resources and capacity building, and facilitated to participate actively in the process of the empowerment of women. Their participation in effective societal reorientation towards women will also be ensured.

17. *Gender Development Indices* : Gender Development Indices will be developed by Government by networking with specialised agencies and be based on specially established criteria to support planning, implementation, monitoring, review and evaluation of laws, policies, plans, programmes and for determination of resource devolution from a gender just standpoint.

18. *Gender Disaggregated Data* : Gender disaggregated data will be collected by the primary data collecting agencies of the Central and State Governments as well as Research and Academic institutions in the pubic and private sector. Data and information gaps in vital areas reflecting the status of women will also be filled in by these Agencies.

All Ministries/Departments/Corporations/Banks and financial institutions etc., will collect, collate and maintain/publish data related to programmes and benefits on a gender disaggregated basis.

19. *International Cooperation* : International, regional and sub-regional cooperation towards the empowerment of women will continue to be encouraged, through sharing of experiences, exchange of ideas and technology, networking with institutions and organisations and through bilateral and multi-lateral partnerships.

Strategies and Action Points

1. *Grass-Roots Level*: At the grass-roots, women will be helped by government through its programmes to organise into self-help groups at the Anganwadi/ Village/Town level. Existing women's groups and women's organisations working at the grass-roots level will also be appropriately strengthened. The womens' groups will be helped to institutionalize themselves into registered societies and to federate at the Panchayat/Municipal level. These societies will bring about synergistic implementation of all the social and economic development programmes by drawing resources made available through Government and non-Government channels, including banks and financial institutions and by establishing a close interface with the Panchayats/ Municipalities.

2. *District and Sub-District Levels* : At the District and Sub-District levels, the services of the existing agencies, Zilla Parishads/District Rural Development Agencies/Municipal Bodies will be available to the womens' groups for co-ordination and facilitating smooth flow of resources for the advancement and empowerment of women.

3. *State and National Levels*

3.1 At the National and State levels there will be Councils for the Empowerment of Women to review implementation of recommendations of National and State Commissions for women and to give broad policy advice, guidance and direction; these National and State Councils will also oversee the operationalisation of the Policy on a regular basis. The National Council will be headed by the Prime Minister and the State Councils by the Chief Ministers. The Councils will be broad in their composition, having representatives from the concerned Departments/Ministries, heads of the National and State Commissions for Women and Social Welfare Boards, representatives of Non-Government Organisations, Women's organisations, Corporate Sector, Trade Unions, financial institutions, academics, experts and social activists, etc.

3.2 All Central and State Ministries will draw up time bound Action Plans for translating the Policy into a set of concrete actions, in consultation with the Centre/State Departments of Women and Child Development and National/State Commissions for Women. These action plans will be reviewed at regular intervals. The Plans will specifically include the following :

3.2.1 Commitment of resources for women in key sectors relating to education, vocational training, employment and income generation, health, all support services, gender sensitization programmes and information dissemination etc.

3.2.2 Time targets to achieve the mandates, strategies and action points of the Policy, for the short term and the long term after determining relevant priorities.

3.2.3 Fixing up responsibilities for implementation of action points.

3.2.4 Structures and mechanisms to ensure efficient implementation, monitoring and review of action points.

3.3 To ensure mainstreaming of women's concerns and issues, every Ministry/Department of the Centre/State will provide for the equal participation of women in their programmes/activities, as catalysts, participants and recipients.

3.4 The National Development Council will review all development programmes and targets on the basis of gender disaggregated data and ensure, with the support of the Planning Commission, flow of funds for programmes undertaken for women in various sectors.

3.5 Planning Commission/State Planning Boards/Commissions, will ensure that the Central and State Governments identify separately, specific physical and financial resources for women and men, in all sectors, particularly in health, nutrition, education, housing, water, sanitation, environmental conservation, training, skill development and employment/income generation in agriculture, industries and allied sectors.

3.6 Every Ministry/Department at the Centre/State will ensure equal flow of benefits in physical and financial terms to women, including specially disadvantaged groups of women, through their different plans and programmes, executed directly, or through autonomous organisations and public undertakings working under it and will report annually to Parliament/State Legislatures in this regard.

3.7 To affirm the full and equal participation of women of all sections and categories and to ensure women's rights, equal access and equal control over resources, the following will be undertaken :

3.7.1 All existing laws, including personal, customary and tribal laws, subordinate legislation, related rules as well as executive and administrative regulations, will be reviewed in consultation with the National/State Commissions for Women.

3.7.2 All new laws, subordinate legislation, related rules as well as executive and administrative regulations will be formulated with a gender perspective.

3.7.3 All existing policies, including sectoral policies, plans and programmes will be reviewed.

3.7.4 All new policies, including sectoral policies, plans and programmes will be formulated with a gender perspective.

3.8 The contribution of all sectoral policies, plans and programmes to the development, advancement and empowerment of women will be subject to Parliamentary and Legislative review by an appropriate mechanism and structure to be created in Parliament and in State Legislatures. Suitable structures and processes will also be created in Panchayats and Municipalities to enable them to oversee and monitor the implementation of sectoral policies on women.

3.9 Women's rights will be guaranteed by strict enforcement of all relevant legal provisions and speedy redressal of grievances, with a special focus of violence and gender related atrocities. Measures will also be taken to prevent and punish sexual harassment at the place of work.

3.10 Crimes against women, their incidence, prevention, investigation, detection and prosecution will be regularly reviewed at all Crime Review Fora and Conferences at the Central. State and District levels and by the Home Ministry/Department.

3.11 Recognised, local, voluntary organisations will be authorised to lodge complaints and facilitate registration, investigations and legal proceedings related to violence and atrocities against girls and women.

3.12 There will be strengthening and expansion of Women's Cells in Police Stations, All Women Police Stations, Family Courts, Mahila Courts, Counselling Centres, Legal Aid Centres and Nyaya Panchayats, to eliminate violence and atrocities against women.

3.13 There will be widespread dissemination of information on all aspects of legal rights, human rights and other entitlements of women, through specially designed legal literacy programmes and rights information programmes. Legal literacy will be included in the academic curricula of schools and colleges.

3.14 All steps will be taken to protect the interests of the girl-child and adolescent girls according to the Convention on Rights of the Child and the Decadal National /State Plans of Action for the Girl-Child.

3.15 There will be affirmative action, by way of reservations and quotas, as may be considered appropriate, in all bodies of the public and private sector, including the law making bodies, to facilitate active power-sharing by women and their meaningful participation in decision making at all levels.

3.16 Gender Sensitization programmes will include :

3.16.1 Training of Personnel of executive, legislative and judicial wings of the State, with a special focus on policy and programme framers, implementation and development agencies, law enforcement machinery and the judiciary as well as non-Governmental Organisations.

3.16.2 Societal awareness to gender issues and human rights of women.

3.16.3 Review of curriculum and educational materials to include gender education and human rights issues.

3.16.4 Removal of all references derogatory to the dignity of women from all public documents and legal instruments.

3.16.5 Use of different forms of mass media to communicate social messages relating to women's equality and empowerment.

3.17 There will be strict enforcement of laws and codes of conduct relating to positive protrayal of women in the mass-media, so that commodification of women and demeaning images of women are effectively checked. Suitable measures will be considered to check public utterances derogatory to the dignity of women.

3.18 To ensure that women are provided with all support services, drinking water, and sanitation, sectoral policies will be suitably reviewed and amended.

3.19 To improve the nutritional status of girls and women and provide them with food security, awareness generation and other related programmes will be strengthened.

3.20 Women will be actively associated in the conservation of the environment and in the management of common property resources specially relating to fuel and fodder collection so as to utilise them optimally and in a sustainable manner.

3.21 Labour protection for women workers in the organised and unorganized sector will be ensured. There will be strict enforcement of relevant laws such as Equal Remuneration Act and Minimum Wages Act, scientific measurement of women's work for determination of their wages and review of all labour legislation from a gender—just standpoint.

3.22 Skills related to technology management will be imparted to women through appropriate programmes, governmental and non-governmental so as to enable them to utilise effectively, among others, infrastructure/services provided by development projects, e.g. those relating to provision of drinking water, irrigation, non-conventional energy sources etc.

3.23 The progress in the advancement of the status of women will be reviewed once in five years. These reviews will be based on objective criteria and Gender Development Indices (GDIs), and also carry Situational Profiles on the status of women at the National and State levels. These reviews will coincide with the Five Year Plans. Appraisals at shorter intervals than five years many also be undertaken, as may be required from time to time.

3.24 To analyse and study relevant Gender Development Indices, gender auditing and evaluation mechanisms will be established. Information derived there from will be widely disseminated.

3.25 National and State Resource Centres will be established with mandates for collection and dissemination of information, undertaking research work, conducting surveys, implementing training and awareness generation programmes, etc. These Centres will link up with Womens' Studies Centres, research and academic institutions through suitable information networking systems.

3.26 Institutional mechanisms which exist at the Central and State levels, to promote the advancement of women, will be strengthened. These will be through interventions as may be appropriate and will relate to, among others, provision of adequate resources, staff training and advocacy skills, to effectively influence macro-policies, legislations, programmes etc., to achieve the empowerment of women.

26

TRANSPORT AND COMMUNICATIONS

Telecommunications

India has a network of over 20,455 exchanges with a capacity of 128.4 lakh lines and 106 lakh working connections as on November 30, 1995. The network grew at a rate of 22.8 per cent during 1994-95. A switching capacity of 22.3 lakh lines was added during 1994-95, 22.1 per cent more than 1993-94. About 25 per cent of the total capacity was added in Delhi, Bombay, Calcutta and Madras.

The annual growth rate of providing new telephone connections has been increasing steadily from 9.8 per cent in 1988-89 to 18.3 per cent in 1993-94. During 1994-95, it recorded a growth of 22 per cent. The number of new telephone connections provided in 1994-95 was 17.7 lakh. The number of people waiting for new connections as on March 31, 1995 was 21.53 lakhs, 13.8 per cent lower than the number in the previous year. During 1994-95, 47,659 villages were provided with telephone facilities. This was 44.4 per cent more than the achievement in 1993-94. During 1994-95, 171.5 lakh conductor kilometers (LCKMS) of cables were laid, 25 per cent more than in 1993-94.

Until 1991 telecom equipment production was reserved for public sector, although opened to some extent to the private sector in 1984 by allowing private participation in the production of customer premises telephone equipments. The liberalisation of the economy since July 1991 has placed the entire telecom equipment manufacture industry under the delicensed and dereserved sector and has allowed automatic approval of foreign equity upto 51 per cent by foreign investors in the manufacture of all telecom equipments.

The National Telecom Policy (NTP) was announced in May 1994. The most important feature of the policy is provision for participation of companies registered in India in basic telecom services with a view to supplementing the efforts of the Department. The other major features of the NTP are : telephone should be available on demand by the 1997; all villages should be covered by 1997; installation of one Public Call Office (PCO) per 500 persons in urban areas by 1997; introduction of value-added services available internationally in India within the Eighth Plan period; the country emerging as a major manufacturing base and a major exporter of telecom equipment and encouragement to pilot projects to access new technologies in both basic and value-added services.

On the basis of licences issued in 1994 for four metro cities viz. Delhi, Bombay, Calcutta and Madras, cellular mobile phones service were started on a commercial basis in these cities. Tenders were also invited for award of licences for providing cellular mobile telephone services for 10 years in various areas. Letters of Intent were issued to 11 successful bidders to operate in 17 circles (service areas). Thus the cellular mobile telephone service was likely to be operational almost over the whole country by the end of 1996-97.

The Radio Paging service has now become operational in 23 major cities and it is expected that the radio paging service will be available in most cities throughout the country by the end of 1996-97.

Reforms in Telecommunications

— Customer premises equipment industry opened to the private sector in 1984.

— Value-added services (VAS) opened to the private sector in 1992. These services include Cellular Mobile Phones, Radio Paging, Electronic Mail, Voice Mail, Audio Text Services, Video Text Services, Data Services, Video Conferencing, and Credit Card Authorisation Services.

— The National Telecom Policy (NTP) was announced in May 1994 with the main objective of providing telephone on demand reaching all the villages in India at the earliest possible and at affordable and reasonable prices; to provide widest range of word standard level telecom services at reasonable prices, to ensure India's emergence as a major manufacturing base and major exporter of telecom equipment and protecting the defence and security interests of the country.

— For value added services, Government has permitted maximum foreign equity of 51 per cent and this limit is fixed at 49 per cent for basic services, cellular mobile and radio paging.

— Licences to private sector for entry into basic telecom services are to be on circle basis.

— The Government has decided to set up a statutory Telecom Regulatory Authority of India to separate the regulatory function from policy formulation and operational functions. Its terms of reference are : price regulation, ensuring technical compatibility among different service providers, fixation of access charges, protection of consumer interest resolution of disputes between service providers and ensuring time frames for making available local and DOT long distance circuits between service providers.

Posts

The National Postal Network with more than 1.5 lakh Post Offices by March 1995, is the largest in the World. The long term objective is to locate a post office within 3 kms of every village and to provide the facility of a letter box in every village with a population of over 500. As on 31.3.1995 it is estimated that there were approximately 1,09,800 Gram Panchayat Villages which did not have a Post Office. During the first three years of the Eighth Five Year Plan 1306 extra departmental post offices and 262 departmental sub post offices had been sanctioned.

Department of Post has also taken up projects for computerisation of other aspects of postal operations like mail processing, savings bank and materials management. During 1994-95 Metro Channel Service linking the six metros, the Rajdhani Channel linking Delhi with most of State Capitals, and a Business Channel with exclusive treatment to pin-coded business mail were introduced. Green Channel, which gives priority to local mail was also introduced.

A new channel-periodicals channel—was introduced in major cities to ensure timely transmission of daily newspaper and periodicals. An integrated automatic mail processing plant was set up in Bombay in April 1993. Such plants at Madras, Delhi, Bangalore and other major centres are under consideration.

Money order services provide a socially useful means of cash transfer. In order to speed up money order transmission, a project for the use of satellite channels is under implementation. 26 VSAT (Very Small Aperture Terminals) centres were successfully set up in 1994-95, and 49 more such centres were being installed in 1995-96. The network of VSATs is being used for providing value added services like hybrid mail involving open message and data transfer and corporate money order service, involving corporate cash transfer, introduced last year.

Speed Post traffic continues to show healthy annual increase. The accent in 1994-95 was on consolidating existing clientele by offering additional facilities like proof of delivery. Other facilities proposed to be extended include bulk discounting, packaging services, insurance and the facility of refund in cases of delay in delivery of speed post articles. To improve monitoring of speed post articles from the point of receipt to the point of delivery, the Department of Post is setting up a Track and Trace System. In 1994-95 this facility had been introduced for articles emanating to and from Delhi and Bombay. During 1994-95 the total revenue earned by speed post was Rs. 54.2 crore and the traffic generated was 124.7 lakh articles.

Postal Life Insurance (PLI) consists of over 21 lakh policies with a sum assured of Rs. 4776 crore. During 1994-95 the Government extended PLI to cover rural areas and the target is to generate a business of Rs. 500 crore sum assured through the Rural PLI Scheme.

Post Office Savings Bank (POSB) operates through the wide network of post offices, of which 89 per cent are located in rural areas. The total outstanding balance during 1994-95 through various savings schemes was Rs. 78,908 crore and operations of POSB are now being computerised. Mahila Samriddhi Yojana scheme introduced in October 1993, in order to empower adult rural women financially, generated Rs. 81.2 crore in 84.4 lakh accounts as on 31.3.1995. During 1995-96 the Department introduced a new value added service i.e. Premium Savings Bank Service in order to facilitate savings bank account holders to access cash more easily. This facility, through a Smart Card based pilot project initially covers 15 post offices in Delhi from November 1995 and is proposed to be extended to 6 more cities from 1996-97.

Railways

The Indian Railways consist of an extensive network spread over 62,660 kms-comprising Broad Gauge (39,612 kms), Meter Gauge (19,210 kms) and Narrow Gauge (3,838 kms). Electrified networks with 11,793 kms., account for 18.8 per cent of the total Route Kilometrage. The thrust areas identified for the Eighth Plan period include replacement and renewal of over aged assets; augmentation of terminal and rolling stock capacities; gauge conversion and electrification. Indian Railways completed gauge conversion of 1,351 kms. in 1992-93, 1,619 kms. in 1993-94, 1805 kms. in 1994-95 and set a target of 1,000 kms. for 1995-96.

During 1994-95, the revenue earning freight traffic moved by the railways was 365 million tonnes. This was only 1.7 per cent higher than the performance in 1993-94. The freight traffic carried during April-November 1995-96 at 245.3 million tonnes, increased by 5.7 per cent over April-November, 1994. The growth had mainly been in coal, raw materials for steel plants, foodgrains, fertilisers, iron ore for export, POL, etc. However, there was a major decline in cement and pig iron and finished steel from steel plants (Table 26.1).

TABLE 26.1. Performance of the Railways

			*April-November**		*Change over previous year*	
	1993-94	*1994-95**	*1994*	*1995*	*1994-95*	*1995-96@*
						(per cent)
Total revenue earning freight traffic (million tonnes)	358.7	365.0	232.2	245.3	1.7	5.7
(i) Coal	167.0	172.4	110.4	115.0	3.2	4.1
(ii) Raw Materials for steel plants (excl. coal)	33.4	36.6	23.3	25.0	9.6	7.3
(iii) Pig iron & finished steel from steel plants	12.1	12.0	7.6	7.6	-0.5	-0.4
(iv) Iron ore for export	10.5	9.8	6.4	6.5	-6.2	1.6
(v) Cement	32.5	31.5	20.5	20.2	-3.3	-1.2
(vi) Foodgrains	26.7	20.7	12.6	16.4	22.3	29.6
(vii) Fertilizers	19.5	21.5	13.5	14.7	10.2	8.8
(viii) POL	26.0	27.7	18.1	19.1	6.8	5.3
(ix) Balance (other goods)	31.1	32.8	19.6	20.8	5.3	6.1
2. Net tonne kilometers (billion)	252.4	249.6	159.8	172.5	-1.1	7.9
3. Net tonne kilometers per wagon per day (broad gauge)	1506.0	1590.0	1479.0	1657.0	5.6	12.0
4. Passenger traffic originating (million) $	3708.0	3914.9	1921.2	1989.5	5.6	3.6
5. Passenger kilometers (billion) $	296.2	319.4	157.1	161.8	7.8	3.0

* Provisional. @ April-November. $ April-September

Existing modal shares between rail and road do not conform to optimal shares as judged by least economic cost. The railways have devised a new marketing strategy following economic reforms, to attract freight traffic now going by road which is more energy intensive and less environment friendly.

The railways employ about 16 lakh workers, the largest number for any undertaking in the country. A comprehensive plan for human resource development is required to upgrade skills, retrain workers and achieve higher productivity. Indian Railways have taken certain concrete steps in this direction such as training and development of management, strategy for improvement in performance and productivity of assets. UNDP is assisting Indian Railways for organisational development and system changes in order to improve efficiency, productivity and quality. The project focuses on major areas like total quality management, management information systems, marketing, work force motivation, project management and restructuring. The budgetary support to the Railways declined continuously from 75 per cent of the Railways Plan outlay in the Fifth Plan to 42 per cent of outlay in the Seventh Plan and further to 23 per cent of the outlay during the first four years of the Eighth Plan.

Civil Aviation

The activities of Civil Aviation are broadly divided into three areas : operational, infrastructural and regulatory-cum-developmental. On the operational side, India Airlines Limited, and private air lines (Scheduled and Non-Scheduled) provide domestic air services. Air India Limited provides international air services. India Airlines Limited also provide air services to neighbouring countries. Pawan Hans Limited provides helicopter support services, primarily to the petroleum sector. Infrastructural facilities are provided by the Airports Authority of India (AAI). The two authorities viz., International Airports Authority of India (IAAI) and the National Airports Authority (NAA) have been merged with effect from 1.4.1995 to form a single authority viz. Airports Authority of India as a result of enactment of Airport Authority of India Act, 1994. The regulatory and developmental functions are looked after by the Ministry of Civil Aviation and the offices of the Directorate General of Civil Aviation.

The Air Corporation Act, 1953, repealed on March 1, 1994, ended the monopoly of Indian Airlines, Air India and Vayudoot over scheduled air transport services. Six private operators, who were hitherto operating as air taxis, have since been granted scheduled airlines status. In addition, 19 air taxi operators were given permit for charter/non-scheduled air transport services.

The competitive environmental on domestic services has been, in effect, existent since April, 1993. By November 1995, 28 aircraft in the 120 plus category, belonging to private air taxis, were in operation. The natural consequence of creating a competitive environment in this sector was that, by March 1995, 35.6 per cent of the market was being catered to by private air taxis. The number of passengers carried by air taxi operators increased from 15,000 in 1990 in 4.1 lakh in 1992, 29.2 lakh in 1993 and 36 lakhs during 1994.

The year 1994-95 continued to be a difficult year for Indian Airlines Ltd., but despite the stiff competition, it was able to maintain its market share of 63.7 per cent. The year 1994-95 witnessed Operating profit of Rs. 36.24 crore. The company was able to arrest its losses mainly due to enhanced operations to international sectors especially at Gulf routes.

During 1994-95 the company increased its fares with effect from 25th July, 1994 ranging from 10 to 20 per cent. But even this was not sufficient to meet with spiralling costs of fuel and oil, airport landing and parking fees, interest charges, insurance, depreciation, spare parts repairs etc., which account for about 87 per cent of the total cost and is beyond the conrol of the company. Following the all round increase in costs, the company revised its domestic rupee fare with effect from October 1, 1995 by 20 per cent on an average and revised its dollar fares with effect from January 1, 1996. The revenue and expenditure of Indian Airlines Limited during April-February, 1994-95, increased by 14 per cent and 8.9 per cent respectively. The net loss during this period was Rs. 189 crore, as compared to Rs. 235 crore during April-February, 1993-94. During April-September 1995 total revenue of Indian Airlines Limited increased by 15.52 per cent whereas the total expenses increased by 11.52 per cent as compared to the corresponding period of the previous year, thereby bringing down the loss from Rs. 136 crore to Rs. 113 crore.

The net profit of Air India Ltd., for the year 1994-95 was about Rs. 41 crore as against Rs. 200 crore in 1993-94. However the company incurred a loss of Rs. 69.5 crore during the period April-September, 1995. During the year 1994-95 total revenue of the company was Rs. 2989 crore as compared to Rs. 2581.8 crore for 1993-94 representing an increase of 15.8 per cent; Likewise the total operating expenditure of the company was Rs. 2920.1 crore as compared to Rs.2460 crore for 1993-94 representing an increase of 18.7 per cent. The main reasons for drop in profits were the factors such as frequent industrial unrest leading to cancellation of flights and disruption of flight schedules; incidence of depreciation and interest on account of acquisition of four 747-400 aircraft; increase in expenditure by 18.7 per cent due to insurance, fuel oil, landing, lease, rental and hire charges; increase in allowances payable to the employees and payment of additional perquisites as per he Memorandum of Understanding reached with the unions, associations, guilds; outbreak of plague epidemic in October, 1994 resulting in large number of flight cancellations and cancellations of booking for subsequent few months and the drop in yield by 18.6 per cent as compared to 20.1 per cent in previous year. Air India's overall load factor of 57.3 per cent is low compared to other international airlines. Its share of international traffic originating from India came down from 42 per cent in 1981 to 35 per cent in 1991 and 20.4 per cent in 1994.

Pawan Hans Limited (PHL) basically provides helicopter support services to the petroleum sector including ONGC and Oil India Limited and connects remote and inaccessible areas. It also provides air support services to several customers which includes NTPC, Government of Punjab and Madhya Pradesh, Lakshadweep Administration, GAIL, BSF and also caters to private sector. The total revenue flying hours during 1994-95 was 18,577 compared to about 18,127 during 1993-94. The revenue earnings and net profits during 1994-95 were Rs. 143.2 crore and Rs. 40 crore respectively, compared to Rs. 131.4 crore and Rs. 33.6 crore respectively in 1993-94. The flying hours during April-September, 1995 were 9,265 and revenue and net profit were Rs. 72.8 crore and Rs. 53 crore respectively.

The International Airports Division (IAD) of Airports Authority of India (AAI) manages, operates and develops the five international airports at Bombay, Calcutta, Delhi, Madras and Thiruvananthapuram. Net profit of IAD at Rs. 97.7 crore in 1994-95 was higher by 94.6 per cent of the net profit of Rs. 50.2 crore during 1993-94. During 1994-95 expenditure grew by 10 per cent, whereas revenue increased by 26 per cent. Passenger and Cargo traffic at 228.9 lakh and 494 lakh tonnes during 1994-95 were higher by 9.2 per cent and 12.9 per cent respectively than in 1993-94. IAD has declared a dividend of Rs. 15.3 crore (25 per cent) for 1994-95, as against Rs. 14.7 crore (24 per cent) for 1993-94.

During April-September 1995, the revenue and expenditure of IAD increased by 14.9 per cent and 14.7 per cent respectively, thus accruing the net profit of Rs. 71.6 crore which was 24.2 per cent higher than in April-September, 1994. The number of passengers and cargo handled by it during the period increased by 11 per cent and 12.2 per cent respectively. The new domestic terminal at Calcutta commenced in January 1995. The work at international terminal (Phase III) at Bombay was in progress.

The net profit of National Airports Division (NAD) of Airports Authority of India at 94.15 crore (before tax) in 1994-95 was 76.3 per cent higher than in 1993-94. During April-September, 1995, the revenue increased by 18.7 per cent and expenditure by 31.2 per cent, resulting in profit of Rs. 56 crore (before tax) as compared to Rs. 60 crore during April-September, 1994.

Road and Road Transport

With a network of two million kilometers India has the third largest road network in the world. Half of this is made up of unsurfaced roads. The National Highways network of 34,058 Km at the end of 1994-95 constitutes less than two per cent of the total road net work, but carries nearly 40 per cent of total road traffic.

It is estimated that road traffic, which accounts for 80 per cent of passenger traffic and 60 per cent of goods traffic, will account for 87 and 65 per cent of passenger and goods traffic respectively by the year 2000. To meet a traffic expansion of such magnitude, the National Highway network must be greatly improved. A large section has inadequate road pavement thickness. Other deficiencies are inadequate capacity, poor riding quality, weak and distressed bridges/culverts, congested city sections, too many railway level crossings, lack of wayside amenities and weak road safety measures. About 20 per cent of National Highways need widening from single to double lanes and about 70 per cent of two lane roads have to be strengthened, and selected corridors on national highways need conversion into Expressways.

Reforms in Road Sector

— Pathkar abolished by all State Governments and octroi by many of them to reduce overall transit time and to help free flow of traffic on roads;

— The Motor Vehicle Act, 1988 amended, which has come into force with effect from November 14, 1994 with a view to simplify procedures and to give more powers to the State Government in the matter of granting driving licences and permits for motor vehicles;

— Road sector declared an industry to facilitate borrowing on easy terms and to permit floating of bonds.

— MRTP provisions relaxed to enable large firms to enter the highway sector;

— National Highways Act amended to enable levy of a fee on national highways, bridges and tunnels.

— Customs duties on construction equipment reduced and procedures streamlined.

Consequent to the amendment of National Highway Act in 1995 to allow private sector participation, steps have been and are being taken to identify and take up the national highway projects through private sector financing.

Additional budgetary support is being obtained for the improvement of National Highways through loan assistance from international agencies such as the World Bank, Asian Development Bank and Overseas Economic Cooperation of Japan. The Government of India has also decided to activate the National Highways Authority, which will have an independent and autonomous status and will be entrusted with externally aided projects with a view to accelerate their pace of implementation.

The State Road Transport Undertakings operate a fleet of nearly one lakh buses employing 8.3 lakh workers. The undertakings, with a few exceptions, face serious financial constraints due to various factors such as the social commitment to operate even on uneconomic routes, absence of cost-based fare structures, overmanning, poor management and widespread inefficiencies.

Shipping

Indian vessels carried about 33.6 per cent of the total sea-borne cargo during 1993-94. The share of Indian vessels in 1993-94 in POL was 61 per cent, in bulk carriers 20 per cent, and in liner traffic 9 per cent. Long term targets for Indian shares in bulk carrier and liner traffic are 50 and 40 per cent respectively. The fleet strength at the end of November, 1995 was 471 vessels of 7 million Gross Registered tonnage (GRT), against 438 vessels of 6.4 million GRT in October, 1994. Overseas trade during 1993-94 was 137 million tonnes against 122.3 million tonnes during 1992-93.

The Shipping Corporation of India (SCI) showed a better financial performance during 1994-95. Its gross tonnage as on October 31, 1995 was 3 million GRT (about 50 per cent of the total fleet). SCI's gross internal resources rose to Rs. 353 crore in 1994-95, as against Rs. 286 crore in 1993-94. Its net profit after tax at Rs. 201 crore in 1994-95 registered an increase of 19 per cent over 1993-94. During April-September 1995, the profit after tax was provisionally estimated at Rs. 115 crore. There are two major public sector ship building yards, Hindustan Shipyards Limited, and Cochin Shipyards Limited.

In order to promote the development of Indian shipping, a new shipping policy was initiated in 1990-91. Several policy measures initiated since then are summarised here :

Reforms in Shipping Sector

— Automatic approval is now given for : (i) Acquisition of all categories of ships except Crude Tankers and Offshore Supply Vessels (OSVs) by Private Shipping companies, (ii) Acquisition of replacement tonnage.
— No approval is required for sale of ships and acquisition of ships from an Indian shipyard.
— Shipping companies allowed to retain sale proceeds of their ships abroad and utilise them for fresh acquisition.
— Shipping companies given freedom to time charters out Indian ships.
— Shipping companies are allowed to acquire vessels through bare boat charter-cum-demise method.
— The shipping companies permitted to get their ships repaired in any shipyard without seeking prior approval from the Government.
— Quarterly Block Allocation Scheme for repaid of ships has been dispensed with entirely and Reserve Bank of India now releases foreign exchange for ship repair/drydocking and spares for imported capital goods without any value limit.
— Certain sections of Merchant Shipping Act have been amended to facilitate Indian shipping companies to raise external commercial borrowings for foreign ship acquisitions.
— As per the recent amendments to Section 42 of the Merchant Shipping Act, 1958 from October 1993 no prior permission from Directorate General of Shipping is required for sale of vessels either for further trading or scrapping by the Indian shipping companies.

Ports

There are eleven major ports and 139 operable minor ports located along the 5560 km long coastline of the country. During 1994-95, the total cargo handled at major ports was 197.3 million tonnes, registering a growth of 10 per cent over 1993-94, constituting about 92 per cent of total traffic handled by Port Sector. Dry and liquid bulk make up 80 per cent of the port traffic in volume with more valuable general cargo constituting 20 per cent of the tonnage. During April-November, 1995 major ports handled 137 million tonnes of charge which was 11.1 per cent higher than the performance achieved in April-November, 1994. (Table 26.2). Major increases in traffic were observed in respect of foodgrains (202 per cent), vegetable oil (146.8 per cent), fertilisers and raw materials (25.1 per cent) and containerised cargo (14.5 per cent). The composition of traffic has undergone significant changes in recent years and there is a need to restructure port capacities accordingly.

TABLE 26.2. Trends in Traffic at Major Ports

	1993-94	*1994-95**	*April-November** *1994*	*1995*	*Change over previous year* *1994-95*	*1995-96@*
	(Million tonnes)					*(per cent)*
1. POL	76.9	82.2	52.7	59.4	6.8	12.7
2. Iron Ore	34.1	34.8	19.5	21.4	2.1	9.9
3. Fertiliser & raw materials	7.4	8.5	5.1	6.4	14.2	25.1
4. Foodgrains	1.4	0.9	0.5	1.4	-61.1	202.1
5. Coal	26.4	29.9	19.2	20.4	13.1	6.0
6. Vegetable oil	0.4	0.6	0.5	1.2	72.2	146.8
7. Other liquids	3.5	4.9	3.2	3.6	39.3	11.5
8. Containerised cargo	12.3	15.4	9.6	11.0	26.0	14.5
9. Others	16.5	20.1	13.0	12.2	22.0	-6.1
Total	179.3	197.3	123.3	136.9	10.0	11.1

* Provisional. @ April-November.

27

DIVERSE ISSUES

27.1 ENVIRONMENTAL CONSERVATION AND PROTECTION

The rapid increase in industrialisation and urbanisation has exerted pressures on the infrastructural facilities which are manifested in terms of increased incidence of air, water and noise pollution.

The ambient air quality of major towns and cities in the country are being monitored under the National Ambient Air Quality Monitoring (NAAQM) Programme. The monitoring results indicate the sulphur dioxide and Nitrogen dioxide levels are mostly within the permissible limits whereas Suspended Particulate Matter (SPM) values are higher than the prescribed limits at some places due to vehicular and air pollution, burning of fossil fuel and natural dusty conditions.

The data on Ambient water quality of rivers reveals that levels of coliform count and Biological Oxygen Demand (BOD) are generally high, resulting in deterioration of water quality. This is primarily due to inadequate sanitation facilities and discharge of waster water into the surface water bodies without proper treatment.

Urban noise levels in major cities also indicate an increasing trend due to rise in human population, automobiles and industrial activities. Specific studies reveal that noise levels in industrial areas are generally within the prescribed limits but exceed the standard in respect of commercial, residential and silence zones during certain hours.

Increasing population, alongwith widespread poverty, has generated pressure on natural resources and thus contributing to degradation of the environment. Of the 329 million hectares (m.ha) of total land area in the country, it is estimated that about 174 m.ha is degraded; this consists of agricultural as well as non agricultural lands, and forests. The forest resources are threatened due to overgrazing and other forms of over exploitation, both for commercial and household needs, encroachments, unsustainable practices like unscientific shifting cultivation and developmental activities. The recorded forest cover in the country is 75 m.ha which works out to 19.5 per cent of the total geographical area as against the broad national goal of 33 per cent for the plain area and 66 per cent for the hilly region. Withdrawals from the forests are much beyond the sustainable levels. It is estimated that the total fuelwood removal from forests exceeds 235 million cubic metres per year, as against a sustainable level of production of only 48 million cubic metres. In large parts of forests, natural regeneration is inadequate due to excessive grazing of livestock, whose population is estimated at around 450 million. However, despite such heavy removals and biotic pressures from forest, the biennial forest surveys of the Forest Survey of India have shown a reversal of declining trend in forest cover.

Over exploitation and loss of habitat constitute a threat to the rich biological diversity available in the country. India possesses the widest variety of biomass and over 75,000 species of fauna and 45,000 species of flora. Many of these are, however, endangered. Among the large animals, 79 species of mammals, as well as 44 of birds, 15 of reptiles and 3 of amphibians are threatened. Nearly 1500 plant species are considered endangered.

The fragile eco-systems of the country also face pressures. Coral reefs, which are very productive marine eco-systems, are adversely affected by their indiscriminate exploitation for production of lime, recreational use and ornamental trade. An area of 6700 Sq. Km., under mangroves is under biotic pressure due to fishing, land use changes in land-sea interface, and pollution of water. The country's unique wetlands, covering an area of 1.45 million hectares, are facing problems of weed infestation, siltation pressures of agriculture and encroachment, chemical and organic pollution, conversion to industrial sites, urbanisation and habitation. Out of the 85 wetlands of international importance in the country, 45 per cent are subject to moderate or high threats. Similarly, the fragile environs of island eco-systems have been subjected to pressures of various forms, including migration of people from the mainland.

To contain the degradation of the environment, the ongoing initiatives of the Government include preventive as well as promotive measures such as conservation of natural resources, prevention and control of pollution, prior environmental impact assessment of industrial and other projects, regeneration of degraded forests with peoples' participation and environmental awareness campaigns.

To encourage the installation of appropriate pollution abatement equipments, the Government has provided fiscal and monetary incentives and punitive measures are also initiated against the defaulting units. To achieve the goal of pollution abatement, emission and efficient standards for air, water and noise have been formulated and notified. More stringent norms for vehicular emissions have been notified under the Central Motor Vehicle Rules which would come into effect from April 1996. A major initiative has been taken to supply unleaded petrol in four metropolitan cities with effect from April 1995 for use in four wheel vehicles fitted with catalytic convertors. Seventeen highly polluting industries have been identified for special monitoring and enforcement efforts, and a substantial majority of the identified units have duly installed the requisite pollution control equipment. According to the data collected by Central Pollution Board till 1995, out of 1551 units belonging to the 17 specified categories of industries, 1186 units had facilities to comply with the environmental standards, 121 were closed and 244 were not having the adequate facilities. Area specific management plans have been prepared to improve the quality of environment in designated 24 critically polluted areas in different parts of the country. The objective of ushering in clean technologies for waste minimisation and environmentally safe production is being attended to, under the ongoing World Bank assisted Industrial Pollution Control Project. An "Eco-mark" scheme is in operation to certify products of industries which fulfil prescribed pollution control standards and achieve high environment friendliness in production, packaging and waste disposal.

The forest conservation strategy has evolved, from dependence on strict regulation of access to and exploitation of forest areas, to incorporating a range of instruments and approaches tailored to specific local situations. The National Forest Policy explicitly recognises the multiple use of forests, the rights of local populations and the role that forests play in the survival strategies of the poor. The task of regenerating the degraded forest areas and lands adjoining forest areas and other protected and ecologically fragile areas and implementation of eco-development programmes is being undertaken by the National Afforestation and Eco-Development Board. During 1994-95 an area of 9,84,102 ha of public land was brought under vegetative cover in the country and 10,810 lakh seedlings were distributed for planting on private land under the 20-Point Programme. The 1995-96 targets for the same are 11,23,784 ha and 11,335 lakh respectively.

Major schemes in the Wildlife sector concentrate on conservation, protection and development of wildlife and its habitat. The main strategy for conservation of bio-diversity is protection of viable habitats in representative eco-systems. A wide network of 75 National Parks, 421 Wildlife Sanctuaries, 21 Project Tiger areas and 8 Biosphere reserves have contributed greatly towards conservation of these species. Ex-Situ conservation is another thrust area in the Government's conservation efforts.

An important thrust towards abatement of river pollution has been the Ganga Action Plan (GAP) to clean up the river Ganga. The phase I of GAP tackled 25 class I towns along the river in the three basin states of Uttar Pradesh, Bihar and West Bengal while the phase II covers tributaries viz. Yamuna and Gomati and the residual pollution load from class I and class II towns. Following the success of Ganga Action Plan, a wider scheme called National River Action Plan covering pollution abatement works for grossly polluted stretches in 18 major rivers in ten States has been approved and the work begun. The thrust of the programme has been popularising the low cost technologies which are easy to operate and maintain and to seek peoples participation in keeping the river clean. A programme for conservation of selected lakes is also under formulation.

The National Environmental Tribunal Act providing relief, compensation and restitution to victims of accidents, while handling hazardous substances and for environmental damages came into force from June, 1995. The Act provides (i) strict liability for damages arising out of any accident while handling any hazardous substance, (ii) the establishment of a National Environmental Tribunal for effective and expeditious disposal of cases arising from such accidents with a view to give relief and compensation for damages to persons, property and the environment, and (iii) matters connected therewith or incidental thereto.

With a view to mitigate the adverse environmental effects of development projects and to integrate environmental concern into development, prior environmental clearance of development projects based on impact assessment is being increasingly emphasised. Such clearance has been made mandatory for 29 specified categories of development projects through a notification issued in January, 1994. This mechanism will also help in catalysing the process of inducting cleaner environmentally friendly technologies into the development process. Other initiatives taken to motivate environmentally oriented technologies and practices include submission by industries of an environmental statement every year and setting up of a Clean Technology Division in the Ministry to identify cleaner technologies that can be introduced in different sectors.

To enhance general awareness of environmental issues a National Environmental Awareness Campaign is conducted every year on a selected theme. The Ministry has also constituted in November, 1995, a Social Audit Panel to assess general public awareness and appreciation of its programmes and to take corrective action, wherever needed, to model them to suit people's requirements and to mobilise there support and participation.

27.2 HOUSING

The formulation and implementation of the housing programmes rests with the state Governments. The Central Government, however, supplements the efforts of the State Government by implementing some central and centrally sponsored programmes. The centrally sponsored schemes are mainly operated for providing institutional and research support to the housing sector.

The scheme for allotment of house-sites-cum-construction assistance as part of the Minimum Needs Programme in rural areas is under the purview of State Sector. The Indira Awas Yojana (IAY) was introduced in 1985-86 in the Central Sector for the poorest of the poor belonging to Scheduled Castes and Scheduled Tribes and freed bonded labourers in the rural areas. Non-SC/ST poor families are also eligible now under the scheme, subject to certain conditions. Houses under the Indira Awas Yojana, as far as possible, are built in clusters along a micro-habitat approach, so that common facilities can be provided for the clusters. Under IAY, 3.72 lakh houses were built during 1994-95, as against the target of 2.54 lakh for which an expenditure of Rs. 474.26 crore was incurred. During 1995-96, the central allocation for this scheme has been enhanced to Rs. 1000 crore as against Rs. 400 crore in 1994-95, with the objective of constructing one million houses. By the end of November 1995, about 2.88 lakh houses were constructed and the construction of about 5.71 lakh houses were in progress for which an expenditure of Rs. 491.35 crore had been incurred.

The physical performance under the scheme of rural house sites-cum-construction assistance indicates that the weaker sections have been given due priority (Table 27.1). The achievement of 1.17 lakh dwelling units well exceeded the target of 0.90 lakh units in 1994-95 for economically weaker sections. For the urban housing the following schemes are being implemented by the central Government ;

(a) Shelter upgradation under Nehru Rozgar Yojana,

(b) Night shelter and sanitation scheme for the urban Footpath Dwellers, and

(c) National Network of Building Centres.

Up to November 1995, a total number of 6.76 lakh dwelling units had been sanctioned under shelter upgradation under NRY, 53 Night Shelters and sanitation schemes to benefit over 21 thousand number of urban footpath dwellers and 210 building centres have become operational.

To augment the flow of institutional credit for the housing sector and to promote and regulate housing finance institutions, the National Housing Bank (NHB) was established in July 1988 as a subsidiary to the Reserve Bank of India. It mobilises resources and channelises them to various schemes.

TABLE 27.1. Performance of Rural Housing for Weaker Sections and Lower Income Groups

(In Lakh)

Scheme	*1993-94*	*1994-95*		*1995-96*	
	Achievement	*Target*	*Achievement*	*Target*	*Achievement (upto July 1995)*
1. Rural House-sites cum House Construction :					
(a) House-sites (Families)	9.21	6.26	9.02	6.46	2.07
(b) Construction Assistance (Families)	4.46	3.64	4.32	2.95	0.63
2. Economically Weaker Sections (Dwelling Units)	1.23	0.90	1.17	0.75	0.19
3. Low Income Group Housing (Dwelling Units)	0.60	0.39	0.40	0.36	0.03

Source : Department of Programme Implementation, Govt. of India.

27.3 LABOUR

Labour Welfare Measures : The thrust of the activities of the Ministry of Labour during the year 1995-96 was on measures for improving the welfare of the workers in the organised and unorganised sector. Thus on 3.11.95, two Ordinances were promulgated on—(i) The Building and Other Construction Workers (Regulation of Employment & Conditions of Service) Ordinance, 1995 and (ii) The Building and Other Construction Workers (Welfare Cess) Ordinance, 1995. These two Ordinances were promulgated for giving protection to building and other construction worker in the country, for regulating employment and conditions of service and for collection of welfare cess. It is estimated that this would benefit about 8.5 million building and construction workers in India mostly in the unorganised sector. These two Ordinances together would facilitate creation of Tripartite Boards for dealing with all issues relating to Labour Protection and Welfare and levy of cess upto 1% of the cost of building and other works for creation of a Welfare Fund from which social security benefits would be disbursed to the workers.

Another major step initiated for the first time after Independence was to introduce a Pension Scheme for the Subscribers to the Employees Provident Fund. The Employees Pension Scheme was notified on 16.11.95. Nearly 19 million provident fund subscribers are expected to benefit from the Scheme. The Scheme provides for the payment of a monthly pension in contingencies like superannuation on attaining the age of 58 years, retirement, permanent disablement, death during service, death after retirement etc. Any subscriber, who puts in a minimum of 10 years membership of the Fund becomes entitled to the Pension. There is also a provision for children's Pension and Orphan's Pension.

Special attention is being paid to the problem of Child Labour. Pursuant to the announcement made by the Prime Minister in August, '94 for the elimination of child labour in hazardous employments by the year 2002 special action was taken in this regard. Collectors from about 100 child labour endemic districts in 12 states of the country which are estimated to account for more than 90% of the child labour population in India were invited to Delhi for discussion in September, 1995 and to finalise the modalities for implementing the Child Labour Projects at the district levels. 63 National Child Labour Projects with an annual expenditure of Rs. 40.50 crores were sanctioned, which are expected to benefit 1.50 lakh children.

Industrial Relations : Maintenance of industrial peace and harmony is essential for sustained economic growth and continued productive employment of workers. The industrial relations situation continued to show a steady improvement during the year because of Government's pro-active role, despite the difficult phase of industrial restructuring. The total number of strikes and lockouts decreased from 1201 in 1994 to 815 in 1995. The number of workers who were involved in strikes and lockouts declined from 8.46 lakh in 1994 to 6.36 lakhs in 1995. As a result of this the number of mandays lost due to strikes and lockouts declined from 20.98 million in 1994 to 11.27 million in 1995. Central Industrial Relations Machinery (CIRM) played an active role in maintaining industrial peace in important sectors like air transport, banks, coal Industry, non-coal Mines, oil Industry, telephone Sector and insurance Sector.

27.4 MEDICAL AND HEALTH CARE

The Eighth Plan has focussed attention on promoting health care to the vulnerable sections of society through consolidating and operationalising the primary health care infrastructure and strengthening referral system through District Health care models.

Since the introduction of economic reforms, the Central Plan outlay for programmes of the Department of Health has been stepped up from Rs. 302 crore (BE) in 1992-93 to Rs. 670 crore in 1995-96 (BE). A substantial portion of plan outlay includes allocations for the control of major communicable diseases. During 1995-96, out of the Central Plan outlay of Rs. 670 crore, outlays have been earmarked for control of major diseases like malaria (Rs. 139 crore), tuberculosis (Rs. 50 crore), leprosy (Rs. 80 crore), blindness (Rs. 72 crore) and AIDS (Rs. 80 crore).

For effective control of malaria in the economically weaker sections of the society in hilly and difficult terrain areas, State Governments have been requested to accord priority. The central assistance for Malaria control has been raised to 100 per cent with effect from December 1994 in seven North

Eastern States which were finding it difficult to finance Malaria Control Programme. Specific efforts have been made to ensure that the ongoing reforms do not lead to any adverse effect on provision of essential care to meet the health needs of the disadvantaged segments of the population. Some of the measures include allocation of funds under the Social Safety Net Scheme to improve Maternal and Child Health (MCH) infrastructure beginning with 90 poorly performed districts in a phased manner.

Specific efforts have also been made to promote the Indian System of Medicine because of its traditional acceptance by the population and local availability of personnel belonging to these systems. A Committee has been set up by the Planning Commission to comprehensively review the existing public health system in India and suggest measures for its improvement.

A High Power Committee on Urban Solid Waste Management set up by the Planning Commission has recommended waste reduction, reuse and recycling, utilising appropriate technology, avoidance of risk transference from one source to other, reduction in the potential risk to human health and environmental degradation. Conservation of energy or its generation through non-conventional sources are the major thrust areas to check environmental degradation resulting from Urban Solid Waste as recommended by the Committee.

To intensify the disease control programme and to strengthen secondary and tertiary level hospitals, assistance has been sought from external agencies like World Bank, DANIDA, SIDA, WHO etc., with a view to harnessing all the available resources for the health care, especially for the poor. It has been envisaged to develop public private partnership through a joint sector approach in collaboration with corporate bodies, non governmental organisations and public sector units.

There has been marked expansion in infrastructure for the health sector (Table 27.2).

27.5 POPULATION AND FAMILY WELFARE

The commitment to containing population growth is one of the priority areas of the Eighth Five Year Plan. India's policies and programmes regarding population and development are in accordance with the recommendations contained in the programme of Action of the International Conference on Population and Development (ICPD), 1994.

Total Fertility Rate has dropped from 5.2 in 1971 to 3.5 in 1993 as per the estimates of Sample Registration System (SRS). The Crude Birth Rate has dropped from 41.2 per thousand population in 1971 to 28.6 in 1994 as per the provisional estimates of the SRS. The Crude Death Rate has also declined from 19 per thousand population to 9.2 over the same period. The Infant Mortality Rate decline from 129 per thousand live births in 1971 to 73 in 1994. The annual population growth rate works out at 2.14 per cent during 1981-91—marginally lower than 2.22 per cent during 1971-81. The population continues to grow as the decline in birth rate has not been as rapid as he decline in the death rate.

The Universal Immunization Programme (UIP) was launched in 1985 to provide universal coverage of infants and pregnant women with immunization

TABLE 27.2 Expansion of Health Services

(In numbers)

	Item	*1951*	*1961*	*1971*	*1981*	*1991*	*1992*	*1993*	*1994*	*1995@@*
1.	Medical Colleges**	28*	60	98	111	128	146	146	NA	NA
2.	Hospitals**	2694	3094	3862	6804	11174	13692	NA	NA	NA
2.	Dispensaries**	6515	9406	12180	16751	27431	27403	NA	NA	NA
4.	Community Health Centres @	0	0	0	217	2071	2193	2289	2321	2385
5.	Primary Health Centres @	725	2565	5112	5740	20450	20719	21009	21155	21693
6.	Sub-Centres @	–	–	28489	51405	130958	131454	131470	131471	131900
7.	Hospital beds (all types)**	117178	230000	348655	569495	810548	NA	NA	NA	NA
8.	Doctors**	61840	83756	151129	268712	394068	410875	NA	NA	NA
9.	Dentists**	3290	3582	5512	8648	10751	11300	19523	NA	NA
10.	Nurses**	16550	35584	80620	154280	340208	385410	449351	NA	NA

NA- Not available. * Pertains to 1950. ** As on December, 31. @ As on March 31. @@ as on 30.6.95.

Source : Ministry of Health and Family Welfare.

against identified vaccine preventable diseases. From the year 1992-93, the UIP has been strengthened and expanded into the Child Survival and Safe Motherhood (CSSM) Project. It involves sustaining the high immunization coverage level under UIP, and augmenting activities under oral rehydration therapy, prophylaxis for control of blindness in children and control of acute respiratory infections. Under the Safe Motherhood component, training of traditional birth attendants, provision of aseptic delivery kits and strengthening of first referral units to deal with high risk and obstetric emergencies are being taken up. Currently, 9 Area Projects are being implemented in 16 districts and the National Capital Territory of Delhi at a total cost of Rs. 1378.35 crore. A new initiative taken up in the year 1995-96 is removal of contraceptive method specific targets, on pilot basis, in 3 States/UT (Tamil Nadu, Kerala and Chandigarh) and 18 districts of 14 other States.

The World Health Organisation (WHO) has set a global goal of eradication of poliomyelitis (polio), a major crippling childhood disease, by the year 2000 A.D. Encouraged by the consistently high level of routine immunisation against polio achieved over the last several years, the Government has taken up "Pulse Polio Immunization" (PPI) from the year 1995-96. The PPI initiative would involve administration of Oral Polio Vaccine (OPV) on the same day to about 75 million children aged 0-3 years in the country twice, once on the 9th December 1995 and then on the 20th January 1996, irrespective of routine OPV immunization status of the infant/child. This exercise will be repeated in the subsequent years also, to achieve the global goal of eradication of polio by 2000 A.D.

In keeping with global trends, the family welfare programme is being reoriented to incorporate additional elements of the 'reproductive and child health' approach. The Central Plan outlay (BE) for family welfare programme has been raised from Rs. 1000 crore in 1992-93 to Rs. 1581 crore in 1995-96, showing an increase of 58 per cent.

Information, Education and Communication (IEC) efforts are being maintained to secure voluntary acceptance of the small family norm by all sections of the population. Counselling is being introduced into the Family Welfare Programme. Greater stress is being placed on the involvement of Non-Governmental Organisations (NGOs) and of the organised sector.

27.6 SPORTS AND PHYSICAL EDUCATION

Sports and Physication are looked after by the Department of Youth Affairs and Sports of the Ministry of Human Resource Department, Government of India.

During the year 1994-95, India hosted the VII SAF Games at Madras from 18th to 27th December 1995. India was at the top of the medals tally.

The Sports Authority of India (SAI), set up in 1984 in the nodal agency for popularising sports and physical education in the country. It was established six Regional Centres at Bangalore, Calcutta, Chandigarh, Delhi, Gandhinagar and Imphal. The SAI has also created wide range of sports infrastructure and facilities necessary for the preparation of our national teams for major international tournaments and for running of National Coaching Camps at Senior/Junior/Sub-junior levels in priority disciplines.

The main schemes of SAI are : (1) National Sports Talent Contest (NSTC), (2) Special Area Games (SAG), (3) Special Projects Development Area (SPDA), (4) Sports Hostel Scheme, (5) Boys Sports Companies in the Army, (6) National Coaching Scheme, (7) Sports Science Research Fellowship Scheme.

27.7 YOUTH PROGRAMMES

The Department of Youth Affairs and Sports, Ministry of Human Resource Development, Government of India is responsible for youth programmes.

National Youth Policy : The youth policy 1988 as approved in 1992 is being implemented. It has the following objectives :

1. To instill in youth a deep awareness of and respect for the principles and values enshrined in our constitution.
2. To help in youth the awareness of our historical and cultural heritage and imbue then with a sense of pride and national identity.
3. To provide youth with maximum access to education which apart from developing their all-round personality, would equip them with professional and vocational training for employment and self-employment opportunities.
4. To make youth aware of international issues and involve them in promoting world peace.

Committee for National Youth Programmes : As per the guidelines of the national youth policy, a Committee for National Youth Programmes was constituted in 1994. The Committee is headed by the Prime Minister held two meetings on August 22, 1994 and on January 13, 1995.

National Service Scheme (NSS) : The scheme launched in 1969, had in 1995 over 12 lakh student volunteers on the rolls, spread over 158 universities and senior secondary schools. The expenditure on programmes of NSS is shared between the Control and the State Government, in the ratio of 7:5. Following local areas have been identified for NSS work; (i) National integration and social harmony, (ii) Literacy, (iii) Gender justice, (iv) Village adoption, (v) Life style education and wasteland development and watershed management.

Indira Gandhi National Awards were introduced in 1994 to provide incentive to NSS functionaries and volunteers.

Nehru Yuva Kendra Sangathan (NYKS) : NYKS, an autonomous organisation under the Department of Youth Affairs and Sports to cater to the needs of more than 8 million non-student rural youth in the age-group 15-35 years enrolled through 2 lakh village based youth clubs. It undertakes the following activities, (1) Training in self-employment, (2) Youth leadership training programmes, (3) Cultural programmes, (4) Work camps, (5) Sports, (6) Celebration of national and international days, (7) Vocational training, (8) Social campaigns, and (9) Youth awareness drive.

The NYKS organised 'Manvata Yatra' (Humanity pilgrimage) on 2nd October 1995 from Kirti Mandir, Porbander to spread Gandhiji's message of peace, communal harmony, social justice and peace. In this programme our 15 lakh youth participated).

CICIL LIST

CONCEPTS IN COMMUNICATION, INFORMATICS & LIBRARIANSHIP

(CICIL)

General Editor: **S.P. AGRAWAL**

CICIL-1 Development of Library Services in India: Social Science Information/**S.P. Agrawal** Rs. 150

CICIL-2 Development of Documentation in India: Social Science Information/**S.P. Agrawal** Rs. 250

CICIL-3 UNESCO and Social Sciences: Retrospect and Prospect/**S.P. Agrawal** and **J.C. Aggarwal** Rs. 250

CICIL-4 INDIANA : A Bibliography of Bibliographical Sources/**M.K. Jain** Rs. 200

CICIL-5 Dimensions of Library and Information Science: Kaula Festschrift/**V. Venkatappaiah** (Eds.) Rs. 600

CICIL-6 Book Numbers: Some Indian Methods/**M.P. Satija** and **S.P. Agrawal** Rs. 100

CICIL-7 National Policy for University Libraries in India: Problems and Perspectives /**N.B. Inamdar** and **L.S. Ramaiah** (Ed.) Rs. 250

CICIL-8 Media Utilisation for the Development of Women and Children/**B.S. Thakur** and **Binod C. Agrawal** Rs. 150

CICIL-9 Terrorism: An Annotated Bibliography/**Susheela Bhan** (Ed.) Rs. 275

CICIL-10 Transnational Library Relations: The Indo-American Experience/**M.B. Konnur** Rs. 175

CICIL-11 Geography of Marketing and Commercial Activities in India (Documentation on Research Information)/**R.S. Dixit** Rs. 130

CICIL-12 Information India 1988: Global View/**S.P. Agrawal** and **J.C. Aggarwal** Rs. 200

CICIL-13 Women's Education in India: Historical Review, Present Status and Perspective Plan/**S.P. Agrawal** and **J.C. Aggarwal** Rs. 360

CICIL-14 Cultural Communication in India: Role and Impact of Phonograms/**J.M. Ojha** Rs. 220

CICIL-15 Second Historical Survey of Educational Development in India: Select Documents 1985-1989/**S.P. Agrawal** and **J.C. Aggarwal** Rs. 490

CICIL-16 Documentation Encyclopaedia of UNESCO and Education/**J.C. Aggarwal** and **S.P. Agrawal** Rs. 800 (set of 2 parts)

CICIL-17 Attitude Towards Information: A Study of Post-Graduate Teachers and Researchers in Social Sciences/**N.G. Satish** (in press)

CICIL-18 Librarianship and Bureaucratic Organisation: A Study in the Sociology of Library Profession in India/**P.K. Jayaswal** Rs. 175

CICIL-19 Literature Search/**K.A. Isaac** Rs. 150

CICIL-20 Child Education in India: Index to Scholarly Writings in Indian Educational Journals and Newspapers since independence/**S.P. Agrawal** and **Naresh Kanta** Rs. 100

CICIL-21 Lok Sabha and Vidhan Sabha Elections in India 1989 & 1990: Process and Results with Comparative Study of Manifestos/**S.P. Agrawal** and **J.C. Aggarwal** Rs. 250

CICIL-22 Islamic Studies in India: A Survey of Human, Institutional and Documentary Sources/**Mohamed Taher** Rs. 180

CICIL-23 Panchayati Raj: An Annotated Bibliography/**N.B. Inamdar, N.G. Satish** and **Anil Takalkar** 290

CICIL-24 Information India 1989-90: Global View/**S.P. Agrawal** and **J.C. Aggarwal** Rs. 500

CICIL-25 First Handbook of Psychological and Social Instruments/**Udai Pareek** and **T. Venkateswara Rao** Rs. 500

CICIL-26 Educational and Social Uplift of Backward Classes: At What Cost and How? Mandal Commission and After/**S.P. Agrawal** and **J.C. Aggarwal** Rs. 275

CICIL-27 Mass Media and New Horizons: Impact of TV & Video an Urban Milieu/**H.R. Trivedi** Rs. 180

CICIL-28 Indian Writings on Education : An Indicator to Indian Educational Journals Grouped by Subject Deseriptors 1979 to 1986 (in two parts) **S.P. Agarwal** Rs. 900 (per set)

CICIL-29 Nation in Crisis/**S.P. Agrawal** and **J.C. Aggarwal** Rs. 200

CICIL-30 Information India 1990-91: Global View/**S.P. Agrawal** and **J.C. Aggarwal** Rs. 500

CICIL-31 Development of University Libraries in India after Independence/**O.P. Gupta** Rs. 270

CICIL-32 Handbook on Child : With Historical Background/**Pramila Pandit Barooah** Rs. 320

CICIL-33 Weaker Section in Indian Society : Undiscovered Past, Uncertain Present and Unpredictable Future : Index to Writings in Indian Scholarly Journals and 10 National Newspapers Classified under 1500 Descriptors 1886-1990/**S.P. Agrawal** and **Rajeev Kumar Sharma** Rs. 600

CICIL-34 Communication Informatics and Librarianship in India : An Introductory Guide to Publications Based on a Survey of Libraries in Capital City of India/**S.P. Agrawal** and **Pushpa Rani Sharma** Rs. 720

CICIL-35 Problems of Collection Development in Special Libraries/**M.S. Sridhar** Rs. 225

CICIL-36 National Information Resources for Social Sciences in India : Mobilisation, Dispersal and International Enhancement/**S.P. Agrawal** Rs. 225

CICIL-37 Modern History of Punjab : A Look Back into Ancient Peaceful Punjab Focusing Confrontation and Failures Leading to Present Punjab Problem, and a Peep Ahead : Relevant Select Documents/**J.C. Aggarwal** and **S.P. Agrawal** Rs. 400

CICIL-38 India Information Sources : Economics and Business/**Kyllikki Ruokonen** and **Manohar Lal** Rs.

CICIL-39 Educational Planning in India : With a Slant to Educational Financing and Administration, Vol. 1, Reports of Committees and Commissions, Five Year Plans, Statistical Tables/**J.C. Aggarwal** and **S.P. Agrawal** Rs. 650

CICIL-40 Integrated Library System : Two Case Studies : Latin America and India **Maria Luiza Rigo Pasquarelli, Rosaly Favero Krzyanowski, Ines Maria M. Imperatriz** and **S.P. Agrawal** Rs. 160

CICIL-41 Social Science Information in India: Effort towards Bibliographical Control/**S.D. Vyas** Rs. 300

CICIL-42 Higher Education in India Since Independence: U.G.C. and Its Approach **O.P. Gupta** Rs. 360

CICIL-43 Government and Politics in India: A Bibliographical Study of Contemporary Scenario Chronicling Rajiv Gandhi Era/**S.P. Agrawal** and **Rajeev Kumar Sharma** Rs. 500

CICIL-44 Second Handbook of Psychological and Social Instruments/**D.M. Pestonjee** Rs. 300

CICIL-45 Development/Digression Diary of India; 3D Companion Volume to Information India: 1990-91/**S.P. Agrawal** Rs. 200

CICIL-46 Development/Digression Diary of India; 3D Companion Volume to Information India: 1991-92/**S.P. Agrawal** Rs. 300

CICIL-47 Information India 1991-92: Global View/**S.P. Agrawal** and **J.C. Aggarwal** Rs. 500

CICIL-48 Committees and Commissions in India 1974, A Concept's Project, Compiled by a team of professionals guided/ **Virender Kumar** (Vol. 12) Rs. 450

CICIL-49 Committees and Commissions in India 1975, A Concept's Project, Compiled by a team of professionals guided/**Virender Kumar** (Vol. 13) Rs. 450

CICIL-50 Committees and Commissions in India 1976, A Concept's Project, Compiled by a team of professionals guided/**Virender Kumar** (Vol. 14) Rs. 450

CICIL-51 Committees and Commissions in India 1977, A Concept's Project, Compiled by a team of professionals guided/**Virender Kumar** (Vol. 15) (in four parts) Rs. 450 each

CICIL-52 Committees and Commissions in India 1978, A Concept's Project, Compiled by a team of professionals guided/**Virender Kumar** (Vol. 16) (in two parts) Rs. 450 each

CICIL-53 Subject Guide to Communication, Informatics and Librarianship in India (Based on a Survey of Library Holdings in Capital City of India)/**S.P. Agrawal** and **Pushpa Rani Sharma** Rs. 400

CICIL-54 Restructurring of Library and Information Science Curriculum/**A. Tejomurty** Rs. 250

CICIL-55 Committees and Commissions in India 1979, A Concept's Project, Compiled by a team of professionals guided/**Virender Kumar** (Vol. 17) (in two parts) Rs. 450 each

CICIL-56 Committees and Commissions in India 1980, A Concept's Project, Compiled by a team of professionals guided /**Virender Kumar** (Vol. 18) (in two parts) Rs. 450 each

CICIL-57 Third Historical Survey of Educational Development in India/**S.P. Agrawal** and **J.C. Aggarwal** Rs. 700

CICIL-58 Model Library Legislation/**Velaga Venkatappaiah** Rs. 400

CICIL-59 Indian Library and Information Science Literature (1990-91)/**Sewa Singh** Rs. 525

CICIL-60 Librarianship and Library Science in India/**Mohamed Taher** and **Donald Gordon Davis, Jr**. Rs. 350

CICIL-61 Comprehensive Glossary for Library & Information Science/**O.P. Gupta** Rs.300

CICIL-62 Information India 1992-93:/**S.P. Agrawal** and **J. C. Aggarwal** Rs. 500.

CICIL-63 Automation of Libraries and Information Science/**R.K. Shukla** Rs. 250

CICIL-64 Modern History of Jammu and Kashmir
J.C. Aggarwal and **S.P. Agrawal** Rs. 1500 (per set of 2 vols.)

CICIL-65 Library and Information Science: Emerging Trends:/**Sister M. Esperanza,** A. C. Rs. 250

CICIL-66 Mental Retardation in India (A Bibliography)/**S. Venkatesan** and **V.G.D. Vepuri** Rs. 275

CICIL-67 Information India 1993-94: Global View/**S.P. Agrawal** and **J.C. Aggarwal** Rs. 500

CICIL-68 Information Behaviour of Scientists and Engineers:/**M.S. Sridhar** Rs. 500

CICIL-69 Uttarakhand: Past, Present and Future/**J.C. Aggarwal** and **S.P. Agrawal** Rs. 750

CICIL-70 National Information System in Education: A Comparative Study/**S. L. Verma** Rs. 650

CICIL-71 Not Published by us.

CICIL-72 Not Published by us.

CICIL-73 Second Historical Survey of Women's Education in India/**S.P. Agrawal** and **J.C. Aggarwal** Rs. 600

CICIL-74 Library and Information Science: Parameters and Perspectives/**R.G. Prasher** (Ed.) 2 Vols. Set Rs. 1500
Vol. 1: Library and Information Science: Basic
Vol. 2: Information Science, Information Technology and Its Application

CICIL-75 Third Handbook of Psychological and Social Instruments/**D.M. Pestonjee** (in two volumes) Rs. 1100 per set

CICIL-76 Information India: Global Views 1994-95 & 1995-96/**S.P. Agrawal** and **J.C. Aggarwal** Rs. 500

CICIL-77 Development of Education in India: Selected Documents 1993-94/**S.P. Agrawal** and **J.C. Aggarwal**